THE CORNWELL CHRONICLES

Tales of an American Life on the Erie Canal, Building Chicago, in the Volunteer Civil War Western Army, on the Farm, in a Country Store

Edited by *John M. Wearmouth*

HERITAGE BOOKS
2015

HERITAGE BOOKS
AN IMPRINT OF HERITAGE BOOKS, INC.

Books, CDs, and more—Worldwide

For our listing of thousands of titles see our website
at
www.HeritageBooks.com

Published 2015 by
HERITAGE BOOKS, INC.
Publishing Division
5810 Ruatan Street
Berwyn Heights, Md. 20740

Copyright © 1998 John M. Wearmouth

Other Heritage Books by John M. and Roberta J. Wearmouth:
Thomas A. Jones: Chief Agent of the Confederate Secret Service in Maryland

All rights reserved. No part of this book may be reproduced or transmitted in any form or by any means, electronic or mechanical, including photocopying, recording or by any information storage and retrieval system without written permission from the author, except for the inclusion of brief quotations in a review.

International Standard Book Numbers
Paperbound: 978-0-7884-1083-3
Clothbound: 978-0-7884-6173-6

TABLE OF CONTENTS

List of Illustrations vii
Acknowledgments xi
Preface.. xiii
Introduction... 1

I -- C.1849 and 1859-1860...Erie Canal...Lincoln-Douglas debates... Bloomington, Illinois ...Springfield, Illinois...Chicago, Illinois 3

II -- 1860-1861...Fort Sumter...Chicago friends.. 9

III -- Lincoln's call and a 90-day enlistment... New York State and very early first loves...Springfield-Camp Yates and down to Cairo 15

IV -- Cairo and organization of the "Old 8th"...Uncle "Dick" Oglesby and close-order drill according to Scott, at $21 per month 21

V -- 1861 at Cairo...cow-napping and nocturnal liquid refreshment, parade ground drill...a c.1885 GAR event in Allegan County, Michigan...country store shenanigans...Illinois infantry volunteers in Missouri, 1862-3 27

VI -- A basket of pies...Post of Cairo...Colonel Bird across Big Muddy...those Mexican War Vets...almost an action...panic preparation 35

VII -- Squire Lawrence and sons...the three-blanket caper 39

VIII-- End of the 90-day enlistment...reconstitution of the 8th Illinois Vols...1859 carpentering in Chicago...Bloomington's new normal school...lost wages 43

IX -- An almost-duel on the river bank...foils, cutlass or broadsword?...Dave's chief military blunder...The Cornwell brothers in Co. K.. 47

X -- At 18 years of age, a carpenter in Chicago...Carville railroad shops...new friend in music ...flute and fiddle fun-times...high times in the new Meeker House and Mr. Meeker himself... 51

XI -- Big-boy sport and fisticuffs...last of the Meeker connection...north to St. Johns and Port Clinton...a grand Lake Michigan fishing haul... 57

XII -- Late summer 1861... "three years unless sooner discharged."...Highland Park revisited ...1855 introduction to carpentering at 16 years of age...moonlight walks and corn shocks ...two weeks and back to Cairo camp life 61

XIII-- Successful recruiting for the 8th...plenty of three-year troopers...Cornwell the drillmaster ...unpretentious Grant arrives, 1 September '61...Kentucky incursion...the Old Dan Rice One Horse Show tents on the parade grounds 67

XIV -- Missouri Waltz...Bird's Point and a new life in tents... first-blood for the 8th... bugle boy of Co. K...a brief cavalry stint 73

XV	-- Nov. 1861 Missouri expedition of Oglesby with four Illinois Regiments plus artillery and cavalry support units...Bloomfield print shop and first issue of *The Stars and Stripes* ...Cape Girardeau and Belmont events	79
XVI	-- Brother Frank...McAllister's Chicago Battery and Fort Holt ...Grant and Belmont ...Christmas 1861 and boxes from home...January 1862 Kentucky visit near Columbus	87
XVII	-- Back to Allegan County, Michigan...timbering and farming... late 1860's and '70's ...oxen, wife and young son...country scenes and folk along bucolic byways...the great squirrel standoff at "Uncle Charley Gibson's place"...leaving Cairo for the Tennessee and other points to the South... February 1862...Fort Henry, Rebel Columbiads and Union gunboats...from Henry overland to Donelson...lead by the 8th ...blunt appraisal of Union staff officers at Donelson... their lack of courage and command capability ...needless butchery of Northern soldiers	91
XVIII	-- Preparing to assault Donelson...costly victory...critique	97
XIX	-- Cornwell country store at Monterey Center, Allegan County, Michigan (c.1883-1903) ...business, spiritualism, seances and apparitions	105
XX	-- Early March...Donelson left behind and back to the Tennessee transports headed up-river...whiskey in the river and when Riley fell overboard...Pittsburg Landing and the camp near Shiloh Church...a brief rest and time for introducing the desiccated potato	111
XXI	-- Sunday sunrise and an unpleasant surprise...April 6, 1862... rout and disaster at the Landing...McClernand's division at center	115
XXII	-- From Michigan farm into big business at Monterey Center... 1883 and a new challenge ...up with buttermilk from a bucket	123
XXIII	-- Next day at Shiloh...Don Carlos saves Grant's Army... band music and stragglers... night storm and stiff tent-mates...rout of Rebs	127
XXIV	-- Shiloh critique...major actors, Grant, Sherman, Buell, C.F.Smith, Johnston, Wallace... a couple of Yankee heros during the Sunday trouncing	133
XXV	-- Father Joshua's cavalry career ends...a transfer to the light artillery...inching down to Corinth...Sheridan appears... games of chuck-a-luck...a fiddle-faddle parade-ground concerto and a fair snakewood bow	139
XXVI	-- Grant returns to command...life in the Battery with new pals...Odd Fellow pranks...a new mess cook, Big Jack	145
XXVII	-- Detailed boys in McAllister's Battery...a colonel's military wife...a beneficial lie... ending a wholesome amusement	149
XXVIII	-- A mania for gambling...honestly played games impracticable... outsharping a sharp ...the euchre tournament	153

XXIX	-- December 1862 and on to Vicksburg...CSA Van Dorn and the Holly Springs disaster...a hungry battery...chicken feast... spirited "good looker" Dixie concerto at Oxford	157
XXX	-- Back into Tennessee...on the Tallahatchee...Scott in calf binding...rifling a corner stone...a major interrogation... the mule breakers	163
XXXI	-- Down Ol' Miss...February 1863...Lake Providence campground ... a Bully encounter ...perks of a bugler...yams, beans and corn ... a bugle gets a handsome curtain cord (still together in 1998	169
XXXII	-- Pretext for dealing with Bully...blood and coffee grounds...counterfeiting confederates ...fake bills, cheats and low finance...and "genwine Lincum greenbacks"	175
XXXIII	-- The great catfish expedition...up to 100 pounds... cruising and spearing in flooded cotton fields	181
XXXIV	-- McPherson's Corps drops downriver to Milliken's Bend... General Lorenzo Thomas announces plan to recruit Blacks into the Army...going after a commission... captaincy preferred...new 1st Lieutenant in 9th Regiment of Louisiana Infantry (African Descent)	185
XXXV	-- New camp on Richmond road...Colonel Herman Lieb... Recruiter Jack Jackson and the plantation drafts... Mississippi recruiting drive... "get in dem ranks dar, faud ma'ch" ...return to Milliken's Bend	195
XXXVI	-- Drilling and equipping the new troops...a new, orderly camp near the levee ...muskets, targets and cartridges... sometimes aimless practice	203
XXXVII	-- The African Brigade...9th Louisiana pokes westward toward Rebels...action of June 6...first charge of company B... save us boys...green Negro troopers rescue Illinois cavalrymen ...back to camp	207
XXXVIII	-- Big battle at the Bend, June 7, 1863...bayonets, mayhem and guts along the levee ...non-stop assault and desperate defense for about six hours...Confederates break contact about noon...official battle reports	211
XXXIX	-- Milliken's Bend aftermath and Cornwell critique...long-after peculiar and conflicting reports...eye-witness accounts	223
XL	-- Back to Michigan...last years in Allegan City... pleasant fishing in the looping Kalamazoo River near the downtown dam c.1910	231
XLI	-- Bend wound...hospital boat to Memphis...healing in hospital and Memphis parks... Chicago recuperation... south to Vicksburg late September 1863, and return to Lieb's command...building a new heavy artillery regiment out of Bend battle remnants still with the old 9th Louisiana	237

XLII -- A new captain takes command of Co. B of the 9th at new camp on south edge of Vicksburg...B Company troopers named ... as of June 6, fourteen of them still with the company at Vicksburg...at last financially very comfortable 243

XLIII -- Settling down in new Headquarters...a new horse...a lieutenant and his milk goat enliven Sunday in Vicksburg...permanent OD and regimental drillmaster...guard duty...a major from November 1863...now commanding 3rd battalion of the 5th.... 249

XLIV -- Heavy artillery tactics training...a Columbiad vs women of business...the trials of sweet Maud...just like Jericho...successful evacuation at last...a Chickasaw Bayou address...dress parades, cornet band...brigade drill confusion...a prize case of wine ...importance of appearance of garrison soldiers 257

XLV -- Staff of 3rd Battalion, 5th Heavy Artillery...commanders of the department at Memphis and Vicksburg district...Lieb schemes for field duty... Battery Castle photograph...a new district inspector--an acting assistant inspector general..... 267

XLVI -- I.G. for about a year for the Vicksburg district... inspection at Davis' Bend (the house that Jeff built)...the beautiful Mrs. Sloan...Mrs. Sloan and missed opportunities... done in by General Washburn 273

XLVII -- A January 1865 inspection at Natchez...reunion with General Mason Brayman...a District change of command...Major Cornwell returns to Vicksburg...inspection of a battalion of regulars...early 1866-Lieb travels to Washington, D.C....Cornwell's I.G. duties end... "Sir, your whiskey is without color, strength or flavor"... wars and opportunities for cheats and profiteering 279

XLVIII -- General Maltby's large, black show horse...Major Cornwell on parade...the Major shows off...run-down on the good old boys of the old 8th Illinois...post-war lives of Oglesby, Wheaton and Caldwell...prospects for early freedom - 1866... business partnership at Vicksburg...nothing beyond the planning stage...released 20 May 1866 after 5 years and 25 days of continuous honorable service, including three full years of active duty with Negro troops... biographical sketch on General Herman Lieb 285

Postscript 290

Addendums:
A: Obituary 293
B: McCulloch's Report on Milliken's Bend 397
C: Elias S. Dennis' Report 303
D: Cornwall in 1901 307
E: Letter 309
F: The Negro in the War 313
G: Epilogue 315

INDEX 317

LIST OF ILLUSTRATIONS

David Cornwell c.1862 .... Cover and xix

Western Tennessee by *Harper's Weekly,* February 22, 1862 8

Cornwell's Civil War experiences were connected in many ways to the Mississippi, from Cairo to Natchez, along often uncertain meandering, as "Big Muddy" reached for its terminal at the Gulf of Mexico 14

Excellent land- and water-scape across mouth of the Ohio River from Fort Holt's artillery in Kentucky, which commanded a critical major river junction. Cairo may be seen directly across the Ohio's mouth 26

Admiral Andrew Foote's Mississippi gunboat flotilla gathering way "under full head of steam," perhaps heading for the Tennessee River and tough shore bombardment missions in support of the volunteer Union regiments heading upriver 34

Colonel Henry Dougherty's 22nd Illinois Volunteers deal with slave hunters at Bird's Point, Missouri, on the Mississippi River, probably late 1861. The Point lay almost directly across the river from Cairo, Illinois 38

The Union Army's advance into the heart of the trans-Appalachian South was supported by land and river depots and resupply points from the Ohio River to Vicksburg. These supply installations were often isolated and very vulnerable to smash and run Rebel cavalry swoops 56

Pages 1 and 2 of the first (and only) issue of *The Stars and Stripes,* Nov. 9, 1861, printed at Bloomfield, Missouri, by soldier-printers in Colonel Richard Oglesby's brief expedition into Rebel-held regions of this tormented border State 82

General John McClernand's troops (including 8th Illinois Vols.) boarding boats at Cairo, Illinois. These soldiers were part of Grant's new command that eventually would invest and capture Vicksburg and again open the Mississippi to Union commerce from northern Minnesota southward to the Gulf and then on to ports world-wide 90

Union gunboats bombarding Fort Henry from the Tennessee River 96

Already well-bloodied Yankee troops storm Confederate artillery at Fort Donelson where very green commanders and combat-new Union infantry paid an extremely high price for a first significant victory gained by frontal assaults against well armed and entrenched Confederates 104

Plaque at National Park Service information center at Fort Donelson shows that Oglesby's Brigade, including 8th Illinois, suffered very high casualties, as described by Cornwell in these chronicles. The Donelson baptism in combat horror was still fresh in his mind during the Shiloh disaster about two months afterward 109

Second Illinois Light Artillery (including McAllister's Battery) heavily involved before Donelson 114

A Sunday morning in Tennessee....April 6, 1862, near Shiloh Church. Sketch depicts Oglesby's Brigade of McClernand's Division near center of Union line, probably just before the rout began that ended with a "meltdown" of effective Yankee resistance. Most of Grant's forces stumbled over each other in panic as they desperately hoped to gain some protection from the Tennessee River and whatever Navy guns might be afloat there. Cornwell's 8th Illinois was near the middle of this scene. A *Leslie's Illustrated* artist incorrectly placed the 8th Indiana in line where in fact the 8th Illinois stood 122

Union General Don Carlos Buell...the hero of Shiloh. His Army of the Cumberland rescued the demoralized remnants of Grant's command that littered the west bank of the Tennessee at Pittsburg Landing the morning of April 7, 1862. Cornwell and shattered odds and ends of the combined 8th and 18th Illinois Regiments provided an exhausted, meager but greatly relieved reserve. The battle-drained Illinois troopers lived to see the flower of the Confederate Army of the West flee the Shiloh field as precipitately as Grant's men had done the day before when scrambling down the river's west bank 132

Farmer David Cornwell in 1878, now 39 years of age and fighting primitive conditions on a small, hard-scrabble farm in Salem Township, Allegan County, southwestern Michigan. Living now with first wife Frances and three children 138

Fort Donelson post-battle scenes 144

The Union Blue Box: The contents of this desk comprise a remarkable wealth of background material at Cornwell's grasp as he wrote his memoirs 165

Frank Leslie's Illustrated Newspaper, January 16, 1864, showing respectful sketches of Negroes serving in the Union Armies of the west during their first year of Federal military involvement 224

David's "Annie," Sarah Ann Stanclift Cornwell, his third and last wife. They were married in December 1888 in the Herman Lieb home in Chicago. This and the following photo of David doubtless were taken on the occasion of their wedding (left) 234

David at age 50 when in Chicago to be wedded to Sarah Ann. They lived together as man and wife for 23 years...longer than either of his previous marriages (right) 234

The Cornwell store at Monterey Center, Michigan c.1883-1903 (top) 235

David and Sarah sitting on porch of the store about 1895. Much has been done to the store building and surroundings since the Cornwells began housekeeping here (bottom) 235

Two *Leslie's* sketches showing early 1863 deployments and occupations of Negroes in the Mississippi River Valley. Their heavy engagement as infantry at the Battle of Milliken's Bend June 7 had to be considered the centerpiece of the Black man's contribution to Union victory west of the Appalachians.
(Top) "In The Trenches" 241
(Bottom) "Govrnt. Blacksmiths' Shop" 241

This 1864 photograph of Herman Lieb's staff was taken at Battery Castle near Vicksburg. All White officers of the 5th U.S.C. Artillery (Heavy) Regiment. The 3rd battalion commander, Major D. Cornwell, is the third figure in line with Lieb and to his left (to reader's right)... 255

1873 outline map of Allegan County, Michigan 265

1873 map of Monterey Township, Allegan County, Michigan.. 277

Title page of 1873 Allegan County Titus Atlas 291

Charity Conklyn Lazier Cornwell, mother of David and Frank, and another son and two daughters. Born in Prince Edward County, Ontario, Canada. Married Joshua Cornwell there about 1830. Photo taken at Picton, Ontario, about 1870. Her husband and two sons saw service in the Union Army 292

The Cornwells in their new brick home at 414 Cedar Street in Allegan about 1910...all very comfortable, steam heat, electricity, extensive library, and doubtless, a telephone (top).... 296

Photo taken March 26, 1910 in front of the Mission at San Diego, California. Cornwells marked by arrows. All most fashionably "dolled up" (bottom)... 296

Cornwell's last entrepreneurial hurrah dealt with ambitious plans to connect Allegan and Grand Rapids by rail. His 1901 diary shows clearly that acquiring railway rights of way for the new-fangled electric cars took a good bit of energy and enterprise. In the end all came to naught when capitalization fell short of needs 306

Frank Leslie's Illustrated Newspaper, January 16, 1864, showing respectful sketches of Negroes serving in the Union Armies of the west during their first year of Federal military involvement 312

ACKNOWLEDGMENTS

First of all and most of all...my heartfelt thanks to my wife Roberta Jeanne Clark Wearmouth for always keeping the faith as we sought to find a publisher. And not the least of her contributions...sound editorial assistance, valuable design ideas, and professional copy preparation.

To daughter Ann Owen Wearmouth, my gratitude for composition help and patience in dealing with aged parents struggling to fit into even the basic elements of today's computer capabilities for preparing manuscript for publishing.

Appreciation and profound gratitude to first cousin Judith A. Sanford Beal of Edina, Minnesota for allowing me to use her copy of the Cornwell manuscript and photographs of Cornwell family members.

And to the most senior living descendant of David Cornwell, his granddaughter Alice Antoinette Owen Sanford of San Diego, California whose long-term encouragement has helped much in keeping our hopes alive for publication. She was five years old when the old major passed away and she remembers bits and pieces about him, albeit somewhat dimly.

PREFACE

The David Cornwell Memoirs have been "sleeping" for many years. A northern Civil War veteran wrote them about the turn of the century with every intention of publishing them. They were for him the culmination of an intensive, deeply felt effort probably underway for a couple of decades. The manuscript seems to have been written in the early years of this century in the small rural town of Allegan, seat of a county of the same name, in southwestern Michigan. Here David Cornwell lived from 1867 until his death in 1911. As farmer, carpenter, merchant, census taker, sometime G.A.R. member, the salty iconoclastic veteran never forgot his wartime experiences and his Union Army companions. In fact, he corresponded with many of them for a couple of decades before finishing his manuscript. A remarkable contribution of these memoirs is that the Cornwell story, while shaped primarily around the Civil War campaigns and figures, goes into warm, often amusing details about the events leading to and following the author's wartime adventures. Cornwell's excellent memory and his brash, no-holds-barred accounts afford today's historians a raw, blunt look at several aspects of wartime services, 1861-66.

Cornwell thought somehow there might be a measure of advantage or increased credibility, or even propriety, attached to using a name other than his own to identify the main character in the story. The name used, Dan Caverno, would lead even the most unimaginative reader to conclude that perhaps writer Cornwell just might be describing his own experiences. This fanciful bit of literary "acting" proves not very effective, however. It seems clear enough all the way that the memoirs are doubtlessly autobiographical, beginning with his droll, sometimes even shocking accounts of life in western New York State (where he was born in 1839) in the Watertown to Rome area, and along the up-and-down stretches of the yet quite new Erie Canal. From very early boyhood in western New York precincts Cornwell seems always to have rebelled against authority and all those who in his eyes seemed fearsome or ridiculous symbols of authority, whether family members, the law, the church, or even a governor of New York. Young Dave surely must have appeared to many to be a veritable "Peck's Bad Boy" of those neighborhoods where his family lived during the 1840's and 50's. Cornwell's in-house rascality and often violent relationships with other members of the Joshua and Charity Conklin Lazier Cornwell family eventually impelled David to leave for points west late in 1854, at about age 15. A rough life as a crewman on his father's Erie Canal boat had hardened him early and prepared him for surviving out on the frontier. He settled in Chicago, however, choosing one of the west's most metropolitan, civilized communities over the absolutely primitive, sparsely settled regions of the far West. Here he invested most of his cash stake in a set of carpenter tools and assumed an immediate but fragile competency in that craft.

The memoirs bring a bit of intimacy and increased comprehension of the times and personalities that maneuvered at center stage in Illinois during the two or three years preceding Lincoln's April 1861 call for the 90-day volunteers. Cornwell seems to have become comfortable with life in Illinois rather quickly. Never, after settling down in the Chicago area, does he look back towards New York State, and never does he mention his family left behind. While David never alludes to abolitionist sentiments, he seems to have had rather forceful, lively opinions about the consequences of rebellion against the government of the United States of America. In fact, his Union-Cause patriotism never flickered during the war. At the same time, his opinion of Confederate forces and efforts were never belittled or described with any degree of disrespect...except for the surrender of Fort Donelson where he felt southern commanders acted in a treasonous manner in giving up this Tennessee bastion. Cornwell was much more critical of parts played by Union field commanders and their staffs, from Fort Henry through Milliken's Bend in June 1863.

After enlisting in April 1861 in the 8th Illinois Volunteer Infantry Regiment, David began a long, somewhat undistinguished (but often exciting) service as an enlisted man. Mostly through his own blunder (administrative), he was not promoted to sergeant until early 1863. A sad but interesting note here: When David enlisted for 90 days in April 1861, he volunteered the services in absentia of his younger brother, Frank, then living in Chicago. During a November 1861 brief excursion into Missouri, Frank apparently contracted pneumonia while on guard duty and consequently died in a service hospital in June 1863 as a result of lung damage caused by this illness. And, just as notable, David's father, Joshua, had come west from New York about 1860 to take up a homestead in Allegan County, Michigan, a most significant factor in family history. In August 1861, Joshua, at about age 52, enlisted in the 3rd Michigan Cavalry at Allegan. How he got accepted is anybody's guess...a member of his regiment some years later told son David that Joshua looked even older than his true age and never should have been taken into service. He was mustered out in Detroit in 1862 because of injuries received in a fall from a mule while on a 3rd Michigan Cavalry junket into Missouri early in 1862. So, for a brief period, the Cornwell family from Watertown, New York, had three members in the Union Army.

At Cairo, Illinois, where the 8th Illinois trained and was encamped for most of its 1861 service, David turned down an offer of the job of company orderly because he was then very uncertain about how he would behave in battle...the connection here is not really easy to understand. As things turned out, Cornwell stood up well under combat conditions. In our 20th Century army, he surely would have been recommended for the Silver Star at least twice-- Shiloh and Milliken's Bend affair. It wasn't until Washington decided to begin seriously to recruit and train Negroes for combat that Sergeant Cornwell was able to move up into the ranks of commissioned officers. He had long thought he could command...at least at company level, and had once so informed his company commander. When, about April 1863, word from the Adjutant General's office reached the Army of the Tennessee that Black troops were to be brought into the Union Army, Cornwell saw at long last a way of becoming a commissioned officer.

He applied for a commission and was accepted and made a first lieutenant in Company B, 9th Louisiana Infantry Regiment (African Descent). Then began a long, always challenging association with Black troops that lasted until May 1866. Few White officers saw such a variety of assignments with Black soldiers during the Civil War...from kidnaping (almost) directly from newly liberated plantations, training, outfitting, rifle (musket) range practice, leading "green darkies" in their first combat exposure, commanding two companies in bloody, hand-to-hand bayonet combat with veteran White Confederates, helping organize and train a new heavy artillery regiment for garrison duty in Mississippi, and long-term duty with colored troops in a thoroughly staunch, White, unsubmissive Mississippi (Vicksburg) community, for well over two years.

In recent years several works have been published that shed long-dimmed light on participation of Negro troops in the American Civil War. One of the more scholarly and extensively researched was *Forged in Battle, the Civil War Alliance of Black Soldiers and White Officers,* by Joseph T. Glatthaar, an associate professor of history at the University of Houston, Texas. It was published by The Penguin Group, Meridian Books, N.Y., N.Y. Glatthaar deals with the action at Milliken's Bend in appropriate detail. He drew generously on the unpublished Cornwell manuscript at the United States Army Military History Institute,

Carlisle Barracks, Pennsylvania. In citing this work the author simply refers to "David Cornwell's memoirs, Dan Caverno," CWMC—seventeen times. Nowhere does he explain who Cornwell was and why his comments are considered credible or even pertinent. The name doesn't even appear in the index. Cornwell's experience and bloody battle exposures are not mentioned, nor is the fact he was badly wounded in the Bend battle while commanding Colonel Herman Lieb's two-company, thin reserve force that plugged a nearly disastrous breakthrough by Confederates on the African Brigade's left flank at noon June 7.

The comment next to the Milliken's Bend map near page 147, "...Despite being in military service for only a month, the black troops fought a vicious hand-to-hand battle with the Confederates and held on even after white Union soldiers had fled from the field." This statement surely would have unsettled the white officers summarily executed by the Confederates within hours after the battle simply for having commanded Negro soldiers. Cornwell's company commander at the Bend, Captain Corydon Heath, was one of these. He and Cornwell had organized and commanded Company B, 9th Louisiana Infantry Regiment (African Descent), which suffered heavier casualties than any other Yankee unit in the battle.

In the early autumn of 1863 the few remnants of this incredibly courageous regiment were folded into a just-established unit designated the 5th U.S.C. Artillery (Heavy) Regiment. When Lieutenant David Cornwell returned to Colonel Herman Lieb's command in late summer of 1863 he was promoted to Captain. A few weeks later he was promoted to Major and commander of one of the artillery battalions in the new 5th. He served with this unit almost continuously until mustered out in May 1866.

The Negro in the Civil War by Benjamin Quarles, (Little, Brown and Company, Boston, 1953), includes colorful, detailed descriptions of Negroes in combat along the Mississippi River, from Port Hudson to Milliken's Bend, about ten miles north of Vicksburg, on the west side of the river. He states that the four Texas regiments ordered to wipe out the African Brigade at the Bend had hoped to do this by 8:00 a.m. on the day of the assault. It did not quite happen this way. When the Texans met the Black troopers there ensued a long hand-to-hand brawl that then and now is considered one of the most bitter and hotly contested actions of the Civil War. Bayonets and musket butts were used with exceedingly brutal effect by both sides, in part because the Black soldiers were far from expert in reloading their muskets, which were in many cases defective imports from Europe. The hot fight went on until noon in the most protracted hand-to-hand action of the war. After noon on June 7th broken, bloody Black and White bodies carpeted the levees. The assault commander, Confederate Brigadier General Henry McCulloch, said in his action report that wounds sustained by his men were more severe, with fewer of them being slight, than those in any other engagement he had witnessed.

Quarles's account of Milliken's Bend suggests this author understood both the nature and significance of this incredibly costly bit of combat. He states that, ...If the record of casualties is the best gauge of severe and gallant action, the Black soldiers [at the Bend] truly distinguished themselves on that sweltering [95-degree] June morning. Lieb's 9th Louisiana suffered 60 percent of its strength in dead and wounded, 60 killed in action and 98 wounded...more than any other Union unit lost in a single fight during the Civil War. Only 21 were counted missing. The 9th began the battle with 285 in action. First Lieutenant David Cornwell was second in command of this regiment's B Company. He remained close to his soldiers throughout the fight and left the field only at the end when ordered to do so by Colonel Lieb because of a disabling wound. From early summer dawn until noon (likely about six to seven hours) the opposing White and Black infantry slugged it out in repetitive bayonet assaults. When it was over Admiral David D. Porter reported to U.S. Grant that his visit to the scene shortly after disclosed that "...dead Negroes lined the ditch inside of the parapet or levee and were mostly shot on the top of the head. In front of them, close to the levee, lay an equal number of rebels, stinking in the sun."

Reverberations from the battle at Milliken's Bend continued a long time for Cornwell and African Brigade commander Herman Lieb. About twenty years afterward Cornwell, at the request of Lieb, corrected a defamatory controversy over who commanded at the Bend, the combat conduct of Lieb, and the mystery of the missing White officers of the 11th Louisiana who panicked and left the immediate ground of combat during the fight. The Colonel of this regiment actually deserted it early in the fray and swam his horse out into the river and took refuge aboard the gunboat *Choctaw*. He resigned his commission soon after. Conflicting accounts of command deficiencies at the Bend were first published in a leading Illinois journal late in 1884. The Cornwell-Lieb version carried the day. Much later an exchange of 1907-08 letters published in the *National Tribune* again stirred the embers of conflict over Milliken's Bend. Once more Cornwell jumped in and publicly flayed those whose memories were faulty in the extreme, to say the least.

Perhaps the most significant contribution of the Cornwell memoirs is the picture David sketches of the between-battle life of Union Army troops in the trans-Appalachia theaters of operation along the Tennessee and Mississippi Rivers. Compared to the seasoned veterans of the Army of the Potomac, the western soldiers of Grant, Sherman, MacPherson, Wallace, Buell and others commanding along the roads from Fort Henry to Vicksburg were somewhat unique. Except for those recently arrived from eastern states, the troops of the Western armies were products of less orderly, rather unsophisticated frontier society...less disciplined, more aggressive, physically usually more durable, more accustomed to hardships of all kinds. Also, these soldiers were less adapted to regimentation and were generally more keenly attuned to the exigencies and demands of the frontier life-styles and philosophies. Western troops would fight extremely well when led by respected, competent commanders. Command competency often was questioned by the ranks, and the western soldier was at his proud, independent best when led by those who understood him. This comes through in the Cornwell story, which seems to reflect the attitudes of quite a number of troops in the Western Army commanded by Grant and Sherman through the siege and fall of Vicksburg.

The memoirs disclosed a peculiar officer-noncommissioned soldier relationship, that at worst sometimes bordered on insubordination, or at least on an unprofessional, unsoldierly relationship. In World War II, at least, an enlisted soldier never casually drifted into a company commander's tent just for friendly conversation. In Cornwell's army, this could happen...at least when a brassy, articulate soldier like him never became overly impressed by the position or presence of the commissioned ranks. Cornwell's one-man Army flanking action at Shiloh was condoned by his company commander and even received some faint praise. He appears, regardless of rank or lack of it, to have been a leader respected in combat by his peers. Surely, he went places and did things that no commander would have dared order him to go or do. Often walking just beyond the boundary of insubordination, or at least in the shade of supercilious contempt, Cornwell managed time after time to earn a good measure of esteem from his commanding officers.

David Cornwell was a complex man. Inside a rough-and-ready crusty frontier-shaped character was a very sensitive person who loved and longed for the "good things" life offered then in a cultured, comfortable setting. His family never knew how or where he acquired his love of music and literature. Even before military service, he played the violin, alone or in concert with others. He served at times as company bugler while in the 8th and in McAllister's battery of the 2nd Illinois Light Artillery. And he mentions playing a piano in a deserted, southern plantation house. He "liberated" a set of Sir Walter Scott volumes in calf binding from a home in Mississippi and found a safe, dry storage room for them in an artillery caisson by throwing out an axle jack...he highly respected what was universally then considered fine in literature, music, and manners. Indeed, once long after the war, he played his violin with the prominent Norwegian violin virtuoso Ole Bull while visiting in Chicago. Even after the turn of the century, he played his violin while accompanied by his pianist daughter, Emma Owen, in Allegan, Michigan. And somewhere along the line during his tempestuous youth he found time to pick up more than a smattering of formal education. During his carpenter days in Chicago, before the war, he spent winters in a community north of town enrolled in a public school. His memoirs alone reflect an active, cultured, sensitive intellect. The quality of his prose often surpasses that attained by many college graduates today. Of course, one has to keep in mind that the author is writing about his life of forty or more years earlier in a style of prose developed during the Victorian Era, and it reflects a dusting of southwestern Michigan speech patterns and terms popular there between about 1880 and 1910.

One unique feature of the memoirs is that they throw more light on some of the routine activities in the day-to-day lives of Western soldiers. The "little things," such as handling of the individual messes, clothing, rations, training, shelter, recreation, transportation, pay, crimes and punishments, all get some attention in Cornwell's story. Relationships between White northern troops and White southern society, between Union Army White soldiers and Union Army Black troops, are described in warm, interesting detail, with a stimulating sense of humor surfacing regularly throughout these accounts. Cornwell's description of how he (when a major) "moved out" a group of prostitutes from a house coveted by the army at Vicksburg is especially humorous and told in an earthy, descriptive manner in no way Victorian or military in style.

David Cornwell's service with Colored Troops (USCT) was lengthy and included a spicy, fascinating variety of assignments, from the heat of hand-to-hand, desperate, bloody combat at Milliken's Bend June 7, 1863, to garrison duty in and near Vicksburg after September 1863. It must be reasonably doubted that not more than a handful of White Union Army soldiers worked more closely with Black soldiers than did Cornwell. As a new first lieutenant, he commanded a two-company reserve force at the Bend battle and stood by his "Darkie" troops during the entire assault by General "Dick" Taylor's Confederate infantry and cavalry. He was fortunate that he was only wounded seriously here. His company commander in the 9th Louisiana Regiment was taken prisoner and executed by the Confederates simply for having fought alongside colored troops and commanding them. Cornwell returned to active duty in the fall of '63 along with an almost completely useless right arm, still carrying a musket ball souvenir close to the shoulder. This lead intruder remained in his arm and was lowered with him into his final resting place many years later. At least he died possessing both arms. An eager, young surgeon had wanted to amputate the shattered member on a river boat shortly after the Bend engagement. But Lieutenant Dave would have none of this.

In the fall of '63, Colonel Herman Lieb, commander of the African Brigade at the Bend, was ordered to convert the shattered remnants of the 9th Louisiana Regiment into a Heavy Artillery Regiment as quickly as possible. This unit was then to become a major military force responsible for protection of Vicksburg. So, Dave Cornwell, with only the slightest acquaintance with artillery gained during non-combat association with light field pieces of the Illinois 2nd Light Artillery Regiment, Battery D, during the weeks between Shiloh and Milliken's Bend, now did everything he could possibly do to back up Lieb's assignment. Lieb now had to produce an effective Black artillery regiment using troops only two or three months away from slavery in the nearby cotton fields along the mud fringes of the sluggish Mississippi.

The welding together of all the forces and factors involved required a firm, experienced, sympathetic hand on the part of White officers. Cornwell was fortunate to have had with him a small, dedicated cadre of Black troops who had survived the Bend conflict. (The 9th Louisiana Infantry at the Bend had 60% casualties.) They respected his performance at the Bend...one of relatively few White officers who did not "drift off" during the heat of "touch and go," eyeball-to-eyeball confrontations along the levee. The new unit became the 5th U. S. Heavy Artillery Regiment (African Descent) armed with 10-inch Columbiads that weighed four tons each.

Cornwell's services continued in the Vicksburg District until he was mustered out in May 1866. For a while, as a major, still under Colonel Lieb's command, he served as the Inspector General of the Department. He seems to have greatly enjoyed the change of pace in this duty, and especially the increased prestige and broader latitude it gave him in exercising his by now rather broad understanding of the Army and of what was expected of soldiers at most levels of responsibility and command. The major continued his long-nurtured interest in developing the Black man into a valued, skilled, proud member of the Army establishment. Cornwell describes how that was done over a period of about two years. It seems to have been his philosophy that the solider who felt he looked like a soldier surely could be depended upon to act like one, and appear to others to be one. And this was a critical element of training in the lives of the Black garrison soldiers who now for the first time moved freely along the public byways and major thoroughfares of Mississippi, both on and off duty. How these troops appeared to local society, both Black and White, had to have been uppermost in the minds of the White officers who trained and commanded them. The Union Army regiments "of African Descent," formed the core of the occupation force along the Mississippi River. Crack, experienced White regiments were with Sherman. They could not be spared in the effort needed to overrun and consolidate Confederate real estate "liberated" by the Armies of the Tennessee and the Cumberland.

Major Cornwell's long association with Colonel Herman Lieb began early in the war when each served as a private in the 8th Illinois Volunteer Infantry Regiment during the initial 90-day stint. Apparently, during the Donelson and Shiloh fights, Lieb displayed a special military talent and command ability that placed him on the road to early commissioning. He had gained some military experience in Europe in the late 1840's. The Cornwell memoirs leave no doubt that Dave admired Lieb and seemed always comfortable about being under his capable command. This had not been true of many other officers Cornwell had served under. The two had observed each other in action at Milliken's Bend and that experience doubtlessly cemented a friendship that endured long after the war. Lieb's apparently fearless command from horseback at the Bend vividly impressed all who saw him and marveled that he did not get blasted from horseback as the battle progressed. Cornwell admired greatly Lieb's courage and skill in combat. But the Colonel's appearance, his distinguished presence and bearing, his cultural and literary background, his European aristocratic connections, all added up to the totality of manhood that Cornwell found very impressive. Dave had no time for wimps and slackers of whatever rank, but was quick to note and admire what he considered to be most desirable in the overall makeup of a human being struggling to perform well and courageously under the often terrifying stress of battle. Herman Lieb on his part reciprocated the friendship and respect shown himself by the cocky, young officer volunteer from Chicago and "the Old 8th."

For the serious student of Civil War history, as well as for those just beginning to explore this tragic, epic national blunder, the memory of Brevet Lieutenant Colonel David Cornwell takes the reader down a fascinating path that continually casts fresh, new light on the nature of the human being involved. Even his usually light, humorous recollections of farm life and country general store management comprise a warm, sharp look at what happened to many officer veterans of the Grand Army. The sudden depreciation in quality of life style must have tested the soul and nerve of many mustered out officer veterans. To move from the rather pleasing existence of a garrison officer living with family in comfortable, permanent quarters in a sophisticated southern town to the rigors and gross uncertainties of farm life in southwestern Michigan must have been very hard indeed. Dave had never really farmed for a living...he had been a carpenter and the wound from Milliken's Bend had pretty much destroyed the career of a right-handed craftsman. Accidents of wartime misadventures and geography combined to settle him on a small Michigan farm in Allegan County's Salem Township early in 1867. He inherited this place from Michigan cavalry veteran Joshua Cornwell, who died in January 1867, never having returned to wife Charity and three children in western New York State. Dave himself had married Frances Millen of Chicago about 1864 and their first child, Frank, was born in Mississippi. So, it was a family of three that settled in Allegan County on the Salem Township plains, just south of the Big Rabbit River. Even amidst all the bleakness and relative poverty during his early years here, Cornwell remained in contact with Herman Lieb who settled in the Chicago area...back to being a big city businessman in the kind of world he had left in 1861.

An especially interesting account in the memoirs relates the final Lieb-Cornwell skirmish having to do with the Civil War. A White officer veteran of Milliken's Bend published in a Springfield, Illinois newspaper about 1885 a base, untrue, disparaging account of Lieb's role at the Bend. Dave was informed about the article and Lieb suggested that he, the old major, do something to set the record straight, which he did, quickly and satisfactorily and in no uncertain terms, very much to Lieb's complete, public vindication and personal pleasure.

As the oldest surviving great-grandchild of David Cornwell, I take considerable pride in presenting these memoirs, which probably should have been published many years ago. But perhaps now will be a more favorable moment. The iconoclasts of yesteryear sometimes may simply have been misunderstood prophets.

JMW
1998

David Cornwell C.1862

INTRODUCTION

In offering this book to the public, I might say in excuse for it being devoid of literary flavor that during my lifetime I have been much too busy earning a living to qualify myself for authorship. The inspiration did not take hold of me until in my old age I got out of a job and felt a need of some pleasant occupation to while away the time.

Of my boyhood days, my life on the farm and in the country store, I have given the humorous side only, but have at times struck a serious vein in describing military maneuvers and battles from the viewpoint of both a non-commissioned and regimental staff officer.

Stories of Army life written by literary people are for the most part creatures of their imagination and convey a very erroneous idea of real warfare. The "panorama" at Gettysburg is no doubt artistically fine, but as a representation of actual warfare, it is in many respects strictly absurd. The same may be said of most of the war pictures displayed in the print shops.

During my service in the Volunteer Army from April 1861 to May 1866 I do not remember that I swelled up with pride at every glimpse of "Old Glory floating in the breeze." Our carried regimental colors kept one man from using a gun and disclosed our position to the enemy. The screeching of the fifes, and the beating of drums did not thrill me with determination to do and die for my country, but only with the disposition to make a bonfire of those instruments of torture and soldiers of the torturers. And I readily overcame that feeling of dependence upon the commissioned officers that I had brought into the service with me, for a better acquaintance (with them) taught me that many were in all respects inferior to some of the privates in the ranks. Also, I could see no use of a chaplain wearing an officer's uniform and drawing the pay of a half dozen soldiers and boring us with dull sermons. I couldn't imagine the soul of a solider who had died in the defense of his country being consigned to an orthodox hell, whatever his opinion might be of a plan of salvation. One can scarcely respect a man who voluntarily enlists in a war and then persistently sends up petitions to the throne of grace for protection from the dangers incident thereto.

In war it is the duty of a soldier to kill as many of the enemy as possible, and take every practical precaution against the enemy killing him and his comrades. Every soldier killed is a dead loss to himself, and a large money loss to the government. Yet, some of our generals sacrificed their men by the thousands through imbecility, or to make a reputation as fierce fighters.

That the reader many not tire of campaigning I will sandwich in many stories of other days without regard to chronological sequence.

David Cornwell.

Allegan, Mich.
(c. 1908)

CHAPTER I

One day during the winter of 1859 and '60 I heard it reported on the streets of Bloomington, Illinois that Abraham Lincoln would speak at Empire Hall that evening. I had never seen Mr. Lincoln, knew little of him, but thought he was much over-rated by the Republicans of central Illinois. I dropped in late, which resulted in my having to stand up.

Very soon a party came down the aisle led by David Davis, then circuit judge of McLean County, and later Chief Justice of the U.S. Supreme Court and U.S. Senator. And on his arm was a tall man whom I recognized as Mr. Lincoln. They were followed by Leonard Swett and his law partner William W. Orme, Banker Gridley, and others. They all took seats on the stage and Mr. Swett at once introduced the speaker.

Mr. Lincoln stepped to the footlights and was received with a round of hearty applause. He was homely, ungainly, slow of speech, choice of words, and careful in the construction of his sentences. I would have been glad to have him give way to young Orme, whom I very much admired.

I do not remember if it was before or after this date that Orme had his debate with Attorney Williams from this platform. The latter had publicly accused Orme of voting against a popular bill while a member of the state assembly, and this Orme indignantly denied. And here he produced the official records of the session, which proved that the vote was on a motion to lay on the table, and that he was recorded with the ayes.

"So you see, my fellow citizens," exclaimed Orme, "that I did not vote against this bill at all, but simply to lay it on the table where it would be convenient to take it up at the proper time and pass it, and not be put away in a pigeon-hole where it would never be seen again."

It was just the other evening [c. 1905] that I heard Senator [Robert] LaFollette from the lecture platform explain that a vote to lay on the table is a vote to kill the bill. So I mention this fact that the young reader may not miss the fallacy and humor of Orme's contention, as many of us young Republicans did on that occasion in Bloomington.

Mr. Lincoln soon finished the dull preliminaries and made a point that brought forth vigorous applause. Then I began to pay better attention. He went after another and he got it, too. He was getting interesting now and they came faster and hotter. His general appearance was undergoing a change for the better; his awkwardness had deserted him. His step had become firm and at times he would clench his hands and shake his fist at us as if he knew what he was talking about and meant exactly what he said. His eyes snapped when he referred to a declaration of Senator Stephen A. Douglass that those who made the system of slavery a subject of public discussion should be imprisoned.

"I," said Mr. Lincoln, "discuss the institution whenever I feel inclined and shall continue to do so, and if anyone attempts to arrest me for exercising the right of free speech they will find themselves engaged in a fight that they will only be too glad to crawl out of."

When he concluded there was a storm of applause and I was quite willing to concede him the leadership of the Illinois Republicans.

The next time I saw Mr. Lincoln it was on the fair grounds at Springfield the next summer [1860]. He had received the nomination of his party and we went down there to have a big blowout. The crowd was estimated as high as 75,000, but I think fifty would have been nearer correct. Speaking was going on at several stands when he unexpectedly arrived on horseback, accompanied by a small escort, and alighted at the stand nearest the entrance; that is, he evidently intended to, but as a matter of fact he alighted on the shoulder of a gang of lunatics who conveyed him to the speaking stand.

There was then a grand rush from all parts of the grounds, and the various speakers vaulted over the railing of their stands and sprinted along with their crowds.

When the multitude got out of breath and ceased their yelling Mr. Lincoln said that he had rode out to see us and let us see him; that he well understood that it was the principles that he represented, and not himself personally, that had produced this boundless enthusiasm, and that he hoped we would all call at his residence before we left the city, that he might have the pleasure of taking us by the hand. That is not all that he said but it happens to be all that I remember of it. And I think he got about all he could stand of the hand shaking function, for he looked pretty well fagged when I gave him the Republican grip.

One of the speakers at the fair grounds corralled old man Hanks [old friend of Mr. Lincoln] of rail splitting renown and told his crowd that he had him up there on his stand and that he would bring him forward and have him tell us the whole story. But they found the old fellow a tough proposition--tougher than any of the rails that he and Abe had split for it took a man on each side to steer him and two pushers in the rear to get him up where we could see him. And then he nearly collapsed and could only say "Yes gentlemen, it is true, me and Abe did split together."

We spent the evening at the Wigwam listening to campaign songs by the Lombard boys and vehement and fiery harangues from Senator Trumbull, Owen Lovejoy, and Senator Doolittle of Wisconsin. The latter must have carried a bottle in his pocket to have kept up such a pressure of steam. He said that in November we would consign the damned rotten old Democratic party to the lowest depths of hell.

It was near midnight when we boarded the box and platform railroad cars in which we came, a tired and sleepy community, and headed back home.

Senator Douglass later came through Bloomington on a special and had with him a couple of body-guards, and a field gun mounted on a platform car. He came up to the Ashley House in an open carriage from which he spoke a few moments after finishing his dinner.

Schuyler Colfax was at the time talking from a stand on the courthouse square, and for this reason the Little Giant did not attract as much attention as he otherwise would have.

I recall a story told by Senator Douglass at a picnic dinner at Highland Park, given by his Chicago friends, where the toasts were drunk in champagne. He was running for Congress or some other office, and made a trip to a public work where there was a gang of Irish moving real estate with pick, shovel and wheelbarrow.

He obtained permission from the Boss, and made them a speech as they sat around on their barrows, and when he had finished one of them asked him if there was any Scotch blood in him.

"On my father's side," replied the candidate.

"Did ye descend from the Duglises of Scotland?" asked another.

"Yes, certainly," responded Stephen A.

Then another old fellow butted in with, "by the holy St. Patrick but you made a hell of a descent."

Caleb B. Smith of Indiana spoke at Bloomington also and I thought him the most forceful and accomplished orator of them all. Tom Corwin of Ohio was also there during the campaign. I remember him as a large, florid-faced man, very fluent of speech and somewhat given to humor. I cannot recall any of his stories upon this occasion, but will give one of his old ones, which is worth repeating and will probably be new to the young reader.

He was then Judge Corwin, and while making a horseback ride on his circuit he put up one night at a country tavern where the beds were full, and he was compelled to double-up with an Irishman. He quizzed "Larry" about the economic conditions of the Emerald Isle, his family connections and personal prospects, and learned that he was a single man, had been in America only a year, had had poor luck and was seriously thinking of going back to the old sod. He had not in fact formed a very good opinion of "the Land of the Free and the Home of the Brave."

This was Tom's opportunity and he at once sang him a song about this gloriously free and easy country of ours, where every man stands upon an equality with his neighbor, with full liberty to down him if he can; where he is free to aspire to any office with the chances much in his favor of his perspiring and coughing up very freely, and then getting left at the polls. And then with much modesty he referred to his own case of a farmer's boy who through his own efforts had worked his way up to his present position of Circuit Judge. And unfortunately he added,

"Now Larry! you would have lived a long time in the Old Country before you would have had the honor of sleeping with a judge", and "Larry" told him (Corwin) that he would have had to live there a long time before he would have been a judge.

The candidates for Illinois governor, the only and old genuine Dick Yates and another man with John A. Logan and Owen Lovejoy, talked from the same stand one afternoon. The two former were fair speakers, and the last two were originals.

I can recall but one little pleasantry of the occasion, which came about from Logan's saying that Lovejoy so hated a Democrat, that had he to choose between one and the devil, he would prefer the latter. Lovejoy's rejoinder was that the rule of choosing the least of two evils would compel him to do so.

Richard J. Oglesby of Decatur, candidate for the state senate, was a very popular and able talker, and was much in evidence in McLean County during the campaign.

Later I heard "Long John" Wentworth introduce William H. Seward to several acres of people near the Wigwam in Chicago, where Mr. Lincoln was nominated, and listened to that oration, commencing with "All Hail the Great State of Illinois."..."All Hail the Great City of Chicago."

He looked like a dwarf beside "Long John," but his nose was large and he could deliver an oration as perfect in construction as a chapter of Macaulay's History of England.

The first time I saw John Wentworth was in the spring of 1855. He was then the City's Mayor and was testing a steam fire engine in the vicinity of the Sherman House. They were a new thing, and very few of them had been tried, some in Cincinnati, I believe.

This machine bore the name of "Long John," and it threw a large stream on the roof of the Sherman. It must have proved very satisfactory, for the city was soon after supplied with them, and the old hand-brake concerns with volunteer firemen were soon mustered out of the service.

At that time Chicago had about sixty-five thousand people. The surrounding country was full of deer, the prairies alive with chickens, and the timber lands along the north shore of the lake were full of squirrels and partridges. One winter day a large buck came pacing in on West Randolph Street, and was cornered and killed near the old West Market.

The city was at that time built out about a mile west of the Chicago River, and beyond was endless prairies, largely utilized by the herding of milch cows owned in the city. A herder would ride out over certain streets each morning, and as he came along the people turned their own Bossies out to him. He would keep them out on the prairie all day and bring the bunch back in about sundown. Then each cow would of her own accord drop out at her stable or yard.

There were men living there at that time who thought Chicago had seen its best days. A shoemaker who had a shop of his own and was doing a good business sold out and bought forty acres of prairie land on which he barely subsisted by much hard labor, and when he died his land had only increased in value 25% while the lots he parted with in the city had appreciated one thousand percent. Another was a mover of buildings in a small way whose outfit cost about one thousand dollars. One day he came to the conclusion that he had moved all the buildings that needed moving, and so he sold his house and lot for 13,000 cash, went into the country and died skin poor. But he lived long enough to see that city lot he had sold worth 125,000.

To go back to William H. Seward, I first made his acquaintance by "proxy" when I was nine or ten years of age. At the time my father [Joshua Cornwell] was the owner and captain of a scow boat on Erie Canal, and took me along to do the driving [of mules or horses along the towpath bordering the canal]. Mr. Seward had a better job for he was the Empire State's Governor. Our boat was of but sixty-five tons burden and bore the name of Blue Jacket, suggested by the color of her cabins. We used but one pair of horses and tied up the boat at nights. We lived in the stern cabin and the bow cabin was the team's stable.

That father of mine had a streak of eccentricity running through his corporate system, and one day he got a small pig and turned it loose in the horse cabin. After it had got familiar with its surroundings I scraped its acquaintance with a curry comb and soon had it lying across my knees while I sat on the bow deck and polished it with the horse brush. The bowsman named it Roxanna, after his Buffalo sweetheart, and in the course of time it answered to the name of Roxey by coming at my call and following me about.

This resulted in a strong attachment growing up between us, and when it backed off into the canal one day I immediately jumped in after it and would have drowned had not the bowsman fished me out with a pikepole. Roxey would have taken me ashore, had I sense enough to have caught it by the tail.

The bowsman would frequently madden me by hinting that Roxey was about large enough to kill. I would admit that it might be all right to kill the ordinary sort of pig, but would insist that Roxey was not one of the kind. And I had a scheme for picking up old rope and iron to sell and pay my father what the pig cost him, and then she would be mine. That would end forever the talk about killing Roxey.

We were lying at Albany unloading lumber one day about 1848, when my father stepped onto the bow of the boat followed by a tall, freckled-faced Irishman. He told me to call Roxey up and I did so. And I was about to put her through some of her stunts for their edification when this son of Limerick drew a grain sack from the sag of his blouse and my father reached for the pig. I at once kicked Roxey down the bridge into the horse cabin, and squared myself across the gangway and asked my father what he was up to. He said he had given the pig to Governor Seward for a roaster. "The hell you have," I exclaimed, and then turning to the Irishman I yelled, "You red mouthed son of a ----- get off this boat or I will kill you."

My father hoisted me on the cabin deck and disappeared down into the stable after Roxey. When I heard her squeal, I was fired with rage and sprang for a pike-pole and got it and myself back on the cabin deck just in time to crack that Irishman on the head as he started for shore on the gangplank. Into the canal he went, pig and all, I was still after him with the pole when the bowsman grabbed me and held me fast.

The Irishman hung onto Roxey and scrambled out. Then he made for a nearby saloon and here the pig escaped and dashed through the window into the street. There was a span of drivers harnessed to a carriage at the curb, and at the breaking of the glass accompanied by Roxey's squealing they tore loose, went down the thoroughfare flying, and riddled the carriage against the truck wagons on the route.

I could not at that time understand why my father should be such a fool as to give a fine pig to Gov. Seward who had a good job while he himself was always in debt to the butcher. Then, too, my father was a Democrat while Seward may have been a Whig. But I doubt not but that my paternal ancestor would have readily flopped over for almost any little old office.

The last I saw of the Irishman he was walking with a policeman off down town, and it has been a consolation to believe that Roxey cost Seward several hundred dollars. And, he never got her either. I searched for her constantly during the two days that we remained in Albany, but without success. No doubt some of the numerous Irish around there had taken care of her.

My father felt it his duty to thrash me for the part I played in this transaction, but the bowsman told him that he better not, and as he was afraid of the bowsman, I got clear.

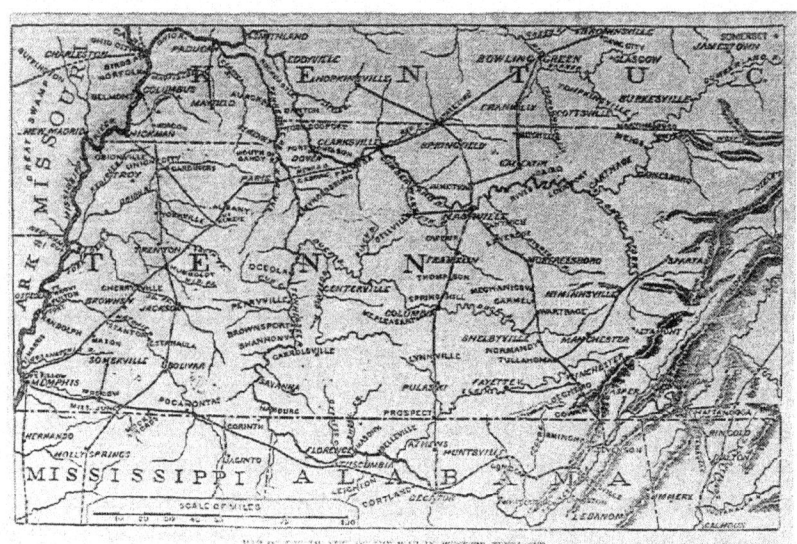

Harper's Weekley map of western Tennessee, February 1862... just when the Union Army began its move up the Tennessee River.

CHAPTER II

Election day rolled around and I cast my first vote for the whole Republican ticket. And I have always been satisfied with myself for so doing as it was creditable to be a Republican at that time. But there have been times since when I have thought it was not, and since then I have stood aloof from parties and been an Independent.

Winter [1860-61] came on and building was suspended. I could not afford to loaf three or four months, and blow in what little I had saved up, and so I took a tramp out among the farmers and helped them husk their corn. A younger brother, Frank, came down from Lake County, and we worked together by the job. The crop was excellent but the price was only eighteen cents per bushel delivered at a railroad elevator, and the farmers were not very jolly over their prosperity.

Then the currency was in a fearful condition. State bank bills, mostly southern, would depreciate twenty-five percent while one was crossing the street, so we took due bills for most of our pay, and realized on them later when conditions had improved.

When Spring came, and building commenced again, I secured my old job and Frank engaged to a farmer.

The April attack on Fort Sumter knocked all disposition to work out of me and I packed my kit and took to the street. I wrote Ward H. Lamon, Prosecuting Attorney for the County, who with Colonel Elmer E. Ellsworth had accompanied Mr. Lincoln to Washington as body guard, for some information about enlisting. Lamon was physically a fine specimen of a Kentuckian, and he said he had studied law with Lincoln. I made his acquaintance while doing some work on his house. I never heard of him afterward except through the papers and from them I gleaned that he started out to do some recruiting in West Virginia with a view of securing an appointment of Brigadier General. Failing in this he secured the appointment of U. S. Marshal of the District of Columbia.

We boys read extracts copied from southern journals, wherein they characterized the northern people as cowardly mudsills, a dozen of whom a gallant southerner would put to flight and much more such rot, and would read this stuff over and rave and cuss like a band of pirates. Then I bought the best revolver in a gunshop, filled my pockets with ammunition, and would go out mornings to a grove a couple of miles from the city and shoot at a mark. The second trip out I took a short but wide board with me and nailed it to a tree. With a piece of blue chalk I sketched a crude representation of a southern fire eater and talked to it and shot at it alternately. My mouth and revolver would run somewhat in this fashion:

"Hello Kernal, Good morning; you are from Alabama you say and personal friend of Jeff Davis. You are going to bust this Union all to smash, I understand. Now let me tell you something. You will likely get smashed yourself before you are through with that job. I believe I will take a pop at you right now." --Crack-- "There goes some of your chin whiskers," --Pop-- "and the end of your nose," --Bang-- "there you have it in the butt of the ear and may go bury yourself. Good bye Kernal, give my regards to the Devil when you get there.

"Now we will see if it will take three shots to polish off this old Nigger Driver from Georgia. You are the chap who says that the Yankees will run like sheep before the southerners. Maybe they will if you don't stand your ground. If you do, there will be a square fight: if you don't they will take after you for sure. We don't wear our hair as long as you do, nor brag as much, but we can cock a gun quite as quick and hit the broad side of a barn as often as you can. And to prove this I will take one shot at you just for luck." --Zip-- "There you have it in the jaw and won't waste any more corn dodgers for awhile. Now you may go back to your plantation and let your niggers feed you with a spoon while I attend to this blood sucker from South Carolina.

"Here we have the only genuine and original 'Ten-to-Onester' and I will try and bring him down the first shot; Ready-Aim-Fire-! Gee whiz, but I missed him -- Crack-- guess he's bullet proof; steady now --Bang-- there got him in the shoulder and he may go to the hospital.

"I must lead up and take a pop at that half-breed blackguard from Louisiana [Beauregard] who bossed that fight at Fort Sumter; steady now --Zip-- a dead shot. Now for the Texas Terror --Bang-- another center shot. I think these Lincolnites will amount to something after they have had a little practice."

I heard a suppressed laugh behind me and turning about saw a gentleman sitting on a down tree. I said, "Hello there; good morning," and then walked back and took a seat beside him.

His face was in his hands and he was choking with laughter. As soon as he had recovered his composure he said,

"What do you think you are doing here anyway?"

I explained to him that I was a candidate for the Army; was waiting for a letter from Washington to tell me where to go to enlist, and as I needed something to do to pass away the time thought a little pistol practice would be the correct thing.

"Well boy," he replied, "when you can shoot as straight as you can swear you will be a good marksman."

I thanked him for his encouragement and we sat there and talked for an hour or more.

When I arose to go he said he would drive in [to Chicago] after dinner, and he asked me to stay and ride with him.

I accepted his invitation and we walked over to his house and took seats on his porch. Not long after a colored woman called us to lunch and I followed the gentlemen into the dining room. His wife was standing behind her chair at the side of the table, and when I was presented to her she came forward and gave me her hand.

She was a very beautiful young woman of twenty-five, and her husband's face indicated that he was ten years her senior. He took the seat at the end of the table and his wife and I sat on each side. Although there was every evidence of wealth and refinement here, their manner was free from stiffness and formality, and I was soon as much at home in their society as I would have been with people of my own class.

They were both fine talkers, she full of wit and laughter, he quite sober but very droll.

At the close of our repast my host proceeded to enlighten his pretty wife regarding the circumstances of our meeting. He had heard some firing in the grove the previous morning, and being near there about ten o'clock this forenoon, he saw me entering from the direction of the city with a board under my arm.

He said he kept himself out of sight but near enough to observe all my movements, and then he minutely described my maneuvers even to the hunting for a stone hammer to nail up the board, and said I picked it up at the foot of the tree behind which he was standing. And he described how I had with a piece of blue chalk, such as carpenters use on their chalklines, sketched a full-length caricature in profile of a southern fire-eater on the board, and then leisurely loaded a revolver.

And then assuming that a portrait of Henry Clay that hung on the wall opposite him was the target, and taking up the carving fork to represent a revolver, he went through with the whole of that absurd performance of mine in the grove, without skipping a word, or gesture.

I was not only astonished, but delighted with this exhibition, for it was the most perfect acting that I had ever seen. Why, that man never forgot a word of his lines, but possibly put in a few that I had forgotten, and he never cracked a smile although his wife and I were dying with laughter.

I could then plainly realize what a fool I had made of myself, but did not regret it when it had brought about this amusing entertainment. I afterwards learned that my friend, George, had had ten years on the stage.

We sat at the table about two hours, and before we arose I had promised to lunch with them whenever I came out to the grove to practice.

A colored man brought out a pair of well bred matched drivers to a road wagon, and we started a leisurely trip to the city.

On the way I casually remarked that I had noticed none of the accessories of a farm about on his premises and was told that he inherited quite a tract of land, and only gave the farms a general supervision; that his wife was the daughter of a lumber dealer in St. Louis where they spent their winters.

I innocently inquired if she had any younger sisters, and he replied that she was an only daughter.

"Well! I must congratulate you upon having the most beautiful and elegant woman that it was every my good fortune to meet," said I. He said, "I have known thousands of them Dan., and she is the best one that I ever met also. There is not a trace of superstition or vanity about her, and it is not in her nature to be guilty of an inelegant action. The best I can wish you is that you may safely get through the war and find as good a one."

I thanked him for his kind wishes, and with a friendly shake he dropped me at the hotel.

A few days later I went out to the grove again, where I whiled away an hour or more shooting, and then sauntered over to the house and found my friends awaiting me on the porch. We soon after adjourned to the dining room where we satisfied our appetites and as Deacon Primrose would express it, indulged in elevating conversation. Although this handsome and cultured couple, surrounded with elegant appointments, were much superior to one in my humble station in life, their manner was so free from any symptom of pride or affectation that I felt quite at ease in their company. I was unable to detect in the slightest degree, from word or manner, any indication of a sense of superiority on their part, and I especially noticed that the darkey servants were addressed in a low, kind voice.

That I did not maintain my full share of conversation at this pleasant home I freely admit. But I was allowed every opportunity, and was encouraged to do so. These friends simply filled up the time with funny reminiscences that were delightful to listen to.

Upon rising from the table, George produced a box of cigars, and then we took seats on the veranda. After taking a few whiffs of the Perfecto I remarked that this cigar reminded me of a boyish incident back in New York.

"Please tell us about it," said my pretty hostess, and so I went on to say that,

"When about fourteen years of age I was the sole proprietor of an Apple-Cart and Peanut Stand located at Mudge and Doty's corner, in the city of Rome, New York. John Stryker, a wealthy lawyer, had a bright kid of about my age who was always hungry for such truck as I kept in stock, and was one of my best customers. He was quoted in Juvenile Bradstreet A.1, and his credit with my firm was unlimited.

"One day he brought a pocketful of cigars and offered to apply them on his account at the valuation of one cent each. I readily agreed to the proposition and it resulted in my getting one hundred at a net cost of fifty cents.

"Later Young Johnny said that he couldn't supply me with any more for his father missed the stock, mistrusted him and he then owned up to it. He said his father had called him a donkey for retailing out his cigars for a cent each when they had cost him ten wholesale.

"They were elegant for a fact, and I smoked the last of them since I came to Illinois. And the flavor of this reminded me of them."

George excused himself and strolled off in the direction of one of his farm houses, and this left me alone with this incomparable beauty. I adroitly led the conversation upon the subject of music, and as soon as an opportunity offered intimated that I would like very much to hear the tone of her grand piano. She laughed merrily, said, "Splendid, I just need a little practice and an auditor," and gaily tripped into the music room, opened up the instrument, gave the stool a left hand twirl, and gracefully seated herself thereon.

I took a seat on her left, in line with the keyboard, and had a profile view of her sweet face and could watch the manipulation of the ivories.

She sat well up, with her elbows above the level of the keyboard, and her hands fell into those fine curves that will make even a coarse hand look quite graceful. The piano is unquestionably a woman's instrument, for there is no other that gives them a pose so utterly becoming, if they will sit up well and hold their hands properly.

There are fine lady violinists it is true, but the curves of their arms and hands are not those of grace and beauty, and there is a seeming lack of muscular strength unless they are of the large and robust sort.

If a woman does not look passably well when properly seated at the piano, then God help her; there is no hope.

I observed that the colored man wore a large ring on each hand and the fingers of his wench were adorned with many of them, with an additional pair in her ears, but their master and mistress did not sport any of these barbaric gewgaws on themselves.

A ring detracts from the beauty of a pretty hand, and upon a homely one it attracts attention to it, and accentuates its ugliness. It is very common to see a ring on the fingers of a man and many on the fingers of a woman, and one must be excused if he exclaims, "Great Scott! In this respect we are not a whit more civilized, and quite as vain and ridiculous as the most ignorant and barbarous races."

As the lady took her seat at the piano, and placed her little white hands on the keys, she presented the prettiest picture in real life that I had ever seen. There was at the Columbian Exposition, in the English Department of the Art Gallery, a painting of a young woman with a harp that was so exquisitely beautiful, that since 1893 I have associated in my mind these two pictures; one of real life, the other of art. Neither of their beautiful forms was marred by jewelry.

But the former had the advantage of life and action, and her pretty fingers commenced rapidly chasing each other, forward and backward, though lightning runs and thrilling trills till my hair tingled at the roots and I was charmed beyond expression.

The concert continued thirty minutes or longer without cessation, during which time she sang a couple of familiar songs, one of them being "Ben Bolt." I have since heard Adelina Patti, while on one of her many farewell tours, warble "Home, Sweet Home," and the "Suwannee River." But this did not enthuse me for I had heard a sweeter voice in 1861. My entertainer would occasionally strike a familiar strain, but I think most of it was improvised. At the conclusion she turned to me and with a smile said,

"I really believe you do enjoy music."

"It is the most delightful half-hour I ever spent," I replied.

"I am pleased to hear you say it, even if it is an exaggeration. I have enjoyed it myself, so it has been time well spent; but must you go now?"

Yes, I had to go then; I was quite sure of that. I knew why, but she did not. When she gave me her lovely little hand at parting, thrills ran through me from stem to stern and I struck the pike in a dazed condition.

Cornwell's Civil War experiences were connected in many ways to the Mississippi, from Cairo to Natchez, along often uncertain meandering, as "Big Muddy" reached for its terminal at the Gulf of Mexico.

CHAPTER III

About the middle of April, the President's call was made for seventy-five thousand men, and a number of us met at the Court House and drew up and signed an enlistment roll. I was number six, and I placed my brother's name beneath my own. Then I took a stroll of about four miles out in the country and found him plowing.

I took the team and started around the field while Frank went to the house to report to his employer and get his pay. This farmer happened to be a Democrat who didn't like war talk and he claimed that he had hired Frank for the season, and that he had to work his time out; then he refused to pay him.

So we put the horses in the stable, and carried my brother's luggage into town. The next day this old farmer drove in, hunted Frank up and paid him.

The enlistment roll soon ran up to one hundred and fifty, and under the direction of a Mr. Harvey, we had each evening a drill in marching. A few days later our company was accepted by Gov. Yates and we were ordered to report to the State Capitol forthwith.

Arrangements were made with the railroad agent for a train the next day at noon, and in the morning I ran out to the grove to bid my charming friends good bye. They were out driving but returned in about a half hour, and we had another pleasant chat on the porch.

The rig was standing at the door and George had intimated that he would drive me back to the city. So I remained with them as long as possible, and feasted my eyes on this incomparable woman. When I arose to go I took her lovely hand and kissed it and saw a tear starting in each of her beautiful eyes, and I hastily turned away to conceal the hundreds that were coming in my own.

For the first time in my life I had fallen in love with a married woman, and I was badly smitten too. George seemed to suspect as much, for he drove rapidly and did not try to draw me into conversation. With a warm pressure of the hand and a hearty invitation to visit them upon my return, he dropped me at the Union House.

Like many other young men I had many flirtations, and at the time thought some were genuine love affairs. The first one I can call to mind was when I was seven or eight years of age and got enamored of a maid of twenty-three. I insisted upon calling on her every evening, and accompanying her to prayer meetings, or wherever her engagements might call her. I much preferred that she remain at home, for there I had a monopoly of her, and I was intensely jealous of every person regardless of sex, who showed her any particular attention in my presence. I especially abhorred the prayers and experience meetings, for I thought that the minister and some of the elders held the hand of Arabella (how I did love that name) much longer than their Christian duty demanded.

It also hurt my feelings to hear her tell of her love for the Savior, of whom I was becoming jealous, also. As a matter of fact, I was gradually working up a grievance against the minister, the deacons and the whole Trinity.

One day Arabella jollied my two grown-up sisters about my infatuation, and related an incident of a few evenings before that which transpired at an experience meeting held in the basement of the Airtight Baptist Church. The Rev. Calkins, who was conducting, had remarked about my regular attendance of late and might have thought that I was to some extent absorbing the divine influence, and also wishing, I think, to conciliate me a little as I had in an instance or two interferred with his manipulation of Arabella's hands, patted me on the head and asked me how I felt, and I replied "bully."

My elder brother and two sisters, who were taking the Wesleyan route to the Holy City, were horrified at my coarse and limited vocabulary, and in the absence of our parents, jumped on me at the breakfast table with all their six big feet.

Their remarks were very sarcastic and threw me into such a rage that I grabbed the stove poker and ran my brother out of the house and two blocks down the street, swearing at him at every jump.

Being distanced, I returned to the house determined to brain my sisters, but they eluded me by retreating to their bedroom, bolting and barricading the door with furniture, and crawling under the bed.

That evening I called as usual upon my Dulcinea and found her alone in the parlor. She was sitting on a couch, industriously knitting new heels and toes into a pair of her father's old socks. I took a seat beside her and got my arm as far around her waist as it would reach, pressed my knee firmly against hers, and resigned myself to perfect bliss.

Before she sent me home she gave me a kiss and asked me if I really loved her. I at once brought my reserve arm into action, hugged her and grunted and declared it was a sure thing that I would never marry any woman but her. She said it was a long engagement and she would agree to it if I would promise not to visit her but once a week; and added that should I at any time change my mind that I would be free to break the engagement.

I replied that the conditions were dang tough, but I would stand them, and that my mind would not change because I wouldn't let it if it wanted to. Then she gave me another kiss and started me for home.

After I had crawled into bed that night I mourned over the hard conditions of my engagement, and had serious doubts about being able to live a week at a time without seeing Arabella; and then I tried to imagine that I had her there in my arms and felt that if it was so, in fact, my happiness would be complete.

A few evenings later I attended a kid party, and in one of the games I was chosen for a partner by a sweet little piece of femininity of nearly my own age, who exhibited toward me a decided preference throughout the whole evening. I wondered I had not noticed before how very pretty she really was. I could now see plainly that she was developing into a very beautiful girl and wondered at my great good fortune in tumbling so suddenly into her good graces. And I said mentally "My!

she really seems to like me and scarcely notices any other boy in the room; what nice little hands, and such a sweet smile when our eyes meet. Gee willikens! but I am getting there this evening all right."

And it turned out that way, too, for when I asked her if I might walk home with her she replied, "Did you think I wanted to walk home alone?" And then she handed me her cloak to adjust to her dainty shoulders, and while fastening the top button my hands came in contact with her little chin. I could hold in no longer and at once caught her in my arms and gave her a smack on her sweet lips. She adroitly slipped from my grasp, and being assured that no one had seen us she called me a very naughty boy and then laughed as if it was the funniest thing that had happened to her in many a day.

I held her hand all the way home (about two blocks) and I think we were the happiest kids in the town. At the door she put up her dainty mouth and I gave her another kiss and was gone in more ways than one.

A few evenings later, about sunset, I espied her on the lawn, and walking up to her I held out both hands. She put her pads into them, which gave me the assurance to tell her that she was looking very pretty and that I had thought of nothing but her since the party and that I was just dying to ask her if she would be my wife as soon as we were old enough to marry.

"Then you like me better than any other girl," she queried.

"You are the only girl that I care a snap for," I replied.

"Oh! I will promise if you will not squeeze my hand quite so hard, there, that is just about right. Say Dan, I have been thinking of you just as you have of me, and isn't it funny, but I knew you liked me best before you told me, for you know what happened in the cloak room and you would not have acted so if you hadn't thought a lot of me." And then she indulged herself in one of those bewitching laughs and continued, "Now isn't it real nice to be engaged for good and know just what is going to happen, and won't we have such lovely times thinking of it and talking about it and keeping it all to ourselves and getting ready for the wedding? And I won't have to have a great big doll every Christmas for when we are married we will buy one or two real live ones. Won't it be lovely fun to take care of them and feed them out of a bottle and hear the little things goo and laugh and doctor them up for what ails them. I know all about taking care of sick babies you see for when they have the mumps they look fat and cute and you mustn't give them any lemon juice nor vinegar. When they cry with the colic just dose them with peppermint and for measles clover tea and when they get wormy you just take a lump of sugar and pour turpentine all over it and drop it into their little mouths for they like sugar and will never know the difference, and as soon as they get well of that and commence crouping why then all you have got to do is to smear them all over with lard or goose grease and dose them with hen oil and they will soon be well again and ready for the-Say Dan there comes Pa and I guess you had better skip."

And I skipped. But wasn't she a sweet little prattler though; the loveliest on Earth, and knew so much and with all so innocent. She had many useful details stowed away in that dear little head of hers, but I was not so simple as she about the "Perpetuation of Species."

A few days had elapsed when one of my big sisters handed me a note which read as follows...

"My dear little Sweetheart

You did not call on me last evening as I expected, and I was very lonely. I was afraid that my little lover was sick, but your sister tells me that you are quite well and so you may come this evening.

From your dear

Arabella."

I read this over with much indifference, for I had not thought of Arabella (what a name) since the kid party. And to think that ancient female would suppose that I cared for her. As far as I was concerned, she was at liberty to distribute her virginal affections among the ministers, class leaders, deacons and the Trinity in any proportion she chose, for she was too much like my older sisters--and I just hated them. It was true that I did use to call on her and sometimes escort her to evening meetings but that was a long time ago and I didn't know very much then. I had recently had a couple of experience meetings of my own and had learned something about the rules of proportion. "No, my dear Arabella," I said mentally, "you are too much for me. I've got something dainty and sweet now," and I scribbled off the following on the margin of her note and handed it back to my sister. "Can't go. Got another girl."

-- ------ --

Soon we arrived at Springfield, and went into camp at the fair grounds, which was known at that time as "Camp Yates."

There we found a regiment of recruits, partly enlisted in the vicinity, and a company of militia doing camp guard duty under the command of a Captain Marsh, who was a very competent officer and a fine judge of good whiskey, or a good judge of fine whiskey, as you may choose.

We were quartered in the cattle sheds and each given a blanket. When my turn came the Quartermaster's Clerk inadvertently yanked two off the pile and I got both of them.

Richard J. Oglesby was on the ground and arranged for ten companies, among which was ours, to comprise a regiment, and got the colonelcy for the asking. He had served as a first lieutenant in Co. C, Fourth Infantry, in the Mexican War.

Frank L. Rhodes, captain of the company from Pekin, who was a private in Co. G of the Fourth, in Mexico and later a steamboat captain on the Illinois River, was chosen for the Lieutenant Colonel of the new regiment.

The candidates for Major were Captains John P. Post and Isaac C. Pugh, both with companies from Decatur. They been in the Mexican War, the former as first lieutenant Co. C. of the 4th Infantry and the latter as his captain. Unfortunately, as will appear later on, Post was selected to be the major.

Captain Charles E. Dennison of the Peoria company should have aspired to one of these field offices for he was a very competent man, who at the expiration of his three-month term, secured a captaincy in the Eighteenth Regular Infantry Regiment, U.S.A.

We were mustered into the service April 25th by Captain John Pope, of the Regular Army, with practically no physical examination. Only seventy-two men to the company were accepted, and as a rule the tallest men of our bunch were retained. My brother and I were of medium height and passed. One half of our number, comprising all the little fellows, were thrown out, and they cried and swore and damned the captain roundly to console themselves for their disappointment. They were all sent back to their homes, but did not have to wait long for an opportunity to get into the service.

The recruits that were there ahead of us were organized into a regiment under Colonel John Cook and took the number seven, and we got number eight. The first six numerals were used in the Mexican War and for historical reasons were not repeated. Otherwise we would have been the second [Regiment]. It was said at the time that Oglesby was the ranking colonel of the state, but if so it availed him little, for Prentiss, Grant, Payne and others were made brigadiers before he secured his star.

As soon as we were fairly organized, we were marched up to the arsenal in the city, armed, accoutered, and cartridged, and immediately after boarded a train, which pulled out for Cairo, Illinois.

CHAPTER IV

We reached Cairo in due time and there we found about 500 militia that had been sent down from Chicago about a week before, a part of which was a four-gun battery of field artillery. Two of these pieces were planted on the levee facing the river in front of the business part of the town and they looked very fine to us when we jumped off the train. The other two were at the extreme point of land where the Mississippi and Ohio Rivers meet, and the cannoneers kept a lookout for boats coming up or going down the Mississippi for the purpose of compelling them to round to and make a landing.

Steamboats were yet permitted to run below Cairo, but they could not carry arms, ammunition, or any article which our authorities thought might be of assistance to the secession conspiracy. So, boats going below were compelled to show their manifest and undergo a search for "contraband of war."

The custom of steamers was that when they intended making a landing they blew a prolonged whistle, and those coming up or down the Mississippi had to run up into the mouth of the Ohio where the wharf-boats were located. In all the cases that I noticed, the pilots would not pull whistle cord until the artillerymen had sent the second shot across their bow. None of them waited for the third, and so we never had the fun of seeing one of them get it amidships.

The principal business street of Cairo was along the Ohio levee, the stores facing the Illinois Central R.R. tracks and river beyond. The building farthest down, and nearest the point where the two six-pounders were planted on the site of an old brewery, was the St. Charles Hotel, a first-class house in a second-class village of only about 2,000 people. The levee extended on beyond the hotel about 200 yards, and there made a right-angle with the Mississippi levee opposite the "Old Brewery Battery."

Our regiment went into camp in some cheap sheds that had been constructed just inside of this Mississippi levee, with our front facing the village and our right resting at the angle noted above. None of the village was built farther south than the hotel and we had a commodious drill ground on our front.

We were supplied with the usual camp equipage and rations, and the commissioned officers went to the St. Charles.

Our companies from right to left were as follows:

Company A.	Captain	Isaac C. Pugh	From	Decatur
" B.	"	Henry P. Westerfield	"	"
" C.	"	James M. Ashmore	"	Charleston
" D.	"	John Lynch	"	Olney
" E.	"	Charles E. Dennison	"	Peoria
" F.	"	Joseph M. Hanna	"	Pekin
" G.	"	John McWilliams	"	Griggsville

"	H.	"	Andrew J. McCramer	"	Vandalia
"	I.	"	Daniel Grass	"	Lawrenceville
"	K.	"	William H. Harvey	"	Bloomington

The letter J is omitted, presumably because it has a sound some what like K, yet the tactical maneuvers where such a similarity of sound might cause a misunderstanding, the letters are not used, but the companies are designated from right to left as "First Company," "Second Company," etc.

In a newly organized regiment each company is assigned to its position in line according to the standing of its captain, and if these captains were commissioned on the same date, as might well happened, then their relative rank would be decided by the regimental commander by proof of former rank or military service, or by lot where no such proof existed. With ten captains in a regiment, one of them is senior to the other nine while the one next below him is junior to one and senior to eight. And so it follows that no two officers in a regiment stand upon an exactly even footing for while captains and lieutenants hold the same rank and draw the same pay as many others in their organization, they are junior or senior to each of them. And this should, everything else being even, decide the order of their promotion, and does settle the question of who takes command when out on duty together.

Now a senior captain of a new regiment gets the letter A for his company and has position on the right of the line, while the next to him in rank takes B and his place on the left. From right to left they are lettered as follows: A,F,D,I,C,H,E,K,G,B, but Colonel Richard Oglesby got things mixed somewhat, and while he may have given each captain his proper position in the line, only one company got the right letter, viz. Company A, for he lettered them from right to left as the alphabet runs from A to K, and not fancying the hard sound "K", was known among the boys as Company Q.

After a letter has once been given to a company, for reasons historical it cannot well be changed, and although the relative rank by seniority of company commanders is through promotion, resignation and death is constantly changing, yet as far as I knew companies retained their positions in line originally assigned them.

We had elected our K Company officers before we left Bloomington and William H. Harvey, a baker by trade, had no opposition for the captaincy, for he said he had served in the Mexican War, and had from the first put us through a little drill in alignment and marching. He did not sign the enlistment roll, and would not promise to go with us. So we forced him into it by electing him captain: Then he said that he intended to go all the time. His head was quite level: He knew the difference between thirteen and one twenty five per month and could see a material advantage in getting a good start. He probably did not go into the Mexican War from Illinois as I did not find his name in the roster from that state, but he had evidently been there on active duty.

Price Keith, a sort of a doctor, who lodged and had his office in a 6 by 8 room in one of the business blocks of Bloomington, and who was consulted chiefly by men and boys who had contracted sexual diseases, was so filled with patriotism that he offered to sacrifice his entire practice and his brilliant future prospects if we would make him our first lieutenant. We jumped at the chance and elected him. Another worthless jay with the euphonious name of Abram Handenburg secured enough votes to be elected to the second lieutenancy.

These lieutenancies we boys didn't think amounted to much, but when it came to selecting an Orderly Sergeant we looked around for better material and decided that Albert S. Eddy was about the right kind of stuff. He was the son of a Congregational clergyman, a bright handsome fellow, holding down a position in one of the banks, and answered to the name of Dell.

When the regimental staff was announced, just previous to leaving Springfield, Dell came in for the position of Quartermaster Sergeant, and I overhead him remark to one of the boys that he believed that was the office next below the colonel. This is a fact and I could never account for this bright young man entertaining such an absurd notion. So, thereafter we saw but little of Dell as his associates were exclusively commissioned officers.

The Quartermaster could not immediately supply us with uniforms, but the officers, who had to furnish their own, soon blossomed out in fine dark blue, with the regulation welt in the seams of their trousers, and the conventional brass buttons, and never forgetting the shoulder straps to advertise their rank. There was no uniformity in their headgear, some fancying caps and other hats of various styles and patterns.

Captain Harvey chose a black felt with one side looped up and secured in place with a brass eagle, and further ornamented with a plume or feather.

Our first lieutenant, "Doc" Keith, was a tall, spindle-legged jay, with a small head, long thin face and large feet. And he wore such tight boots that they hurt him unmercifully, for it was really painful to see him amble over the parade grounds. He was grave, dignified, and occasionally sober. Among the first to appear in full regimentals, on account of his length, he did not succeed in getting a pair of trousers long enough to fit him, and the bottom of the legs would persist in hitching up towards the top of his bootlegs. To overcome this difficulty he sewed buttons on the bottom of his pant legs, made a couple of elastic bands out of an old suspender, and secured them under the balls of his big feet. The result was that the waist band and his waistcoat parted company and exhibited about six inches of very dirty shirt.

One day as the officers were marching down to the center at the conclusion of a dress parade, one of Keith's buttons flew off and shot a pant leg nigh to the boot top, and on the side next to us dangled a piece of that old suspender about eight inches long. Dress Parade, you know, is a grave and dignified ceremony, and Colonel Oglesby was an officer who felt his responsibility to the utmost and was much irritated when he heard us snickering and talking in a low tone. But "Uncle Dick" had as keen a sense of the ridiculous as we had, and when the officers reached the center, came to a front and were marching up to him, he caught sight of the lieutenant's right leg. He dismissed the parade instantly and turned his face away from us. It must have been in mortification of our ill behavior - or to laugh; I never knew which.

For headgear this lieutenant obtained an article that was not duplicated in our camp, and it would be a safe bet that it could not be in any other either. I do not think it was made to order but rather was a relic of ancient times that had laid in a garret and was presented to him by some wag who was ebullient with humor. The body of it was in the form of a twelve inch length of six inch stove pipe with a slight upward taper and a damper in the top for a crown. At the bottom there projected a horizontal fore piece at the extreme ends of which were large brass buttons supporting a leather strap which he dropped under his chin to support this aesthetic creation and keep it from toppling over. At the apex was a sort of plume which was identical in appearance to a march cattail with a short stem. "Doc" sported a long mustache, waxed and twisted ala Napoleon the III, and a dainty goatee, and was a sure enough one-man show.

There was not a lazy hair on that big head of Colonel Oglesby, and he had the regiment out nearly every day, putting us through the evolutions of battalion drill. He evidently took great delight and felt much glory in sitting astride his large sorrel horse in full regimentals, and roaring out the tactical commands, for he had a voice trained by much stump speaking that was suggestive of a calliope.

But I was always tired and took no interest in such drill as we were getting, and I think with some reason too.

A few years previously, I had seen the Ellsworth Cadets go through their paces at an exhibition drill given on the grounds later known as Camp Douglass while it was occupied by the Illinois State Fair. So I had a faint conception of what a regiment of infantry ought to look like and how they ought to move. We were using the old heavy infantry tactics that had been handed down by Frederick the Great to General Winfield Scott, unimpaired, and which had been discarded by our own Regular Army. But our books on light infantry tactics were compiled by Hardee, whose name they were known by and as he had gone over to the Confederacy, they compelled us to drill in "Scott's" 'til they could get out a new edition with Hardee's name left out.

When we started over that parade ground with the twenty-eight inch step at the rate of ninety a minute, an observer would have had to look sharp to decide whether we were trying to go somewhere, or simply marking time for leg exercise, and would be sure to conclude we would be fine game for an active enemy.

And, then, the manual of arms: Great Scott! It is no wonder they formerly issued a whiskey ration three times a day. And here they put us through those exasperating evolutions and demoralizing manual, and never gave us any whiskey at all.

If we looked as ridiculous as we felt, standing there with those old fazees at a "Carry Arms," Falstaff would have declined a detail from the regiment for his bodyguard. At this tactical position the butts of the old converted flint-locks would rest in the palm of our left hands and could be prevented from toppling over only by giving them a considerable slope to the rear and support against the shoulder.

To escape this torture I volunteered to work on the barracks to be built immediately in front of the sheds we were then occupying, and being very familiar with the use of a square and scratch awl, the quartermaster placed me in charge of a gang and I had a snap while the job lasted.

We were promised extra pay for this work but never got it, from the fact that the quartermaster did not know how to go about getting it for us. It was said that at the close of his three months term, he stuffed all his invoices and receipts into a nail keg and shipped them to the Quartermaster General in Washington. They sent them back with blanks to make proper returns upon, but after racking his brain over them a week or more he again fired them to Washington with a letter stating that he could not make head nor tail out of them.

While the barracks were going up they issued us a uniform of shoddy grey, with light grey felt hats, which answered our purpose very well except that the goods were rather heavy for climate and season.

These barracks were completed about the middle of June, and then our officers, nearly all of them, left the St. Charles and organized officers, messes, or grubbed around with the boys. Officers did not properly draw rations from the government for themselves, but were expected to buy and pay for whatever they required, and they were given a monthly allowance at the paytable in cash, which amounted to about ten dollars a ration. And each officer got an allowance of two or more rations according to his rank. Such stores as the commissaries have they could buy at about cost, but I think that in the earlier part of the war many of them unwittingly or otherwise smuggled much of their grub from Uncle Sam or from their men. Later on I will tell you how it was managed in our company and how it suddenly got knocked out. I will also mention that our commissaries kept supplies that they did not issue to us boys but sold to the officers. And whiskey, in abundance, was one of them.

Dell Eddy was still taking his meals at the St. Charles Hotel and wearing his citizen's clothing; and it was about this time that a Regular Army officer dropped into our quartermaster's office for the purpose of making an inspection. Dell approached him on the subject nearest his heart by saying by way of apology that he was still wearing citizen's dress because he had been unable to find out what the prescribed uniform was for an officer of his rank.

"I can tell you what it is, young man," said the inspecting officer, "have you any uniforms in your warehouse?"

"None but those for enlisted men," replied Dell.

"They will do," said the inspector and he followed Dell into the back room. Taking one of the shoddy grey jackets from a pile that lay on a table and borrowing a piece of chalk, he sketched on the sleeve the prescribed chevron and told Dell to cover those chalk marks with light blue tape a half inch wide, and put a corresponding embellishment on the other sleeve, and then he would have it.

"But what kind of uniform am I to put it on," said Dell.

"On this if it is what regiment is wearing," replied the officer.

"Zounds!" exclaimed Dell, "I thought I was a commissioned officer"

"I guess someone has been guying you," said the Inspector.

"No they haven't. I just thought so," says Dell. "Say Captain, how much pay do I get?"

"Twenty-one dollars per month."

"Twenty-one devils, why here I have been paying a fifty-a-month hotel bill ever since I have been here," groaned Dell.

"Well, well, young man," said the sympathetic inspector, "it can't be helped now. Send home for a hundred, square up and take a new start. It will do you good to live on government rations the balance of your term."

Dell came straight back to the company and put up such a howl that Captain Harvey gave him the place of Orderly again. Then he took one of the uniforms to a local tailor and had him fit it to his model form, and he looked real nice. He took the soldiers' ration with good grace from that time on, and gave the St. Charles Hotel a wide berth. He wrote many an interesting letter for publication to the *Bloomington Pantagraph*, but I doubt that any of them contained an episode of more interest than the one I have just related. I don't suppose that he mentioned it at all.

Excellent land- and water-scape across mouth of the Ohio River from Fort Holt's artillery in Kentucky, which commanded a critical major river junction. Cairo may be seen directly across the Ohio's mouth.

CHAPTER V

Directly in rear of the barracks of Company Q (K), and just back of the levee, lived a German who kept seven or eight cows that had a long and free range up and contiguous to the river. He sold his milk in the retail way, and it was mostly taken by our officers. These cows were rounded up each evening and corralled in a yard between the dwelling and stable.

I happened to awake one morning about two o'clock, and my stomach was so empty that I could not fall asleep again. The moon was shining brightly, and as I lay there on a soft pine mattress with a couple of army blankets wrapped around me, my mind got to running on about the many good things I had eaten in times past, and I wondered if such good things would ever come my way again.

I recalled the three months I had spent in the log cabin of a farmer-hunter in Northern Illinois in the '50's, when deer were plentiful, and the old chap used to bag about seventy-five during the winter hunting season. He would skin out the fore-quarters, wrap the hide about the saddles, and market them in Chicago.

This man was a crack shot and would bring down a deer running across his path with the same certainty as if it were standing broadside and stock still. He always raised a goodly crop of buckwheat and during the three winter months I spent in his little log house while attending a term of country school I did not eat one meal that did not consist almost wholly of buckwheat cakes and venison. And I assert in all sincerity that the last meal was relished as heartily as the first. In truth, it makes my mouth water now to think of the delicious venison gravy with which we used to flood those wholesome flapjacks.

I had passed Col. Dick's quarters the evening before, just as he was about to take his supper, and I saw on the table real nice light biscuits, such as your mother used to make, and a chunk of real butter, and as I caught the old fellow's eye I raised my hat and fired in a complaint about something that quickly came to my mind, with a faint hope that to mollify me he would ask me to sit down and talk it over, and incidentally to help myself to the good things on the table. But Uncle Dick was too sharp for me. He undoubtedly suspected that I stopped for that very purpose. He knew very well if I got a crack at the layout he would have to crawl into his bunk that night hungry.

My mind ran in such channels until I became ravenous. I knew that nothing but cold beans and bread could be found in the mess kitchen, because there was never any pie or cakes left over. Then it occurred to me that if the old German should happen to be awake I might buy a quart of the fluid he dealt in and have a nice little game of bread and milk all by myself.

So I took my boots in hand and quietly slipped out into the kitchen without disturbing the boys. Here I hauled the boots on and secured a quart cup, and then stepped over the levee to reconnoiter.

All was dark about the house and so I walked on down to the corral and found the cows lying there contentedly chewing their cuds. I was getting hungrier every minute, and remembering that I had some practice manipulating cows while stopping with various farmers during my boyhood days, I could see nothing wrong in helping myself and paying the old German the next day.

It was much easier to satisfy my conscience than my appetite, and so I slipped over the fence and gently requested the nearest bossy to please get up and cooperate. Zounds! But I could scarcely get a drop out of her and I rapidly kicked up one after another and barely got the cup full after going through the whole bunch.

As I came back over the fence I saw at the corner diagonally from me a sneak of a fellow with a large pail on his arm, but I didn't stop to hear him swear. I was much too hungry to loiter about there, and then profanity was very distasteful to me anyway.

A day or two later I saw the old German sitting alone on his porch, and as he was not engaged in reading and looked rather lonesome, I strolled up and took a seat beside him, intending to give him a dime before I came away. In due time I adroitly maneuvered the conversation around to the milk business and learned that he had discontinued morning milkings "since the soldiers came" and charged the officers, to whom he sold his fluid, double the price.

That let me out all right and I decided to keep my dime. I wanted to tell him about that fellow who raided his corral with a big pail but could contrive no plausible excuse for being in the vicinity myself, and so kept quiet.

--- ------ ---

Hair clippers were unknown to us at that time, and I think as a rule we wore our hair longer than we do now. As the summer temperature rose we felt the need of having our locks trimmed. So we picked up an old chair somewhere, took up a subscription, and bought a pair of shears and commenced trimming each other.

There was in the company a heavy-set chap with a full face, small head and a shockingly heavy mass of yellow hair. His ears were singularly large and under perfect control for he could flop them as gracefully as a calf.

Queen Victoria boasted that her ancestors had been traced back to King Solomon, but this fellow could make her pedigree look sick, as his surely passed through Adam on back to the ape. I do not remember his name, but we knew him by the nickname of Slyboots.

He settled himself into the chair one day to have his hair trimmed and went to sleep. Jonas Lawrence came by and told the boy who was engaged on the job to cut it off tight to his head.

"But what if he should wake up before I get through," said the boy, who was figuring on a chance of getting away.

"Then I'll hold him while you finish him, so get busy."

Jonas' orders went in company K, and the ground was soon strewn with yellow hair. After the job was completed we all walked around the fellow and viewed him from all points of the compass, and unanimously voted him a "beaut". Then, a rascally private tickled one of his ears just to see it flop, and then he awoke and found the whole company standing about grinning. He thought the joke was on his having gone to sleep, but when he commenced spitting the flies of out his mouth he saw the pile of yellow hair on the ground. Then he slapped his large paw on his topknot and yelled with rage. But Slyboots was not a bloodthirsty fellow and so did not kill the boy.

--- ------ ---

Company drill in the fore-noon and battalion drill in the afternoon was the regular thing, and they gave us no chance to try the shooting qualities of our muskets, while that was the drill we really stood most in need of. It is quite probable that each of us had at some time in his life fired a gun; yet we sadly needed practice with these muskets. To be a good shot is of the highest importance on a battlefield: To be steady and accurate in maneuvering in line and column is of much less consequence, for none of the exacting movements of the parade ground are, or can be, executed in the presence of the enemy.

Against an enemy battalion of equal number, with a knowledge of company and battalion drill that could be acquired in thirty days, but with a practice at target firing that would give five hundred shots to the man, a regiment such as ours with our three-month drilling would stand no show whatever in a fair field fight. We would simply be wiped out in short order if we were fools enough to stand our ground.

On the parade grounds the officers are very much in evidence, for every movement is indicated by a tactical command repeated by the company commander, but on the battlefield the strut is taken out of their gait, and the pomposity of manner is no longer there.

"Attention, Battalion. Shoulder Arms. Forward-Guide Center-March," is seldom or never heard on a battlefield after the action has commenced. The boys generally commence firing as soon as they get within sight and range of the enemy, without waiting for orders from their officers. They instinctively keep a general alignment; and should their change of position be either forward or to the rear, it would not be made in cadenced step, and would have little resemblance to the parade ground maneuvers.

Now, target practice does not appeal to the average commissioned officers for the opportunity to draw his sabre, strut about and bawl out commands is absent. But the boys would enjoy it and as soon as they became skillful enough to plunk the bull's eye nearly every shot, they would be inspired with courage and confidence and itch to try their skill on the enemy.

In excuse it may be said that many of our officers were new to the service; had no military training. But, it would be more truthful to say they had no military sense. Many of them claimed previous service in the Mexican and other wars, but if so they had learned little or forgotten much.

To illustrate this point, allow me to relate a little personal experience of about twenty years ago, when I was keeping a country store. I was a member of our G.A.R. Post, and suggested Fourth of July celebration under their auspices and I offered to be the committee on arrangements and to provide music, speaker, cartridges for a sham fight, fireworks for the evening, get out the bills and post them, build a speaker's platform in my orchard, erect seats, and in fine do all work and pay all the bills.

The boys thought this a pretty fair offer and readily agreed to it, and so I commenced planning devices to relieve the crowd in attendance of as much of their loose change as possible. Among other things I ordered a Winchester target rifle and iron target. General Herman Lieb came from Chicago with his wife and three bright boys, delivered the oration, and took charge of the sham fight. We had a nice bunch of fireworks, and after paying the bills and figuring up the profits, I found myself seventeen dollars to the bad.

So I set about to even up with the target equipment. My store was sixty feet long and I located the target in the back end and thereby added a shooting gallery to my various businesses.

The game was one shot each and the loser buy two nickel cigars. I was not a very good shot myself, but when asked by a caller to let a couple of shots decide which should furnish the smokers, I could scarcely refuse when others were not about.

Squire Bishop, the blacksmith, kept a rifle, was something of a hunter and a good shot. He was also a good smoker, and especially enjoyed the snipes that the other fellow paid for. He burned a few at my expense and he would tilt them up at such an aggravating angle, and would deliver himself of such funny remarks as he sent the circles of smoke tilting up toward the ceiling, that I felt very much humiliated. And I swore that I would take the conceit out of that rascal, regardless of the time or expense.

In one week I had destroyed about one thousand cartridges and was ready to try shots with Bishop or any other man.

The next time our blacksmith dropped into the store he wanted to smoke as usual, so he suggested that we light our La Gracias and then take a crack at the bell and see who would pay for them. We lit up, and then with apparent reluctance I pushed a cartridge into the rifle and passed it over to him.

That beautiful expression of confidence that he carried on his manly mug, did not affect me as it had formerly, for I was quite confident that I knew who would have to settle with the house for the cigars we were smoking. Squire tripped up to the mark with a step as light as that of a school girl, brought up the gun with a flourish, and missed the bell. I then took my shot and missed it by one-half inch.

Bish wanted to shoot again, but a lady came in and I couldn't oblige him, and so he had to pay. A day or two later he came in after "satisfaction" and got it by paying for four more, for we were again interrupted by one of his customers who wanted his horse shod, and so we could carry the game no further at the time.

When Bishop dropped in a few mornings later I could see blood in his eyes, for I well knew that he did not relish being beat at his favorite game by a country cross-roads store keeper. He was in high mettle and at once sang out.

"Well Dan! nothing doing this morning so get out the gun and will show you some shooting. Would you like to hear that bell rung a few times?"

I acknowledged that I would, and suggested that we light up at once so we would know what we were shooting for, and proceeded to pass out the stogas [cigars].

Bish winked a knowing wink or two for the benefit of a couple of fellows who had just dropped in, and intimated that I would not get off for a dime that morning. I had my opinion about it, too, but did not express it.

Shoving a cartridge in the gun, I passed it over to Bish, and he waltzed gaily over to the scratch and took a shot. I then sent one on the other side of the bell that tied him. His next shot was an inch above and mine an inch below.

Then I told him that he was getting nervous and if he was not careful I would beat him yet. He said he would make a ringer this time and I offered to bet him another cigar that he wouldn't. He didn't take the bet nor ring the bell but came very near it, and I tied him again.

He was getting serious now and took a long aim and succeeded in sprinkling a little lead on the bell. He was gaining, but so was I for I got the same tinkle of the bell that he did.

Then his assurance commenced evaporating and as soon as there was room for it, an idea invaded his cranium and he turned on me,

"See here, Dan, I believe you are tieing me a purpose."

"That is just what I am doing Mr. Bishop," I rejoined.

"Well! how long are you going to keep this up? There are eight cigars in the jack pot now. Do you intend to keep me away from the shop all day and work off your whole store on me? I want to tell you, Mr. Caverno, if that has been your game, it is about time that you quit."

"All right!" I replied, "if you feel that way I will shoot her off this time."

But this time Squire got a ringer and I said that I couldn't shoot it off when he made such shots as that, to which he answered that he guessed it was shot off already. I promptly offered to lay a side bet that it was not but the answer I got was "shoot".

I took a ringer also and made another tie.

"Now I want to know when this game is going to stop," said Bish.

"Whenever you miss that bell," I answered.

"Do you mean to say that you can hit that bell whenever you try?"

"That's just the size of it, Squire."

"Well! I want to tell you one thing, Mr. Caverno, when I shoot, I shoots the best I can like a gentleman, and I ain't going to miss that bell a purpose."

"And I won't anymore, so go ahead."

Bish failed to get a ringer that shot and I took one and ended the game with a dozen cigars on him. Of course, he would never shoot with me any more.

On the corner opposite the store I had a well for the watering of horses, and one morning a half dozen of us were standing on the front porch, when one of them called my attention to a lot of butterflies that were extracting moisture from the wet ground about there, and remarked that there were about as many of them as there were of those English Sparrows when I took that shot out of the old musket that kicked me through the light of glass.

I said I had a different gun now and could get those butterflies by the taking one at a shot.

The late James McAlpine was of the party and he said,

"Pshaw, Dan! you don't pretend that you can hit one of those butterflies with that target rifle of yours, do you?"

"Wait just a moment and see," I answered, and at once stepped in the store and brought out the gun and hand full of cartridges.

I grazed the first one and it went off with an unnatural wobble. Then I sent in six shots in rapid succession, and we walked over and picked up six of the little beauties.

The distance was sixty-five feet. At that time I could up to the point-blank range of the gun, hit any spot that I could see, and do it repeatedly and with the greatest ease. I never felt that I was liable to miss. It seemed to me that I couldn't.

That is the feeling that a soldier ought to carry about with him. He has a coarser gun and shoots a longer distance but then he has a larger object to shoot at and ought to hit it oftener than once in five hundred shots. It would scarcely seem possible that our officers were such idiots as to utterly neglect the essential, and much the most important branch of a soldier's education, but they were, and as far as I observed, little attention was paid to target practice throughout the war.

If soldiers could go into battle with the confidence in their skill that I felt when peppering those little butterflies, it would give them courage and a feeling of self-reliance that no amount of battalion drill could convey, and if they were trained to take advantage of every covering that the ground afforded, to load on their backs if in the open, and only expose themselves when taking a shot, they would each man of them feel something of "the glory of battle" that vibrates the systems of those officers who stay well to the rear out of personal danger. And, when an opposing force ran against such a lot of boys they would think a cyclone had struck them. And, a month's practice with five hundred cartridges to the man would have accomplished this.

Since writing the above I incidentally turned to an historical sketch of the "Mclean Regiment," the 94th Illinois Infantry. It was recruited in July, 1862, and William W. Orme the young law partner of Leonard Swett (of whom I spoke in a former chapter) took it out as its colonel. Orme was put in charge of a brigade, and in November made brigadier general. Now the management of that regiment devolved upon a Lieut. Col. McNulty. And from this sketch I will take a few extracts, presuming and hoping the history to be truthful:

> "On Sept. 10th the brigade was moved by rail to Rolla, Missouri and thence a few days to Springfield, at that time upon the extreme front of the Union forces. Here six weeks were spent in the most insidious company and battalion drills, the men being especially exercised in firing while lying down and in the skirmish drill, in which they became remarkably proficient, and the result of which was very apparent when they came into action. The advantage of being able to deliver accurate and rapid fire while lying down and almost entirely protected by the slightest irregularity of ground is obvious. Here the drill at Springfield proved its value. Scattered in a long, irregular line, lying flat on their faces, taking advantage of every stump, fence and irregularity of ground, the regiment maintained so destructive a fire that no troops could be brought against them without being cut to pieces, while our men were comparatively unharmed. Colonel McNulty contributed largely to this result by riding constantly up and down the lines urging the men to lie close and fire low, utterly regardless of his own exposure. It was owing to this policy that our loss was so trifling, one killed and twenty-six wounded, compared with regiments at our side who were not so well handled.

> "Returning through Missouri to near Rolla, the regiment drilled and recruited until June 1863, when it was sent down the river to Vicksburg. It was stationed below the city on the left of our line, and assisted in all the siege operations terminating with the capture of that stronghold on the 4th of July. Here again the indefatigable McNulty was constantly among his men in the trenches, rapping them on the head when they needlessly exposed themselves. Although exposed for two weeks to a hot fire in the trenches and with their camp almost constantly under the range of the enemy's shells, the regiment sustained only the loss of one man killed and five wounded, showing how much a prudent and sagacious commander can do to prevent needless sacrifice of life."

The 94th served just three years, marched 1,200 miles, traveled by railroad 610 miles and by steamer 6,000 miles. It took part in nine battles, sieges and skirmishes and lost during its service 11 men killed in battle and 45 wounded. If this is true, and I hope it is, Colonel McNulty was a model regimental commander.

The 7th Illinois Infantry, under Colonel Richard Rowett, bought at their own expense of fifty dollars each, sixteen-shot Henry rifles and became invincible. At Altoona Pass, with three other regiments, they were attacked by General French's division of 6,000 Confederates. They not only defeated them but killed and wounded more of them than they had men in their own command.

All honor to such regimental commanders as Colonels McNulty and Rowett.

Admiral Andrew Foote's Mississippi gunboat flotilla gathering way "under full head of steam," perhaps heading for the Tennessee River and tough shore bombardment missions in support of the volunteer Union regiments heading upriver.

CHAPTER VI

At Cairo a German baker would each morning come down the line in front of our quarters with a basket of pies, which he would sell at a bit, 12 1/2 cents each. After a time, one of our boys who was long on appetite and short on cash asked him to give him one on tick, and he handed it out without hesitation. Soon others followed suit, and as they were never refused, this easy little pieman had to run a hand cart to supply our regiment alone. My company K would generally take his last pie, and he never asked for a name and took no account of his sales whatever.

We also had a sutler where we could obtain credit, and he was liberally patronized, too. It was understood among us that his bills would be collected at the pay table, but I had currency enough for my needs and took only a general interest in the subject. When pay day came the privates were each handed their thirty-three dollars in gold and silver and the sutler got left.

I felt much sympathy for the amiable little pieman, and after the boys had got away I called at his bakery to console with him and read him a lecture on the evils of credit system. I found him carrying bricks and mortar for a couple of masons who were enlarging his oven. In reply to a question from me he said,

"Dose was mighty good boys; dey givs me more money as dot da owe me; big intrust an more as dot too. I's going to have big bakery now and gets me a horse and pretty soon I be rich man I tells you."

Bird's Point lies directly across the Mississippi River from Cairo in the state of Missouri, and "Colonel" Bird's mansion stood near the river in plain view of our camp. The distance was about a mile and through a field glass the valiant colonel could frequently be seen pacing his veranda and shaking his cane at us, presumably daring us to come over there.

The "Post of Cairo" was commanded by Brigadier General Benjamin F. Prentiss of Quincy, Illinois who had been adjutant of Colonel Harding's First Illinois Infantry that went to Mexico, and who came into the present 1861 service as colonel of the Tenth Infantry for three months. About the middle of May he was made a Brigadier General, and assigned to this post.

The Ninth Infantry, commanded ostensibly by Eleasor (Heaven protect that name) A. Payne, but in fact by Lieutenant Colonel Augustus Mersey, a German who had had foreign service and kept the organization well in hand, was camped on our immediate left.

Colonel Payne graduated at West Point and served in Mexico. He was intensely patriotic and loyal to the Union, and if he had diligently applied himself to the business he might have made a respectable farmer. He thought, however, that he would like to try brigadier generaling awhile and the authorities humored his whim and gave him the appointment. But he didn't have the ability to make his loyalty effective. Yet he had no cause to feel lonesome; they were making many such promotions about that time in the Union and Confederate service both.

Colonel Oglesby would not speak of him as General Payne, but would substitute "that damn fool" for his legal title. Bearing in mind that "Uncle Dick" was the ranking colonel of the state, and as much of a Mexican Vet as any of them, it is not to be wondered at that he could not with complacency see such mediocrities as Grant and Payne promoted over his head. It was enough to make a saint swear, though "Dick" was no saint. Much less provocation would set him going. He should have been a master of languages to enable him to switch off on another as soon as he had exhausted the English swear words. This would have saved him much repetition, and been the source of great amusement for those within the range of his voice, say about one-half mile.

It would appear that the brightest thing learned by our boys in the Mexican War was to look sharp and get a good start in this one. Each was favored by the fact that we held him in high esteem- he who had actually planted his foot on Mexican soil, had seen with his own eyes old "Fuss and Feathers" in all his glory, had never obtained a position in that service above that of an ambulance driver or sutler's clerk. Yet when a commission now was in sight, he had only to reach out his hand and take it. Among these Mexican Vets, many made worthy officers, but as many more made worthless ones.

The reference to the great General Winfield "Fuss and Feathers" Scott recalled an incident reported about a presidential reception in Washington, when in the crowd Henry Clay incidentally brushed against Winfield's arm, and he with a mock grimace of pain said, "Ah! Senator you forget Lundy's lane!" To which the Kentuckian, who did not hold the old hero in very high esteem, replied,

"I had forgotten it, but evidently you never will."

I think it was about the last part of June when Major General George B. McClellen came to Cairo and had us out on review. He was cut off a trifle short but looked quite stylish when mounted on a good horse. He wore a cap and this fact would no doubt have settled the discussion about the proper head piece to place on his statue, about which they were quarreling a couple of years ago. I mentioned this to a friend and he suggested that I write to the monument commission (U.S.) and insist upon their putting a cap on the fellow. But I had no inclination to interfere as I had known several corporals I thought more worthy of a statue than he was.

There were many Southern sympathizers in the vicinity of the Big Muddy Bridge on the Illinois Central Railroad, and we kept it well guarded by a company of infantry. Company K went up and remained a week or more. One evening I was posted as a guard at the lower end of the bridge. Capt. Harvey himself gave me unqualified orders to shoot any person I saw approaching. It was a bright moonlit night and about ten o'clock I saw a man walking rapidly up the track towards me. I drew a bead on him once or twice at long range, and concluded to kill him near by, so that I might see him struggle, and catch his last words. By the time he got up close I became a little confused, and instead of shooting him as I was told to I bawled out:

"Hello there! what in hell do you want here?"

He immediately halted and said he wanted to see the commanding officer. I told him to remain where he was and I would call the corporal of the guard. He was conducted to the Captain's tent and soon after piloted a detail under a lieutenant who captured a couple of local "Secesh" who were sent to Cairo under guard by the first train.

I was never court-martialed for this disobedience of orders, not even reprimanded. In fact, I don't think the captain ever after thought of the vicious instructions he had given me; and it is probable that if I had obeyed him and killed that honest fellow, Harvey would have denied giving any such orders, and I would have had a good long term in a military prison. And I think I would have deserved it too.

It was in 1865, I think, that part of the Marine Brigade camped at Vicksburg became unmanageable, claiming that according to terms of their enlistment their time had expired. Their arms were taken from them, and a guard of Colored soldiers was posted about their camp. These "Darkey" guards had strict orders and knew no better than to obey them, and the result was that when one of the Marines passed outside the line and refused to return he was shot and killed. There was no question but that this guard strictly obeyed orders that he had received, and his character as a soldier was A number 1. Yet he went to a military prison for a term of five years.

After the 1861 episode at Big Muddy Bridge (over the Mississippi) I concluded I knew just about as much as any of the Mexican War Veterans, and that I would obey their orders only when they agreed with my judgment. And when they didn't I wouldn't.

--- ----- ---

One fine day late in the fall, General Prentiss sent a detachment of troops over the river to Bird's Point, much to the disgust of the crusty old Rebel colonel, and the commanding officer obtained permission to establish his headquarters in the Bird mansion. Southern hospitality would not permit this old fire-eater Bird to kick the officer out, but it did not require his remaining there to entertain him, and so he spread his wings and flew away. That was the last we ever heard of him.

There was a line of railroads terminating there, but the river was cutting the point away rapidly, and the depot, and a section of the track, and finally old Bird's house, went into the drink. While here, the pickets thrown out around the Point were spiritedly attacked one night, and they had a right lively scrap. The rattling sound of the musketry came over the river, apparently increasing in volume in its passage over the muddy stream, and as soon as it struck our camp we tumbled out of our bunks in a beautiful state of excitement. Some of us fell in with guns, but no accoutrements; others had both but did not stop to dress. There was a continual scurrying back and forth from ranks to bunks for fifteen minutes or more- all were excited, some to the extent that their teeth chattered even though the skirmish was a mile away with the broad Mississippi running between us.

I enjoyed the excitement and discomfiture of the other boys very much for I had kept so cool over the matter that I did not have to return to quarters for clothing and equipment more than six times. I had the presence of mind to bring out my musket on the first trip. Then, when I went back after my pants some cuss stole my gun, and while looking about for it, another stepped on my toes and I discovered myself bare footed. I yelled and made a break for quarters after my boots and stole a gun on the way out. I also picked up a large plug of tobacco that had been dropped, and shoved that in one of my pockets. A big corporal had accidentally got his trousers on hind-side-afore and I buttoned them up for him and said nothing, which made him my life long friend.

While we were thus scurrying about and getting good and ready to fight, down came the Ninth Infantry in column of company across the front of our camp, led by Lieut. Col. Mersey, who reported for duty at Post Headquarters. By this time the firing had subsided and we all returned to our bunks.

Upon Payne's promotion to a brigadier, Mersey became full Colonel of the 9th, reorganized the regiment after their three months service, and commanded it with great credit for three years.

We had a cornet band at Cairo which came down from Decatur or Peoria, and we enjoyed their music very much. The leader was an artist and would give us a solo each evening as a prelude to the tattoo. Tipp Prentiss, a son of the General, who usually accompanied him, was the finest snare drummer I ever heard. The skill and taste he displayed in embellishing those fine airs with smooth, undulating rolls and accentuated taps, stamped him a snare drum genius of the first order. He disappeared at the close of the three months service and I never heard of him after that.

Colonel Henry Dougherty's 22nd Illinois Volunteers deal with slave hunters at Bird's Point, Missouri, on the Mississippi River, probably late 1861. The Point lay almost directly across the river from Cairo, Illinois.

SLAVE-HUNTERS EXPELLED FROM THE CAMP OF THE TWENTY-SECOND ILLINOIS VOLUNTEERS AT BIRD'S POINT, MISSOURI.—[SKETCHED BY MR. BILL TRAVIS.]

CHAPTER VII

We had two of the Lawrence boys in our company, Jonas and "Toll." Their father was for many years a justice of the peace in Bloomington, and was held in such high esteem for his sound judgment and integrity that I have little doubt he held down that position 'til the day he skipped out after his heavenly harp. He was not a scholarly man, had never been admitted to the bar, and therefore was not in the line of promotion to a higher position.

I witnessed an amusing case that came before him one day, which was that of a very honest appearing old farmer, who brought suit against the teacher of his district school for damages to his team and rig, which he laid at forty-five dollars.

They waived a jury and the pedagogue announced that he would manage his own case. The simple farmer chose a bright young man who was studying law in one of the city offices, who no doubt was highly pleased with a chance to air his knowledge of Blackstone and Tiffany and rake in, say three dollars spending money.

This young man appeared quite modest for one who had spent any considerable time in the atmosphere of a lawyer's office, but it could scarcely be doubted that he would be able to overcome that weakness by the time he was duly admitted to the bar. He opened the case by saying that the defendant came to his client and engaged a rig for the purpose of taking a drive one Saturday afternoon, for which he agreed to pay one dollar and fifty cents, that his client wished him to take the older horses as they were more steady and safe, but the defendant insisted upon a pair of colts that he had seen driven together; and that he recommended himself as an experienced and careful horseman, that his client was by such statements persuaded to hitch these colts to a pair of double-seated light bob sleds, repeatedly cautioning the defendant about their friskiness, and charged him not to leave them without securely tying them both. And that the defendant drove to a certain farm house and took in two young women, and went from there to another and picked up one more; then, returning one-half mile, he drove west two miles to a country cross-roads store. Here he drew rein and handing the ribbons to the youngest miss in the bunch, who was occupying the front seat with him, he jumped out, entered the store and ordered ten cents worth of cheap mixed candy. And, that while the dealer was filling this liberal order, the colts started and made a circle to the left, and just before it was completed the bobs careened on their side and the girls all went out in a pile screaming, and fortunately landed in a snow drift unhurt...

That the sleighs righted themselves and the colts ran home and into the barn-yard gates which were smashed, and there the rig was also smashed. That the colts made a few circles of the yards and then were caught by the farmer and his boy.

That the gallant educator, upon seeing the girls piled out in the snow, and the colts flying down the road toward home, rushed out of the back door of the store and disappeared, and that he has since stubbornly refused to pay the farmer either for the use of the rig or for the damage he had caused.

The farmer gave his testimony and then his boy of about twelve took the stand and the schoolmaster immediately tackled him.

"Do you understand the nature of an oath?" which was answered in the affirmative.

"What would be done to you if you swore to a lie?"

"I'm not going to swear to a lie," answered the kid.

"Well, but if you did what would be done to you?"

"I supposed they might put me in jail."

"But what would become of you after you die?" said the educator.

"Hold on there," interposed Squire Lawrence, "we don't want any of those fool questions here; this court has no jurisdiction over dead people."

After the boy had given his testimony, the pedagogue tried his best to make him lie, but did not succeed. Then the storekeeper told what he saw of the affair, and the plaintiff's case was closed.

The defendant had no witnesses and so the young student took the floor and lambasted the schoolmaster in fine shape. He had the stuff in him for a lawyer all right for he shoved his fist in that fellow's face and called him every vile name that can be found in Webster's unabridged, and several that have been incorporated in the language since Webster died.

But it did not phase this pedagogue for he happened to be insensible to shame. He only cared to win the verdict of the court to save him the money involved in the suit. He was a born orator himself and was wholly depending on his eloquence to carry the squire off his feet and get a verdict in his favor.

He arose with great dignity and leisurely shoved his long dirty fingers through his longer dirty hair, and said "Your Honor."

He then commenced a harrangue of forty minutes duration that was simply indescribable. The proprietorship of that speech on Edison phonograph records to kinetoscope films to run in unison, would be a fortune to the vaudette manager.

When he became exhausted and dropped into a chair the clothing he wore was wet with perspiration. His collar, necktie, vest and coat were dry, however, for he had discarded them as he warmed up in his masterly effort.

In his appeals to the Justice, he used every title that he had ever heard or read, among which were: Your Excellency, Your Grace, Your Lordship, Your Royal Highness, Your Majesty, etc. Sire was used about forty times.

Referring to the instructions of the farmer about hitching the colts, he said that his language was so ungrammatical that to a gentlemen of his refinement and education it was quite unintelligible. He quoted history, poetry, and scripture and proved by a mathematical demonstration in algebra that not being nearer than two miles from the plaintiff's house when and where the wreck occurred, it was not in the nature of things that he could be held responsible for it. And he implied the fault was entirely with the farmer who had neglected to teach his colts to stop when they came to a gate, and wait until it was opened and they were invited to pass through. He "proved" from scripture that all things were fore-ordained, and therefore known from the beginning, and that this thing was bound to happen just as it did, and then he asked his "Majesty" if he dare condemn him for what God himself had decreed. This being clearly the case, it was of course an act of Providence that he could not be held accountable for.

He quoted "Judge not, lest ye also be judged," and warned Squire Lawrence that if he did not give him justice he would roast during all eternity in flames of brimstone fire. And Squire remarked in an undertone, "Don't worry, you will get it all right."

Then he assumed that he was being tried for a crime, and asserted that no evil intent on his part had been proven, and therefore he was innocent as an unborn babe. And he wound up with a pathetic allusion to the death of his parents who left him an orphan at the tender age of twenty-seven, in an unsympathetic world. Here his sympathy for himself took a violent turn, which carried him off his feet. Tears streamed from his large bulging eyes and he was so overcome with emotions he had raised within himself that he sank into a chair, sobbing like a sick calf.

He was given time to recover himself, and when he finished mopping his face and glanced about the room to note the effect of his eloquence, he saw that the court, the student and we auditors had all been affected to tears also, and the discovery brought a triumphant grin on his beautiful mug. He was quite convinced that he had won his case by his shrewd reasoning, sublime eloquence and gestures, and he arose from the chair and proceeded to don the garments that he had discarded with an air that suggested that he now felt himself in the class with Demosthenes and Cicero.

The Justice had his feet on one of the tables, and without removing them, or waiting for the law student to take another crack at the pedagogue, said,

"It is the judgment of the court that the defendant pay the plaintiff forty-five dollars, and settle the cost of this suit."

"Why, this is an outrage, your majesty," yelled the astonished schoolmaster, as he sprang from his seat. "Didn't I show you that I couldn't be held respons---," and that is as far as he got for "His Royal Highness" had his worshipful fist under his plebeian nose so quickly it took his breath away:

"You contemptible puppy, if you say another word I'll send you to jail for contempt of court. Now, settle up quick and get away from here before I throw you out of a window."

The schoolmaster hastily paid the costs in currency, gave the farmer an order on the school treasurer for the judgment, and flew the court room.

"Squire, how did you manage your countenance so well during that flow of oratory?" I asked.

"Gad! did you ever see anything like it? His gestures were simply terrible. It's a wonder his arms are not disjointed and his back-bone cracked. I never had so much suffering fun come in a pile since I held office."

Jonas, the squire's eldest boy, was a manly fellow, a blacksmith by trade and by profession a pugilist. He was six feet, well-built with hard muscles, small head and ears, large short neck, and with a reputation of never avoiding a scrap. Still I did not think him quarrelsome, at least he was not with the boys of the company, for whatever he said went with us.

Shortly after we reached Cairo, one of the company reported to Jonas that his blanket had been stolen, and intimated to him that I had two. It was known that I got them both on the draw at Springfield, but he suggested that I let him have one of them, and so I turned it over. A day or two after, in obedience to a hint, I made the rounds of the saloons, and found the stolen blanket, which had been pawned for a bottle of whiskey. I redeemed it for four bits. I took the case to Jonas and he said that the owner had pawned it himself, for he had had a taste of the whiskey. He called the fellow out and sent him back after my blanket. Then I offered him his own for the half-dollar it had cost me, but he had no money with which to redeem it. So then I had three blankets.

Then Jonas' fun came in. He took that fellow by the scruff of his jacket with one hand, and with the other he slapped five dollars worth of stuffing out of him. Then he led up to the Orderly and told him to draw him a blanket and have it charged up to him.

At the close of our three-month term Jonas went home, and I heard that he went out again as a first lieutenant of cavalry. His brother Toll didn't amount to much. I was told that they had both been arrested and taken before their father, and his parental affection had resulted in their getting the full extent of the law. On one occasion the squire fined Jonas twenty-five dollars, or thirty days in jail, and Jonas elected to serve his time. This was too much for the old gentleman. He could have resorted to a suspension of sentence during good behavior. But Squire Lawrence could not do this. Instead he went down in his own pocket and fished up the twenty-five dollars himself. Then he pounded Jonas so that they had to send him home on a dray, and he wasn't able to shoe a horse for a week.

CHAPTER VIII

The end of our enlistment was drawing nigh, and efforts were being made to re-enlist us "for three years unless sooner discharged." Colonel Dick's plan was to retain all company commanders who could re-enlist one-half of their men.

He talked very eloquently and forcibly to us from the back of his old sorrel horse, for he was a born orator and a fighter. His mouth, as his fists, was always at full cock. If put to his trumps he could have delivered a convincing speech while standing on his head and gesturing with his legs.

And this reminds me that when I came to Michigan after the war a delegate to a Republican convention to be held in Philadelphia asked me who were the leading Republicans in Illinois and I answered that Oglesby and Logan stood at the head of the list. He didn't know much of "Uncle Dick" and thought me a little off in rating him among the leaders. But when he returned from Philadelphia he told me that Richard Oglesby was the grandest man there, and that he made "the speech" of the convention.

In this talk to us at Cairo he promised to begin using the light infantry drill, and add a sergeant and four more corporals to each company. He said he would make an effort to get another lieutenant also. I had no idea how he expected to secure that third lieutenant, but Colonel Dick was a politician, and a very shrewd one, too. He knew that a little bait like that would catch many recruits. And it did, too, for about every second man who was subsequently enlisted had one eye on that "third lieutenancy." I don't think he ever asked for it. It was something that he should not have wanted, and must have known that he could not get.

It soon became evident that our Company K could not re-enlist one fourth of their men. Our lieutenants were of course out of the game, but Captain Harvey was well liked at regimental headquarters, and fairly well by the boys of the company. But, for various reasons only a few of them were inclined to stay. Many of them had a grievance against the captain for not starting to build an officers' mess when our barracks were finished.

He had boarded at the St. Charles Hotel during half of the term, which took half of his pay during the time he was there, and being a poor man with a family to support he was no doubt trying to get through the term with the least possible expense. So he messed with us, and I considered the honor of his company a fair equivalent for such tough board. And some of the company would have thought otherwise had they not wanted some pretext for not re-enlisting.

When I stopped off at Bloomington for a couple of days while on furlough, a couple of weeks after the company boys reached home, I found that this complaint about Harvey had been circulated about the city quite generally, and I swore that it was a damned lie and just an excuse by some to come home. Then Harvey's stock went up with a jump.

To show how the re-enlisted panned out, I will give the result by companies:

Company A. Capt. Pugh and Lieut. Martin stepped out, and 2nd Lieut. Bruce took the captaincy and re-enlisted 13 men.

Company B. Private Herman Lieb took the captaincy, Private Peter Schlosser the 1st Lieut'cy and held six of their men.

Company C. Capt. Ashmore remained, and 2nd lieut. Daniel Sayer went to 1st, and they got nine.

Company D. 1st Lt. Luther Startsman, and 2nd Lt. Joseph W. Roberts each went up a notch, and Private Joseph B. Jones went to 2nd and they held 9 men.

Company E. 1st Lt. John Wetzell, Orderly Lloyd Wheaton and Corporal Samuel Caldwell took the commissions in the above orders and got seven of their own men and one from Co. K.

Company F. Captain Joseph M. Hanna stood pat, and Lt. Josiah Sheets went to first, with seven men.

Company G. 1st Lt. James S. Barnard gobbled the captaincy, 1st Sergt. E. Jones the 1st Lieut'cy, and 2nd Sergt. W. P. Sutton the 2nd Lieut'cy, and they kept 12 men.

Company H. 1st Lieut. R. H. Sturgess drew the captaincy, Private John L. Shaw the 1st Lieutenancy, and Corporal A. G. Bishop the 2nd Lieutenancy with just enough men to fill the rank of sergeant...5.

Company I. Officers and men all went home. Sergeant Robert Wilson of Co. E and Wm. Zeigler of Co. F assumed the responsibility for recruiting a full company - succeeded - and filled the two top offices in the order named.

Company K. Capt. Wm. H. Harvey remained. Private Joseph G. Howell came next followed by Private Noah W. Dennison and six men.

The field and staff all stayed in the 8th except the Quartermaster and Chaplain.

A total of 712 officers and men had served in the regiment three months in comfortable quarters; had never fired their muskets, except to unload them after a tour of guard duty, and the war had barely commenced. The regimental officers were capable and popular. In fact Col. Richard Oglesby was exceedingly so.

Now why was it that only 105 officers and men could be prevailed upon to remain with their companies? Simply because they wanted a change, and hoped thereby to better their positions. There seemed to be no difficulty in persuading enough of them to remain to fill the commissions and sergeant ranks but as soon as these positions were promised, there seemed to be an air-brake set on the recruiting business. The rank of corporal is not very attractive, though as a matter of fact it is worth taking, there being many little advantages in the way of duty and puts one in the line of promotion.

There were those who were bright enough to notice what a pull the "Mex Vets" had on the commissions already issued, on pretensions of military knowledge acquired in former service, and they wondered if with three months service to their credit they would not be in demand in some of the new organizations about to be put in the field. And I think their heads were quite level.

Some of them appeared from their conversation to be somewhat home sick and tired of the life, and tried to satisfy themselves that they had done their duty and could creditably go home and stay there, but I think they soon got their fill of mother's hot biscuits and cold apple pies, that they found the work on the farm and in the shop unusually tiresome and monotonous, that they got but little credit from their friends and neighbors for their camp-guard campaigns, and eventually drifted into the Army again.

Unlike them, I did not get home sick for the good reason that I had no home to get sick for. One does not get sick for a boarding house where he has to shell out four or five dollars every Saturday night for the privilege of eating three bum meals a day and sleeping on bumpy mattresses. He is only sick for a change and never goes back to what he has served in before. While three months was a short term to serve in the Army, it would have been a long one in some of the boarding houses I have known. Among the tough places into which I had stumbled was the boarding shanty at Bloomington when the principal school building was going up.

In the fall of '59 I was in Chicago where I had spent the summer at the carpenter's trade, and when winter came on and no job in sight, Mr. Lonsbury, whose house I had worked on, who was a general agent for several insurance companies, heard me remark at his house that if I could not get a job for the winter I would go out in the country where I could get cheap board and attend school. His little girl was sitting on my knee and I was conversing with his wife. He turned on his heel, facing me, and butted in.

"Why, Dan, they don't have any good schools out in the country. Go to one of our city schools and stay with us. Then you won't have any board bill to pay."

He kept a man to drive his carriage and do the work about the house so I could not see clearly how I could make myself useful to him. A day or two later, when I had about concluded that I could stand the arrangement if he could, I heard of a man who was hiring carpenters to work on the normal school building at Bloomington.

I found him at a shop on the West Side and struck a bargain to work during the winter months for one dollar per day and board, but no cash 'til Spring, after which time he said he would have plenty of currency. I left on a midnight train, and the kind Lonsbury family all sat up to see me off and say good bye. A week later I wrote to the Madame, thanking them for all the kindness I had received at their hands, and it was the beginning of a correspondence that continued 'til they left that city for St. Louis. I never heard from them again.

The normal school contractor was an Englishman by the name of Thomas H. Soper. He kept a couple of pimps about the shanty, one as assistant cook and the other a roustabout, to spy on us boys and make reports to him. He kept a room full of stuff to sell at exorbitant prices, but failed to work any of it off on me, and a coolness arose between us. The board was tough and by the first of March the situation had become unendurable, so I packed my kit and asked for a settlement.

During a fierce gale one afternoon that made the unstayed walls sway, every one left the building except six of us and the expert foreman who was from Cincinnati. We worked like tigers 'til dark, staying the walls with long heavy joists and lashing down lumber that had been elevated to the roof for sheathing. Soper, his grown-up son, his two pimps and two thirds of the workmen, would not go near the building and yet he did not show the slightest appreciation of this service. The foreman praised us heartily and said that if we had not stood by him the walls would have gone down in ruins.

We worked through that roaring gale at the imminent danger of our lives 'til it was so dark that we could scarcely find our way out of the building, and I was so incensed at the ingratitude exhibited on the part of the contractor that I swore I would quit the job the minute my contract expired.

Soper denied the agreement and refused to pay until fall and so I sued him before Justice Lawrence and relied on one of the boys who was present when the bargain was made as my witness. This chap had come from New York City about a year earlier, and the wintering in this shanty made him wish himself back again. So Soper had only to buy him a ticket and give him his balance in cash and truck to get him out of the way. The old knave and his roustabout swore that I agreed to wait until fall for my pay, and that I was non-suited. I only realized twenty dollars out of that winters work. The roustabout was in Chicago when the bargain was struck, but was at that time downtown, and did not see me in the city at all, which goes to prove that perjury is the commonest of crimes.

CHAPTER IX

I had not committed myself on the re-enlistment question when our comical lieutenant "Doc" called me out on the side, and asked me if I was going home with him and the boys. I told him that I had not yet decided, but if I did go back I should take another train, for I had too much self-respect to go with his gang.

"Do you mean that as an insult, sir?"

"I mean just what I said and you are at liberty to take it as an insult if you wish."

"Damn me if I will take such talk from any man," said this fierce chevalier, hissing his words between his teeth like the stage villain, "you have grossly insulted me and I demand satisfaction."

"All right! Let's get over the levee out of sight and you can have your block knocked off in about a minute."

"This is not the satisfaction due a gentleman; it will take blood to wipe out your remarks."

"That's a new idea to me, in fact two of them."

"What the devil do you mean by that?"

"Why, that you are a gentleman and that a little of your blood will wipe out reflections on your character. If that is all you want I can draw the claret out of that nose of yours the first round."

"By God, I have had enough of your insults and now I want to know if you will meet me on the river bank at the break of day tomorrow and give me the satisfaction due a gentleman?"

"I'll be there all right but I don't think you will. You will fill up with whiskey and go to talking, and that will bring about your arrest for issuing a challenge. But if you get over there you will find me on the ground, and say, you won't mind if I dump your carcass into the river to avoid any explanations about the affair?"

He made no reply to this cold blooded proposition except to say if I did not meet him as agreed, he would denounce me as a coward to the company. And then he ambled off in the direction of the St. Charles Hotel.

My game was pure bluff but he had called it, and at the break of day I had to be on the river bank and show my hand. And it is needless to confess that I was not happy over the turn of affairs at all. We both carried revolvers and no doubt he expected we would use them, for he was in excellent practice as well as myself, and I was aware that they were dangerous weapons to fool with.

I had underrated "Doc" and needlessly insulted him, and had got myself in a predicament. I didn't want to kill the cuss, nor want him to kill me, and my disposition was to get out of this scrape in some way other than backing out. I suffered untold misery over the situation for a couple of hours. Then I received an inspiration and was happy again.

I had had much practice with the foils and was handy in the cutlass or broad-sword exercise, and the chances were not one in a hundred that "Doc" knew anything about the game. Nothing had been said about weapons, and being the challenged party I had a right to choose cavalry sabres, for they were military and dueling tools all right. With these I was confident I could readily do him up without hurting him, by a stroke on the side of the head with the flat of the blade. I had only to borrow the swords of the cavalry, have them on the ground, give him his choice and he would have to take one of them and make the best of it.

The camp of Baker's Dragoons was above the 9th Infantry, and I had frequently been up there looking their outfit over, for I had a fondness for horses, and had thought of getting into that branch of the service. I had made several acquaintances, and so here I went at the dusk of the evening and borrowed from an Orderly Sergeant a pair of sabres under the pretense that a couple of us wanted to try a little sword play. They were extras and he said I might keep them a week, or 'til he called for them. It was dark when I returned to quarters, and I succeeded in getting them into my bunk without being seen.

I turned in that night with the load off my stomach and a cheerful feeling, for I felt certain that the chance of "Doc's" knowing anything about the broad sword exercise was not one in a thousand, and I had no more fear of meeting him in that manner, than with my fists. So I chucked a few chuckles and went slumbering off into dreamland, and did not wake up 'til someone shook me by the shoulder and whispered,

"Get up Dan. I want to see you outside," and then immediately disappeared.

"What the devil is up?" said I as I pulled on my boots and shoved the revolver in my hip pocket, "I wonder if this thing has been given away." When I stepped outside I saw the form of a man standing out on the parade grounds, and when I reached him I discovered it was "Doc".

The affair had worked on his mind so that he could not sleep, and he had come down to call it off. We shook hands at parting, and acknowledged much respect for each other. Then he started back to the St. Charles Hotel to get some sleep, while I rolled into my bunk and returned to dreamland again.

When the boys alighted from the train at Bloomington they were persuaded to fall into line and march up to the city under the command of these lieutenants, for whom they could have had no respect whatever, a mistake which they no doubt afterward regretted.

Doc entered the service again as a private, and I think served in the ranks 'til the close of the war. I have no doubt that in that capacity he made a fair soldier.

--- ------ ---

Captain Harvey sent for me one morning and I reported to his quarters and found him alone. He said he hoped to retain the organization (Company K) and recruit it to the limit, and he wanted my brother Frank and me to stay with him. I asked him who he had selected for his First Lieutenant, and his countenance fell as he replied, "I would like Joe Howell."

"All right, if he takes it we will stay," and he immediately jumped to his feet and hugged me.

"You will be Orderly, Dan, and it won't be long before there will be straps on your shoulders," and he placed both hands on my jackets where the straps would be located.

"But I don't want to be Orderly" said I.

"Oh! but you must be for we have settled on that."

"How could you before I had decided to stay?"

"Easy enough; we said that if you would stay with us you should be the Orderly."

"Well, I didn't say so and don't want it."

"Sure thing; you can depend on that."

Then the Captain gave me another hug, and asked me to think over the matter of Orderly and he would see me again about it.

That day Joe Howell took me out for a walk. I liked this boy exceedingly well, and his selection for the First Lieutenant was what decided me to stay. Yet he could not persuade me to take the Orderly position, though I reluctantly agreed to take the next lower step.

This was the chief blunder in my military career. A month later I was on the lookout for a buck nigger that I could employ to kick me up and down the parade grounds for my contemptible stupidity. I can only explain this singular conduct by saying that I had avoided drills and tactical instruction, and really considered myself incapable of creditably holding the position. And I was sensible too, that I had not inherited an over-supply of courage and was fearful that I might not be able to acquit myself with credit on a battlefield. I believed that an inconspicuous position would be the best, until I got better acquainted with myself.

Now at this time I was not much afraid of a fist encounter with the average man, for from boyhood up I had many scraps, and whatever the result, I never regretted that I had waded in and did my level best. When worsted, I felt the better for the exercise, and to this day I like a man who will not submit to insult and wrong, but will fight on all proper occasions. Since I had gotten a little coaching, which I will describe in the next chapter, I had generally come out on the upper side.

CHAPTER X

It was in September, 1856 that I got a job of house carpentering in Chicago. The location was then known as Carville, a settlement built up contiguous to the carshops of the Illinois Central Railroad, over which Harriman and Fish are now (c. 1905) making a gallant fight for proxies. This was about three miles from the City Hall, and in going there one had to cross quite a bit of prairie.

I was eighteen years of age and had spent the previous summer and the following spring on heavy frame-work, and got a couple of month's experience on a country farm house. Then I bought a few tools, built a pretentious looking chest to hold them, and recommended myself as a workman. And I got a job too and held it down 'til winter came on and house carpenters were laid off. Then I procured work in the railroad carshops at advanced wages and held the job down for two months. That seemed to be my limit for good behavior, for I then fractured one of the shop rules and got fired.

I had a room-mate at the boarding house by the name of Tom Whelan, who was foreman on a large residential building nearby, and he gave me a job with him. Tom was the most accomplished scamp that I ever met. He had a few virtues and many vices ingeniously combined with a fine form and an attractive face. He had black eyes, straight and black hair, wore the conventional mustache, and was at all times a well-dressed handsome fellow, but in no respect a dude or fop.

An exemplary young lady at the boarding house told me that she could never marry a man who was not religious, and free from all the common vices. But she got badly smitten by Tom, and when she discovered that the attention he paid her was just for pastime, her little heart very near broke.

He occasionally attended the Congregational Church nearby, and would walk home with the beautiful young daughter of one of the wealthy members who welcomed him to his house at all times. When he felt in the mood he would attend a prayer meeting and take a prominent part in the exercises, and when he returned to our room he would haul me out of bed and rehearse the performance for my edification.

These church members evidently thought Tom a very holy young man and I quite agreed with them, for I knew that he had more holes in his character than there were mosquitoes on Montezuma Marsh.

Tom played the flute with about the same degree of skill that I did the fiddle, and we gave ourselves many concerts in our private room. Our pious landlady would not invite us to use her parlor for our concerts, or allow her daughters to accompany us on their piano, because our music was all memorized and secular. As I had not succeeded in getting into society, and Tom only with the holy cult, we were not invited out as often as we would have liked. Our musical tastes and talents were singularly alike, for we had memorized identical music to a degree that was phenomenal. When Tom would lead out with "Old Dog Tray," or "Nellie Gray," I would hop in at the second bar and carry the refrain through in perfect harmony. And when I struck up "The Widow McCrea" or "Mrs. McDonald's Reel," Tom would send the fine-cut spray into the blow-hole of his old flute and finish two bars ahead of me. We would habitually leave "The Devil's Dream" for the finish, for the run of scales was very easy and we would race it through to see which could get it out first.

The old Irish woman who did the rough work about the boarding house was waiting on the table one day and said,

"Mr. Whelin, what is the last dehune [tune] it is that ye byes play before you go to bed for the night?"

"I guess it is `The Devil's Dream'," replied Tom.

"I guess it must be for ye play it like hell," she returned.

There was an insignificant, middle-aged man occupying a little room in rear of ours who was a sort of roustabout in the moulder's department of the car works. He had left a family somewhere in Jersey, with little intention of going back to them, but his heart had softened and he was dying for an invitation to return. One fine Sunday morning he came into our room and poured his grievances into my ear, and in a way expressed his hopes and fears, and then requested me to write to his wife and ascertain her feelings toward him.

I complied with his request and told her that her husband had repented of leaving her as he did, and that I believed a little encouragement from her would at once bring him back into the bosom of his family.

She immediately replied that she could give him no encouragement to come East, but hoped I would induce him to think his fortune lay in the far West and get him headed in that direction. Chicago was too near New Jersey to give her that peace of mind and comfortable feeling that would possess her the moment she heard he had reached a point so far from Jersey that it was unlikely he could ever get back again. In fine, he was too insignificant for a woman like herself and she had no earthly use for him whatever.

I didn't read this letter to him for fear he would collapse on my hands, but put him off with a few lies and said he must hustle and get a few hundred dollars ahead before going back again.

A week later he came into my room and requested a violin solo. As I lifted the "Strad" from the case I asked him what he would like to hear, and he gravely replied, "Do They Miss Me at Home, Do They Miss Me."

Tom and I kept a pair of foils in the use of which we were quite evenly matched, but with the gloves Tom was in his element and had given me many a hard jolt. One Sunday we stepped out of the boarding house with the foils for the purpose of having some exercise over at the house we were building, and saw the congregation filtering out of the church a square away.

The wealthy member - who was an Englishman - and his beautiful young daughter would be among them. Tom had said that he (the Englishman) was extremely ceremonious and polite, and that it put him (Tom) to his trumps to match his Chesterfieldian airs. Here was his opportunity to show off, and so he handed me the foils and told me to take the other side of the street.

I crossed over, and Tom walked airily up to meet the elect. He tipped his hat gracefully to all he met, and when he arrived at the church his friend and daughter had just stepped from the platform to the walk.

When their eyes met, the Johnny Bull's stove pipe and Tom's cap came off in unison, and their heads went down on a level with their knees. Then the Englishman side-stepped to the right and made another low bow, while opposite him Tom took a left side-step and matched him with an equally low salaam. Then they sidled toward the opposite flank with a perceptible advance, and down went their noses again nearly to the ground. Then, the gentlemen shook hands and Tom got his away from the old duffer as quickly as possible and secured the little hand of the daughter, which he held 'til they separated, which was as ceremonious as their meeting; bowing, scraping of their shoes on the walk and backing away.

We met at the next corner and Tom dryly remarked that no damned blooming Englishman should give him points when it come to slinging style. This was just a trifle droll because Tom's parents were English and he reached the United States from Canada at the age of ten.

One of his greatest delights was to spend an evening in the cottage of an Irishman or Scotchman who could brew a good whiskey punch, tell a good story and sing a song. He sang well himself, and his favorite was of the barber who gave the paddy a gratuitous shave. As this song is quite funny and out of date, I will give what I remember of it, which will be sufficient to convey the humor:

The barber kept an old bum razor especially for credit customers and dead beats and one day an Irishman was passing that way;

His beard had been growing for many a day.
He said to the barber, as he lay down his hod,
Can't you give me a shave for the pure love of God.
It's divil a cent have I in my purse,
If you give me a shave, you'll be none the worse.
He spread the lather on Paddy's broad chin.
With his old rusty razor, to work did begin.
Howld on! Bloody nouns! Now what's that yur doin'?
If you don't lave off, my jaws you will ruin.
One day when Pat heard a donkey roar,
He thought the noise came from the barber shop door.
Arrah now! that barber, the villain and knave's
Givin' some poor devil a 'love of God shave.'

Tom was a well-read fellow and could converse intelligently upon a great variety of subjects. He cornered our pious landlady - who was a clergyman's widow - on the history of her own church and talked literature and poetry with her eldest daughter. He was also a fine mechanic. But hardened sinner as I was fast becoming, I did not enjoy his reading the letters he received from young women with whom he had been much too familiar in his rambling life, for they were the beings, and the only ones, I worshipped. I have always held the fair sex in high esteem, though more than once in my life have I been done to a turn by the dear creatures. Tom seemed to have no sincere regard for them, but applied to them such approbatious terms as chits, baggages and heifers, all of which was distasteful to me.

While working one morning in the Meeker House, Tom sent out for a pint of whiskey and when Sam, the Scot boss plasterer came in, Tom passed the bottle and the Scotchman asked what it was for.

"Washington's birthday," gravely replied Tom.

"That's a fact," says Sam, "but it had slipped me mind;" and then he squared himself about, spread his feet apart, and gave this toast:

"Here is to the American Eagle; may it take flight around the Earth and drop tail-feathers on both Ireland and Scotland."

Tom and I applauded and told him to drink hearty, which he did. At this juncture in walked a well-dressed, good-looking young Irishman of Sam's acquaintance, and as the latter was still holding the bottle, he proffered it to him. Strangely enough the young Hibernian declined with thanks, but Sam was persistent in urging him to take a little for once to the memory of the father of our country, and his importunities finally prevailed, for this young Mickey at last seized the bottle and drained it.

As he emptied the last swallow into his gullet, the expression on Sam's face was indescribable. He was already thirsting for another drink and had seen the last drop disappear down that young Irishman's throat.

As soon as the young man left, Tom sent out and had the bottle refilled, for he was bent on getting Scotchman Sam good and drunk.

When Sam had downed another horn, he became voluble and commenced to brag. He had been a member of some organization of Scottish Guards, and when a neighboring regiment sent them a challenge for a broad-sword contest, his colonel had selected him to defend the reputation and honor of his regiment. He accepted the responsibility, and defeated his antagonist.

Out of mock curiosity, Tom got him to take a lath and exhibit some of the cuts and guards, and to illustrate it with better effect, he got me around there with another lath.

We crossed sticks and Sam told me to hit him on the head, which I did instantly. Sam rubbed his head and said I had taken him when off his guard that time, but that I could not do it again.

Then he put up his guard and told me to try it again. Of course I couldn't hit him a down stroke on the top of his head, after he had deliberately put up his guard, and so I gave him a vigorous punch in his bread basket. When he grunted "Ow there," and dropped his guard, I reached his head easily. But not so easily as I might or should have done, however, for my lath flew into several pieces, and for an instant Sam saw constellations galore.

As I stepped to the lath pile to get another and a tougher foil, for I was now getting interested and commencing to enjoy the sport, Sam made a dive for me and I retreated around the work bench. Tom gave me a signal to pitch into him, but I refused to see it, and had no thought except to keep out of his reach.

Sam gave up the chase when he got 'round to where the bottle was standing, and didn't leave enough in it to cock a school boy. Then he meandered off into one of the back rooms where his work lay.

Tom and I had taken only fake drinks, and were as straight as a fiddle string while Sam was about as tight.

We put the bottle out of sight in a tool chest and were engaged with our work again when the owner of the building - Mr. Meeker - came in. He talked a few minutes with Tom, and then as was his custom started out on a tour of inspection of the various rooms to note what had been done since his last visit.

He noted that the hod carrier came out of one of the rooms with a broad grin on his face, and immediately closed the door behind him. So he stepped up, quietly opened the door, and stood aghast at the sight before him. There was Sam, with his back to the door, hawk and trowel in his hands, slinging plaster on three sides of the room and the ceiling. He had plastered one of the windows entirely over and daubed himself from head to foot. When Mr. Meeker had sufficiently recovered his breath to speak, Sam was so astonished that he wheeled about, and the trowel full of plaster that he intended to put somewhere else, struck Mr. Meeker square on his shirt front.

Sam was so dumbfounded at what he had done that he instantly collapsed, fell into the plaster which was left on the mortar-board, and the hawk emptied itself onto his neck.

Mr. Meeker came back where Tom and I were, and we cleaned him up as well as we could. We had the mortar-mixer, who lived in a shanty on the lot, take Sam in charge. Meeker returned to the building again the next day and found Sam removing the superfluous plaster from the room he had decorated the day before.

Meeker at once discharged him but Sam begged like a presiding elder at a quarterly meeting, and when he was asked what possessed him to commence drinking that morning he replied that it being Washington's birthday he just drank to the memory of the father of the country.

"Washington fiddlesticks," exclaimed Meeker. "His birthday comes in February and it is nearly the first of April. Now understand; if you touch another drop of liquor while you are on this job, out you go."

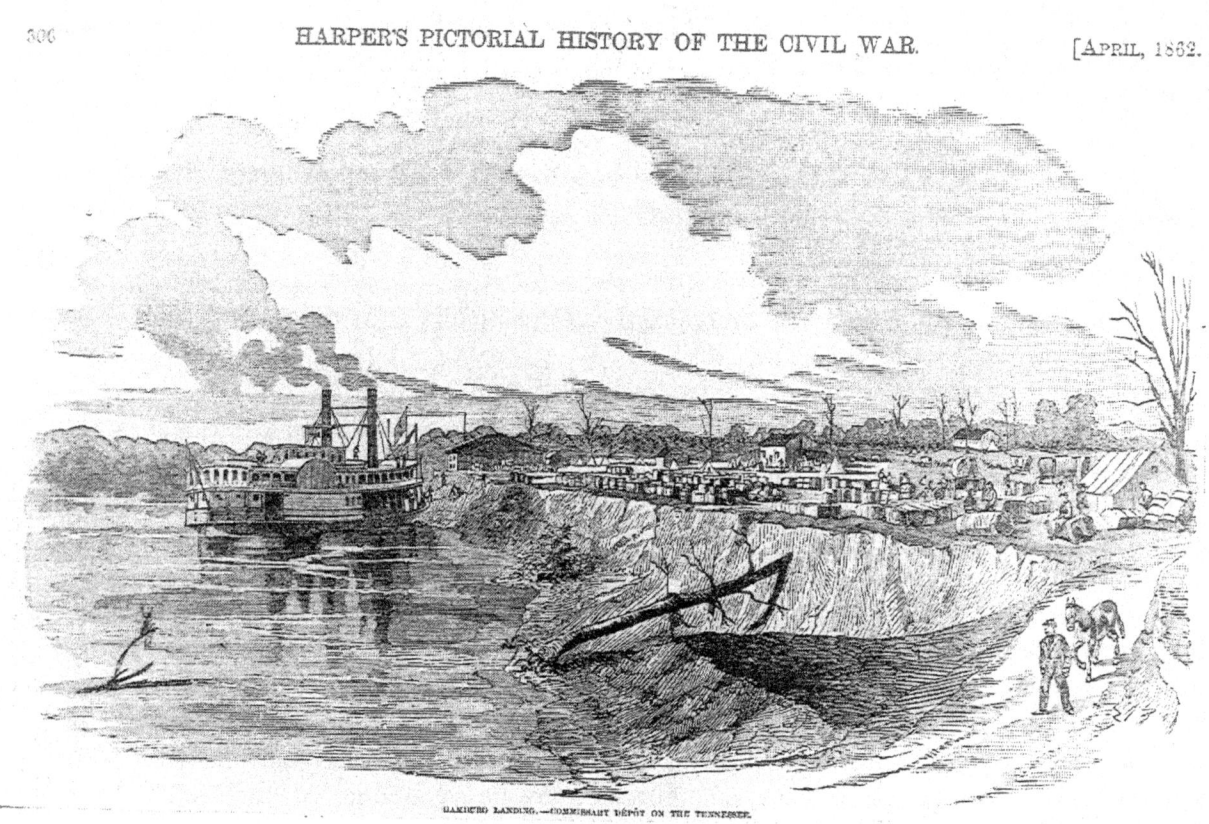

The Union Army's advance into the heart of the trans-Appalachian South was supported by land and river depots and resupply points from the Ohio River to Vicksburg. These supply installations were often isolated and very vulnerable to smash and run Rebel cavalry swoops.

CHAPTER XI

One of the amusements that we indulged in at the Meeker House was that of kicking from one foot. You raised one foot and kept it clear from the floor. Then you spring on the other foot and with it kicked as high as you could and get back on this same foot with which you made the kick. The one foot was used for standing, kicking and alighting. The other was not used at all. Try it once if you never have. The first time I did, I could get about fifteen inches from the floor, but at this time I could reach about that much higher than my head, and Tom could do still better.

Another little diversion we indulged in was the composing of doggerel, and recording our inspirations on blocks of wood with a pencil.

But a little fun of another nature transpired the second or third day after Sam's drunk. While in our room at the boarding house Tom had asked me why I did not tackle Sam when he chased me 'round the work bench, and I replied that I would be no match for that big fellow.

"There is where you are fooling yourself," said Tom. "You could do him up with your punches as easily as you did with the sticks. Let me tell you how I got a start.

"I was living at home in Rochester, N.Y., and was a year younger than yourself when my father, who was an ugly brute when he had a few drinks in him, upon a trifling pretext, dragged me out to the stable to horsewhip me. When he reached for the whip I caught the back of his coat collar and dumped him on the floor as neat as anything you ever saw and then pounded him so that he had to be helped to the house by one of the neighbors.

"He couldn't wait 'til he got well to get his revenge, but sent for my uncle, who was also a large man, quite as ugly, and a few years younger. I was expecting him and was in my room above trying to get a load into a little pocket pistol when he strode in and caught me by the collar of my jacket. Down the stairs we went together and out to the stable. I had unbuttoned my jacket, intending to slip out of it and run, but he shut the door behind us, and so the instant I freed myself I gave him a right hander under the ear, a left to the chin and then a backward push over a tool box. He fell hard and I kicked him into insensibility in less than a minute.

"It took four men and an express wagon to get that blooming uncle of mine back into the bosom of his family again.

"My mother said nothing but I could see that she was not displeased with me, and thought that I had been worth raising. The next day she packed a carpet bag for me, gave me ten dollars, and I bid her good bye.

"I brought up at Kingston, Canada, where I lived when a small boy, remained there a week with people I had known, but did not succeed in getting a job. I then took the stage for Belleville [Ontario] where I had heard of an opening I might get into, and I happened to be the only passenger out.

"When we changed horses I jumped out and walked into the public house and there was an English officer with some hand baggage. When the fresh horses were hitched, the driver blew his horn and I followed the officer to the coach. Although it was raining quite hard this officer ordered me to get up and ride with the driver.

"I will take my carpet bag then, I said, and when I reached for it I caught him by the wrist and yanked him out flat in the mud. He arose twice, and each time I knocked him down again. Then he cried for quarter and said I was a blooming fine lad and might ride inside with him. I told him he was a blooming hog and could go up and sit with the driver, and he had to go."

This ended Tom's story, and then he added, "All you need is a little more sand, you could do him up as easily with your knockers as you did with the sticks."

I said that if he ever tackled me again I would buckle into him.

The next morning I was in the second story casing a door when Sam came up with blood in his eye. He had met Tom below and had asked him how he supposed Mr. Meeker had got on to him so easily that day and Tom told him that when Meeker came in and inquired for Sam I had told him that he would find him in the back room drunk. Then Tom followed Sam upstairs to see the fun.

"I understand me boy that you told Mishter Maker the other day that I was in the back room drunk."

"I understand that you are a bully and a liar," I retorted.

"I'll take that from no living man," said Sam.

"You will have to take it from me, and I will give you something to go with it," and I sprang from the step ladder and handed him a jolt on the chin, followed by two more in rapid succession, when down he went and in an instant I had him by the throat. He gave up at once. That ended the affair as I supposed, and since that time I have not had much fear of an encounter with the ordinary man.

Did you ever hear the term "crafty" applied to a Scotsman? My trouble with Sam did not end where I supposed it had. That fellow, with much ingenuity, with Tom as his subject, composed a piece of doggerel on a wood block in imitation of my hand, and left it on Tom's bench. As soon as the latter saw it he recognized the writing and brought it to me. It was exceedingly funny, and my laughing increased his anger. If the joke had been on me I would have laughed at the wit and the ingenuous rhyming, and so would Tom, but it being on him he could see no fun in it, only malice. One verse described an incident that was not supposed to be known by anyone around the building except Tom and me.

"Did you write that damned stuff?" asked Tom.

"The imitation of my hand is so nearly perfect, that I suppose it will be useless to deny it, but it would be impossible for me to compose it. I would give ten dollars to be able to write this verse."

Then I read it to him and asked him if he had ever seen a neater turn in versification, and then he got madder than ever and said it was an insulting piece of stuff from beginning to end, and that anyone could write it, if they were low lived enough.

Then I said, "I never saw it 'til you handed it to me, and you can believe this or not, just as you please."

The next time Mr. Meeker came to the building I lost my job.

I at once packed my kit and went out on the Chicago and Milwaukee Railroad to a spot on the lake [Lake Michigan] shore called St. Johns, which was about a mile north of Port Clinton. The latter burg had a store, a blacksmith shop, an excuse for a hotel, and possibly a dozen dwellings. It had had a warehouse on the bank of the lake that I helped build, but it was soon taken down and shipped across Lake Michigan to St. Joseph, Michigan.

About half way between there and Highland Park lived Doctor Myers, who had a beautiful daughter of about sixteen whom I used to stop and look at occasionally, but that was as far as I ever got with her. She had many admirers and I was too near her age and too bashful to be successful there. Her oldest brother Hank was single, about twenty-five, and lived with the family, putting in his time hunting and fishing.

The spring we were building the warehouse Hank had a skiff and a seine net that was probably fifty feet long, and with this gear had made some very good hauls of white fish that ran in schools near the shore. But he had provided no means of curing or putting them on the market, and so all the families about there helped themselves. Hank never got down to the shore very early mornings, and a few of us boys thought we would try a haul ourselves before he arrived.

So we loaded his seine in his boat, and giving one end to a boy to hold near the shore where the water was about waist deep, we struck out a circular course paying out the seine as we went. When the net was all out we jumped into the water with that end and commenced slowly drawing it in toward shore.

It soon became evident that we had caught a school of them all right. Some of us were in the water up to our necks pushing on the net, when we heard a yell from up the bank that would have been a credit to a Comanche Indian. There stood Hank, fairly paralyzed over our impudence in taking such liberties with his property. The oaths soon commenced to roll down the bank mixed up with orders to drop that seine and threats to kill every one of us, but we had a lot of fish there and didn't propose to let them go. So, we just ignored Hank and pulled and heaved on the seine. When he was half down the bank he saw the net was full, and many were flopping over the top, and then his tune changed to "hang on to her boys, push up you fellows there in the middle, pull up there on the further end now, what are you doing, now jump in and throw them out on the shore before they break the net. You are a bully lot of boys; that is the biggest catch of fish ever taken out of Lake Michigan."

Before A. C. Hessing put up his pressed brick machine at St. Johns, there was nothing there but a blacksmith shop and a shanty. Charles Dole was the financial backer of the concern, and I worked here for a month or two and then went to Evanston. The boss carpenter soon went busted and then I went next to Glencoe and worked for the Gurnies for a year or more.

In the early fall, I went back to the city to do some trading, and on the way down from the depot, then on the north-west side, I passed down Lake Street, and looking into one of the store buildings where I heard some hammering I saw Tom Whelan there at work. I walked in, and after a warm greeting he threw off his apron, donned his coat, and we started out on the street together.

We strolled down to the lake front, stretched ourselves out on the grass and gave an account of ourselves since our parting.

"Dan, I got onto that d----d Scotsman at last, and fixed his flute for him."

"Who are you talking about?"

"Why Sam, there at the Meeker House, who wrote that insulting stuff about me."

"Did he write stuff about you too?"

"He was the fellow that got up those insulting verses."

"Oh go to, I wrote them myself and got fired for it.

"You're a liar by the clock; now let up 'til I tell you. After Sam left, Irish Billy told me all about it, and a month later I met Sam on Clark Street and got him into Mulligan's wholesale whiskey house for a drink. I gave the boys the wink and steered him down in the basement and there I batted him about among the high wine casks 'til he couldn't get up any more. When I finished him, he didn't look much like a Scotch poet. Say Dan, how do you suppose he got hold of that affair over at the Prairie Queen?"

Tom parted with me at the depot that evening, and that was the last I saw or heard of him.

July 25th, 1861 arrived and we were mustered out of the 90-day service: Citizens again.

CHAPTER XII

When the boys got away on the train from Cairo those that remained behind called on the mustering officer and were sworn in for "three years unless sooner discharged." Then we returned to the barracks and held an election, all voting according to the program cut out in advance, with an exception.

Lawrence Roberts was sworn in with us and had been promised the first corporalcy, but the meeting was adjourned as soon as the sergeants had been elected and Roberts was left a private in violation of a well understood agreement. It was a piece of bad faith that I can't account for. I tried to convince Roberts that the captain would give him the place when we filled the corporalcies, but he was so incensed at this little piece of treachery that he swore he would not stay with Company K under any conditions. So he took his furlough and never returned, and as a consequence was reported as a deserter, and this stands as such on the records of the Adjutant General's Office of Illinois. I would bet dollars against peanuts that the boy entered the service again, in which case he was no more of a deserter than myself, and there was no wrong in the action either. He had a right to choose a company that had a captain he could respect.

I was left in charge of the barracks, and the others went home after recruits. Colonel "Dick" remained with us, and as he felt mighty kindly toward us boys who were staying with him, and had plenty of leisure, he made us very welcome at his quarters. The refreshments served were cigars and commissary whiskey, but my drafts on the latter were light as I had not yet got the habit very strong.

Soon recruits commenced coming in - four or more in a squad, and I would have them sworn in by the mustering officer, give them uniforms and muskets, and drill them. I had secured a copy of Hardee's Light Infantry Tactics, and was getting posted. Because Hardee went with the South when the war began, the War Department was averse to scattering his tactics through our Union Army. They then issued an edition in one volume with his name left out, and it was known as the Authorized, or Cameron, edition. A year or more later Brigadier General Silas Casey revised and improved them [the tactics], and they were published in three handy volumes and distributed throughout the Army.

In a couple of weeks our company and the regiment were nearly full again, and when one of our sergeants came back I turned things over to him and asked for a furlough. From a book of forms Col. Oglesby filled out an order for transportation on the Illinois Central R.R. to Chicago via Bloomington, and wished me a good time.

"But I have no furlough here and nothing to indicate how long I may stay."

"Stay as long as you want to and come back when you get ready, Sergeant." I thanked him and said I would not stay over-time. Then I took the first train out, shifted at Centralia to a freight that was bound up the main line and reached Bloomington some time the next day.

Two or three days later I boarded another Illinois Central freight, and in due time landed in Chicago, where I spent a couple more days and then went out to Highland Park where I knew the country and people for miles about.

At a little burg built up about a cross-roads a few miles from the Park, at the edge of the prairie, I had obtained my first job of carpenter work in the early summer of 1855. I was then sixteen, but not very sweet. I had been on the job less than a week, and was taking an after dinner smoke in the shade of a tree when I was approached by a comely looking female of about my own age, who said she would be happy to make my acquaintance.

After recovering from my embarrassment, I assured her that the felicity was mutual and gave her my chair. Then I planted my back against the tree, looked her over critically, and took her dimensions with much care.

She was of medium height, had a profusion of brown hair, grey eyes, regular features somewhat tanned, as were her shapely hands. In reply to her questioning, I informed her that I had been in the West six months, and in the neighborhood three days; and thought I would be very fond of the society of young ladies, though so far I had had but little to do with them.

That seemed to please her for she told me that Illinois young ladies, at least some of them, were not starchy and stuck-up, and were very glad to make the acquaintance of young gentlemen from the East. She then invited me to call upon her - an invitation that I readily accepted, and we made a date for the coming Sunday.

On the place where I worked was a young man employed by the year, whose name was Alick. He was not a smart alick, but a level headed, sensible fellow, who was born on a farm in the vicinity, and much respected by all. I chanced to meet him a few months earlier at Port Clinton, and when I turned up on this job, we remembered each other and were chummy from the start. He was six or eight years my senior and had planned to introduce me into the best society the country afforded.

He had observed the young lady and me engaged in conversation under the old oak on the lawn, and asked when and where I had made her acquaintance. I innocently related the circumstance and he laughed 'til the top button flew off his overalls. I had thought myself in great good luck, and was slightly irritated at his excessive mirth. I had not confessed making a date with her, and now I was very glad that I had kept that item to myself. At the table he was usually voluble and full of good natured humor, and I was fearful he would give me away in the presence of all the family, but my fears proved groundless. He took occasion to hint that he had in his mind a very pretty young woman whom he knew would just please me and said that we would call on her soon - probably Sunday evening.

Sunday came at last, and directly after a two o'clock dinner I took a stroll down the highway, passed through a farm gate and on beyond the barns, and then followed a path for eighty rods or more that led to a log house around which stood three or four shade trees. Under one of them sat my Dulcinea, in her best attire, awaiting me.

I planted myself in the vacant chair facing her, and we sat there and talked nonsense and told lies 'til sundown. I caught glimpses of her parents, and noted that they both had ridiculously large noses, and wondered that the girl did not resemble them. Her brothers passed in and out of the house, but none of the bunch came near us, and so it was quite evident that the girl was queen of the Ranche.

She asked for my name and when I had given it to her she said she was going to call me her Dan. Then I thought it was the proper thing to ask for her name and she said that the whole of it was Polonica Cristine Abigail Cameron Thompson. I did not quite faint and tumble off my chair, but I came mighty nigh to it.

As the sun went down I recalled what Alick had said about calling on No. 2, and reached for my hat, but as if she had read my thoughts, she reached for it too and got it. She declared that I should not go yet; that I must wait and take a walk with her by moonlight - she just doted on moonlight walks. I was not averse to them myself and so I invented a few more lies to pass away the time 'til the sunlight had got out of our way.

When its last rays had disappeared she handed me my hat, took my arm, and we sauntered up the path through the wheatfield, as I had come. We soon had our arms around each other's waists with our hands locked in front and presented a lovely sight to the gentleman in the moon. As we were about to pass out the wheat field onto a piece of meadow land we halted and stood there kissing, hugging and grunting, and I was having such a good time I was in no hurry for her to break away and start back home.

She was of about my mind for she said it was early yet and suggested that we sit down by one of the wheat shocks and visit a little longer. I was quite bashful at that time and incapable of advancing such proposition or declining it either for that matter. I knew well that it was a dangerous proceeding, but I never could resist temptation.

Then she looked so very lovely by moonlight that I was loathe to part with her. So the motion was carried unanimously and we backed up to a shock and sat down.

It is said that a bashful man when in society does not know what to do with his hands and feet, but I kept my hands busy holding hers and pulling her head over on my shoulder. I had no particular use for my feet just then and so I let them stick out in the stubble.

It must have been about midnight when we tore ourselves apart and started for our respective homes. We were both in the best of humor, and another date was made but I did not keep it. A few evenings later, Alick took me with him to call on No. 2, and chat with this modest little beauty drove the devilment all out of me. I determined then and there to devote myself to her, but before I had made much progress, No. 1 heard of my maneuvering and gave me clean away. She accused me of making improper overtures toward her, and all that sort of thing, although I am sure I behaved remarkably well under the circumstances. It might have been overlooked but for a couple of homely old spinsters - who for the past twenty years had looked under their bed every might, hoping to find a man there. They were amazed, horrified, scandalized and shocked at the accusation by No. 1 and their influence was strong enough to have me turned down and out.

I ought to have gone back to No. 1 but I was much of a boy and didn't have much manly sense. When I met her on the highway she stopped and acted real nice to me, but I imagined I had a grievance against her, when as a matter of fact I ought to have been kicked into the middle of Lake Michigan for the ingratitude I had shown her. She told this story on me to keep me away from No. 2, and get me back again. Living off the road, she stood at a great disadvantage in catching beaux, and had slipped her lariat on me in a mistressly manner, and was entitled to me for a reasonable length of time. She was as virtuous as any girl in the community, only fearless and indiscreet, and was deserving of fair treatment. How much happiness we miss in life by harboring imaginary grievances.

My hopes of getting into "society" having vanished, I spent my spare time in the timber with a gun - game being very plentiful - and sawing on an old fiddle in my sleeping room evenings. At the conclusion of the job here I went to Waukegan and worked on the ravine bridges and Catholic Church 'til winter, and then came back here and engaged board of a farmer about a mile away and attended a three-months term of school.

I remained about this territory three or four years. A new crop of girls grew up and the 1855 summer escapade with No. 1 was overlooked or forgotten.

This neighborhood was somewhat affected with spiritualism, watercure, a graham and vegetable diet, and the influence of C. S. Fowler was very much in evidence in the community.

Two years after attending school here in the Highland Park neighborhood, I took another term in an adjoining township and so had a large acquaintance round and about there, and here is where I elected to spend a couple of weeks of my furlough.

There were many young and pretty misses about here whose society was really charming after my three month debarment from female companionship. And many of the older people had shown me kindnesses in the past, and not having seen them for about a year, it was quite a pleasure to call on them all and accept their hospitality, which was unbounded.

Things had improved somewhat since my first visit into the community. Some had died from too much graham and cold water, and others had lost their health for the same reason. But these often thought they needed a change of climate instead of diet, and emigrated to California, bloomers and all. The general store dealer found it to his interest to add a meat market to his establishment, the Water-Cure Journal and Graham-diet Advocate ceased coming to the local post office, and the youngsters were now growing up healthy, happy and handsome.

I spent the furlough weeks with these good people, and enjoyed every moment of the time. If there was a disagreeable incident, or an unpleasant word spoken, I cannot recall it. "No. 1" had married a stranger, and "No. 2" my friend Alick. I kissed all the pretty girls I met, and repeated it as often as a good opportunity offered, and never met a rebuff. They were so intensely patriotic and grateful to "The Brave Soldier Boys," that they could not find it in their warm hearts to deny us such innocent and harmless pleasure.

The elders were interested in the details of camp life, and the early hours of the evening would be spent in general conversation, and if there was a pretty girl in the family, the others would considerately retire at their usual hour and leave us together.

Of course, it goes without saying that we would soon be sitting side by side on the settee, talking silly nothings and telling harmless lies between kisses and endearing embraces, and midnight would come upon us before we had seemingly been left together an hour.

And such spreads as these good matrons would lay before a fellow who had subsisted on pork, beans and sour bread for the past ninety days: Light fluffy biscuit with yellow butter and honey; real cream for the coffee; mashed potatoes with rich milk gravy; a large platter of fried fresh eggs; delicious cake and yellow custard pies. This was the sort of fare these hospitable people stuffed me with during my stay among them.

That I survived two weeks of this diet is probably due to the fact that I would sleep over the breakfast hour, and only turn out in the time to take a sprint before dinner. The first time I turned into a soft bed, I pronounced it luxurious, but still I was restless and did not drop off to sleep as usual. After tumbling about awhile it occurred to me that it was a pretty sudden change from sleeping on a board, so I yanked a blanket from the bed, spread it around me, lay down on the floor with my boots for a pillow and was sound asleep in less than no time.

Under the liberal verbal terms of my furlough, I might have prolonged my stay much beyond the two-week limit I had imposed upon myself, but the truth is I had begun to tire of this heavenly existence and was quite ready to go back to camp life again.

So I ran into the city one morning, took a sleeper that evening on the Air Line to Centralia and slept over the route. The porter gave me the first report I had of the death of Union General Nathaniel Lyon at Wilson's Creek, Missouri, August 10, 1861.

CHAPTER XIII

Upon arrival at Cairo I found my brother Frank, who by the way was third duty sergeant and had spent his vacation with some friends in Wisconsin, had got back a few days ahead of me. He left a week or more before I did, so he got in full time.

The officers had been very successful in recruiting, in spite of the stories circulated about Company K's Capt. Harvey by the three-months boys. The company now was filled to the maximum--say 84 privates, making about 100 head all told. Only 64 privates were allowed in the former organization, with 4 corporals, and 4 sergeants, which with the three commissioned officers made 75 men for a full company under the old heavy infantry arrangement. In all respects we were very much improved. The proportion of commissioned officers to the enlisted men was less, and that was not the least of the improvements. Too many officers without guns weakens a command rather than strengthening it. If all the company officers had slung their toad stickers away and procured the best rifles that could be purchased at that time, it would have added greatly to the efficiency of our Army.

There were too many non-combatants connected with our Armies; musicians, clerks, color bearers and chaplains. All ought to have been armed and sent to the firing line. And in a measure, the company officers are in the same class; they stand about and get shot at but send back nothing in return. Occasionally an officer would take the equipment of one of the wounded or dead soldiers, step up on a line with the boys and get busy. And you might every time mark that man down as a No. 1, and never make a mistake.

Cairo soon had quite a garrison of three-year troops: Among them were the:

Eighth	Illinois Infantry	Col. R. J. Oglesby
Ninth	" "	" E. A. Paine
Eleventh	" "	" D. J. Morgan
Fourteenth	" "	" J. M. Palmer
Thirty-first	" "	" John A. Logan

There may have been other regiments here that I cannot recall; certainly some artillery and cavalry. Col. Dick was in command of the Cairo Post, so Lieut. Col. Rhodes had charge of our regiment.

In the drill we had to start from the bottom again, for the officers had the light infantry tactics to learn and the men were all new and had to commence with the "School of the Soldier." But the new drill was so much more sensible and more pleasant than the old, we took great interest in it, and for one I studied the tactics so earnestly, and drilled myself in the manual of arms, and in the marchings by measurements of the steps and timing by the watch, 'til I could step off 100 paces of 28 inches each in a minute, almost to a dot, both in time and distance.

The result of this was that drilling of the company was practically turned over to me, and this gave me every opportunity to perfect myself. It seemed very hard for Capt. Harvey to unlearn the old drill, rather difficult for 1st. Lieut. Joe Howell to learn the new, and the 2nd. Lieut. preferred to play marbles with Johnny Dawson. Howell would take a gun and get into the ranks, and in time he could take out the company and put them through their paces in fair shape, but the other two never became competent "Drill Masters."

I can recall but two commissioned officers who mastered the new tactics promptly, and they were 1st. Lieut. Loyd Wheaton and 2nd. Lieut. Samuel Caldwell, both of Co. E.

The former came out on the parade grounds one morning and watched me maneuvering the company until I got nervous. I moved farther away and he came along too, and it became evident that I couldn't get away from him. Then I conceived an idea that for the moment I mistook for inspiration, and wheeling the company about, sent them down upon him on a double quick. Instead of moving off in the direction of one of the flanks as I supposed he would, he folded his arms and stood his ground and I roared out, "Company-Right-about, March," just in time to avoid a collision.

I let the boys get far enough away to be out of the hearing, and brought them to a "rest." Then I walked up to the lieutenant who instead of reprimanding me for trying to run him off the parade, paid me a very nice compliment and said it was the only correct drilling he had seen on the grounds. The boys believed that he had called me down for trying to run over him, and I let them think so. It was better than to have the reputation of a liar.

Now it was the regular thing at this time, and for months afterward, that the men had to submit to drilling in movements and by tactical commands that they knew were wrong. As a rule the men of our company knew the drill better than their officers, and when one of them took them in charge and commenced slinging any of the old heavy infantry orders at them, they got out of humor and would not perform well. They couldn't talk back even to a petty second lieutenant, for they were the ones who drew the sharpest distinction between themselves and the enlisted men.

I never hesitated in approaching Oglesby, Rhoads or Wheaton with anything I had in mind, and expressing a free opinion that would have brought about a skirmish with many an insignificant second lieutenant.

It must have been nearly a year before we got rid of the exasperating "Mex Vets." Oglesby had the good sense to see clearly that he should not undertake any battalion drill until he had mastered the new tactics, and so he got a leave, went home and put in a couple of weeks studying. When he came back he was ready for business but was exceedingly careful not to try any maneuvers that he had not thoroughly worked out.

In the old tactics, if a company was standing in line faced to the front and you wished it to face to the right, you would say, "Company: *By the Right Flank*, Right Face." The new tactics omitted the underscored part, but it seemed as if many of these old Vets would never omit it, nor anything else they learned that was useless and ridiculous.

I was crossing the drill grounds one morning and saw Col. Rhoads trying to drill his company officers in the manual of arms. He brought them to a "Present" and looking down the line observed that the pieces did not line up as they should. The rule is to take the musket with the left hand halfway between the guide sight and the lower band, and keep the left fore-arm horizontal, but regardless of this he passed down the line and raised the pieces of the short officers and lowered these of the taller ones 'til he had them all on a level.

I immediately saw his difficulty and raising my hat said, "Colonel, may I speak with you a moment?" and stepped back a few paces out of hearing of the company officers. Rhoads brought them to an order and came back to where I was standing. I said to him, "I noticed the difficulty you were having in making these guns line up, and if you will not take it amiss I will tell you how that thing is done." "Of course I won't take it amiss. How is it Sergeant, anyhow?" "I see you have arranged your officers in line according to their rank. Now arrange them according to their height so they will taper down from right to left and then if each will hold his piece in the tactical position they will range to a dot." "Why of course they will; why didn't I think of that? Am much obliged, Sergeant." And he at once commenced rearranging his line.

I started on down to the city and my head commenced to swell so that I was fearful if I did not get a larger hat that I would soon have corns on my head.

About the first of September General Ulysses S. Grant came to Cairo and took command. He was an unpretentious person--a sort of an office general--and we boys saw very little of him.

The Confederate General Leonidas Polk had fortified Columbus--a strip of high land on the Kentucky side of the river about twenty-five miles below--and was about to garrison Paducah, fifty miles up the Ohio River. They had already commenced accumulating military stores there, and Rebel Gen. Gideon J. Pillow was on his way from Columbus with five thousand men, when we dropped off there and took possession.

There were only two thousand of us under General Charles F. Smith, and C.S.A. General Pillow might have come right along and gobbled us up after a stiff fight. But he probably imagined that there were ten thousand of us, and so turned about and went back. So we kept the city and his army supplies with it. More troops soon followed, and our regiment (8th) returned to its old quarters at Cairo.

It was along about this time that Dan Rice, the showman, came up from below on a steamer and pitched his tent on the north side of the parade grounds.

The first recollection I have of Dan was way back in the 1840's when he hit Rome, N.Y. with his "One Horse Show," which was transported on three Erie Canal boats. He had previously had much trouble with one Van Arnum, who he made the subject of a song, and he warbled this off in great voice, with an orchestra accompaniment.

I can recall only these fragments of the poem:

"Van Arnum you know is a thief and a liar,

And that I will prove for I can.
He stole my horse, he stole my show,
and he robbed me of every cent."

He also said that in this fracas with Van Arnum he got landed in "The Rochester Blue Eagle Jail."

"To break me again it's no go," he made rhyme with, "Dan Rice and his One-horse Show."

We found him the same Dan of ten or twelve years before, with the same old nose and a trifle stockier, with about the same equipment as formerly, and still filling the anomalous position of proprietor and clown. And it was impossible to rid our minds of the notion that if that dignified, elegantly appareled and scrumptious individual, who from general appearance would be entitled to the proprietorship of the layout, should happen to miscalculate the distance between himself and the clown's shins, when cracking his whip at him so spitefully, that it would not be beyond the range of probability that he would suddenly discover himself walking ties in search of another job.

Dan had one ring, one performance at a time, and you could see and hear everything. The moderate size of the outfit enabled him to stop at places that later day combinations have to pass by; and while the riding and tumbling were good, we were sure to have a plentiful supply of pure fun.

There was always a neat speech and a good song coming from the clown proprietor, and in the closing acts he would introduce a pair of ingeniously educated shetlands that would drive around the ring a couple of times very handsomely, but when you tried to send them around the third time they would invariably balk, kick the dashboard into slivers, and scare the driver into fits.

And then they would bring out an innocent looking jack or jenny and tempt some hard up individual out of the crowd to ride it by offering him five dollars if he made three circuits of the ring. Of course he could never accomplish it for if the critter failed to buck the rider off, he would lie down and roll on him 'til he was smothered in sawdust. Generally though, the animal would succeed in sending the boy over its ears and landing him outside the ring.

Dan got out of the Confederacy in the nick of time. His was the last boat that came up the river. He lived to the good old age of seventy-seven and died at Long Branch, N. J. in 1899.

A few of us were in the habit of going down to the river in front of the battery on the point and take a swim in the Ohio, above where it joins the muddy current of the Mississippi. The water here was fairly clean and of slow current, compared with the latter, which contained about ten per cent sediment and ran so rapidly that it had no time to settle 'til it reached the Gulf of Mexico.

Often, we would put our clothing in a rowboat and swim for the Kentucky shore, which was three fourths of a mile away. The trip was made by a few of us after a trial or two, but Lieutenant Howell could not make more than half the distance. He was gritty though--steadily improving--and would not hesitate in striking out with us and swimming as far as he could and then crawl into the rowboat, which we took along with us.

The Kentucky side was low bank covered with heavy timber to the water edge, and we found it very pleasant to sit there in the shade, far from roll calls and squad drills, loaf away time.

Howell and I started across in the boat one afternoon, intending to bathe from the Kentucky shore, but when we reached the middle of the river we concluded to go in there. So we dropped our uniforms and plunged in. After swimming awhile we crawled into the boat and took a sun bath. Presently, Howell took a dive from the stern and I followed him. It so happened that the boat was headed down stream, and the kicks we gave it as we dove into the water put it in motion and it immediately commenced leaving us.

We leisurely struck out after it and I thought of no danger 'til Howell asked me if I could catch the boat. I assured him I could, and went after it at a lively clip, but could see that I was gaining very slowly on the boat but rapidly leaving the lieutenant behind. I could also see that the boat was not far from the Mississippi current, and if it struck that it would be whirled down the dirty stream beyond recovery. While I could reach the nearest shore by myself, it would be impossible for me to save Joe. He sang out in a faint voice. . .

"Hurry up, Dan."

"Take it easy, I'll be there in a minute," and I went for that boat hand over hand and caught it. With a spring I landed inside, and dropping in the oars, shot her backward with all the power I had left. Joe's head was under water when I caught him by the hair, and we were down the Mississippi a half mile before we could get wind enough between us to land him in the boat.

We landed on the Kentucky side, and after an hour spent in regaining our strength we pulled back to the Ohio. Because I was much the best swimmer Joe had depended on me to manage our trip and it was through my stupidity that his life was placed in such danger. But he refused to take that view of it, and never missed an opportunity to do me a good turn. In camp we spent hours together, and on the march we would roll in together for the night. Nothing could disturb our friendship from that date.

CHAPTER XIV

In late fall of '61 the 8th and a couple of other regiments of infantry and a troop of cavalry, were ferried over to Bird's Point in Missouri and went into camp for the first time in tents. Later, our regiment moved down the river six miles and established an outpost that was known as Norwalk, or Norfalk, and the little top heavy steamer *Rob Roy* that plied between Cairo and Bird's Point made two daily trips to our landing.

While there, a little scare was raised by a report of some rebel cavalry scouts, and our Company K that evening was thrown out in a bunch to picket near the river. We took positions in the timber just as the light of day was fading. Then the wind came up and gradually increased in force 'til it blew like a hurricane. It was darker than the hide of Henry, the captain's darkey cook. Limbs were snapped from the trees and strewn on the ground around us. Trees came up by their roots and went down with a crash. A few steps to the river bank would have put us out of danger of falling timber, for the wind came over the river from Kentucky. But these steps were not taken.

Then the electric lights were turned on from above -- the devil's artillery cut loose. We could stand this easier. The wind had subsided and we were no longer in danger of falling timber. This heavenly bombardment continued half an hour and then water commenced coming down. It increased in volume 'til it quite replaced the atmospheric air, and we were nearly strangled.

About midnight it let up and we proceeded to wring the water out of our clothing. Our guns and accoutrements lay on the ground, soaked to the limit of absorption.

As we twisted the brine out of Captain Harvey's trousers, I suggested that we go at once to camp, as it would be impossible for any of the enemy to be about after such a deluge, but the captain would not listen to such a proposition, although it was rapidly growing cold. Then I asked permission to go into camp and get a company to relieve us, but he would not give it. He did hope though that they would think of us and send one out. Of course, we were not remembered, but left there to freeze 'til morning. Harvey was a machine soldier who thought he must obey orders whether there was any sense in them or not. If we had gone into camp without new orders it would have been considered the proper thing. In fact, no notice would have been taken of it. Strict literal obedience to orders cannot always be had in an army, for no commander can foresee everything that is going to happen. The Articles of War require obedience to lawful orders, and, in case of refusal to obey, the court martial that might intervene would no doubt decide whether or not orders were reasonable, as well as lawful.

Suppose your regiment were part of a force that had charged the enemy's breastworks, and had met with the usual repulse, and that the color-bearer had been shot down on the retreat and was lying with the flag within point blank-range of the enemy's rifle pits. And then just suppose your fool of a drunken colonel would ride up to you and say,

"Lieutenant, take a few men with you, rush forward and recover our flag."

If you were an idiot you would attempt it. If not, you would probably say that the colors were an inanimate and useless thing and not worth sacrifice of any more lives. So saying, you would take your chance on a court martial for disobedience of orders rather than face certain death on a fool's mission.

Every officer and soldier should judge for himself whether the orders he receives are lawful and reasonable, and when he gets beyond sight and hearing of his commander he is in a measure an independent commander himself, and should act upon his own judgment.

Company E was commanded by Capt. John Wetzell, a gruff old fellow who was believed fearless as a badger, and I had discovered from observation that he was just about as intelligent. His lieutenants, Wheaton and Caldwell, whom I have already mentioned were about the brightest officers in the regiment. When their captain got a leave of absence they took advantage of it and taught their company the correct drill.

They went about it in this way. The men were told not to obey any non-article order, but to stand fast 'til the proper command was given.

It was amusing to watch them drill, which I did on several occasions. Some of them would not stir at a correct command, but step off promptly at a wrong one, and leave the balance of the company behind. Then they would have to return to their places. Those who did not move when the order was correctly given would have to come up and take their places with those who were better posted. The utmost good nature prevailed and they were not held to strict silence and the usual rigid discipline. So they all enjoyed it and were willing to drill overtime on account of the fun they got out of it.

It was a fine school for them, and when Capt. Wetzell returned they were a pretty well drilled company, though he no doubt thought that they had gone backward in both drill and discipline.

On occasion of the first dress parade after his return, the company orderly formed the men in front of their quarters, dressed them up and brought them to a parade rest to await the appearance of their bold commander.

After an unusually long wait, purposely for effect no doubt, out from the captain's tent strode Wetzell in a brand new uniform. The orderly commanded "Attention-Shoulder Arms," and when the captain had strutted out to his position in front of the center, the orderly called out "Present Arms," stepped into the front rank and came to a present himself.

Capt. Wetzell acknowledged the compliment by the tip of his cap, and then with a fierce expression on his countenance drew his sabre. Leisurely bringing it to a vertical position, he sang out, "Company,...Shoulder arms." That worked all right, but when he added, "Company, by the right flank, right face," not a boy budged.

An expression of astonishment overspread the coarse features of the doughty captain, but as soon as he could get his breath, he roared out,

"Did you hear what I said to you or have you forgotten all I learned you before I went away? I say-by the right flank, right face."

But the men remained stubborn and would not move, and so we can only conjecture what would have happened next had not Lieutenant Wheaton stepped around the right flank of the company and revoked the order he had made. Then Wetzell told them there would be no more such tom foolery going on in his company, and they soon got away to the colors.

About a mile inland was a small stream spanned by a roadway bridge where we habitually kept a picket post. Lieutenant Jones of Company D was in charge. One cloudy, dark night a little past midnight, the pickets heard the tread of horses on the far side of the bridge, and a husky voice in a low tone saying, "Close up, close up."

When the head of the column reached the bridge, a dozen pickets were lined up facing them twenty paces away, and getting the direction by sound they blazed into them. Then that same voice bawled out, "FALL BACK, FALL BACK."

Two wounded were all we got out of it, but it was the "first-blood" for the "eighth" and Jones and his men were the lions of the camp for a few days.

Guards were relieved about nine o'clock a.m. and they often arrived in camp ravenously hungry and exceedingly cross. Lieut. Jones brought in a brace of chickens that morning and told his cook to get them into the skillet as quickly as possible for he was starving.

Our Chaplain, the Reverend Samuel Day from Macon County, surprising as it may appear, had a singular weakness for poultry. He could smell a frying pullet one and one half miles distant if the wind happened to be blowing in his direction. This morning he was lying on his cot sound asleep not more than one thousand yards away from the skillet when the aroma was wafted by the gentle breeze to his sensitive nostrils. He immediately arose, put on his coat and hat, and followed the scent unerringly to the quarters of Jones, where he arrived just as the cook had dumped the first skillet full of chicken on Jones' plate.

"Good mawning, Lieutenant Jones," said the Rev. Samuel Day, "I hear you got a few Rebels while on picket last night."

"Yep," grunted Jones with a scowl, "got a couple of um," and he drew a drumstick through his mouth, dropped the bone on the ground, and reached for a chunk of white meat.

"Ah! I see that you have a fine chicken for your breakfast, lieutenant," said this follower of the Meek and Lowly, in a tone of surprise to convey the impression that he had just then tumbled onto this fact. "I believe I will sit down and enjoy it with you while we discuss the picket fight."

"Not by a damned sight," roared Jones, "You've heard all about that picket fight, so get out of here. I can't talk and eat at the same time and there ain't no more chicken here than I want myself."

We soon after moved back to Bird's Point, helped throw up a line of breastworks from the river above to river below, and here the army gave us our first whiskey ration. I was young and green and didn't like the taste of it. So I handed it over to my friend and crony, Bill Miller, who always proved himself equal to any emergency.

After the entrenchments were completed, steamers went up the river and brought down second-growth cottonwood logs with which we built comfortable winter quarters.

Our Orderly Sergeant had left on sick leave, or some other pretext, and for the first time I was asked to draw rations for the boys. I counted up the enlisted men present and made out the requisition accordingly. I was aware that rations habitually were given the officers' cook, but did not know which was getting beat, the boys or the government.

When the chuck [chow] was piled up on the issuing table, the first one there with his dishes was the captain's cook, Henry.

"Well, what are you after?" I asked.

"Maw reshens, sah. Dat whut I's efter," replied the Darkey with much assurance.

"Oh, I see!" said I. "Are you in the habit of getting your supply before the men get theirs?"

"Yessah. Segent Merclum alers gibs me my reshens fust, an' I gets de bes' dar is. I wants my beef right off dat der part, war de good steak is."

"The hell you do!" I returned. (I was figuring on getting some of that myself.) "Say, who do you draw rations for, anyway?"

"I gets reshens for Cap'in Hervy, Lieutn't Heul, Lieutn't Denshum an' my ownself," replied Henry.

"Well, I guess I will reverse the order of procedure today, if you know what that means, and after I get through issuing to the enlisted men, you may have all there is left."

The company was divided into five or six messes of a dozen or more men each, and one of the number in each mess cooked for his group and was excused from ordinary company duty. We made these arrangements for ourselves without interference of officers and each man paid the mess cook one dollar per month out of his regular pay. These cooks had to keep their fighting equipment, turn out for inspections, and were expected to be on the firing line when the enemy appeared. We found, however, that after they got interested in their job it was difficult to separate them from their pots and kettles.

The cooks came out with their mess pans to receive their chuck, and I divided it among them according to the number of men in each mess at the time. When the last one had his allowance, the table was swept clean and then the captain's cook broke out,

"See heah, Segent whars I goen to get maw reshens, dat whut I wan's to know?"

"That is what I would like to know, too," I remarked. The captain never referred to this matter except indirectly. A few days later I stepped into his quarters to borrow his copy of the "Army Regulations" and he bluntly told me that I couldn't have them. The reason he gave was that I had read them too much already. I thanked him for the compliment and got them from Company I. Lieutenant Joe Howell was present at the time and noted the incident. A week later he made me a present of a copy that he had obtained somewhere, remarking that I couldn't read them any too much to suit him. It was quite evident that he preferred to pay for his supplies like "an officer and a gentlemen," rather than sponge them out of the men or Uncle Sam.

Our Company K Orderly came back after a month's absence, and his first appearance before the company was about as embarrassing as that of Capt. Wetzell. The occasion was the evening of roll-call, and the air was quite chilly. I was in the habit of running the roster rapidly from memory, and many of the boys would step in line without stopping to put on their jackets.

But this time, to the surprise of many of them, there stood orderly Tom with a lantern and his roll-call book. He commenced drawing out the names and checking them off at the rate of about ten per minute. One of the men said, "hurry up there." That only made the matter worse for he spent a full minute trying to discover the author of the impertinence. Failing in this, he drawled out,

"I want you to remember that this is Orderly Thomas J. McClung that is calling this roll now."

"The devil it is," said Corporal Shennisy. "I thought you were trying to muster us out of the sarvice, or fraze us out by the time yur taking. If ye don't hurry up now we'll lave ye here to yerself and ye can call the roll of the stars."

Tom knew who this was very well but wilted and as soon as the laughing subsided, another voice in imitation of the orderly sang out, "Break-Ranks--March." And we all broke for quarters.

About this time I got hold of a bugle and soon mastered skirmish calls and commenced drilling the company by them. Although now out of favor with Capt. Harvey I was still held to the drilling of the company. I was very glad to do it. When you know it from A to Z and can handle a company so that officers will come out on the parade and compliment you. It is fun.

Capt. Robert D. Wellman's troop of the Illinois 1st Cavalry was part of our Cairo garrison, and they had occasionally exchanged shots with C.S.A. General Jeff Thompson's Missouri Raiders. One day Lieut. Howell went out with them on scouting and they chanced to get into a little scrap...just nothing much, but enough to catch the music of a bullet whistling past an ear, and having the privilege of exhilarating the Rebs in return, and seeing them run.

Those little affairs were very exciting, and from the suddenness with which they broke upon you, often made your gizzard jump into your throat and hair stand on end. But I did not know it at this time, and the next day I went out with the cavalry boys, myself.

They gave me a good horse, a carbine (I can't remember the pattern [model]) and a pair of Colt's army revolvers, carried in holsters on each side of the saddle front. They offered me a saber, which I declined. I didn't believe them, then, and I don't now. For short, quick work, an army revolver in the hands of a man of nerve and practice was the ugliest thing known at the time.

I rode beside a sergeant at the rear of the troop. Directly in front of me was a German trooper who appeared to be extremely nervous. I questioned the sergeant about him and he said he was always that way and that at the first crack of a gun he would wheel about and streak for camp.

"Why do you bring him along?" I said.

"I can't say--just for the fun of it, I suppose. I had hoped he would get over it but am afraid he never will. He could stay in camp if he would work and make himself useful, but he won't do it. He is all right for a mile or two and then his nerve leaves him. He thinks it will wear off after a while, but it never will. Some day he will run against a tree and kill himself. Then we will be rid of him."

Just then there was a cracking of brush in the timber on our left, caused by some browsing cattle, and the fellow sunk in his saddle and pulled his steed half 'round.

"Get back in your place," roared the Sergeant, and then he chuckled.

I enjoyed this ride very much and Captain Wellman said he would get me transferred if I would join him. But Joe Howell talked me out of the notion.

CHAPTER XV

Monday, November 4th, 1861, the following troops made up an expedition under the command of Col. Oglesby, embarked upon transports, and started up the river:

8th	Ill.	Infty.,	Lieut.Col.	Frank Rhodes	commanding
11th	"	"	Col.	W.H.L.Wallace	"
18th	"	"	Col.	M.K.Lawler	"
29th	"	"	Col.	James S. Rearden	"
Battery E, 2nd Ill. Lt.Art.,			Capt.	Adolph Swartz	"
Troop H, 1st Ill. Cav.,			Capt.	Robert D. Wellman	"

We landed at Cape Girardeau and as soon as the bow of our boat (the leading boat) hit the bank, our scout, who was sitting astride his thoroughbred on the forecastle, rode ashore and soon disappeared over the high bank above. He carried a saber, a pair of holstered revolvers, and a magazine (repeater) rifle. The revolvers were of the Colt Army pattern and differed from the Navy in having a longer barrel, but they were all called "navies." The powder of the cartridge was covered with a film and connected with the bullet, and was forced into the front end of the six barreled cylinder by a lever, and was fired by an ordinary gun cap. They would not stand inspection at the present day, but were then a most formidable weapon in the hands of a cool man.

I had frequently seen this scout ride aboard the little *Rob Roy* at Cairo and go ashore at Bird's Point before any troops were stationed there, and it must be admitted that it took nerve to scout that section alone, without a camp on that shore to fall back on.

He returned in about an hour and dismounted at the water's edge. One of our boys stepped up to hold his horse but he waved him back, saying that he preferred to hold it himself. And then he added, "He will not leave me unless I tell him to, and then won't go far away. When I give him the right whistle he will come like a shot. He will lie down at the word and spring up with me in the saddle." Then he washed blood from his saber and dried the blade on his handkerchief.

This set us wild with curiosity and we persuaded him to relate his adventure since he left the boat. And he told us,

> "When I reached the top of the bank, I took a look about and then walked my horse down the street that leads out on the Bloomfield road. Soon I saw a man ride out from a stable and take a gentle lope down the road ahead of me. I kept him at about the same distance 'til he was well out on the Bloomfield turnpike, then I suspected he was carrying the report of our landing to Jeff Thompson.

> "When I began to crawl up on him he increased his gait, but the distance between us got less just the same, and he soon had his animal on a dead run. Now I was cock sure I was after the right man and told Prince to catch him. He at once lay back his ears and commenced splitting the wind. There is none of them that can get away from him. When within twenty yards I told him to pull up, when out came his

pistol and he took a shot at me. In about four jumps Prince was at his side and I lifted him off his horse with my sabre."

We were encumbered with far too much luggage and transportation for such an expedition. The notion of catching Jeff Thompson with such a clumsy outfit was the limit of absurdity. The baggage wagons and artillery carriages were all taken apart and stowed in the holds of the boats, and I am not right sure but that some of the mules were dumped in also.

There were plenty of steamers at Cairo and such mismanagement was inexcusable. It took many hours to reassemble these vehicles, and get started from Cape Girardeau. It is quite possible that before we got up the bank with all that truck, Jeff knew all about us that he cared to know.

In order to fool him we did not take the short and best route, but went almost directly south. When we got opposite Bloomfield we slightly disappeared into Nigger Wool Swamp, and had a lovely time floundering through the mud with the artillery carriages and transportation wagons.

This swamp got its name from a moss or creeping plant that runs on the ground and which is almost identical with nigger wool. What a location for a stuffed furniture plant.

Our regiment was very fortunate from the start in getting very competent medical officers, and we did not have a man die in the three-months service. Silas T. Trowbridge was surgeon, and John M. Pipps, assistant. They were both kind hearted, able, and energetic, and were highly regarded by all.

The latter was about thirty years of age, of athletic build and nervous temperament, and could not remain idle when anything was doing. So he threw off his coat, took an axe, and helped corduroy the soft spots in the swamp.

Some of the boys nicknamed him "Quinine," and although this appellation was not in general use among us, all knew who it was meant for and no doubt Dr. Pipps had heard it himself.

Here a smart jay who was about to drive his mule team over a short piece of corduroy that the strenuous doctor helped make sang out:

"Hello Quinine! Struck a job, have you?"

In five seconds Pipps yanked that mule puncher from his saddle mule and pushed him into that black mushy soil 'til he begged for mercy. We gave him a lusty cheer when he hoisted the fellow to his feet, kicked him in the direction of his mule team, and resumed his chopping.

We got through at last and immediately came into Bloomfield, Missouri, which was of enough importance to support a weekly newspaper. It had a wooden building they called the court house, so it was probably the seat of Stoddard County, and it might have had a population of one thousand before the war. It lay south of Cape Girardeau, and was but little farther from Bird's Point. Why we went around the way we did and endured the task of twice loading and unloading these river steamers, can only be explained by a strategist. Common sense could never account for it.

Some of our boys took possession of the abandoned printing office and got out an issue of three pages that measured eight inches by twelve. It was made up of complimentary remarks about ourselves, and mean allusions and flings at Jeff Thompson and his men because they were not foolish enough to remain and welcome us when we came up out of the swamp. I have no doubt that they had other business to attend to, and it was no concern of ours when they left. I guess Jeff ranked Oglesby and Grant also, and he didn't have to obtain their permission to exercise his horses.

Here is the way it was captioned.

THE STARS AND STRIPES.
The Union Must and Shall be Preserved.
Bloomfield, Mo.   Saturday, November 9th, 1861   Vol.1 No.1

It was a grand thing--that is, the boys who got the edition said it was--and so put a copy of it in my pocket and am now waiting for a good offer from some curio collector. [Editor Wearmouth now has this rare item.]

We were here about three days when a courier arrived. He handed Oglesby a dispatch, which the colonel hastily read, and then exclaimed, "My God."

Orders to break camp were immediately given and we hustled our traps into the wagons and got into line. We were not steered into the swamp though, but took the direct road to Cape Girardeau, on high and dry ground. The road led us to the edge of the swamp on ground higher than the nigger-wool forest, and it gave us an interesting view.

Our dignified Orderly had remained at Bird's Point and I was performing his duties. When the night came on we halted near a filthy frog pond that was so vile that we could not even drink strong coffee made from the water. No other could be obtained and so we had to go without. We should have marched on 'til we found water that was usable. The company was shy on hard tack now, and I took a couple of boys along and hunted up the commissary.

I had behaved myself pretty well so far on the trip, but now I was mad about the water and just dying for a row with someone. So I asked this officer if he was responsible for our going into camp by this filthy old frog pond where we could not even get the water for making coffee. He replied that he thought that the water would do for coffee. I bet him five dollars that he hadn't a mule in his train that would drink a bucket of it.

He didn't take the bet but asked me if I wanted anything and I said I was after hard tack. As a matter of fact I had heard that he was nearly out and expected he would try and put me off 'til we got to the river, and that would give me a pretext for a tilt with him, for I had failed to raise his temper about the nasty water. But he handed me out a box so quick that the only show I had was to demand another and so I told him that I wanted one more.

THE STARS & STRIPES.

BLOOMFIELD, NOV. 9, 1861.

EDWARDS & ATHERTON, PUBLISHERS.

R. F. Stewart, } Editors
W. A. Rusk,

THE STARS AND STRIPES. — Once there were towns loyal to patriotism and Honor — The Union Spirit of Illinois has planted its seed in the hearts of secessionists, and the Glorious old flag waves over Bloomfield Missouri!

Our heart trembles over the paper, till all our pretensions refuses to touch it, as the dear and memories of the Sanctum come back to us, in the midst of an enemy's land. We again see the dusty paper and around the walls, and the cob-web hanging from the corners, like the ghosts of our ruined energy when our misrepresentations have blessed! But we are against the press! Through the distinguished kindness of our commander, Col. R. J. Oglesby, we are permitted to take temporary possession of the office of the *Bloomfield Herald*, and print a paper; but it is with different feelings, and from different motives than those which led us into our first field of action.

We now feel that we must atone for the past, — that we must tell the causes which we must speak from the heart, — tell in the brave; and to the soldiers in our expedition we would say, that there is no lack of competency on the part of their officers, if they with only obey their commands.

We should all remember that we have not started out to destroy a country, but to save one, — that we are fighting neither for fun nor for glory but for "God and our Rights". We have hearts that are ready and willing, and .... forward and let the .... our-selves (Cowardly in some .... Sublime Confederacy) in .... about the "army wagons" in this morning's issue.

☞ Those watching the *Stars and Stripes*, can obtain it by leaving their names with the Captain.

☞ Below we publish a list of the names of the so-called "Missouri State Guards," of whom the present expedition are now in search. Unfortunately the manuscript which came into our possession does not give the names or the places they are guarding. However, if they are Missouri Guards, we presume they will turn up before long.

Col. Oglesby's Expedition.

The 8th, 11th, 18th, and 29th Regts. of Illinois Volunteers, Capt. Noleman's Cavalry, and Swartz's Artillery, — commanded by Col. R. J. Oglesby, left Cairo on Monday morning, the 4th for this place, and are now encamped on the branch south of town; each Regiment does credit to their Colonels and Company commanders, — and judging from their appearance, as they marched through town, preceded by Aleck Smarts 16th Regiment Brass Band, will never allow the laurels won for Illinois, by her first six Regiments in Mexico, to be trailed in the dust.

It made our hearts glad to see the noble sons of our native Prairie State marching out to battle for their Country and their Country's rights.

Dear the curse......, some kind friend and let modesty hide its blush;—For even while laboring for the Benefit of our fellow men, we should never forget that "self preservation is the first law of nature."

The companies composing the 29th Regiment, should feel deeply indebted to Col. Jas. E. Rearden for the serious manner in which he has commanded them, and his unflinching adherence to the laws and justice, in all cases.

And the Captains — well they're a whole team. — Capt. Ferrell — beg your pardon Captain — we meant Major, — makes the men mind and they all like him. Capt. McKinnie don't care whether they do or not, just so he does his duty, and all the rest of the Captains are clever men. — So far as we know.

☞ If the command of Southeast Missouri would come through the *ostrich* printers here and Commerce, it would believe every word we say.

INFANTRY COMPANY B.

Benjamin J. Farmer, *Capt.*
John Taylor, *1st Lieut.*
Millington Offutt, *2d Lieut.*
Clay Taylor, *3d Lieut.*

Wilson, Andrew   Wilson, Wm. G.
Stewart, Elijah   Street, Wm. L.
Bright, John   Singleton Jas., P
Hentscreek, Smith   Gatem, John
Hill, Jinks   Sarad, James M
Jose, John W.   Goate, Henry M

FIRST DIVISION COMPANY D. Home Guard

Jessee Blisse
Jacob Kieder

FIRST DIVISION Mo. STATE GUARDS STODDARD COUNTY RANGERS.

S. G. Kitchen, *Capt.*
Van W. Hale, *1st Lieut.*
J. J. Miller, *2d Lieut.*
Reuben Harper, *3d Lieut.*
E. W. Hill, *Ordly.*

Thos. A. Wright   S. J. Bartlett
A. J. Ploien   G. W. Miller
J. R. Jackson   John W. Leech
W. W. Miller   N. R. Wilber
M. D. Wright   A. L. McLean
R. W. Carter   W. E. Settle
J. Y. Walburn   Wm. Culberson
Jas. L. Hale   A. E. Carter
F. F. Lee   John L. Clark
Carroll McLard   E. B. Taylor
R. W. Wommics   David Fisher
R. T. ....   H. H. Bedford
H. Hicon   Col. A. D. Hill
T. G. Welch   James Williams
W. C. McDaniel   Collins Morgan
R. J. Whitehead   Wm. Rieger
Wm. Welborn   J. M. Johnson
John D. Smith   Isaac Jesse
L. C. Holliday   Chas. Baldridge
N. R. McLain   David B. Miers
E. Gitchell   Robert Hill
T. J. Myers
Ay. Ellison

THE STARS & STRIPES.

THE UNION. "IT MUST AND SHALL BE PRESERVED."

VOL. I.   BLOOMFIELD, MO., SATURDAY, NOVEMBER 9, 1861.   NO. 1.

E PLURIBUS UNUM.

Though many and bright are the stars that appear
In the sky of our country unfurled;
And the stars that float in majesty there
Like a rainbow adorning the world.

Their lights are unsullied as those in the sky,
By deeds that our fathers have done,
And are leagued in as true and holy a tie,
In their motto of many in one.

Let it up! with that banner wherever it may call
Our millions shall rally around,
A nation as freeman that woman shall fall
When the stars shall be trailed to the ground.

ARMY WAGGONS.

On the present expedition of United States forces from Cairo Ill's, under command of Col. R. J. Oglesby, of the 8th Illinois Regiment by way of Commerce, Col. Hunters farm and the black jack "nigger wool" swamp to Bloomfield Mo, a fair test of the utility of Regulation army stores, camp equipage and two horse waggons for expeditions and rapid movements the small waggon is far superior to the large heavy four and six horse waggon. Having mustered the rear guard on the 7th inst on which day the writer stuck eleven times yesterday the roads very clearly to the satisfaction of the writer, that although the road was rough, very crooked, filled with stumps and deeply cut waggon ruts, and seemed to require that the stoutest and heaviest waggons should be used, yet the small two horse waggons with from twelve to sixteen hundred pounds were the most successful in passing the swamps in both safety and speed, the large waggons does not carry more than double the weight of the small waggon but where twice the number, and often thrice the number of horses or mules to draw them. I recommend to all officers the use of the small waggons whether for long or short routes, if the country is level or swampy, dry hilly roads where there is rock of heavy gravel the large waggons may be superior, but I doubt it.

☞ Since our arrival in Bloomfield, or in fact before we reached it, we could easily account for the assumed bravery of the southern army. Their "bushwackers" remind us of the success of prisoners at their officer, the only difference being enough of the ......d suckers at Fred ericksb..g. Enip for the Bushers.

☞ A Gen. — What do Jeff Thompson and his troops resemble?

Ans. — The Irishmen flee, when you think you have them they're no there, but running like the d—l.

☞ Jeff Thompson's rebels showed a good pair of heels in their retreat from Bloomfield, if they did not show good stout hearts. We understand Jeff waved his men to show fight, but they informed him that they had seen quite enough of the ....

☞ A HAPPY REPLY. — An incident, the Memphis *Appeal*, is related on last Sunday occurred between the officials of Columbus, the other day. After the preliminaries were arranged, a repast was partaken of, during which one of the Fed'ral officers, round, propose "The memory of George Washington. The company instantly rose, when Gen. Pollk responded. "The memory of George Washingt....., *the first rebel*." The toast our informant says, was drunk in unanimous silence by the Federal officers who were present. The story is too good not to be true, — so to be true. — *Pocohontas (Ark.) Advertiser and Herald.*

The above is only one of the numerous rumors, from the patriot body.

☞ Cotton reports, that still breathe. "Almighty God, in Dr. ladustic wisdom, (and we have no right to doubt it.) did know that there would never be so deep and dark and damning a crime as secession from so glorious a Union, and that such foul misrepresentations and jealousies lost, against the Father or the Gods, or would be the result of it — we cannot understand why there had not been some better piece than Hell, to receive the polluted brains that could commit such damning, willful lies, out thereby deceive honest, unsuspecting Union citizens into their abominable pit, in the belief that no other could lease protection.

☞ We are under many obligations to Lieut. Wakefield, acting Adjutant of the 29th Regiment, for the favors while getting up his issue.

☞ While speaking of the 18th and 29th Regiments of Ill. Vol., who were with Col. Oglesby's expedition, we should not forget to mention the 8th and 11th Regiments, of them it is enough to say, they are all that could be expected, even under such distinguished commanders.

Pages 1 and 2 of the first (and only) issue of *The Stars and Stripes*, Nov. 9, 1861, printed at Bloomfield, Missouri, by soldier-printers in Colonel Richard Oglesby's brief expedition into Rebel-held regions of this tormented border State.

This was refused, but I swore I would not leave 'til he passed it out, and he finally did to get rid of me, saying that he would report me to the colonel in the morning.

When the boys had all helped themselves, there was a full box left, and I started with it to the company wagon but changed my mind and took it back to the quartermaster. So I guess he never reported me to the colonel.

Lieutenant Joe Howell found me, and we selected a nest at the foot of a large tree. It was dark as pitch and we simply felt that it was a very good place to stop. A couple of boys, lying not far away, were still talking and one asked the other why the Orderly was not with us on this trip, and the reply was,

"Oh, damn him! We don't want him along. If he had been here we wouldn't have hard tack for our haversacks. They can't bluff Dan, he's enough for any of them."

After we settled down, Joe asked me what the boy meant in his reference to hard tack, and I told him all I thought necessary about it. He then remarked,

"Dang it! We had you listed for Orderly from the very start and you ought not to have smashed the slate the way you did." I answered,

"Well, I didn't know as much then as I do now except in one respect; I don't know yet if I have sand [grit] enough to stick when it comes to a fight." Howell replied,

"That don't cut any ice. We are all cowards and if we had no pride we would all run. When we ran into that Rebel cavalry troop up at Charleston, Missouri, the day I was out with Capt. Wellman every hair on my head stood up and near lifted my cap. And yet I hope you don't imagine that I ever thought of running away. It is pride not insensibility to fear that holds us to the rack. Don't you think that you have the average allowance of pride and self respect?"

I answered, "I hope so, let's go to sleep."

When we reached Cape Girardeau the next day we heard about the fight down at Belmont [Missouri] General Grant called it a Union victory, but all the boys I talked with about it seemed to think they had gotten licked. Lieut. Campion of the 20th Illinois Infantry, who was a boarding house friend of mine in Bloomington, was taken prisoner and soon after exchanged. If he ever had any fight in him, it was all gone now, and he declared that we could never whip the South...never.

General Grant says in his *Memoirs* that when he started down the river he had no intention of attacking Belmont. He landed part of his force six miles above Columbus on the Kentucky shore. He had previously ordered General C. F. Smith with the Paducah garrison to threaten Columbus from the east, and he was at this time menacing them from the north. While Grant's transports were lying here at the river bank, with part of the troops ashore, he says he learned that the enemy was crossing troops from Columbus to the Mississippi west bank to be dispatched, presumably, after the Oglesby expedition.

At this time Oglesby was at Bloomfield, fifty miles from Columbus, and was doing no harm to anyone, Union or Confederate. To suppose for a moment that Rebels at Columbus, threatened from two points of the compass, would concern themselves about him, and weaken its garrison to send an expedition against him, is too absurd for a moment's consideration. Grant further says, by way of excuse for his attack on Belmont, that his officers and men were so keen for a fight that he did not see how he could maintain discipline, or retain the confidence of his command, unless he gave them one.

Now, as a matter of fact, up to this time he had never gained the confidence of his men, for it was mighty little they knew about him. He was sort of an office general, and was seldom seen by us. He never visited our quarters or the hospitals, and was not seen riding about making himself familiar with his surroundings.

We felt we knew officers such as Oglesby and Logan, for they were men of force, energy and activity, as well as being approachable. So the real credit for our discipline was due to the subordinate commanders and not to General Grant at all.

He re-embarked the troops that he had landed and commenced dropping down the river at the hour that his attack on the camp should have been sprung; that is, at the break of day. They landed in broad daylight, about two miles from Columbus and in plain view of the Confederates. The assault commenced about nine a.m. Gradually, Union troops drove the enemy back toward their camp near the river bank, into their camp, through it, and at last over the bank. Now it will occur to the most civil of civilians that our men had only to approach the river bank to force the Rebels to surrender.

Instead, Grant says our men threw down their arms and commenced plundering the camp. Meanwhile, the enemy crept up the river below the bank and came out on level ground again between the Union soldiers and their transports. Can you imagine what General Grant was doing at this critical period? Why was he not with these men, exercising the discipline he boasts of, to capture or push into the river the Johnnies who had dropped behind the bank?

If he had been present on the battleground, as he would have been if he had had the spirit of a true soldier, he could have captured very nearly the whole Confederate garrison. Instead, Grant says in his *Memoirs* that some of his officers thought they were surrounded and would have to surrender, and that he told them that they had cut their way in they could cut it back out. And, he says, this bright remark seemed a revelation to them. It was no doubt a revelation to them many years later when they read of it in his *Memoirs*.

Well, they got out of there by a hair's breadth, followed all the way to their transports by the Johnnies. Grant still called it a victory. That was all right at the time, however. He probably did not make the people believe it, and they needed something to cheer them up. Nevertheless, it was hardly fair to make such absurd statements to a generous and confiding public in the year 1885, upon the release of the *Memoirs*. Grant used much space in his *Memoirs* to tell of the part he took personally in this fight and of the narrow escapes he had. Some of the boys who were there at Belmont told me that they never saw him at all. Others said they merely glimpsed him sitting on his horse out in a corn field.

We hustled aboard the transports awaiting us at Cape Girardeau, and were soon back in our log quarters at Bird's Point. Here we met and conversed with many officers and men who had been at the Columbus-Belmont affair. They spoke of the gallantry displayed by Logan, Lauman, Buford, Dougherty and others, and made no more mention of Grant and McClernand than if they had not been with the expedition at all. During the long military careers of these officers they were never able to prove proximity to the enemy in battle by exhibiting any wounds received in military action. Later on I discovered that they were rendering Providence material assistance in protecting their valuable lives.

CHAPTER XVI

The night we camped at the filthy frog pond, my brother, Frank, went on duty as sergeant of the guard, and while asleep on the ground a rain shower came up and he caught a severe cold. Soon after we got back to the Point, he went back across the river to the regimental hospital at Cairo and never returned to the company again. He endured a surgical operation, lost one of his lungs, and became an invalid. I was excused from company duties now and visited him daily in Cairo 'til we started on the Donelson Campaign. I would have been allowed to remain with him had I chosen to stay. As it was, soon after we left Cairo, Frank was sent to Camp Dennison, Cincinnati, where he died in June 1863 while I was at Milliken's Bend, Louisiana.

Frank was a quiet, good boy of fair education, and was popular with the officers and men. Up to the date of his misfortune, he had displayed no special taste or talent for army life. He had one excellent quality for a soldier, however, that only I knew, and for which I envied him. From a small boy up, he was never afraid of anything, alive or dead, and I knew that he could go through the severest military engagement without a tremor. When we were small boys, and near of a size, we had many a tussle. He would never give up though, and these scraps would always end in my defeat, least to the extent of my running to get away from him.

When he was about sixteen and living with an Illinois farmer, there was a fat girl past his age making a prolonged visit here. She constantly embarrassed him with her unwelcome attentions. This was at a time when he was somewhat devoted to a younger and daintier piece of femininity at a neighboring farm house. His employer had two daughters and the trio conceived a playful scheme to give Frank a fright so that he would be loathe to go out after dark, thereby giving them more of his society.

About ten o'clock one star-lit evening, this silly fat girl slipped out of bed, wrapped a sheet around her plump form, toiled up the highway a few rods and sat down in the angle of a rail fence. If that foolish young woman had known that boy as I knew him, she wouldn't have been out there at that time of night, togged out in such flimsy apparel and snickering over the fun that she imagined was in store for her. Instead, she would have been snugly in bed, if not sound asleep.

Soon Frank came strolling along, whistling as was his habit, and would have passed her by if she had not risen to her feet and given a groan. Without an interruption in his gait he walked up to the apparition and seized the robe at the back of the neck. The undergarments were included in his grasp and with a yank, everything came off at one time and one motion.

If nothing had happened to Frank, he would no doubt have risen to the rank of captain, if not higher, for he had none of that genius for making trouble and enemies that I possessed so strongly.

--- ------ ---

Opposite us on the Kentucky Point the heavy timber had been removed and an earthwork constructed that was known as Fort Holt. Battery D of the First Illinois Light Artillery garrisoned it with four 24-pound howitzers. These differed from the usual field gun or cannon in having a powder chamber much smaller than the bore of the piece. These were made of bronze, intended for field service, and each was drawn by eight horses. Originally, it was known as the Chicago Battery and went by the name of its first commander, Edward McAllister. Its officers were Captain McAllister from Plainfield, Illinois, 1st Lieutenant Matthew W. Boreland from Joliet, Illinois, and 2nd Lieutenant Uzziel P. Smith. Half a dozen of the men were the only original members from the Garden City. Other men came from several Illinois towns, six from Michigan, and twenty from Indiana. There were several from Ohio. Other recruits were from New York, Wyoming, Iowa, Vermont, Tennessee, Pennsylvania and Ontario, Canada.

At least up to the Vicksburg campaign, this battery was part of the Second Regiment, Illinois Light Artillery.

One of the Confederate gunboats ran up from Columbus after the Belmont fracas, sent a couple of shells in the direction of Fort Holt and then hastily skedaddled. Such fool play was unworthy of brave men. Come to think of it, they didn't have many Bob Evanses [Fighting Bob Evans of the Spanish-American War Naval Exploits] in the Confederate Navy. There was no patrol boat stationed down river to bring us warning of an attack, and so their coming was an absolute surprise, and they might have come up abreast of us, knocked a few holes into Fort Holt, shelled our camp at Bird's Point fearfully, sent a few shells into the shipping at Cairo, and then got away before our gunboats could have gotten into action.

So it is no easier to account for such timidity in Confederate officers than it is for some of the senseless movements of our own. General Charles Halleck, our department commander, who was holding forth in St. Louis, was in mortal fear of an attack from this direction, yet this was the only such demonstration the Rebels ever made. And no doubt this was encouraged by the ease with which they hustled Grant out of Belmont a few days before.

Referring again to Grant's *Memoirs*' account of the Belmont affair, he wishes the reader to think that he was the last man to board the last transport when they made their escape and that he rode his horse fearlessly down a nearly perpendicular bank and up a plank from shore to boat. If he had shouldered his steed and carried him aboard the boat, or had he kicked him down the bank the first kick, and aboard the steamer the second, this would have been something worth bragging about, but any trooper would have done what he says he did and thought nothing of it. The plank he says his horse walked aboard on was a strong bridge at least three and one-half feet wide.

He had been recognized by the boat captain who told the engineer not the start the engine, when as a matter of fact he couldn't have told the engineer anything without going down two flights of stairs and then walking nearly the length of the boat, back of the boilers, for he was without a doubt on the hurricane deck in front of the pilot house where he belonged. The captains held no communication with the engineers, but gave their orders to the pilot, and the engineers got their signals from him.

These signals are communicated by bells connected by cord or wire to the pilot house, and there could be no possible use of a signal to "not start the engines." They are never started except when they get the signal to "Go Ahead," or "Back Her." Grant went immediately to the captain's room and threw himself on a cot, for he must have been worn out sitting out there in the cornfield all alone, during the three or four hours the boys were peppering it to the Johnnies. And this before they were quite done with them, for Confederates were still sending bullets into the steamers, and one would scarcely suppose that he would have a disposition to lie down until the affair was entirely over. But he acknowledges that he did, though he says that he got up in less than a moment "to go out on deck to observe what was going on." Why didn't he stay on deck "to observe what was going on?" Any other kind of general would have done so.

When I read these remarkable *Memoirs* for the first time [about 1885] I could not understand how Grant could have gone into the cabin at that time, and thrown himself down on a cot unless he felt humiliated and crushed by his defeat, and was ashamed to appear among his officers and men. But he was no sooner down then up again. I am just mean enough to conjecture that the moment he lay down a bullet went through the cabin, and that is what suddenly inspired him "to go out on deck to observe what was going on."

I never heard of Grant losing his horse until I read of it in the *Memoirs*, and I have wondered if he was really shot, or did he die of colic from eating too much green corn in that cornfield?

At this time, we had several river gunboats in commission, and Commodore Andrew H. Foote was in command. I somewhere read a very flattering sketch of this officer, and he was represented to have been a brave, Christian gentleman. One day I saw him commit an act that may have been brave and Christian-like, but it seemed to me inhuman and unworthy of an officer and a gentleman. Foote was passing over the deck of one of the gunboats and wished to ascend a short flight of steps that were being scrubbed by one of the Jackeys. The man was standing at the foot of these steps leaning over, supporting himself with one hand and briskly scrubbing with the other, and beside him was a bucket of water. He certainly did not suspect the approach of this doughty commodore 'til he got a vigorous kick from his boot in the seat of his trousers.

This man felt so outraged by this dastardly treatment that he straightened up, dealt Foote a swinging blow under the ear, and the old son-of-a-gun went bowling over the rail into the Ohio River. At least that is what he ought to have done, but he didn't. He no doubt knew that if he resented this gross indignity in such a strenuous manner it would cost him life or long imprisonment. A gentleman would not kick a dog out of his path, unless he knew the cur was aware of his approach. Is it singular that enlisted men desert? Is it not singular that more of them do not?

About Christmas time 1861 the people at home commenced sending down large boxes filled with good things for the boys, and for a couple of weeks we lived high. The edible contents were given to the cooks and we all shared alike in the benefits. I remember one selfish fellow who failed to follow the generous example set by the other, and lost the whole outfit while on guard duty.

Each man got a comforter for his bunk, Frank and I included. We also each got a box filled with pies and cakes, jam and chickens galore. Neither of us could figure out who sent them and so were relieved of the trouble of writing letters of thanks. Poor Frank! He could not enjoy his box the same way that the rest of us did, but he had opened it up in his ward, and took much pleasure in having those about him walk up and help themselves.

In January 1862 about 6,000 of us landed a few miles above Columbus and tramped around that section for a week in snow and rain. They called it a reconnaissance. At night we would build a long fire against a down tree and sleep with our feet toward it, each taking a turn watching fire and sleepers.

I believe we were at one time within two miles of enemy rifle pits about Columbus, and they must have felt quite confident we intended to attack them in their works, for they lay low and never disturbed us. They probably had as many or more men than we had, and if they had half our number they should not have permitted us to return to the river without fighting our way back.

The notion that prevailed in the South at the beginning of the war was that in generalship and fighting ability they were greatly superior to the Northerners. This was the most absurd conceit ever possessed by a civilized people.

We were soon back in our comfortable quarters but were not destined to remain there long.

General John McClernand's troops (including 8th Illinois Vols.) boarding boats at Cairo, Illinois. These soldiers were part of Grant's new command that eventually would invest and capture Vicksburg and again open the Mississippi to Union commerce from northern Minnesota southward to the Gulf and then on to ports world-wide.

CHAPTER XVII

Before we go up the Tennessee River let us skip a few years and talk about farming. Too much war history is like too much cabbage, hard on the digestive organs. I am quite aware that chicken farming is the most popular with city people, but at the time I have in mind I was not that far advanced, I was still in the woods, and had to chop my way out. About thirty five years ago [1872] I was clearing up a timber farm in Allegan County, Michigan. My only team was a large pair of oxen, and my family consisted of a wife and a boy of six. The kid stubbed around among the stumps, logs and brush and was healthy and appeared to enjoy himself as well as any of the pampered pets of fortune. His grandmother came out to see how he was thriving one day and happened to see him give the dog a kick and hear him swear at him. [The six year old son was Frank, born in Mississippi, January 29, 1866.]

"Why Frank, is it possible that you swear?" asked the astonished old lady

"Of course, I do," was his reply, "you have to here in the woods. How could you drive oxen without swearing, I'd like to know?"

At the table one evening I remarked that a certain person was so dense that he didn't know where the sun rose and set.

"Why, I know that much my own self," said the kid. I had my doubts about it and asked him to tell us what he knew about the subject. He replied,

"Why, hain't you seen it? It rises down to John Bacon's and sets up at old Beck's."

It seemed a little risky to bring up a lad with such an environment, but the neighbors and the ministers all agreed that he was a good boy--remarkably so, considering the father he had--and it turned out that he grew up into quite a respectable young man, even if he did leave for Kansas while quite young.

About the time he became of age, he decided to go west and grow up with the country, and I called his attention to four general principles of life to ever keep in view, viz.

1st. Don't marry 'til you are past thirty and have enough to support a wife without drudgery. Then get a young woman of twenty and keep her nice so that you will not get tired of her.

2nd. Keep out of secret societies--they are no good, and take much of your time and money.

3rd. Churches are organized to flimflam, frighten and fleece society. The preachers know no more about a future world than you do. Give them the hook.

4th. When you put money into a life insurance company, you acknowledge that you lack brains and ability to take care of your savings and make your own investments. Give them the hook, also.

When I had gotten these four cardinal principles well driven into him I settled up with him and let him go. He lit in a fine little city in Hutchinson, Kansas and is there yet.

Within a year he married a girl about his own age and before he was worth a hundred dollars joined the Odd Fellows, the Methodist Church, and got his valuable life insured.

But he is a good boy just the same and has promised me a visit the coming fall [about 1907]. He has been away about twenty years and has a family of four children, the eldest being eighteen.

One Saturday afternoon I started out afoot [about a four mile hike] for Monterey Center, Allegan County, to get the weekly mail, and soon after I hit the Allegan road, lawyer Hannibal Hart in his buggy overtook me and asked me to ride with him. He was on his way to Allegan from Burnip's Corners, where he had been trying a suit, and he made a life-long friend of me by picking me up as he did.

I knew Hannibal by sight and reputation, but he knew nothing of me whatever, for he never before had occasion to notice me. I hadn't enough reputation at the time to attract anyone's attention. But I was gritty and independent and would have walked all the way rather than have asked a favor of him.

Twenty-five or more years later, now Judge Hart and I traversed that thoroughfare again. However, this time I owned the rig. He was again returning from Burnip's where he had defended a suit and won his case. At the very spot where he had picked me up and given me a pleasant ride so many years before, I handed him a ten-dollar note for managing my suit so successfully at Burnip's. We jogged along for a mile and one half 'til we came to the farm house of Charles Gibson, where there appeared to be something going on.

Just south of the house the road is cut out of the hillside so that on the west of the pike there is an abrupt bank and on the other side a sharp decline to a piece of bottom land through which there is a running brook. At the foot of this slope were a few trees standing just beyond a rail fence.

They were threshing at "Uncle Charlie's," and the gang was strolling out of the house after partaking of a five o'clock supper. A kid had spied a black squirrel in one of the trees mentioned, and proceeded to shy stones at it, while two dogs stationed themselves at the base of the tree to cut off all chance of escape.

The roadway stood on a level with the lower limbs of the tree and stones of convenient size were plentiful. The distance was just right and so the fun was tempting. The threshers all gathered about and kept that squirrel constantly on the jump.

You would expect such a game would be of short duration, but there you would be off. That squirrel was not born to be killed by a stone--not on that day at least. Hundreds were thrown, but none hit him.

A team drove up from the south with a hay rack and a few men on and among them was a young fellow who lived at Burnip's. Before the team was brought to a halt he commenced manipulating his mouth...

"Why don't you hit him? Why in the devil don't you hit him? Why in hell don't you knock him out of there? You are a fine lot of chumps, you are."

"And you are so damned smart that you had better come down here and try it yourself," said one of the threshers.

The smart Burnipian dropped on the gravel, gathered up a choice lot of stones, and squared himself opposite the squirrel.

The threshers stepped back out of his way, and when he got to work, they commenced guying him.

"I thought you were going to knock him out the first shot."

"You are a great thrower, you are!"

"You couldn't hit a cow!"

"The squirrel has gone to sleep. You haven't made him move in the last six throws!"

"Go and take a rest. You can't hit nothing!"

"Take a shot at the barn there and see if you can hit that!"

Burnip's was getting desperate now and had to do something quick for the threshers were about to take a hand in the game again. So he gathered up another handful of stones and hopped over the rail fence. The squirrel was directly above him and he took a vertical shot. The stone struck a limb, rebounded, and took him square in the mouth.

A yell of delight went up from the gang. The squirrel skipped to the top of the tree and took a look about to see what had happened, while Burnip's made a sneak to the brook to soak his face.

The crowd had all got busy again when Mr. Gibson appeared and said to his two grown-up boys,

"Jasper, you and Fletcher go to the barn."

The old gentleman was grave and dignified, and would not himself allow any of his family to abbreviate or "nick" any of their names. In the family they were distinguished as Isaac, Jasper, Fletcher and Clinton. But outside, Ike, Jap, Fletch, and Clint brought prompt recognition. The balance of the gang were his neighbors whom he could not presume to order about but he hoped they would take a broad hint and hike themselves to the machine as there was much threshing to be done yet.

But they didn't; they were having too much fun, and each and every son-of-a-gun of them was determined to remain in the game to the finish.

When "Uncle Charlie" saw that his ruse was not working he intimated that he would soon put a stop to that nonsense, and at once started for the house. Soon he came out with a rifle in his hand and the boys knew that their sport was spoiled unless they could keep that squirrel jumping so that the old gentleman couldn't hit him. And they were not right sure he couldn't singe him on the run. He was an old hunter from way back near the red school house in Ohio, and had killed a fine string of deer since he came to Michigan. If the old gentleman had not been religious and truthful, he would probably have told the biggest hunting stories ever heard in Monterey Center.

Uncle Charlie gravely walked down near the tree, and deliberately loaded his rifle with powder and ball, and the gang was busy loading themselves with cobble stones. When Mr. Gibson drew the gun to his cheek the boys all cut loose together and the squirrel flew about that tree so fast that Uncle Charlie could only occasionally catch a glimpse of him. But when some of them had to stop for more ammunition, there was a lull in the firing, the squirrel stopped for an instant, and the rifle cracked.

Then, of course, the squirrel came tumbling to the ground? Not on your life: It just skipped up to the top of the tree again. The most astonished man there was Uncle Charlie himself. He looked straight ahead for a minute, then set his teeth firmly together and commenced reloading.

When he was ready the boys ceased firing and stepped back, for the old gentleman had always commanded their respect and now had their sympathy. The squirrel sat on a branch in full view. The dogs had caught some of the ill-aimed stones, and had sneaked off.

Then the rifle cracked. This time the squirrel came down on the limb on which he was sitting and scooted across the flat land. He jumped the creek and made for a large tree standing on high ground beyond: Quite safe at last.

--- ------ ---

I enjoy writing on agricultural topics, and now feeling much refreshed am ready to again pitch into the serious business of following our "great commander" up the Tennessee River with the 8th.

About the first of February 1862, we had quite an Army gathered about Cairo, and we started out to take Forts Henry and Donelson, on the Tennessee and Cumberland Rivers respectively. Col. Richard Oglesby took the lead with a large brigade, and had our regiment with him on the advance transport. When we came in sight of Fort Heiman, which was perched on a high bluff opposite Henry, we were directly in the rear of the leading gunboat. Two mounted C.S.A. officers came galloping down from the fort, halted on the low bank a half mile above, and surveyed us with field glasses.

From a small bronze cannon mounted on an iron carriage similar in model to a field gun carriage, which was standing forward on the deck of the gunboat, we sent a shell that burst apparently over the heads of these officers. They decamped with a suddenness that might have been taken for fright if they had been common soldiers. But it was just as well for them to get out of there when they did for the line shot was perfect, and the gunner would have corrected the elevation if he could have gotten another pop at them.

We were set ashore on the right bank which, as we were now headed up-stream, was on our left-the Fort Henry side. We pitched our tents about three miles below that fort. More troops came pouring in for a day or two, and in the meantime our regiment went up opposite the fort and within about a half mile of the enemy entrenchments. An escort to Lieut. James B. McPherson, of the Engineer Corps, was now making sketches of the roads and surrounding country.

We ran bump against Rebel cavalry pickets who fired into us quite unexpectedly, and I experienced the sensations Lieut. Howell so graphically described as his own when he got into that cavalry fight near Charleston, Missouri. And I presume the others were similarly affected. For a wonder they didn't happen to hit any of us, but we hit a large burly "Butternut" with a shot in the forehead. The second day after we again traversed this same road, for the purpose of investing the fort, the Confederate forces were about as follows: In Fort Heiman, 500 men; Fort Henry, 3000; in Fort Donelson, 12 miles from Fort Henry on the Cumberland River, ten or twelve thousand.

It was evidently our plan to invest Henry and not let a man escape to fight us at Donelson. We had plenty of troops to do this, and to place a strong force on the Donelson road to head off any interference from that quarter while we dealt with Henry.

We could not count with any degree of certainty on bagging the Heiman bunch, for they were not likely to stand for a fight. They would likely retreat up the river and not go to Donelson, and so we had little concern about them. But it was different at Henry. There was a formidable fort there at a commanding point on the river with ten guns, the largest being a ten-inch Columbiad and a large rifled cannon. The powerful Rebel camp was enclosed with a semi-circular rifle pit from river above to river below for the protection of the infantry and field guns.

Beyond a question they intended to fight. When they left their quarters for the rifle pits they took nothing with them but their fighting tools.

Now this is the way it was actually managed. By suggestion of General Grant the gunboats started as soon as the Army, and engaged the fort before we were fairly underway, and compelled them to run up the white flag before we had covered one third of the distance. Then the men in the rifle pits hiked for Fort Donelson.

My! but was not that a great victory for our Army?

When Grant "invented" his *Memoirs* he must have felt that this great victory needed some elaboration, and so he says the roads to Henry had become almost impassable. If he had been very bright he would not have made up that story for that was only an additional reason for keeping the gunboats back 'til he had the garrison securely invested. But when a man gets going in a certain way he doesn't know where to stop, and so he casually remarks, as though it was a matter of no particular importance, that Gen. Tilghman, C.S.A., intended to evacuate Henry from the beginning and put up the fight against the gunboats to gain more time for his men to get away.

This does not accord with the facts nor with common sense. The soil was gravelly, the roads were good, and there was no unusual delay on that score. If Gen. Tilghman had not intended to defend Henry he had plenty of time after our army hove in sight to move to Donelson and take everything with him except his big guns. Had he luckily defeated the gunboats, as they did at Donelson, we would have had to fight his infantry at their rifle pits.

The enemy got away at the last moment with nothing but their guns and equipment, and it stands to a reasonable certainty that they did not get the order to go 'til their 64-pounder was hit in its face and dismounted, the Columbiad had choked, and their rifled gun had burst. After these mishaps any further defense was useless, and Gen. Tilghman should have gone to Donelson with his men. Why he surrendered himself and his cannoneers as prisoners of war cannot be explained by any requirement of soldierly honor or military necessity.

One would suppose that a man who attained the eminence that Grant reached, could afford to tell the truth and not fill his *Memoirs* with such puerile stuff in an absurd attempt to cover the blunders of his early career.

The sight in the fort was gruesome: Guns and carriages were upset, smashed and scattered about. A shot or shell from a small gun had clipped the flagstaff at the splice in the center, and the upper half stood at an angle of twenty degrees out of plumb. Bodies of half a dozen or more gunners were stretched out on the esplanade.

Union gunboats bombarding Fort Henry from the Tennessee River.

CHAPTER XVIII

Wednesday morning, February 11, 1862, we started toward Fort Donelson, our 8th Illinois Regiment leading the infantry in the wake of a squadron of cavalry. About noon, within a mile of the Confederate rifle pits, we ran into their outlying pickets and received a hair-raising volley, which we returned across the ravine separating us.

The land was more than half covered with standing timber and was also hilly. In these respects it was very favorable for our approach. Near their breastworks much of this timber had been felled for abatis. We maneuvered about that afternoon and the next two days getting into position. This called for a little skirmish fighting at times, but nothing grand enough to be called a battle occurred 'til Saturday morning the 15th.

Friday evening we had stacked our muskets within long rifle range of Rebel rifle pits. The 18th Illinois was on our right, and held the right of our entire line. We had our knapsacks, overcoats, blankets, and a haversack of chuck, which consisted of hardtack, fried bacon and coffee. Although there had been snow in the air and it was steadily growing colder, we were not allowed to start fires. Therefore, we could have no coffee nor get any heat to warm our frames. At dark we ate what we could get down and then rolled ourselves in our blankets and went to sleep--those who could.

About midnight the pickets commenced firing quite sharply and we were routed out of our warm nests. There had fallen a blanket of snow, which made us very comfortable. We took our arms from the stacks and stood in line 'til the firing ceased, then stacked them again and lay down. But we didn't lie there long, however. We were chilled and could not get warm and only grew colder. We were forced to jump up and exercise violently to keep from freezing. Soon I made a large circle of snow, and after making a few rounds thought it a good thing. As an invitation to the boys to join me, I sang out "Fall In."

The words were instantly caught up and went right and left along the line, and I think the whole Army broke their stacks again. Off on the left for a half mile or more I could hear those doleful words, "Fall in...Fall in." I think I was the only fellow there who could identify the ass that started that false alarm.

Colonel Oglesby had seen fit to detail Lieutenant Joe Howell to temporarily serve on his staff, and Capt. Harvey thought it up to him to make a lieutenant for the vacancy out of the company Orderly. We had no more use for such a lieutenant than the regiment had for another chaplain. And I became the new acting Orderly.

This change took me from the left to the right of the company, and as it turned out from the coolest to the hottest place in the regiment. It gave the new lieutenant an opportunity to keep himself comparatively out of danger. During a fight my tactical position was now in the line of file closers, but I wouldn't take it and remained in the front rank.

After it was over I swore by all the gods, devils and my illustrious ancestors that it would take a bigger man than Capt. Harvey to ever again make me take up any duties of that contemptible Orderly position.

In front of our regiment was heavy timber with some underbrush except where our Co. K was in line. Here was clear, open ground to the enemy's breastworks, except for a strip of undergrowth running through the lowest point of the valley over which we had a clear view of the line of rebel fortifications.

Morning came at last and the Johnnies with it. They poured out over their works in plain view, thicker than flies around a cider mill, and deployed in double-quick. Then they moved forward down the decline, crossed the bottom and commenced the incline. All this without a shot being fired in either direction.

When they came within 200 yards, we cut loose on them, and they dropped behind a natural rise of ground that gave them much protection. And they returned our compliments in full...volley after volley.

Our position was on the crest of a moderate ridge behind which we might have had protection, but our company officers seemed to be so fearful that we would not stand our ground that they pushed us over the crest in plain view of the enemy, from our caps to our toes, and they never suggested even that we lie down as the Johnnies had done from the start. It looked as if they thought we were a good buffer for themselves so long as we stood up in the front of them.

We were all green enough to do as we were told, but our officers could never handle us in that manner again.

The enemy did not line up in the opening in front of our company but rolled back inside the timber line to protect themselves, and cracked it to us across the opening at a slight right oblique. And as if we were not already getting it hot enough, standing there exposed as we were, they had to run up a field piece just inside their rifle pit and open up on us with that.

When they jerked the lanyard on the first cartridge the shell cut the branches out of the trees behind us. The next one came much nearer our heads. These cannoneers were not exposed to any fire themselves and so kept on the jump and sent their rounds in at a rate of about five shells a minute. Their fourth shot went into the ground in front of us. The next took off the foot of a corporal of Co. I, standing at my right hand, and then they sent one just over our heads again. A call had been sent in for some artillery and a gun was coming up on the left of our company. The next shot shattered the file at my right.

Ritter and Riddle, both large brave fellows on my left hand, had been killed, and feeling that it would certainly be my turn next, and knowing that such slaughter was unnecessary, I went for Captain Harvey. I found him about twenty paces to the rear of the company, and below the danger line.

"Are you going to leave the company standing up there to be butchered in this sort of manner?" I shot at him. The captain replied, "I'll attend to them. You find out if any Rebels are hid in the bushes down in the hollow."

I flew back to my place on the right, pushed out two skirmish files and told them to deploy and skip out at a left oblique. Then I ordered the rest of the company to fall back a little and lie down. As I turned to follow my skirmishers, a shell crashed into the ground in front of me and filled my eyes and mouth with dirt.

I caught the men just in time to drop them behind a large downed tree that lay across the field, and jumping over this I sprinted to a large standing oak fifty paces in front. From here I could see there were no Johnnies in the undergrowth. So I sauntered back to the downed tree.

There was an artillery duel on now and the shells were going over our heads in both directions. Just after I had my mouth filled with dirt, our light artillery opened up on the Johnnies and drew their fire, so our infantry was now "shut" of them. The Rebs did not train their piece on us again, possibly because our men were no longer standing up in plain view of them.

Next, on our left was Col. John A. Logan's Thirty-first Illinois Infantry Regiment, and the battle was raging there with full force. There was such a wide opening between us that the brush, timber and uneven ground hid them entirely from our sight. The downed tree to our company front lay diagonally on the field, slightly to the rear of the Rebel line, and not more than one hundred yards from them. We could see the Rebels plainly and could have cracked it to them from where we were.

The tree made a fine breastwork from which the enemy could not dislodge us except by a rush. And that would have exposed them to a full fire from our entire company above on higher ground. Anyway, if it came to it, we had a good line of retreat in the direction of Logan's right. But I was green and thought the order to reconnoiter had came from Col. Oglesby, for whom I had the greatest regard, and thought he ought to have a prompt report of my observations. The boys wanted to cut loose on the Rebs from behind the downed tree, but I said no. I told them I must get back and report and couldn't leave them, so asked them to come with me. If I had understood then as I did afterward that the order originated with Captain Harvey and that he took that course to get rid of me, I would have kept those boys with me and not joined the company again 'til the battle was over. If we had done so no one would have noticed it or cared anything about it anyway. What a time we could have had, poking it to those "Butternuts," strung out along there in plain sight as they were and us behind a large downed tree, just the right height to shoot from our knees and at point-blank range. I have never forgiven myself for this blunder and I never will.

Taking a cue from the examples set by some of the great general officers of our Army, I should have romanticized a little here, or ignored the incident entirely, I suppose.

We returned to the company around its left flank, and Harvey received my report with thankless indifference. Then we stepped up to the line, emptied our guns in the direction of the enemy, threw ourselves on the ground beside the other boys, and proceeded to re-load while on our backs.

The captain of Co. I at Donelson was an Englishman by the name of Wilson, who took no better care of his men than Capt. Harvey did. But he took no better care of himself either and kept close to the firing line 'til he was wounded. I don't know when his men ceased exposing the whole length of their frames to the enemy's fire, but I presume they did not stand there long after our Co. K had stretched itself on the ground. It so happened that all the men killed by the enemy field gun were on the left of Wilson's company, and their exposure to those shots was the result of stupidity.

Walter F. Evans of Co. I was a clerk at regimental headquarters and he with Ira A. Batterton, and a detail from our company, were left at Fort Henry in charge of the Headquarters stuff. But bright and early the first morning of the Donelson scrap (February 15) Evans turned up and at the opening of the fight took a position behind the upturned roots of a downed tree, well in advance of the left of his company. After a while the enemy discovered him and made the dirt fly about his head in great shape but he held his place to the end of the game and came off without a scratch.

We held our ground 'til about noon. We had robbed our dead and wounded of their cartridges, and they were about all burned up. Grant says there was an abundance of ammunition nearby lying on the ground in boxes, but that our commanders did not know enough to deal it out to us. When things went awry with him he often blamed the stupidity of his commanders. It is more than probable that no ammunition was handed out for he did not look for or plan on any fight that day.

It was not cartridges that we needed, but fresh troops to take our place. For four or five hours we had been under a continuous and heavy fire. Like a decapitated snake, and there were plenty, we were all tail and no head. Some commander on our left attempted to help us out, but those that came upon our rear mistook us for the enemy, gave us a volley and ran. We were then utterly, completely and eternally disgusted.

During this long and hot contest before Fort Donelson none of our generals showed up at all. Grant was off on one of the gunboats, and McClernand instinctively kept himself in the far rear out of all personal danger. As far as any good they were to the Army that day, they may as well have been back in Cairo, though we would have liked to consign them to a much hotter place.

When we left the battlefield at Donelson we did not run, nor did we retreat in battalion formation and in good order--as a distinguished historian has said--but just walked off as a lot of sullen and disgusted men naturally would without having the slightest thought of our officers, or the order of our going.

Capt. Harvey and I were among the last of our company to get started and happened to walk together. We had not gone more than fifty paces when I fell flat on my face. I was not aware of stumbling and for an instant thought myself shot. Capt. Harvey must have thought the same but he kept walking and did not look back. I arose and rejoined him but no remark was made of my mishap.

I was mad all over, at the way our company was needlessly exposed, that we had been left to fight against large odds when there were plenty of idle Union troops nearby, and that no general officer had come near us during this long and hot engagement. And now we were defeated and driven from the field. We had lost our knapsacks, overcoats, blankets, clothing and trinkets, and worst of all had left our wounded and dead with the enemy. I could have killed McClernand, Wallace and Grant without the slightest remorse. Colonel Oglesby had remained constantly with his brigade - often under fire - and I would have made him then the commander of the Army.

I was waiting for an opening and was about ready to explode when Harvey remarked that I had conducted myself to his satisfaction during the battle and then I promptly told him that I was sorry I could not return the compliment.

"You had no earthly use for an acting second lieutenant, but put the Orderly in a cool place and me in a hot one. That was a trick that you can never play on me again. Do you think it was the sensible thing to keep your company on their feet when the enemy were lying on their faces within point-blank range, and with a Rebel field gun playing on them as if they were a lot of tenpins. Why did you crowd them over the crest instead of letting them lie behind it?"

"Why, the boys all lay down when they wanted to. I didn't prevent them."

"Nor did you tell them to. I gave them the order myself."

"I heard it and thought it was all right."

"Why did you send me down to reconnoiter that undergrowth instead of one of your worthless lieutenants who were standing back there out of range doing nothing?"

"Because you can handle the men better than they can. Did you know that Joe Howell was killed?"

God! But that was a stunner.

We came upon a rise of ground and found Colonel Logan in a furious rage. He had gathered in about fifty men and swore he would die right there before he would fall back another inch. I asked Harvey if he was going to stop and he said no. I had no disposition to either and so kept on with him.

I wanted Harvey to open the conversation again. But he wouldn't so I had to.

"Since Joe has gone I shall have no more use for Company "Q", and I take it that the company will not concern itself about me. When I make an application for a transfer, I will expect you to approve it. In the meantime you must not attempt to reduce me to the ranks, for it will not work, nor ask me to do any of the Orderly's duties, for that won't work either."

"I don't want to reduce you to the ranks and you can do just as you please while you stay with the company if you won't talk before the boys."

"Very good! Now I think we understand each other."

Our regiment got together near Wallace's reserve division, about two miles from the enemy's works. When the Captain and I came up, there sat General Grant on his horse, quite alone. No one spoke to him but we all looked him over, made remarks about him in an undertone, and wondered what kind of stuff he was made of. He could not see or hear anything about what was going on in front, and I wondered if he was really sober and realized the critical condition of his Army at this time. He spoke to no one and no one seemed inclined to speak to him. If Oglesby or Logan had been in his place they would have been surrounded by officers and men, but the conditions would have had to be different to have kept either one of them there five minutes. He must have felt the effects of our surly undertones, possibly heard some of them for he soon rode over to the next hill and sat there by himself for I don't know how long.

Later in the war we might easily have been mistaken for a colored battalion of African Descent for our hands and faces were as black as powder could make them. We were in no humor to take an ice water bath, however, and so didn't try to clean up. Neither were we disposed to freeze through another night, and so with only our own permission we started a number of fires and sat around them and dozed as best we could. A nearby regiment gave us one hardtack each, and that had to stand us 'til we went into Donelson the next day.

There was no sense or reason for this surrender, for if the Confederates had remained behind their rifle pits and defended them with the spirit they displayed when fighting us on the outside, they could have held them indefinitely. The bastioned fort on their right next to the river, with water batteries immediately below it, had defeated our gunboats, and they controlled the river above and could get down reinforcements and supplies as readily as we could get them from below. As long as they could muster half our force they could defy our attacks and make our losses four times their own.

Such chumps as C.S.A. Generals Pillow, Floyd and Buckner were a disgrace to the Confederate uniform, and we owed our success at Donelson to the imbecility of this trio...that and the indomitable pluck of our subordinate commanders and the boys under them.

Several reputations were made and unmade in the Eighth at Donelson. That fractious Capt. Wetzell of Co. E made a sneak [deserted] and was forced to resign. His two talented Lieutenants, Loyd Wheaton and Sam Caldwell, both came out with flying colors. Early in the fight, each had strapped on cartridge boxes, taken up a musket and got busy. Sam walked down to a standing oak fifty paces in front of his company and cracked it to them as long as his ammunition held out. The tree that protected him was literally barked by rebel bullets, but only his uniform got wounded. Wheaton kept his men down and his own musket working over their heads and singularly escaped a serious wound.

Major Post strolled off and was captured by some Rebel flankers. He was held prisoner so long that his conduct was overlooked eventually.

Relating to the deportment of Capt. Herman Lieb of Co. B, 8th Illinois Infantry, I take the following extract from a letter dated Nov. 5, 1905 from C. W. Daniels of Co. E (also the 8th) and now of Baxter Springs, Kansas.

"About this time, after we had retired about a quarter of a mile, Capt. Lieb got hot - he fairly yelled - by God, I go back. If I get one man, by God, I go back.

"None of us were anxious to go back just then and he took his sword - which was made of tin or pewter but silver plated - and put his foot on it to break it, he was so mad. He beat it nearly double, and as it had no spring in it, it remained in a shape like this. He then waved it over his head and used language that is not proper to put on paper.

"Capt. Lieb was a fine officer; kind, considerate, warm hearted, and a true patriot, although hasty and impulsive at times."

During the two and a half days before Donelson (Feb. 13, 14, 15) there was quite a little skirmishing going on, and several vicious artillery duels took place. Capt. Adolph Swartz, Battery E, 2nd Illinois Lt. Artillery, had a gun directly in front of us, and he had to stand over his men with a drawn saber to make them work their piece. We were lying on our faces safely behind the ridge and Swartz's lieutenant was borrowing our guns and firing them in rapid succession. Suddenly he clapped his hand on his abdomen and exclaimed,

"Vell poys, they gots me dot time," and then passed back to the rear. But the gallant fellow recovered and later became Captain Conrad Gumbart.

One of our old Company K boys wrote me quite recently that he was one of the 20 men I had out skirmishing with the enemy that first day after our arrival, and while I cannot recall the incident I mention it to show the Captain's habit of sending me out on all occasions, as if unconscious that he had lieutenants that should share some of the duties and risks of the service.

Col. Oglesby got a bullet through his uniform that came from a Reb who had located himself behind a log ahead of their rifle pits. He came to our company and asked for the boy who had done that good shooting at Bird's Point. Sidney Hazelbaker stepped up and said he rather thought himself the chap that was wanted.

"Are you the boy that hit that snag in the river?" asked Uncle Dick. Sid replied that he was the identical fellow, quite at his service.

"Can you shoot as well now as you could then?"

"That's hard to say; there was no one shooting at me then; that may make some difference, you know, with a fellow's nerves," replied Sid.

"Well I will find you a chance to try your nerve if you will come with me," said the Colonel, and they started off together beyond our left flank. Dick pointed out the Rebel's location and they examined it through the Colonel's field glass and saw that he was still holding his little fort and quite ready to take a crack at another Yank. Sid wanted to lessen the distance and also to reach cover and, seeing a standing tree several rods ahead, he got this in line with the Johnnie and made a break for it.

The Rebel took a shot at him as he rushed forward and missed. While lying out of sight reloading, Sid reached the tree and leveled his gun on the little fort. Oglesby's field glass was leveled on the spot, too, and he did not have long to wait. The fellow pushed his gun out over the log and an instant later Sid's musket cracked.

"Come in, boy", called out Dick, "you have fixed the damned son of ---------------."

And sure enough, Mr. Johnnie Reb crawled back inside his lines with Sid's bullet in his shoulder. After the surrender Sid hunted him up and they had a chat over the affair.

Already well-bloodied Yankee troops storm Confederate artillery at Fort Donelson where very green commanders and combat-new Union infantry paid an extremely high price for a first significant victory gained by frontal assaults against well armed and entrenched Confederates

CHAPTER XIX

Before we start on another campaign of carnage and slaughter, let's take a furlough, return to civil life, and discuss things spiritual.

It was ten or twelve years ago, while I was running the Monterey Center store that, Squire Bishop, the farmer/blacksmith/horseman, came in and took a careful survey of the premises. Seeing no one but the proprietor about, he sidled up to the desk where I was writing. He told me he had just been talking with Frank Granger over at the post office.

There was going to be a spiritual seance that evening at Bill Jones' farm house over in the adjoining township of Hopkins, and Frank was commissioned to invite a few of his Monterey friends. He wished Sam Wilcox and us to go and said he would take his brother, John, who was visiting at his house. While we were talking, Sam came in and it was arranged that he go with me, and that Bishop would take his wife.

Later Sam sent word that he was not feeling well and would back out, and so I persuaded Mrs. Caverno [Cornwell] to accompany me.

It was Amos Krug of Hopkins Station who was running the west end of this menagerie, and from him Frank Granger had received his invitation and commission to invite his Monterey friends.

Amos, who is now a resident of Battle Creek, Michigan is a broad shouldered German with the strength of a bull. At one time I had put up a lot of telephone poles [c.1901] along the road adjoining his farm. Two men and a pike lever were required to set them, but Amos alone tipped a half dozen of them into their holes the next morning just to give himself an appetite for breakfast.

He kept the hotel at Hopkins Station a few years, and was there the date of the seance. He was a genuine wag and a shrewd fellow whom it was very difficult to get the best of in any respect. I had just installed a telephone in the office of the hotel, but had not yet made the connection with the switchboard at the exchange, when his dinner bell rang. The telephone was a bridged instrument that would ring on itself, and as I stepped to the sink to wash my hands, Amos walked up to it and apparently sent in a call.

A dozen or more men were in the office, and it attracted the attention of them all. I was the only other person there who knew that he could call no one but himself.

"Hello, Central!" bawled Krug, "Give me Allegan." And a moment later he added "Is this Allegan? Say Allegan, give me #-- #----, (giving the name of a notorious bagnio mistress) quick." Then, having apparently got his party, he said, "Is this you #--; this is Amos Krug: I'll be down on the evening freight. Good bye."

I think this fooled nearly every person in the office. A fellow who stood beside me at the sink remarked in all seriousness:

"If I had as nice a wife as Liz, I wouldn't have anything to do with such women."

We adjourned to the dining room and at the family table with the landlord and his lady were two stylish nieces from Battle Creek, who were paying their Uncle Amos and Aunt Lizzie a visit. During the repast their conversation turned to the packing and keeping of ice, and one of the girls remarked that he father's ice melted very fast that summer.

"Huh!" grunted Amos, "My ice never melts."

"Why, Uncle, how can you keep your ice from melting, I'd like to know?"

"I paint the cakes when I pack them," said Amos gravely, "and they never melt."

"I declare! Who would have thought of it. I'll tell father of it when I get home," said the innocent girl. And I have no doubt but she did. Bishop and I drove over in company and we found the place about a mile east of the "burg" [Hopkins Station]. Krug and wife were there and they had brought with them a large-framed, portly old gentleman, Mr. Roderick, who boarded at the village hotel and bought fruit for shipment. There were many strangers there, but Frank Granger was absent. He had gotten Bish and me started and then characteristically backed himself out.

But there were enough without him, quite as many as the house could accommodate. I looked them over without spotting a suspicious looking character. There was not a long-haired man or a short-haired woman in the bunch. Just good average country people, you know.

The seance operator, Mr. Finney of Grand Rapids [Michigan], directed us to take seats, men and women alternately. Observing an attractive young lady about to seat herself, I immediately approached her and asked permission to occupy the seat at her left hand. This request was pleasantly granted and Mrs. Caverno [Cornwell] dropped in on the other side of me. When all seated we made a complete circle around the room, and we were instructed to join hands and keep the contact unbroken during the seance.

On a small table in the center of the room was a metal horn about thirty inches long, smooth inside and out, with apertures of one and three inches; also a guitar and a tea bell. The medium sat inside the circle, facing a lady whose hands he held. I was quite confident that I could comply with the unbroken chain conditions all right, for if I should use Mrs. Caverno's hand to scratch my nose or bat a mosquito, I felt quite sure she would not let go or giggle. And as a precaution, I slipped a handkerchief in my left coat pocket for fear my confounded proboscis might require attention of another nature.

When all the arrangements had been completed the light was taken from the room and we were left in total darkness. I took a firm grip on the two little hands I was holding (to assure the owners of my protection) shoved my legs forward to the limit, that the operator might stumble over my feet if he attempted to perambulate around the room, and then commenced to feel that it was good for me to be there.

I felt very pleasant vibrations, but I am afraid they were not of the truly spiritualistic sort. They were of a familiar kind. I had had them before, and could always obtain a recurrence of them by persuading some pretty young woman to let me hold her hand. Truly, a fellow cannot be wholly depraved and lost when he is so susceptible to such sweet and heavenly influences.

At the suggestion of the director, someone led off with a hymn in which many joined. I had a very strong voice, but not one cultivated along those lines. So I kept quiet. I had never taken a fancy to gospel music anyway, and thought it quite tame and uninspiring. Somehow, this time it had a salutary effect on me and I didn't feel a bit bored. Connected as I was with this large circle of good people, I presume I was unconsciously absorbing virtue from the other segments.

After a hymn or two the bell tinkled the signal for the orchestra to hush and the curtain to rise on the first act. The performance commenced with the guitar picking itself up and producing in a sweet and even tone a few familiar airs as it floated around the room between our heads and the ceiling. At the finish it carefully placed itself in the corner of the room behind the seats.

The trumpet was next brought into play, and through it came several voices in succession, apparently changing hands as it moved from one person to the next in the circle. When it came to Squire Bishop a hoarse voice said,

"Hello Squire! Do you know who this is?"

"Yes sir, it is Andrew Mallory," replied Bish.

Andrew had for some years been a blacksmith at Monterey Center and Bishop, I think, learned the trade of him, or at least worked with him more or less for some time before he had passed on to the next world. I had also known him well and thought it his voice for sure.

"Well, Squire," said the voice, "You need not worry about the future. Everything is all right over here. Tell my Rose of this, will you? Tell her I'm all right and she will be, too, when she gets here."

For a moment I trembled with joyful excitement, for I had known Andrew Mallory as a rough, profane and godless man, chuck full of fun and all manner of devilment; just the kind our professional soul-savers consign to eternal perdition, unless they repent at the last moment. Now no one ever heard of Andrew Mallory repenting of anything, for he was not one of that kind, and here he turns up back in Allegan County, without a hair singed and says he is having a good time. Jerusalem! But I guess there is some hope for me after all. I took an extra grip on the ladies' hands and felt right sure that it was good to be there.

"Shall I tell Mandy, too?" asked Bish. This time the answer that came back through the trumpet was a big "NO." Mandy had been his widow and had married again, which may account for his unconcern about her.

When the horn reached me a manly voice called out,

"Hello, Major, how are you?"

I told him I was well and happy as a clam. He would guess that much if he could see me sitting there as I was with both hands full of these little women, and vibrations of ecstasy oozing out of every pore of my system. He gave me his name, which I cannot now recall, and said he was the man who brought me water when I was wounded at Milliken's Bend. I remembered the incident but could not recall the man or the name, for which I asked his pardon. I thanked him again for the deed and expressed a hope to meet him on the other side of Jordan and renew our acquaintance. He said he would look out for me, bade me good bye, and I passed the trumpet over to the next one.

A friend of Mrs. Caverno then talked with her a few moments, and closed with the query "have you got that money yet?" followed by a laugh.

The speaking tube had got a little more than half way around the circle when it reached portly Mr. Roderick, who had come over with the Krugs. Amos had attended this sort of entertainment before, and he convinced the old gentleman that it would be quite the proper thing to take hold of the horn and assure himself that no mortal was at the other end of it. He told him that he had done it many a time. So the simple, honest old fellow reached out his big paw and grabbed it.

There was a little tussle in which Roderick lost his hold. The medium called for the light, the trumpet came down on Roderick's head, kerwack, and fell to the floor. And the seance was at an end. This threw Jones (our host) into a rage. He was a large broad-shouldered man with a square jaw, and had a local reputation as a fighter. He paced the room with clenched fists, and told Roderick that he deserved a thrashing, and only his grey hairs saved him; that many of these people had driven miles to witness this seance, and now when only fairly commenced it had been broken up through his idiocy. The old gentleman expressed extreme sorrow for his misconduct but did not give Amos away. If he had, what a picnic we would have had! It would have discounted the "Ruction at Lannegan's Ball," for Krug and Jones were about of an age and evenly matched for weight. We western county fellows apologized most profusely for the old man, and declared that we were well satisfied with the entertainment we had had. And well we might be for we all sat at Roderick's right and had talked with our spirits before he clinched the horn. So we had a good enough time. Of course, those on Roderick's left got left.

When things got quieted down we gave Mr. Finney a half dollar each for his time and expenses, thanked the Joneses for their hospitality, and bid them good night. If there was any skullduggery about this performance I was unable to detect it. The people all appeared sincere and honest-except for that wag Krug, and I have learned since that he is a firm believer in spiritualism. But he can't let a chance for a practical joke pass by, no matter what the consequences may be.

After we had driven about a mile Bish came up alongside and asked me if I had been thoughtful enough to put a little "spirits" in the buggy before I left the store. I certainly had, but had forgotten all about it. I fished it out from under the seat and said we would not drink until the girls had had some, and that we would not start up our rigs until we had had a swig. In order to get home and in bed they took a lady's nip, then Bish and I took a gentleman's size drink and we started for the Center as though we intended to get there.

On the way I asked Mrs. Caverno what the "trumpet" person meant by asking her if she had got that money yet, and by going off with a laugh as he did. She said that during the forenoon Mrs. G. [Granger] had called and in a conversation Mrs. Caverno had enumerated several articles she intended to make herself present of when she got the one hundred and fifty dollars she had loaned Oswald Gates and Jim Holdsworth of Hopkins Station. To justify the pleasantry of the party that talked to her through the trumpet, I will remark that she has never had the opportunity of fooling that money away a second time.

Plaque at National Park Service information center at Fort Donelson shows that Oglesby's Brigade, including 8th Illinois, suffered very high casualties, as described by Cornwell in these chronicles. The Donelson baptism in combat horror was still fresh in his mind during the Shiloh disaster about two months afterward.

CHAPTER XX

About the first of March '62 we trudged back to Fort Henry and immediately went aboard river transports. As they went plowing up the Tennessee River, we were cheered with the report that Grant was under a cloud and would have to remain behind. Col. Oglesby was now in command with headquarters on our leading boat. It was a pretty stream, running through interesting scenery, and we enjoyed the trip greatly.

I recall an incident during this trip that presents a phase in the character of "Uncle Dick" that had much to do with his popularity. Some of the men were getting pretty "full," and it was discovered that in a stack of sutler goods piled up on the boat's forecastle, (on river streamers the forward end of the boat is the boiler deck and its name is pronounced fork-a-sel, with accent on the first) were many cases of bottled whiskey. This was, I think, in violation of orders, for commissioned officers could obtain all the firewater they wanted from the commissary department, which didn't intend us boys should have any.

But some of the men had evidently been getting whiskey all right and without paying for it either, and when the fact was reported to the colonel he ordered the "Officer of the Day" to fish out these cases, open them up, and break the bottles over the gunwale of the boat.

This officer gathered his guards around him and went at it, while Uncle Dick watched them from above on the cabin deck. And all the rest of us were watching them, too, from all three decks, and once more gave proof of our self-denial, loyalty to the old flag, and devotion to discipline in permitting the destruction of so much good stuff before our very eyes. They couldn't do it now; but we were younger then and had not cultivated a strong taste for the "critter." But there happened to be one man on the boat who didn't propose to stand for it. He was a heavy, broad shouldered bull-neck soldier, and he walked up to a case, grabbed a bottle in each hand, and started for the rear of the boat. He was stopped by a couple of the guards when Col. Dick sang out,

"Riley, throw them in the river!" And the answer was "I won't do it."

"I tell you to throw them in the river," roared Dick, "or I will go down there and make you."

"I'm not afraid of you: I licked you once in Decatur," replied Riley.

"Well, you can't do it here," and Dick went down the stairs two at a clip, walked up to the fellow, caught him by the collar of his jacket, yanked him up to the gunwale and again ordered him to shy the bottles into the Tennessee River. But old Riley held fast to them and answered, "Not by a damnsight." Dick gave him six or eight flat-hand slaps on the side of his head, and he tossed one of them in the stream.

"Now, throw the other in," said the colonel, but he didn't. He just hung onto it with both hands, and told Dick he would see him in hell first.

Oglesby changed hands on him and slapped the other side of his face 'til the bottle dropped to the deck. Oglesby then started him for the stern of the boat, and resumed his place on the cabin deck. Later in the day Riley fell overboard and was drowned.

In due time we reached Pittsburg Landing, moved out about two miles from the river and went into camp not far from the old Shiloh Church. As soon as we broke ranks I started a little fire and proceeded to make a cup of coffee and cook a dish of stuff that I had fished out of my haversack.

Lieut. Col. Rhodes, now commanding the regiment, came along, and seeing me stirring something in a cup that looked like cornmeal mush, drew up his horse and said,

"Dan, what is that stuff you are messing with anyway?" I told him I had something there that was right, that I had picked it up at Donelson, and that after eating two or three dishes of it concluded to save the balance of it for a march, and so I had some of it yet.

"Well, what do you call it? Is there no name for it?"

"Of course, it is desiccated potato—whatever that means and I wish you would write to the quartermaster general for a supply of it. I know it would tickle the boys to death. Say, it is the slickest thing you ever put in your mouth, just heavenly, you bet. And it is no trouble at all to prepare it. You just put a handful in a cup like this. I picked up this cup on purpose for the business, pour on a little water and when it comes to a boil let it cook about two minutes, then stir in a little pepper and salt; let it cool off a little and there you have it."

"What did you say the name of it was, desecrated potato?"

"Yes, or something like that. It is a wonderful improvement on the plain article." I sifted a sprinkle of salt and pepper in and passed it up for a taste.

I had always considered Col. Rhodes a level-headed officer who was always gentlemanly and approachable, and the interest he was taking in this little matter, which might possibly please and benefit his regiment, raised him still higher in my estimation.

He took a spoonful, cooled it with his breath, slid it beneath his heavy moustache, rolled it about in his mouth, swallowed a portion of it, tasted the balance again, and then spat it out and said,

"Why, dammit, Dan, it's as tasteless as buckwheat bran."

I reached for the cup, took a mouthful, and found that all the strength and flavor had evaporated. It afterward came to my mind that the package I had taken it from had been lined with sheet lead, and I had kept this nearly two weeks in a cloth sack. I then felt like kicking myself for not eating it while it was good.

A week later I was crossing the parade ground in sight of Colonel Rhodes' tent when he hailed me and called me in. Oglesby had been made a brigadier and Rhodes had just received his appointment as full colonel in command of the 8th and also had a leave of absence. There were a dozen or more officers in there and he was evidently celebrating his commission before starting down the river. He ordered me to take a seat and I dropped into one and wondered what he had up his sleeve for me at that time. He then asked the party if any of them had any knowledge of a ration called desecrated potato. They all confessed ignorance of it and I arose to go, but got orders again to sit down. "But I have no interest in desecrated potatoes," I said.

"Well, you did once and you are the very fellow who called my attention to that nourishing article of diet."

"I didn't think you ate enough of it to find out whether it was nourishing or not."

"No, I took your word for that."

"But you wouldn't take it for being palatable; you said it tasted like buckwheat bran."

"Well, didn't it?"

"I don't know how buckwheat bran tastes; I never had to live on it."

"You ought to be kept on it a week for deceiving me as you did. Sit down, I tell you. If you make a sneak before I get through with you I will send a guard after you."

The colonel was getting in a conversational humor and wanted to talk.

"See here, boys, you say you never heard of these desperated potatoes, and I never did myself 'til the sergeant here called my attention to them. You see, I was riding along and saw Dan making coffee and cooking some stuff that looked like mush in a new tin cup. I pulled up and asked him what it was, and he said it was designated potatoes, the slickest thing he had yet found, that they beat the genuine article to death. He wanted I should write immediately to the Chief Commissary, President Lincoln, and the Secretary of State, and obtain a supply for the regiment. He said the boys would just go wild over it. So I sat there while it was cooking and his mouth kept running on the merits of this new ration, which he said had more intrinsic nutrition in it than any stuff that he had ever eaten."

Here the colonel rose to his feet and with extravagant gestures quoted me as saying...

"Give this ration to the boys and they will drill better, be more alert on picket, march farther in a day, and fight a damnsite harder than they possibly could on hardtack and sowbelly."

"Well, he talked so eloquently on the subject that I began to feel hungry, and was thinking of eating the dish and allowing him to prepare another one for himself, but when he passed it up I very quickly changed my mind for it was as tasteless as sawdust. Say Dan, what was the matter with the damn stuff anyway: did you ever find out?"

"Yes, I will tell you some other time, but I'll have to be going now."

"Not 'til you have had a taste of the Good Samaritan and lit up a stoga; walk right up, Dan, and help yourself."

We had been here about a week and I had not received an order of any kind nor paid any attention to duty, but put in my time roaming about the various camps. About this time I discovered myself getting out of physical condition for the first time since I entered the service. I constantly craved something to eat, but it was a morbid appetite, and nothing that I could get tasted right nor did me any good. I constantly grew weaker and while still able to walk called on Surgeon Trowbridge and he gave me a bottle of the tincture of iron. He told me if I got any weaker to come back and take a cot in his hospital. I went back to the company quarters and remained there for I don't know how long, my chum Bill Miller looking after my needs.

The drum corps of the various regiments kept up an incessant pounding from morning 'til night. I would have burned their instruments of torture and kicked the drummer and fifers into the ranks, where they could have been of some use, but I wasn't strong enough. This drum corps business was one of the humbugs of our Army and the soldiers became very tired of them. They were a useless expense and therefore a detriment to an army. They never play any of their dubious music on the battlefield to inspire the boys to deeds of valor, and no one wants them to. You could never coax a band to play within gunshot of the enemy, anyway. They couldn't if they tried. Every screaming shell or whistling bullet would make them dodge about so that they could not keep in tune together. A good cornet band sounds very pleasant on a clear evening, when there is no enemy within fifty miles, for you can then relax and enjoy it. But when the enemy is nearby you are somewhat strung up and can't relax, you see. And if you could it might make a coward of you, for the tendency is strongly in that direction. The roar of musketry and the roar of artillery fills the entire bill for music on a battlefield, and every other sound is tame and silly in comparison.

POSITION OF TAYLOR'S AND M'ALLISTER'S BATTERIES DURING THE BATTLE AT FORT DONELSON.—Sketched by Mr. Alexander Simplot.—[See Page 168.]

Second Illinois Light Artillery (including McAllister's Battery) heavily involved before Donelson.

CHAPTER XXI

The boys now hustled in and out of the tents getting their guns and accoutrements, and after they were all out I rose and leisurely dressed myself. I could distinctly hear the firing about a mile away to the left and front and concluded that there was a battle on and I was out of it because of my illness. It was clear that our Army was surprised, and as Grant had come up the river and taken command again, I could see but little hope for our side.

I was not much sorry to be out of this for I had scarcely recovered from the horror of the Donelson fight, but decided to take care of my gun and equipment, and possibly take a hand in it when the Rebs reached our camp. So, I buckled on the cartridge-box belt, took my musket out of the rack, and stepped outside the tent. I felt stronger than usual that morning, and as the regiment was just moving off by the right flank I could not resist the impulse to drop into my place on the tail end. Company commander Harvey happened to see me and dropped back and walked with me a moment. He said I was not expected to go out with them, and probably wouldn't stand it long if I did. He was concerned about the company property, especially the headquarters stuff, and said he wished I would go back and take charge of the camp and save as much of it as I could. I told him that I preferred to go with the regiment, but if I had to fall out then I would look after the camp. Then I added, "I am going in today on my own hook and if you want a man for extra dangerous duty, just send Dennison or Orderly McClung, for I'll not be available."

"Do as you please, Dan, and if we both get safely through this battle, I hope we will be good friends in the future." Then Capt. Harvey returned to the head of his company.

Our march was in a left oblique direction from our camp ground, and we made about three-fourths of a mile and went into line of battle. "On right by file into line," and as fast as we got on the line, we commenced firing into the enemy who were coming up a slight grade through open timber.

Behind us, and to our left, was a large open field that had been used so much for a drill ground that it was tread hard and smoothe. We had no regimental officers with us and were taken out by Capt. Ashmore of Co. C. But he skipped out at the first shot and Capt. Harvey took his place. We were all veterans now. That is, we had been through one severe battle and it would be supposed that we were now somewhat hardened and would be a tough regiment to buck against. At Donelson we were green and stood where our officers put us and in some instances were slaughtered through their indifference or stupidity. We had had time to think it over and were bound to look a little out for ourselves. There was little shirking and straggling at Donelson, but there would be a lot of it here today...April 6, 1862.

The enemy did not stop coming but kept up a steady fire, advancing, and as there were no Union troops within sight on either flank, we gave way. In the retreat across the field behind us Capt. William Harvey was shot in the back of the head and killed. Then the command devolved upon Capt. Sturgess of Co. H, 8th Illinois, a gallant officer who soon after became major of the regiment.

I had taken a stand behind an upturned root and got two shots off after the regiment broke. Then I ran like a whitehead deer to the left and rear for some bales of cotton that were stacked up in the center of the field. Here I found two of our company--George W. Carr and Ira A. Batterton. The latter was the regimental headquarters clerk who had been left with Evans of Co. I at Fort Henry when we moved on Donelson. But he had not joined Evans who shouldered his musket and joined us in time to take part in the bloody battle Saturday morning at Fort Donelson.

Ira had much regretted that he had not come with Evans to Donelson for he envied Evans the reputation he had won on that occasion and determined to have a hand in the next fight. So here he was and had made this retreat while I was getting in the last two shots. He was a fine-grained educated man of about twenty-eight, familiar with the printing business, and had got out that little paper at Bloomfield, Missouri under the name of the "THE STARS AND STRIPES" that I referred to in a previous chapter. He was evidently going to make good today at Shiloh.

We plugged it into the right flank of the Johnnies while they were crossing the field to the number of about four cartridges each, and our last shots went into their rear rank. Behind us--two or three hundred yards--was a heavy piece of timber, and from this there suddenly burst out a heavy fire past us after these same Johnnies. The distance was rather long and I should say that most of them took a point blank aim for their shots kicked up a dust the whole length of the parade ground. We were in a bad place if not observed, but I presume we were for we heard none of the bullets strike the cotton bales. But we sprinted out of there during the lull--after the first round--and got out of their range [Union fire] in safety.

We circled the piece of timber through which our regiment had retreated and found them in line on the other side of it, expecting the enemy to appear. But they did not come. Here I saw Evans again ready for business, in an advanced position near a good piece of cover. Batterton joined him, Carr fell in with the company, and I selected a large oak on the left about opposite Evans and Ira.

Histories of the Civil War, or accounts of battles written by ex-general officers, deal with bodies of troops such as brigades, divisions and corps, and historians must obtain their information in the main from the official reports of commanders of such organizations. Considering the source of their information, it is not to be marveled at that the public will never hear much of the truth about these engagements. General officers will not acknowledge themselves [to be] stupid or cowardly, yet many of them were both at Shiloh.

But I am not writing a history of this battle; just giving a soldier's account of what little he saw of it, and with a pledge that there is more truth in it to the square yard than in many of the writings of our general officers, and with a hope that the novelty of such details will prove interesting to the general reader.

There were no friendly troops yet in sight on our left, and I am not sure there were any on our right. Even our brigade commander had not yet shown up and the highest officer in sight was a captain. I became convinced that something had happened to those Johnnies that we were looking for and started up through the timber to see what had become of them. When I came near the field over which we had fled, I ran into a mass of brush that the eye could not penetrate more than ten paces. I stopped and listened attentively for a moment, but could hear nothing beyond, and then pushed my way through. The Johnnies were not in sight. We were now in John A. McClernand's division and organized as the first brigade with the 18th Illinois on our right and the 11th and 13th Iowa on our left, and were supposed to be commanded by one of the Iowa colonels. But we never saw him. So the unit that fired past us boys when we were behind the cotton bales was no doubt one of these Iowa regiments. And I conject that the reason the Rebels did not follow our retreating regiment down through the timber was that they decided to change front to their right and go for the party that was firing on them. And I also conclude from information subsequently obtained, that these Johnnies made them [Iowan's] get too, the same as they had us.

I hastily returned and reported the facts to Capt. Sturgess and he asked me to go back and keep a sharp lookout. Getting a hardtack from one of the boys and a pull at his canteen, I went back to the edge of the field and this time I saw something. A Rebel regiment was moving across this large bare drill ground with their left flank toward me. The accuracy of their alignment, and precision of their step gave them the appearance of a battalion out for a drill, with one exception. The officers were in the rear of the men, in the tactical position for combat. Soon they halted and the three field officers came together for a consultation. Then they resumed their places, the regiment was faced about and started in the opposite direction.

Some of our troops still had grey uniforms and the regimental colors these Confederates carried were much like those lugged about in our own battalions. I had seen these troops in both directions and could not tell for sure which side they belonged to, or where they were headed. I skipped back to our regiment, and when within hearing distance called for Capt. Sturgess. He came up on the run followed by Captains Lieb and Wheaton. When we reached the strip of dense undergrowth, I remarked, "Wait here a moment while I push through and see if the coast is clear." Capt. Wheaton bowed and with a bland smile told me that I was very obliging.

Sturgess exclaimed, "That's a hell of a note," while Lieb sizzed out between his teeth in broken English "by got I guess I see you." Then they all plunged through the thicket and left me to follow them.

When we got to the drillfield opening that fancy Southern regiment was executing a left half wheel, and they moved with the precision of a piece of machinery. When they got around facing us they got the order "forward," and slowly bore down in our direction. Sturgess exclaimed, "They are Rebs all right, let's go back and get ready for them." Lieb went flying to get his company to skirmish them down through the timber, and the other captains started off more leisurely. I backed into the brush a few paces and got busy. When the Rebels reached there they pushed their way through and came on without throwing out a skirmisher. They never fired a gun until Lieb had rallied his skirmishers on that battalion and the regiment gave them a volley. Then they stopped.

How long this fight lasted I'll not guess, but it was long and hot, and continued until the Johnnies got all they wanted of it and left. And they didn't go off in the cadence step either. And I'll bet a fifty dollar counterfeit Confederate note that these troops never before were in a fight and that they never again attempted to hold a dress parade on a field of battle.

Here Captain Loyd Wheaton got a bullet in the shoulder but pluckily remained in command of his company 'til near sundown, when he became so weakened from the loss of blood that he was compelled to give up and go to a hospital. Later he got a "leave," and went north. He rejoined the "Old 8th" while it was in front of Corinth, Mississippi.

Evans was wounded in this scrap, too, and Batterton helped him off the battle field. He never returned to the service but was discharged in August. I will if I don't forget it, give you Batterton's finish in the latter part of this history.

And it was here that "Orderly Thomas J. McClung," who was now a second lieutenant-and since Capt. Harvey had just been killed was likely to take the first-set the men of the company a fine example by making a streak for tall timber, and keeping out of the way 'til the battle was over. The excuse he gave was that he was hit in the back by a piece of a shell, but he could never show a mark, nor had any shell came near us up to this time.

Before starting out from camp in the morning of the 6th Capt. Harvey had noted the absence from the ranks of a fellow who had skulked at Donelson and he sent Sergeant George Marion after him. He got him, put him in the ranks, and was told not to let him get away. While moving up to take our place in the battle line, the roar of musketry was steadily increasing, punctuated at shorter and shorter intervals by the boom of the field guns, and this fellow became dreadfully sick. The disease was known among us as the cannon fever. I presume we all had the symptoms more or less, but this fellow had the real thing exceedingly bad and didn't try to conceal it. On the contrary, he tried to excite pity by vomiting and groaning, and begged to be allowed to step out of ranks a few moments for sanitary reasons.

But George Marion was inexorable, and told him if he left the ranks he would put a bullet through him, and held onto him and got him into this scrap. After it was over I saw he was gone and asked Marion when and how he got away.

"Why it was like this," said George. "I held him to it 'til we got nicely engaged with those fellows, when all of a sudden he dropped his gun and screamed 'oh God, oh God, I'm shot.' and commenced crawling to the rear. It made me feel kind of bad to think I'd got him killed the way I did, but I didn't have to feel that way long for as soon as he got to that old snag back there he jumped up and ran like a jack rabbit. I suppose I ought to have sent a bullet after him, but I didn't."

And now I suppose that that fellow was never again under fire; I will bet a pewter dollar that he never was by hook, crook or any other means. I have forgotten his name and know nothing of what became of him, but the chances are that he received an honorable discharge and reached home safe, well and hearty. He had cost Uncle Sam several hundred dollars, but had not returned him one cent's worth of service. This being the probable case, the spirit of poker playing days comes back to me and I want to wager my other bogus dollar that he was among the first to apply for a pension, and join the Grand Army of the Republic; that he excels in the telling about the fierce fights he has taken part in. If he is a man of family and has children, they no doubt firmly believe that he is the man who put down the Great Rebellion all by himself.

But if we condemn a worthless jay like this fellow, who in time of danger is willing to acknowledge himself a constitutional coward, and unfit to be a private soldier, what shall we say of a commissioned officer wearing shoulder straps and carrying a sword, who will fly the white rag and scurry for cover as this boy's second lieutenant did upon this occasion. Elbert Hubbard with his limitless vocabulary might do the subject well in printable English, but I confess myself unequal to the task. I might possibly do it to my own satisfaction, but I presume this history will be read by many mollycoddles as well as people of nerve and I certainly don't wish to shock anyone's feelings.

At Shiloh my unusual opportunities for burning powder was running me shy of cartridges and Bill Miller got me a supply from the box of one of the dead men, and gave me another hard tack. Instead of growing weaker, I was getting stronger every hour. The excitement in connection with the liberty I took in going where I pleased without interference from officers, and the satisfaction of feeling that I didn't owe Uncle Sam a cent for all he had spent on me, was bringing me out in fine shape, and I felt like a new man.

Four of the boys now were engaged in a game of cards. If any of them were reading their Bibles, I did not notice it. I had just commenced dozing with my head on Marion's knee, when Major Mason Brayman, the Asst. Adjutant General of our division rode up and took us out of there. We were well in advance of the general alignment, and could have been gobbled up if the Confederate officers had been attending to their business.

He conducted us to a new position nearer the river with open timber in our front and I at once sallied out to see what I could find. I did not look for trouble before reaching the crest of a slight ridge about two hundred yards ahead and so strolled along carelessly, and when about half way up the rise a bullet zipped past my head so close that I felt the disturbance it made in the atmosphere. I saw smoke near a tree just over the elevation and stepped behind an oak, drew sight on the spot, and waited. We got about three shots each, alternately, during which time a cannon ball went through my tree about ten feet over my head and dropped bark all over me.

We had both got loaded and were watching for a chance when the Johnny pulled and "killed" me. That is, he thought he had for I jumped so quick that I went backwards over a root and fell outside the tree in his sight. Our boys were all watching the game and they also thought I was done for. But it was a mistake for I was soon on my feet again and looking out from behind the tree. The boys gave a cheer and yelled "plug it to him, Dan."

I know that it excites a prejudice against a man if he acknowledges that he has killed another, but it might not be so in the case of a soldier. He is there for that purpose, and the enemy is there for the purpose of killing him. It is duty as all must acknowledge to send as many of them over the River Jordan as possible, and save himself if he can to send some more over it in the next battle to keep them company.

I don't think that a reasonable person will attempt to dispute this position and I have no sympathy for a man whose conscience was so squeamishly acute as to upbraid a soldier for killing a man in self defense or in a square fight in combat.

This fellow had tried to kill me and thought he had succeeded and like a good soldier that he was, he happily slung his empty gun on his shoulder and was contentedly strolling back to his command.

"It is my turn now. He thinks I am done for. Holy smoke, but won't I astonish him!" I drew a bead on his back and let her flicker. His cap went off over his eyes and he picked it up and pulled it on his head again and gradually disappeared over the ridge without looking about or changing his gait. My intentions were all right but my aim was too high and I am glad of it.

I went on over the ridge and met the enemy coming our way with no skirmishers out as usual. So I skirmished my way back and though in plain sight much of the time never got a return shot. When I got back over the ridge, I hustled back to our line, reported what was coming and made for a down tree to the left and well in advance of our line.

When they hove in sight over the ridge our men let loose on them and they returned the fire but advanced no farther. It was a stiff fight of about even numbers and we tired them out at last and they withdrew. Not a shot came my way that I knew of and so I enjoyed that fight with a peculiar relish. I think it was here that Sergeant Cassidy was killed. He was a model soldier and as fearless as a wildcat.

To keep us on the general alignment we were again moved to the rear, for the enemy had persistently crowded our Army back all day, and this is the first time I remember of our being joined on the right by the 18th Ill. Infty. The fact of our being surprised in the morning attack and left on the field by ourselves to fight everything that came along, which indicated an absence of anything resembling generalship and being overreached as we were by the enemy, disheartened our Army so that desertions were numerous. Our losses in killed and wounded up to this time had not been excessive but now we had not one half the men we came out with. When the 18th joined us there were not enough men altogether to make a decent sized regiment.

We were lined up now on the edge of large openings, and the field that lay in our front was about 500 yards wide. From the farther side of this the enemy infantry opened the ball, and we lay there on our faces and blazed away at their smoke 'til they got tired and quit. I saw Corporal Charles Hayden get a bullet in him when he arose to fire. He crawled back a couple of rods on his hands and knees and died in that position.

After the firing ceased the Iowa regiments of our brigade came from somewhere and formed on our left with an interval of about fifty paces. In this interval two 24 pounder iron siege guns were stationed and a couple of field pieces were placed in battery on the right of the 18th.

These dispositions were no sooner made than the enemy started a fine regiment over the field to drive us from our position with the bayonet. They had got fairly under way when Gen. McClernand and some of his staff rode up in rear of the regiment on our left. This was the first we had seen of him that day, and we were rejoiced to be assured with our own eyes that Providence had up to this time protected him from the cruel bullets of the enemy. Upon reflection I concluded that

Providence was not fool enough to concern itself about the safety of a man so infinitely capable of taking care of himself as was this doughty brigadier general.

Something had roiled his temper for he damned one of those Iowa colonels 'til he wheezed and got out of breath. Then, as the Johnnies were getting closer he wheeled his horse about and rode away to the rear. But one of this staff did not follow him. It was the gallant Major Mason Brayman [later Colonel of the 29th Illinois Infantry] who was here, there and everywhere, over the field that day, encouraging the various commanders and conducting them from one position to another. He rode a beautiful white horse whose color matched his long beard and flowing hair and made him a most conspicuous figure on that battlefield at Shiloh.

When his general turned tail and skipped, Brayman rode to the front of our regiment, took the colors and planted himself fifteen paces in front of our line, asking us not to fire 'til he waved the flag. And he declared that if those Confederates were not driven back he would never leave the ground alive. In the 18th were many Irish and one of them sang out "Never fear Major, but they'll all go back that are able to travel."

They were getting close now, and one after another we got to our feet as the Southerners struck into the double-quick, and the click of our musket locks could be heard along the Union line. What could they be thinking of to blindly run into double their number as they were doing? Their colonel was on his horse a short distance in the rear of his line and he should have seen before this that it would be impossible to drive us from our position with that one regiment. They should have had four of them and then thrown their flanks well forward to put us in a pocket. In that case we might have withdrawn with or without a fight.

But we have no time to speculate now for we can see the white of their eyes and our muskets are at our shoulders with one eye on them and the other on the senior white bearded Major who sat there like a statue with his bridle rein and hat in his left hand and the colors in his right. They are almost upon him. We can't hold in any longer. God! will he never give the sign? There she goes-- and every piece went off as one. We annihilated that splendid Rebel regiment without the loss of a man.

When Division Commander Brigadier General John A. McClernand was told how this affair resulted, surely he could plainly see that he had missed witnessing one of the finest sights ever seen on a battlefield. His presence would have gained him a little reputation for nerve which he so sadly stood in need of without incurring the slightest danger. He must have felt like calling on one of his orderlies to kick the gable end of his uniform pants for about ten minutes. But let's leave this for a pleasanter subject under a new chapter head.

A Sunday morning in Tennessee…April 6, 1862, near Shiloh Church. Sketch depicts Oglesby's Brigade of McClernand's Division near center of Union line, probably just before the rout began that ended with a "meltdown" of effective Yankee resistance. Most of Grant's forces stumbled over each other in panic as they desperately hoped to gain some protection from the Tennessee River and whatever Navy guns might be afloat there. Cornwell's 8th Illinois was near the middle of this scene. A *Leslie's Illustrated* artist incorrectly placed the 8th Indiana in line where in fact the 8th Illinois stood.

CHAPTER XXII

I think it was in 1883 that I left the farm in Salem Township to try my luck at merchandising at Monterey Center. The next year, or the one after, I was buying groceries of a Grand Rapid's house that was represented in my territory by a man named Hudson. He was a fine looking heavy weight with a patronizing, commanding air that was quite irresistible with me at that time for I still retained a flavor of the modesty and diffidence I had brought from the farm.

The old hotel in Monterey Center had been closed for several years, and what little call there was for such accommodations I tried to supply.

Mr. Hudson made fortnightly trips, and was due to arrive at my place about eleven a.m. From that time 'til twelve he would be taking my order and stuffing it with everything he thought I needed, thereby giving me the advantage of his long experience with the trade. He also collected for his house and upon those occasions that I did not pay him in full for his last bill, he would be content to take the order as read off to him.

At a time when I had no clerk, the young woman who kept my house usually came to the store after setting my dinner on the table. But when there were guests she could not leave and therefore I did not eat with them.

One day this young lady said to me,

"What did we get for feeding that man, Hudson?"

"Twenty-five cents," I replied.

"T w e n t y - f i v e c e n t s," exclaimed the girl in apparent astonishment, "You ought to have a dollar at least! Why, that man is a holy terror and I pity his poor wife. I wouldn't marry him if he was single and worth a million. I had a bang-up good dinner ready today and do you know he found fault with everything I set before him? He called for another napkin and made me fry him two more eggs when he already eaten four. He saw our young chickens out by the stable and said they would be just the right size for broilers when he made his next trip, and ordered me to cook one for his next dinner. I have made up my mind that there won't be any next dinner here for him for he's not going to eat up that nice brood of chickens when there are no more of them than you and I want. After all the fault he found with the dinner he ate enough for three harvest hands. If we had him for a steady boarder we would soon go busted."

I was highly amused as well as pleased at the girl's loyalty and spirit and told her I would work him off on a lady in the neighborhood who had once got the better of me, and with whom I was just aching to get even. And I made the arrangement accordingly without the slightest trouble.

When Hudson made his next trip my stable boy took care of his roadsters [team of buggy horses]. After he had stuffed my order to his eminent satisfaction I told him my girl was sick, which was no lie for she was just dead sick of him, and then I pointed out the house where I had engaged his dinner.

This lady was somewhat talented, of engaging manner, and slightly flirtatious. He stayed a full hour and came away with a beaming countenance. He said she was a "charmer" and he hoped I would not take it amiss that he had engaged to dine with her in the future. I feigned a trifle displeasure when he dropped a couple of dimes on the cigar case for ten centers and said it should be the regular thing hereafter. I told him that would be satisfactory with me only the girl always counted so much on having him there to dinner that I was afraid it would hurt her feelings. This was his first suspicion that the girl was mashed on him and so he said she should have a dimesworth of chocolates and remarked that the house would have to stand for it for it would all go in the bill. Then I brightened up and said it was a go and he threw down another dime.

One very hot day in August he drove up at the usual hour in a bad humor.

"Where is the boy to take these horses," he growled.

"I sent him to Hopkins after freight," I replied.

"You keep a fine hotel you do-no one about to take a gentleman's rig when he drives up hot and dusty!"

"Oh, come in and fan yourself; I'll put your team out."

"Put out nothing; I'll go over to the old hotel first."

He seemed to think that they were still doing business over there when they got a chance but he discovered he was wrong after trying a couple of other places. Without meeting with success, he drove back to my barn and found the boy there to take the rig.

When he came into the store he dropped into the chair in front of the grocery counter and proceeded to fan himself and grumble. He spoke of a place on his route no larger than Monterey where he could get anything he wanted and remarked that if he were there now he would be sipping a glass of iced lemonade or buttermilk. I didn't happen to have any lemons in the store but I caught on the buttermilk all right and said,

"Why didn't you tell me you wanted buttermilk? Don't you know that this town is famous for buttermilk? Here, kid, take this pail over to Mrs. Mack's and tell her to fill it and give her this dime. But quick about it now or Hudson will be fainting away!"

I had seen the old lady agitating the cream that morning and knew it was a sure thing, so I at once got a piece of ice from the refrigerator, broke it up and filled a pitcher. The boy returned a moment later with his pail full and I at once dumped some of it on the ice and stirred it with the cheese knife to reduce its temperature.

It quickly dropped to about freezing or a little below while Hudson sat there perspiring, and impatient for me to pour him a glass.

I filled a goblet, which he soon swallowed with the greatest relish and smacked his lips for more, declaring it was fine, finer than silk. So I poured out another and another, then refilled the pitcher with the delicious beverage and went out to take an order from a lady customer who had just driven up.

When I handed out her packages I heard the call "D i n n errr" in a minor key, and saw Hudson's new landlady waving her kerchief from the front porch. I passed the word on to him, but got no reply and when I entered the store I repeated it and he said he could not go just yet as he felt a little sick.

I remarked that he did look some ghostly and surmised that he had over heated himself, and then stepped behind the counter and filled his goblet with buttermilk again. But he only scowled and said that he thought he had had too much already. I told him that was quite impossible for buttermilk was the most wholesome drink on earth-especially Monterey buttermilk.

"How do you know-you haven't drank any of it," he snapped out.

"I'll drink the balance that's in this pail with you, glass for glass if you dare," I said, and reached for another goblet. "What do you say?"

"That you can go to hell, damu!" And then he started for the oil room, planted himself at the back door on a soap box and took his face in his hands.

Just then came a call on my local telephone system with terminal stations in the kitchen and oil room, wherein cigar boxes did duty for both transmitters and receivers. By agitating the fine copper wire with the forefingers, the generators were dispensed with also. I was the sole owner of this telephone line, pole, wire and instruments, and as there were no intermediate stations where inquisitive and idle people could cut in and listen, it would naturally be supposed that here I could get secret service. But I couldn't--for the voice at the other end came pouring out in the oil room in volume equaling an Edison phonograph.

Girl:- Hello Dan--has Hudson gone to dinner yet?

Self:- No, he sits here at the back door on a soap box heaving Jonah.

Hudson:-Won't you shut up da-ahzz--oh my!

Girl:-Why, I can hear him belching from here--the poor little fellow; what have you been giving him anyway?

Self:- Only a little iced buttermilk.

Hudson:- I'll smash that talking box the minute I get up.

Self:- Hudson, don't interrupt my conversation with my housekeeper please, it is not good manners you know.

Hudson:- Confound you! if you had any manners you would shut up.

Girl:- I guess you give him something else; a glass of buttermilk wouldn't have made him sick. Say Dan, where did you get it?

Self:- Over Mrs. Macks.

Girl:- Save me some and I will make you some nice biscuits for supper.

Self:- All right; I only got a four quart pail full and if there is any of it left you can have it.

Girl:- A n y o f i t l e f t ! Heavens! Don't that man know anything at all?

Self:- Not much just now, only that he is feeling mighty bad and his dinner is getting cold. Don't you think you ought to come over and hold his head?

Hudson:- You son-of-a-gun, if I don't get even with you.

Self:- It's wicked to think of revenge when you ought to be repenting your sins, you know.

Hudson:- I'll make you repent of yours as soon as I get out of this.

Self:- Iced buttermilk is a cooling and healthful beverage on a hot day I am quite sure, for I have heard you say so, but I suspect that you took too much of it this time.

Hudson:- Dang you! are you never going to quit?

Girl:- Ask him if it tastes as good coming up as it did going down.

Hudson:- Tell her to go to the devil and take you with her.

From that time on I got along with Hudson swimmingly. Whenever he began to get airy I had only to threaten sending for buttermilk and he would instantly wilt. This little episode cost me seventy-five cents for the girl laughed 'til she split her corset and I gave her a new one out of the stock.

CHAPTER XXIII

I said that we annihilated that splendid Confederate regiment at Shiloh, but I do not wish the statement to be taken literally. They were coming at a fast double-quick with their bayonets to the front and when we fired, their whole line seemed to drop into the earth. We rushed forward, captured a few, and of course some got away. They never fired a shot and as our muskets were empty--and a half minute was consumed in reloading them-- we didn't do much in the line of picking off the fleeing Johnnies.

Nothing daunted, the enemy quickly organized another charging column and commenced moving directly for us from a half-right oblique direction. I could not see why we should not stand our ground and destroy them, too, but it was not in the program and our line was started to the rear again. Here was a chance for me to get in a little independent work, with a minimum of personal danger. I stepped over where the 24-pounder siege guns had been planted, yanked from the bottom of my box a package of ten cartridges, opened them up on a log and commenced firing on this new, advancing column. They came slowly, and being in no danger myself, I enjoyed a few minutes here as I never did before or since in any other place.

When the tenth cartridge was burned I spurted for a ravine to the left and rear and followed this a ways and then came out on the high ground and took a direction that I thought would bring me out at or near the regiment. But it didn't and I did not see a man until I came to the river bank a short distance above the landing. And what a sight! From the bottom of the high bank to the water's edge the ground was covered with men who had not fought at all, or who had fought 'til they became discouraged, and would fight no more.

Transports were ferrying Union General Don Carlos Buell's troops to our side of the river, and as fast as they landed they pushed their way through the human mass at the river's edge and followed the road up the high bank. Half way up this bank now was a man in his shirtsleeves who with wild gesticulation railed at the cowed Union troops below the bank and begged and pleaded with them to return to their regiments and keep the enemy from reaching this point. And he encouraged them by saying that if the Rebels were not driven back it would all end in the greatest massacre of human beings ever known to history. He was probably some sutler whose stock was in the vicinity, and he was fearful of losing it. I looked in vain to see someone shoot him, for lots of the boys had their guns with them.

If Richard Oglesby or John A. Logan could have suddenly appeared on the scene and said "Boys-you have been shamefully treated; you have been kept for a month within a days march of a superior force of the enemy, and were not permitted to throw up a line of breast-works to protect yourselves from an attack. And what is more disgraceful, your generals have lolled around their quarters smoking sutler cigars and drinking commissary whiskey, and permitted themselves and their Army to be surprised, which is the crime unpardonable. The result is that our line of battle is now short and near the river. It is solid and the enemy can't break through it, nor flank us. Soon they will have to withdraw for the night.

"In the morning we will have General Buell's whole Army here and Lew Wallace's division and will greatly out-number them. We will soon have general officers of skill and courage to handle this Army, and long before tomorrow night what is left of this Rebel horde that crowded us so hard today will be tumbling over themselves on the road back to Corinth. Now boys, come up here and fall in. I will take charge of you and see that you have a fair show. You may not have to fight again, but if you do I will be there with you and share the danger. It is better to die like a man than live like a coward. Come up and fall in. To the end of your life you will be glad of it."

An appeal of this sort from a man like Oglesby or Logan would have brought hundreds of these men scurrying up the bank with new courage in their hearts.

A cornet band was blaring out patriotic airs from the top of the bank, and the effect on the stragglers was about as salutary as the ranting of that shirt-sleeved idiot who had taken up his station half-way down the bank. You may talk ever so eloquently and forcibly to the ordinary man about it being his duty to protect his country and sacrifice himself upon an alter of necessity, but if you are not willing to go along and share the dangers with him your discourse will affect him negatively, if at all. The natural expression that would go out from these fellows in answer to these musicians and the hill-side orator would be, "Why the devil don't you get guns and try it yourself?"

It took only a couple of minutes to take in this situation, and for fear of being recognized by someone, I cut back the way I came and reached the main road about forty rods from the river. Near there I found two boys of our company with their guns and equipment and asked them where they were bound. They said they were looking for the regiment. I told them to come on, I was going there myself. Soon we met an Army wagon that had been distributing hard tack and got the information we wanted. It was growing dark and I struck a lively gait and soon found the regiment but the two boys that were following me had slipped away.

After filling up with cartridges and hard tack I asked my chum, Bill Miller, if he could devise some way to keep us out of the storm that was coming up. He was a man of about thirty-five, a resourceful chap who was equal to every occasion. It had been thundering violently for about a half hour and the rain drops were commencing to fall. Bill said, "come on," and I followed. In a few moments it became so dark we could see only by the lightning flashes, and the rain was increasing at a rate that made it certain that we would be soaked before we got anywhere. Then we ran into a piece of luck. A Darkey was standing with his back to a tree holding a canvas cot over himself. Bill saw him in the flash of lightning, took the cot and with that over our heads we started on. We soon came to a hospital tent, and had reached it comparatively dry. We saw by the flashes two men lying apart with blankets over them. Bill immediately crawled in beside one of them and I the other. And without a word we went to sleep.

I did not awake nor make a stir 'til Miller called me about an hour before daylight. The clouds were gone and it was light enough to see objects in the tent. We stretched ourselves with much satisfaction over our dry and comfortable condition compared with the thousands of boys who were soaked to the skin in that pitiless rain. Bill remarked, "We must wake up our partners," and he gave his a roll with his foot. This not being effective, he pulled down the blanket, took a look at his face and said,

"My partner is dead."

I gave mine a couple of kicks and replied,

"So is mine."

We struck out for the regiment and I soon detected Bill in a low chuckle and asked him what was running in that red head of his.

He "allowed" we were fools for not pulling the blankets off those "stiffs" and rolling in together, and I thought as much myself.

Miller said he thought he would know the Darkey who lost his cot, and if he saw him he would tell him where to find it, and another small chuckle escaped him.

When we got back to the company we found a line of Gen. Buell's men in our immediate front, and a general officer who was standing by holding his own horse, said,

"We will try and keep you out of the fight today, boys. You had enough of it yesterday. Just keep along within sight and see us pepper it to them today. I know you will come up if we need you."

We assured him that we would, thanked him for his kind words and admired him for his humanity, confidence and pluck. I regret that I did not catch his name, but it must have been Gen. McCook or one of his brigade commanders.

As we were the right of McClernand's division, it is evident that his whole division was counted out of the attacking force April 7, and the few men still in line were counted as a reserve force only. And it is quite clear that Lew Wallace's fresh division on our right was similarly covering the remnants of Sherman's troops.

Grant says on page 350, vol. 1 of his memorable *Memoirs* that, "The position of the Union troops on the morning of the 7th was as follows: General Lew Wallace on the right; Sherman on his left; then McClernand and then Hurlbut. Nelson, of Buell's Army, was on our extreme left, next to the river. Crittenden was next in line after Nelson and on his right; McCook followed and formed the extreme right of Buell's command. My old command thus formed the right wing, while the troops directly under Buell constituted the left wing of the army. These relative positions were retained during the entire day, or until the enemy was driven from the field."

The above is conspicuously untrue and totally unfair to General Don Carlos Buell and his gallant men who covered the entire front with the sole exception of what was occupied by Lew Wallace's division.

At daylight the new Army commenced the advance in line of battle, and it was a cheerful sight to see their officers riding well up with their men as if they intended to manage things and share some of the dangers of the engagement. We followed along, just to keep them nicely in sight, and after they had gone about a mile they found the Johnnies and opened up on them in great shape. This was the first fight we were in when we were not doing the fighting ourselves. It was a pleasant novelty. None of our general officers were with us. None of them showed up during the entire day. We had no use for them anyway, so I simply mentioned the fact.

We bunched up with the 18th Illinois and made but a small bunch even then. A few of our officers toddled along behind us and had little to say. If one of them gave an order it came in the form of a request, or a plea, and we did as we pleased about the matter. None of us were held to the ranks by authority of our officers. Many of them would have been glad if the balance of their men had straggled, that they might have an excuse to get away themselves. I tell you, this was a fine army Grant had about this time and they would have cut a great figure attacking the enemy that morning in the absence of Buell's army. Yet, that is what Grant says he intended to do and would have done if Buell's forces had not arrived.

Up to about noon the firing was very steady. Then a gap was created in our front and a general officer rode back and asked us to move up and fill it. He remarked,

"We have pushed them back more than a mile and have got them whipped, and will soon have them running."

We promptly went forward on the line, but we were extremely nervous. No enemy appearing in front of us, Capt. Herman Lieb got out a few of his men for a skirmish party, but had the dickens of a time getting them to penetrate some brush that was in our front. Nothing could ever cool Lieb's ardor, and it was strictly amusing to hear him swear at those men in his German-English-American speech style.

Lieut. Dennison was with Co. K yet, and he came to me now and asked me to take charge of the company 'til he came back, saying that he was going over to the right where the heavy firing was. I made no reply and he went off in that direction. But he didn't keep the direction long. Unconsciously I presume, he commenced circling to the right and soon disappeared in a piece of timber that lay between us and our old camp. It is almost excusable for enlisted men to straggle when their officers desert them in this manner.

Later we went slowly forward and while pushing our way up through a piece of timber we ran into a masked battery of three guns and were frightened to the verge of fits. But they must have shot over us for I don't think we lost a man. We ran a few rods, changed our minds, turned about, made a rush for those guns and got them.

If the Rebels had stood by those guns and worked them lively, they could have given us two or three more rounds, for a field gun fully manned was capable of five discharges per minute. I explain it in this way:

Their Army had started to retreat and they had to leave these guns. So they placed them in ambush and when we came up, they jerked the lanyards and ran, without stopping to spike them.

There were no artillery horses about and the cannoneers were seen flying across a field in rear of the guns they deserted.

Some of our men appeared quite familiar with such artillery for they wheeled one of the pieces about and sent a few cases of canister after the retreating enemy. We were nearly opposite a right angle in the main road to Corinth, and Rebel cavalry commenced stringing along on the far side of this field parallel with us. They first appeared at a walk, but when we commenced reaching out after them with our muskets and the captured six-pounder, they began using the spurs on their old nags and rapidly getting them up to a dead run. So much speed did some of them get up, that when they came to the angle in the road they could not make the turn, and went pell-mell into the brush and undergrowth beyond. Occasionally the horse would make the turn all right and only the rider would take a bee-line into the grubs. So hardened, calloused and unsympathetic had we become that we would actually smile at these mishaps, and then take a shot at the next fellow. Some of them were not lucky enough to reach the turn at all unless it was on foot. After they went over their horses' heads we lost all interest in them.

We saw a little white rag appear in the center of this field and wave itself about. Presently a boy arose from the ground and came to us, holding this signal of surrender about his head. The excuse he made was that he had had all the fighting he cared for.

The battle was now virtually over. We had given the Johnnies back the drubbing they had handed us Sunday, and were quite willing to call it quits. It was a very small party of us that were still in the line, and each one of us was glad that we had remained to witness the finish at Shiloh.

After a while we started out for our old camp, which we reached before sundown. Lieutenants Dennison and McClung, and about all of the company that had escaped death or wounds, were there when I brought in my little squad of stayers. They were thirteen in number, and here are their names:

Sergeant Thomas J. Wiley,	Corporal James W. Jessee,
John W. Ayers,	Sidney J. Hazlebaker
John B. Dawson,	Robert L. Grundy,
Lytle R. Hemline,	William Miller,
James M. Rhodes,	John S. Wiley,
George Sutherland,	John Batterton,
James W. Drake,	[and David Cornwell, Commanding]

Although the camp had been outside of our lines parts of two days and one night, I do not remember that anything was disturbed.

Skulking, by both officers and men, was so general that no attention was paid to it, and our company lieutenants, being of that class, promoted mainly those boys who like themselves had taken to the brush. Orderly Robert Mercer, who was still absent, was made 2nd lieut. and Sergt. Tom Wiley took his place.

Personally, I had no fault to find with the battle of Shiloh. I could have remained out of it in whole or part without discredit. I was my own captain, colonel, brigadier and commander-in-chief, and the interest I took in maneuvering myself, and the satisfaction of knowing that I was damaging the enemy to the maximum, with the minimum of personal risk, kept me in unusual good humor. I was free here from that feeling of dread and rage that possessed me at Donelson, where we were unnecessarily exposed, and men were being slaughtered on either side of me by a vicious fire of infantry and artillery. Our boys were not so green here as to act the part of dummies in a base-ball alley on a county fair ground. At Shiloh we kept low and took every advantage the field afforded.

Union General Don Carlos Buell...the hero of Shiloh. His Army of the Cumberland rescued the demoralized remnants of Grant's command that littered the west bank of the Tennessee at Pittsburg Landing the morning of April 7, 1862. Cornwell and shattered odds and ends of the combined 8th and 18th Illinois Regiments provided an exhausted, meager but greatly relieved reserve. The battle-drained Illinois troopers lived to see the flower of the Confederate Army of the West flee the Shiloh field as precipitately as Grant's men had done the day before when scrambling down the river's west bank.

CHAPTER XXIV

It was a matter of general knowledge that the Confederates had commenced concentrating their forces at Corinth immediately after their surrender at Fort Donelson, for I heard of it myself while there and consulted a map to see where it [Corinth] was located.

Our Army had been sent up the Tennessee River to Savannah, Tennessee under General C. F. Smith and he placed a division at Crump's Landing, four miles above him on the enemy's side west of the river, and another five miles above that on the same bank at Pittsburg Landing. He kept the larger part of his force with him near the river at Savannah. These forces were but strong outposts and could have readily been withdrawn to the east side of the river in case of impending attack.

A severe sickness overtook General Smith, and General Grant was unfortunately sent to command the Army again. He had to do something smart and bold immediately. He, therefore, moved the main body of the forces from Savannah to Pittsburg Landing within twenty miles of the enemy's fortified encampment, with no natural or man made obstruction between them. General Buell's Army now was a hundred miles or more away [eastward].

Colonel James B. McPherson must have seen our danger for he went over the nearby ground with a view of fortifying it. But in his *Memoirs* Grant says that nothing was done [to fortify Pittsburg Landing] because this would have left some of our camps on the outside; that he thought this would have a tendency to make soldiers timid, and he was sure he was not engaged in a defensive campaign anyway. The enemy [thought Grant] would not leave their breastworks to fight us in the open field when they were certain that we would attack them in their fortifications whenever we got ready.

These excuses are too silly for comment. We would cheerfully have thrown up a fair line of rifle pits in twenty-four hours and made them formidable in a couple of days more, and then it would have been fun to receive an attack. We could have stood off a force three times the size of our own, while they could not put double our number against us.

The enemy were given to senseless and idiotic bayonet charges, and we could have slaughtered them like sheep with but slight loss to ourselves. Grant was cut out of a similar pattern inasmuch as he always wanted to be the attacking party and was not astute enough to allow for the possibility of the enemy conceiving and executing any novel surprise tactics.

Grant says he once thought well of Confederate General Albert Sidney Johnston, but had since been compelled to materially modify his views of that officer's qualifications as a soldier. Well, the two men were not much alike-that's a fact.

Grant didn't know there was any way to whip an enemy except by cornering them with a superior force and bluffing them into a surrender. He said he personally had known the Rebel officers at Fort Donelson, and took advantage of their imbecility. Albert Sidney evidently knew something about Grant and profited by his stupidity at Shiloh.

Johnston no doubt was as well acquainted with the strength and disposition of our forces as Grant was himself, while it does not appear that Grant knew anything about him whatever. It was a matter of the greatest ease for Darkeys to pass between the opposing forces, and Johnston could have kept himself informed of every move we made. But Grant couldn't see things any way but the way he had understood them. He no doubt got Sherman and other officers thinking his way. McClernand must have thought differently for I heard him say that one of the greatest battles of the war would be fought on our camp grounds there at the Landing.

General Johnston also had ideas. He knew there was more than one way of whipping a superior enemy, and that one of them was to take him when his force was divided and thrash his wings in detail, separately. If we had fortified ourselves he would not have thought of making the attack. But under the inviting conditions he could not do otherwise. A corporal who couldn't see that hole at Shiloh would deserve to be reduced to a mule puncher.

Johnston was busy receiving new troops and supplies and could not leave Corinth 'til the last moment. He evidently got daily reports of exactly where Buell was and planned to hit us Saturday, April 5th, in the morning, which he would have done if things had gone well with him. Some of his division commanders, and [Gen. G.P.T.] Beauregard, his second in command, could not believe they wouldn't find us in entrenchments, ready for them. In fact, some of them favored turning about after they had got well under way in their initial assault.

This feeling, and a violent, heavy rain that caught them on the way, delayed their attack one day, which proved fatal to their campaign. If they had reached us as first planned on Saturday morning, Union General Buell would have had no occasion to cross the Tennessee River, for there would have been no Army of the Tennessee left to help.

It was only through the timely arrival of Nelson's division of Buell's Army that the Confederates were prevented from capturing the Landing Sunday evening. If none of Buell's forces had arrived that night, Beauregard could have advanced in the morning and picked up what was left of us with the greatest of ease. Grant says that Sherman was his best division commander and no doubt he was. Sherman says that he had but one unit left that had retained it organization at the end of April 6 and that what was left was mixed up in all sorts of shapes. And it was the same in the other divisions. Whole companies, regiments and brigades were gone-officers and all-and the few plucky fellows that remained on the battleground were simply hanging around to see how the thing was coming out with but little intention of enduring another hard fight. When Buell's fresh troops were lined up on our front and told us we needed only to keep them in sight and see the fun, we felt grateful and were willing to help them out at the end when they needed little assistance. And we didn't see an officer of our Army above captain during the entire day, and would have conducted ourselves the same way without any officers.

One would infer from the writings of Grant and Sherman that this attack was foreseen and no surprise to them. A surprised commander is a disgraced officer, and as the reputations of these major generals were in great jeopardy, anything one would assert in their mutual defense, the other would promptly swear to.

And this suggests an aphorism: "To lie like a major general."

But, in an apology for William Tecumseh it can be said that he had struck a piece of hard luck in Kentucky and didn't know exactly now what his standing was in the Union Army when he was sent to Paducah to take command of that post. Grant was now playing first violin. Sherman hustled his forces up the Tennessee River to support Grant at Pittsburg Landing.

And it turned out that a warm sympathy and friendship grew up between them, for notwithstanding the lucky turn things took for us at Donelson, it was widely felt that Grant had bungled the affair and would have been disastrously defeated if the enemy had been commanded by a skillful and obstinate officer. Grant was assigned to Fort Henry. His Army was sent up the Tennessee River under the command of General C. F. Smith, a very capable and brave old regular, who sickened and died at Florence [Tennessee], ten miles below Pittsburg Landing. But for this, Grant might never again have commanded the Army of the Tennessee, and the chances were that this disastrous Sunday at Shiloh would never have occurred.

Before the battle Sherman permitted himself to be influenced by Grant's depreciation of the Confederate commanders at Corinth, and his inordinate over-confidence in his own astuteness. General Johnston spent four days moving his whole army from Corinth to Shiloh, formed his line of battle three miles or more long, moved on our camps without Grant having a suspicion that the Rebels had moved out of their works at Corinth.

It could not be expected that Grant would think well of Albert Sidney Johnston. However, he could speak highly of Tilghman and Buckner, who needlessly surrendered to him. Johnston gave him the worse trouncing that any army commander ever got on American soil, and proved himself a consummate general and a gallant and fearless professional officer. Unfortunately, he lost his life, but he would not ask his soldiers to go where he would not dare go himself. Grant would never knowingly expose himself in battle in the slightest degree. I never heard of an instance of it except from himself in his *Memoirs*, and when I read it I was surprised that he would mention the incident of a bullet having hit his saber scabbard in such a battle as we had passed through. I say "incident" because I do not believe it to be a fact. Possibly something happened to his scabbard about that time, but one remembers that his horse fell down with him a few days before, and then clumsy officers sometimes tangle their legs up with their scabbards and fall down on them.

Bearing in mind that the Confederate Commander-in-Chief and several of his general officers were killed and wounded on this field and that only one of our generals--W. H. L. Wallace--was seriously injured, it is quite natural for us to conclude that if our generals did shamefully fail to properly care for their men, they were never at any time unmindful of their own personal safety during the terrible conflict at Shiloh.

It was left for such heroes as the elderly Major Morris Brayman to fearlessly race from point to point--where the battle was raging the hottest--and inspire our troops with courage and a determination to strongly contest every position attacked. The grandest monument in the national cemetery on this field should be erected in memory of his gallantry. Holes in the ground would appropriately commemorate the services of Grant, McClernand and Wallace.

General Grant was not a man who did much talking for he was not overburdened with knowledge of any sort. Many of his subordinates knew as much of military affairs as he did. He was possibly sensible of this fact and was cautious about letting his mouth betray his weakness. Much is made of his curt sayings--many thinking them wise-even profound. At Donelson he said to McClernand and Wallace,

"Gentlemen, the lost ground must be re-taken," and rode off without another word.

Here is about what he might have said if he had had the sense of a corporal and the sand of a duty sergeant:

"Lew, hustle your division to the front and head off those Johnnies on the right. When you sight them give them a couple of shells from one of your batteries in quick succession, and I will have Smith crowd them and keep them busy on the left, and then get right over there and see what you are doing. Get a move on now-you ought to have been there an hour ago. Mack-get your men together and hold them in reserve about a half mile back."

But, according to Wallace all Grant said was, "Gentlemen, the lost ground must be re-taken," and then he rode off and left these two division commanders sitting there on their old plugs with their mouths open, gaping at each other and wondering what to do next.

The next morning, replying to a note from Buckner suggesting the appointment of a commission to arrange terms to surrender, Grant swelled up with a determination to be the whole thing himself and sent back his bombastic demand for an unconditional surrender.

Had Buckner called this bluff by telling Grant that he did not fancy his terms, and that he should feel free to move on his works at any time that suited his convenience. And if Buckner's troops had then fought us from behind rifle pits, with half the spirit they had fought us outside of them, it would have been many a long day, and the cost of many hundreds of lives before we saw the inside of Fort Donelson.

At Shiloh, on Sunday, Grant visited General Benjamin M. Prentiss and thought he should say something and so told him, "Hold your position at all hazards." He should have cautioned him to keep in line with the division on his right and to look carefully to his flanks- though that would probably have been superfluous for Prentiss was no one's fool-yet he did obey Grant's order literally, which resulted in the capture of himself and 2200 of his men.

Speaking of this on page 340, Vol. 1, of his *Memoirs*, Grant says,

"In one of the backward moves on the 6th, the division commanded by General Prentiss did not fall back with the others. This left his flanks exposed and enabled the enemy to capture him with about 2200 of his officers and men." He does not add that it was the result of a fool order that he had given General Prentiss.

"Hold your ground at all hazards" was an easy thing to say, sounded very brave to him, and was therefore a favorite expression of his.

When Grant reached Louisville on his way to take command of the Army of the Cumberland he telegraphed the identical thing to Gen. George H. Thomas, instead of saying that he would be there with help in a few days and to act accordingly. Gen. Thomas would have been the last man to vacate any desirable position, and was the best judge of the moment that it might become utterly untenable. I do not hesitate to say that there are no circumstances in war to justify such an order. Every commander in the absence of his superior is bound to use his own best judgment.

Lew Wallace with a division of 5,000 men was only six miles below us on the same side of the river, and he spent the whole day of the 6th not getting to us. What was he doing? Well, one of Grant's messengers said that Wallace refused his orders because they were not in writing. But Lew says that was a lie. When this officer got back and reported, Grant was too nervous to write an order and so he sent two staff officers hoping they could prevail on Wallace to come up river. When they got to Crump's Landing they learned that he had left on another road that would bring him out on the right of our line, now held by Sherman. So they raced out on this road six miles and found him with his division by the roadside resting themselves. They had hoofed it six miles without stopping, and you know they must have been mighty tired. They could not have been far from Snake Creek Bridge, which would let them onto the battlefield at a point near Sherman's right flank. But a straggler came to them and said that Sherman had been forced back and that they would reach the battlefield behind the enemy's line.

That would have been grand news to a spirited commander, for here was an opportunity to get a nice bunch of Johnnies in a pocket between himself and Sherman, and to smash Johnston's left flank into smithereens. But Lew couldn't see it in that way. He said that if he went in there he would be captured. He wouldn't even risk the chance of cutting his way through their line of battle with 5,000 massed men and reaching Sherman in safety, notwithstanding that the enemy troops he would encounter would be fully occupied with Sherman at their front. So he turned about, toddled back to Crumps Landing, took the river road, and took his place in line near midnight.

Grant afterwards said that if he had placed the next ranking officer in the division, Morgan L. Smith, in command, the division would have been on line of battle by 10 o'clock A.M., and this is the brightest and most truthful remark I ever heard out of him.

It was a serious mistake by Wallace and very unfortunate for the nation that he had military ambition. He should have confined himself to a literary career. Just think of this man in his dotage offering his services to the government for the Spanish-American War, "In a position consistent with my former rank."

Great Scott! wouldn't he have made a lovely commander for such men as Colonel Theodore Roosevelt and his Rough Riders? If there had been no better men than Lew Wallace at the foot of San Juan Hill, the Spaniards would be in possession of the knob today.

Grant delivered himself of another profound expression that was much quoted at the time, when he said, "Let us have peace." And it reminds me that when my boy Frank was six or seven years old he was regularly attending the district school but didn't appear to be learning anything. I had a talk with the teacher about him and she said he was a good boy and appeared bright enough but somehow couldn't retain anything that she had taught him. She suggested that I give him a good talking to and so the next morning at breakfast I said,

"Frank, how are you getting along in school?"

"First rate: I don't have any trouble with anybody."

"I mean with your lessons: Do you study arithmetic?"

"Oh yes, that's easy."

"Good! now how many times are three times two?"

"Seven, I guess, or else it's nine. I forget which."

"Holy smoke! I don't believe you can count the pancakes that are on your plate."

"Gee! what's the use? There won't be any there to count in a minute. Let's eat our breakfast."

Farmer David Cornwell in 1878, now 39 years of age and fighting primitive conditions on a small, hard-scrabble farm in Salem Township, Allegan County, southwestern Michigan. Living now with first wife Frances and three children.

CHAPTER XXV

The next morning, April 8, 1862, a small party of us gathered up the blankets of the boys who had been killed and started out to bury them. We first found the body of Captain Harvey and at the sight of him I sat down and cried like a school girl. He had shown me many acts of kindness, and had he lived I think we would have been friends again.

We rolled him carefully and snugly in his blankets and buried him where he fell, marked the spot with a piece of board inscribed with a pencil. We also found Sergeant Hugh Cassidy, Corporal Charles Hayden, Calvin Smith and Charles Herbert. If there were others I cannot recall them. We gave them the same care we did the Captain, and got back to camp about noon.

After dinner I went down to the Landing and found two of our company wounded on a hospital boat. I at once returned to camp for their effects and got a few of the boys to go back with me to help cheer them up and bid them goodbye. I took the addresses of several of their friends, and promised to write them. So that is what I busied myself at the next day.

I had not had a word with a company officer since the fight until one of them came into the tent one day and said there was a man outside who would like to see me. I stepped out and found Jim Evans, of the firm of Hayes and Evans, builders, of Bloomington, who had come up the river with a metal casket after the body of Captain Harvey. I had worked much for this firm-liked them-and had their promise of steady employment if I was lucky enough to get back again.

So I relieved Evans of any concern about getting the Captain ready for shipment. He wished to take back a few Rebel relics, but the authorities would not permit it. But prohibition is easily evaded and we proceeded to gather up the curiosities (souvenirs). I started the collection with a huge knife picked up at Donelson. It was evidently made to order by a Texas blacksmith, for his name, town, and state, were stamped on one side of the blade, and on the reverse side was roughly engraved,"A Yankee Nightmare Realized."

We made several trips over the battlefield and secured a grand assortment of rifles, revolvers, pistols, shotguns, swords and knives, and selected out the articles of plunder that appealed to the strongest of Jim's fancies. We rolled them in strips of blankets and filled up all the space between the casket and the outer case.

Evans said he would represent Captain Harvey as three hundred pounder, and he could readily manage to get the truck out of the box at Bloomington without the public knowing anything about it. I had put extra cleats on the case, renailed it doubly strong, and after Jim got home he wrote me that it went through as fine as a fiddle.

General [Henry] Halleck soon came up the river and took command and about the same time the Army of General Pope, which had been so successful about Island No. 10, also arrived and pitched their tents at Hamburg, four miles above Pittsburg Landing. At this time my father was a member of the 3rd Michigan Cavalry, which was a part of this command, and not having seen him for several years I got a mount from the Quartermaster and went over to call on him. The old governor had been left in a Cairo hospital, and was later [August 1862] discharged. I took dinner with the boys of his company and they told me he could not stand the life and should not have enlisted. He was about 57 years old when he enlisted, and old for his age. It was surprising that he managed to slip past the mustering officer in Allegan, Michigan, where he joined the 3rd Mich. Cavalry in August 1861.

Soon after Shiloh I heard that the Army was detailing a few men from the infantry to serve in McAllister's Battery, which was still in our (McClernand's) division. Unlike cavalry and infantry, an artillery battery must have the minimum assigned number of men or lay one or more of their guns aside, and when they fell below that number the practice was to borrow men from the infantry. I decided to obtain a detail and if pleased with the artillery service to secure a permanent transfer later.

I strolled over to their camp, talked with a number of the boys, then called on Lieut. Wood, who was in command and had a chat with him.

He seemed pleased to have me join him but remarked that he could not give me the position of sergeant in the battery. I said I had no such expectation nor even desire; that without doubt I would be reduced to the ranks soon after I left Company K, 8th Illinois Infantry Volunteers.

So the lieutenant took down my name and corps, promised to ask for my detail, and I bid him good day. Soon after this, Col. Rhodes sent for me and we had a long talk. He was not present at the battle. All of the recommendations had been sent in before he returned, and he couldn't criticize the action taken. Being assured that I could no longer serve with the old company, he said he would approve the detail and let me go. I received a copy of the order the following day, picked up my traps [gear], reported to Lieut. Wood, was assigned to one of the gun squads, and given the position of No. 3 on the gun.

This Army of 120,000 men lay here a month undergoing a reorganization unsatisfactory to the troops and highly injurious to the command. It was satisfying only to the whims of General Halleck. Then it took another month moving to Corinth, when it should and could have covered the distance in two days and surrounded that place on the third. And the whole thing could and should have been done six weeks earlier. The disaster brought upon us by Grant's stupidity and over-confidence had made Halleck over-cautious to the extent that when he did advance he made a mile a day and fortified every night.

Grant was hung up to dry and we were mighty glad of it and hoped Halleck would keep well so that Grant would not get back into the command again. We could plainly feel the absurdity of our Army hitching along the way they were doing and covering the country with fortifications, but we preferred it to Grant's methods; we had had enough of them and wanted no more.

Grant acknowledges that he had nothing to do, was not consulted about anything, that he was in fact simply ignored by Halleck, and inferentially, by everyone else.

There was a little Regular Army officer [Capt. Philip Sheridan] at Halleck's headquarters who was destined to become the most consummate and irresistible commander on either side during the entire war. He had only contempt for Grant and when an officer introduced him he remarked that he had heard of him and turned and walked out of the tent.

About the time we reached Corinth, Governor Blair of Michigan telegraphed Halleck, asking him to nominate a Regular Army officer to command the 2nd Michigan Cavalry. This resulted in Capt. Philip Sheridan becoming its colonel. He was soon placed in command of a brigade of cavalry and cleaned out everything he went after in the vicinity of Corinth.

A division of troops was ordered to Chattanooga and Sheridan incorporated his brigade into that division, and got ready for the march. General Grant did not want him to go and told him so, but he was a brigadier general now and insisted upon going with Granger's Division, and go he did. Grant had been left in command and Sheridan was determined to get out of his department.

Oglesby and Logan were brigadiers after Donelson, and neither was at the Shiloh fight. They were both back now, the former in charge of a brigade in the left wing and the latter commanding our brigade in McClernand's Division, which was in this advance on Corinth a part of the reserves. So we found the rifle pits all made for us, and all we had to do was to hitch along about a mile a day and play cards.

For the first time as I remember, the game of chuck-a-luck was introduced, and I took much interest in watching the play of others, and at times bucking it myself. The proprietor of the layout, who is called a banker, has a board upon which squares are drawn and numbered from one to six. Upon these numbers we would lay our money. Then the banker would throw three dice, pay off the winners and rake in the balance.

As played by the boys this was evidently a fair sort of a game, for the bankers frequently went broke. If a dollar was placed on each number and doubles or triples were not thrown, the winnings would just pay the losses, but if a pair turned up, the operator would lose three and win four. So possibly the throwing of doubles and triples is to the bank's advantage.

To offset this, the player also had some advantages, and one of these was betting on a number that had not appeared for several throws of the dice, for they said, and with much reason, that if everything was played on the square, in the long run one number would appear about as often as another. Another supposed advantage was in doubling your bet until you won, but this was dangerous play and involved large risk for small prospective gain, which would be only the amount of the first bet unless your number was double or better.

Our games were generally limited by the banker to five dollar bets on one number, which permitted doubling only twice, but I was not long in arriving at the conclusion that if you sat down to an unlimited game, you had better decide a proper limit for yourself and stick to it.

Without giving it much thought one might think that with $500 in his pocket he could drop down at an unlimited layout, and by starting with a five dollar bet beat the bank by the doubling process, but his sixth double would require $320, and there would be but $185 left in his roll. I had a singular example of this many years after at a West Michigan Fair in Grand Rapids while watching the revolutions of a wheel of fortune. The only figures on the wheel were the first six numerals, one of which was bound to win and the others certain to lose. Here they paid the winner only double, which gave the bank a decided advantage, your chance of winning double your bet being only one in six.

Recalling my favorite chuck-a-luck number I watched the five until it had slept eight or ten turns and I put a dollar on that number three times in succession and lost. It lay dormant for two more turns of the wheel. Then I dropped a five and it won.

There was a large horse-shoe shaped counter full of these betting layouts with an attendant at each, and the fellow where I was playing might have been new at the business and slightly confused for he shoved out to me twenty dollars instead of ten. He discovered his error after I had innocently raked it in and tried to recall it, but I was so "deaf" that he could not make me hear without talking loud enough for the proprietor to hear him, and so let it pass.

At that time I had more sense than money and decided to drop out. I went around to another layout and watched the play of others, and on the margin of a sheet of advertising music that had been handed to me I began marking down the winning numbers as they were called off by the man at the wheel. Running them over after several whirls I noticed that my lucky number, five, was not on the margin of my sheet and called the attention of a young Irishman standing by to this fact. He at once began betting on that number five at a good clip and seven whirls of the wheel finished him-no winnings at all.

John Braggington, a sporty merchant of Hopkins Station (Allegan County), was watching the play and took it up where the unlucky Irishman left off. Every time the wheel spun around one of his fives disappeared into the bankers till. This continued for twenty successive twirls. Then John said it had become monotonous and quit.

We three stood rooted and kept our eyes on that wheel of misfortune, wondering if it would ever again stop on that ill-fated number. It did not for a dozen more whirls and then it came four times in succession, missed once, came twice more and seemingly quite frequently thereafter, proving that in the long run one number will win as often as another.

At chuck-a-luck we will suppose that twenty doubles would be the limit and you would not require a very large roll-say only about 5 million. But if your number came single you would gain only the amount of your original bet--say five dollars. It would not be worth the bother. You could make it easier raising cucumbers for a pickle factory.

One morning near Corinth I saw a middle-aged Darkey crossing our campground with a violin case under his arm. I called him to me and asked if there was a fiddle in that box.

"Yessah, un a mighty goodun, suah."

"Let's have a look at it."

He handed it over to me and I opened it. It contained a fair looking shell with strings and a good snakewood bow well filled with dirty hair. I looked it over for openings and found it as tight as a president of a state bank. I owned a violin and had expressed it north to a friend before we left Bird's Point for fear of losing it on a campaign, and I was now itching to get possession of another. Here was my opportunity.

With the edge of my pocket knife I scraped some of the dirt and resin from the hairs of the bow, wiped the strings and shell with my handkerchief, and proceeded to put it in tune. When the bow set the strings vibrating the notes sounded very sweet to me, as will be readily understood by any amateur musician who has had the misfortune to be separated from his instrument for three long months.

I ran the scales up and down, and crosswise on various keys, until by accident I ran bump into "Annie Laurie." I did not offer an apology but simply took her arm and accompanied her to the end of the lane. She never before looked so beautiful, nor did her voice sound so sweet.

In my mind, I had, to start with, set aside five dollars to buy this fiddle, but now without any opposition I had raised my own bid two and a half, and did not feel quite sure but that I would feel compelled to raise myself again before the negotiation was completed.

The Coon asked for something lively and I sawed off "Fisherman's Hornpipe," which brought forth a broad grin on his dark mug, and a few steps from his bare feet.

Again I mentally raised my bid two and half, and it now stood at ten dollars. And I was determined to have that fiddle, but felt I could not spare more than a ten-spot, even for such an indispensable addition to the Battery's equipment. I felt this Darkey was a shrewd chap, and very well knew that I wanted this fiddle badly. What if he should hold me up for twenty-five? I couldn't spare that much for the sufficient reason that I didn't have it. We were not robbers and I could not take it from him forcibly before all the boys in broad daylight; neither did I fancy the notion of luring him off into the swamp and killing him.

I began to see clearly that I had made a fool of myself by putting in some of my best licks in his hearing, as he would not credit it so much to my skill as he would to the virtues of the instrument itself. I must change my tactics. So I assumed an indifferent air and commenced depreciating the violin by comparing it with the one I had sent north, which was made in Germany, while this was only a cheap affair manufactured in New Jersey.

"Wy wats de mattah wid it boss, isn't dat fiddle all right?"

"Well, you see, the bass bar don't line up with the tail piece and the sound post is too large for the inspirator, while the finger board and keys are stained basswood when they should be made of the best ebony. It is pretty hard work to get any music out of an old shell like this."

"Den you's mighty good at ha'd job boss, cos yu mad't soun fust rate. Say, gid us nuder one of den jig tunes, will yer?"

This time I rasped the bow over the strings and played out of tune most shamefully, and had to shake my head at the boys who were standing about to keep them from snickering aloud.

"Say boss, yer did' play's well' yur did afores, yeh is'nt git'n tiad ob de fid'l redy is yer?"

"Well, you see, this is a very cheap fiddle and you can never play a tune twice exactly alike on it." This bit of truth slipped accidentally but as it was not noticed I didn't stop to recall it.

"If you will sell it cheap I will buy it. What do you want for the old thing anyway?"

"Mistah Boss, I wants fo' bits for dat fiddle an I cudn't sel't any che'pr."

"I don't think you could," I replied, but the irony was lost on him. I shoved a dollar greenback into this paw, and he rolled up his eyes and said,

"Boss, I hasn't got a bit ah change; can't yah made it out yerself sumow?"

"Oh, keep the dollar," I generously replied, "There is nothing mean or small about me."

I thought it quite likely that I might have to buy this fiddle again from its rightful owner, but such a party never turned up. I have changed violins several times since, but the snakewood bow I have yet, about forty-five years later [1907].

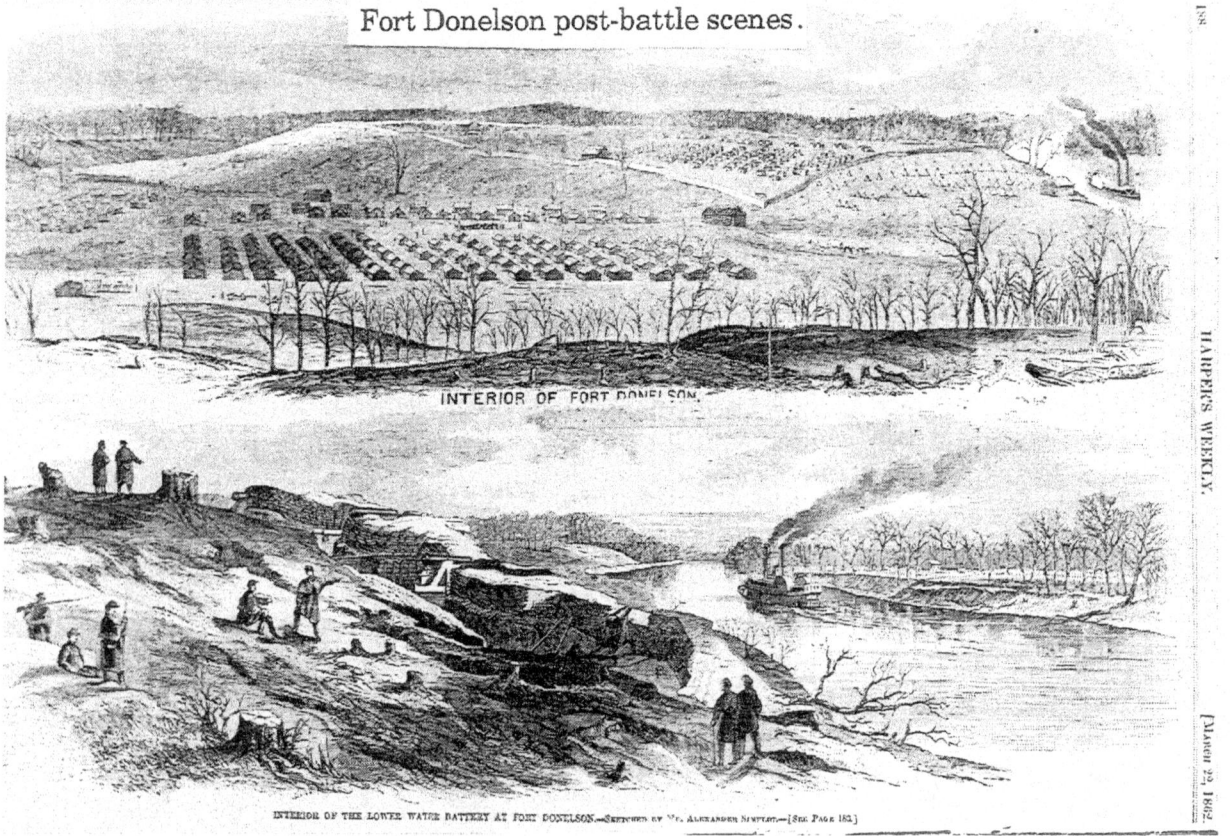

Fort Donelson post-battle scenes.

144

CHAPTER XXVI

Upon arriving at Corinth we found that the enemy had taken leg bail [departed], and General Halleck, having an ear open for a call from Washington to take the position of Commander-in-chief, he felt no officer under him was capable of handling the large army he had gathered about him. He sent General Buell with his Corps back to his old stamping ground around Chattanooga and put the Army of the Tennessee in summer quarter at Corinth and at points along the Mississippi Central Railroad between Grand Junction, Tennessee, and Columbus, Mississippi.

Since Halleck's arrival at Pittsburg Landing, Grant had been on the supernumerary list, and Hallack was at a loss to know what to do with him. He was loathe to send him home for he did not amount to anything in civil life, and possibly thought if he kept him around awhile he might be able to make some kind of use of him. Grant was an amiable man with whom you could not get into a quarrel, and he appeared to wish to do the right thing. He lacked the astuteness to see beyond his nose anything other than the ashes of his cigar. And yet he had the assurance of Sancho Panza [Don Quixote], whose ambition was to govern an island, saying that if the King would give him such an appointment he would make shift to govern it somehow. Surprised and overwhelmed as Grant was at Shiloh, he had failed to exhibit on that disastrous field one mark of genius, generalship, or personal courage, and we boys hoped we had seen the last of him.

Our division was sent to Jackson, Tennessee, and reached there about the first of June. The handsome and accomplished McPherson, now a brigadier, was in command, and Logan was still in our brigade. Our Battery took possession of a pleasant grove on the outskirts of the city, not far from the Hatchie River.

My old friend, Lt. Sam Caldwell of Co. E 8th Ill. joined Oglesby as aide-de-camp about this time. A year later he was promoted captain of his company, but did not take command of it until a short time before the regiment was mustered out in 1866.

We had not been in Jackson long when our orderly, Thomas Henry, duty sergeant Dave Ocher, Oscar Lamson the saddler, a corporal and a private or two, saddled their nags and started out on a lark. After riding about eight miles, they captured a small "burg" without opposition and ransacked an Odd Fellows Hall. When they returned to camp they and horses were covered with Odd Fellows regalia and each animal had a streamer attached to its tail. Each rider carried in his hand a fantastic implement resembling a spear, a shepherds' crook-or something of that sort-harmless tin playthings used in the grave and sublime ceremonies of that mysterious order. They said they turned the goat loose in the street and let him go, for they could pick up a better one near Jackson (Tennessee).

One of this gang, Charles Herbert, intended to secure the largest goat that could be found in the vicinity, and organize an Odd Fellows Lodge in the Battery and have fun initiating new members. There were enough Darkey cooks and teamsters about there to furnish initiates for a month, and it would have been howling fun to witness the blindfolded Blacks bedecked in rich regalia taking their degrees on a bucking billy goat.

But our officers had to butt in and spoil it all, for the next morning General Logan and our Chief Artillery Major Charles J. Stolbrand came to our camp and had all of this paraphernalia gathered up and taken away. After dinner these officers, escorted by a company of cavalry, rode out to this little "burg" and returned the plunder. On the following day the non-commissioned officers connected with the lark were reduced to the ranks. Then Lieutenant Wood sent for me and said if I would get a transfer [from the 8th Ill.] he would appoint me Orderly Sergeant of the Battery. I thanked him, and said I would see what I could do.

I at once interviewed the reduced boys and all others that I thought would have any interest in the case, and without an exception they told me to go for it. Then I drew up an application, and after securing the signature of First Lieut. George J. Wood, took it over to Co. K, having no doubt that Capt. Dennison would be very glad to get rid of me. But he stubbornly refused to sign it even after I told him where it would land me in the Battery.

We had some hot words and he threatened me with arrest. Then I told him that the commissioned officers of Company I were both slinks [deserters] and I would never accept an order from either one of them. He left his tent, presumably after guards to take charge of me, and I walked over to Regimental Headquarters (8th). Colonel Rhodes was highly pleased with my prospects and assured me that he would have Dennison's name on the paper in less than thirty minutes and would take it up to Brigade Headquarters himself. So I left the case with him and returned to the Battery.

Three days later George Cunningham was made Orderly of the Battery. He was a fine young fellow of about my own age, in every respect competent for the position. I wondered why he was not preferred to me in the first place. I called on Lieut. Wood and he passed over to me the returned application for transfer. There was Dennison's approval as Col. Rhodes had promised, also Gen. Logan's, but Gen. McPherson had not stamped it with his approval. I called on Col. Rhodes again and he said he had taken the paper to McPherson himself and was told that since he took command of the Division there had been a hundred applications for transfers, and he felt compelled to veto them all.

So I remained a Sergeant of Co. K and drew a sergeant's pay while doing a private's duty. I felt confident that I would not be reduced to the ranks while Col. Rhodes remained in command of the 8th Illinois Volunteers.

It was about this time our mess got a permanent cook. He was a powerful Darkey-six and one-half feet high-with a hand that measured five and one-half inches across the palm. He had never worn shoes on account of the size of his foot. Had there been a Holland-type[1] settlement about we might have got a pair of cotton-wood clogs made to order, but with a tariff on hides he was doomed to go barefoot. When there was snow on the ground he would tie his feet up in pieces of old blankets and gunny sacks.

---

[1]Allegan County, Michigan contained many settlers from Holland in the latter half of the 19th Century. It still does. Their first settlements were founded in the late 1840's.

As I was taking a stroll down to the river, I met him coming into camp and we sat down by the roadside and talked an hour or more. He had come from the Yazoo district in Mississippi where he had trouble with an overseer about a wench he was fond of and he was not sure but what he had killed him. After hearing his story I hoped he had.

He said the overseer attacked him with the butt end of his cowhide whip, which he caught in his left hand, and then he gave the overseer a "mighty blow on his head wid my left hand, and he drop like a stone. I guess he not fool 'roun Emline eny moah." Then this huge Black picked up an axe and started for the swamp. When he saw an ironwood tree of the right proportion he cut a club, trimmed it out to his taste, and then threw his axe in a water hole. Late in the day he heard hounds on his trail. When they overtook him he was standing on a large downed cottonwood tree.

"I tell yer Mistah Sojah, dem dogs no bisnes foler me up dat way an pitch inter me savage like wen I neber did um eny arm, so I jest killed ebry one ob dem wid dat club."

I quizzed him about the size of the "club" he used, and remarked that the proper name for such a stick would be "handspike." He gave his name as Jack Jackson, and he proved as fearless as Old Hickory [General Andrew Jackson] himself in the months ahead.

Oscar Lamson, the Battery harness-maker, was a wiry little fellow, and the jayhawker-in-chief ["scrounger" in 20th century army slang] of our mess. During one of his daily rambles he had observed a few swarms of bees just inside the roadway fence in front of a suburban dwelling that sat back a hundred feet or more. With help, he proposed to bring one of the hives in to camp. Pat Kalga offered his services and they asked Jack Jackson to come also.

"Phawt th divil we want of the nager," exclaimed Kalga, "They'r no good on the jayhawk."

"To help lug it in," answered Lamson, and the three started off while Grim, Potter, Rhodes and myself took seats about a table for a game of draw.

It was not long before Oscar and Pat came in and reported that they had no sooner entered the gate than the front door of the house was flung open and they were fired on. And what got them was how the old man knew they were there.

"Did Jack come in with you?" I asked, for I had not heard him about.

"Gad! I haven't seen him," said Lamson, "maybe he got plugged."

"Plugged the nager got, is that what yer saying?" broke in Pat, "Its meself that mighy nigh got kilt; the ball didn't cum foot of me head."

"I presume it didn't," dryly remarked Clark Grim, "but where do you think Jack is, anyhow?"

"Ees 'af way to Bolivar by the time it is, for I hered 'im going down the road like the divil was after 'im." And then he turned to Oscar and exclaimed,

"I towled yer nagers was no good on the jayhawk and to lave him here in camp, and now we've lost our cook fur you will niver see that big nager anymore." And then he added, "Hitch yerself along there, mister Rhodes, and you Grim, dale me a hand." And soon after he exclaimed, "An Irishman for luck; three trays and I'll take the pot." He got the next rake-off also, and was in high spirits, when Jack's voice was heard outside the tent.

"Won't some you gemen coms an take dis bee ive off my ed!" Potter and Lamson, being next to the tent flap quickly stepped out. Jim Rhodes snorted like a four-year-old steer. Then Grim innocently asked Kalga where he said Jack was hoofing it to the last he heard of him: Was it Bolivar or Ballingarry?

Pat's eyes were riveted on the tent flap, and on his broad face was an indescribable expression as Oscar Lamson came in and resumed his seat at the table.

Kalga was in such evident misery that he won my sympathy, and to save him from further humiliation I called out,

"Rhodes, ante and shove the buck; Kalga deal the cards."

"Deal thim yerself," replied Pat, "I'm out of the game with the grinning lot of yer; theres' Bother the young spalpeen out there rowling on the sod an killing hisself wid lafter at these circumstances. Be gorry it ul be a sorry day for the likes of you that goes blathing this about th bathery and thrying to ruin me charackter."

CHAPTER XXVII

There were several details [soldiers temporarily assigned to a unit other than their own] besides myself serving with the Battery at this time. James Rhodes, also of Company K, was one of them. He was a large fellow who on account of his size and strength was inclined to be somewhat domineering. Early in the service I had nicknamed him "Bully," and it stuck to him so that he soon answered to it and was known as "Bully Rhodes," except of course on the company records. He was a "stayer" in battle; vain, cunning, unscrupulous, unpopular. He did not like me in either the old company or in this because I had from the first ignored his size.

Clark Grim was a Battery boy from Texas, Illinois, a model soldier full of grit and good humor. George Potter was a clean-cut youth with a smooth face and the complexion of a young woman. He was from Jaris, Indiana, handsome, witty, of good height, correct proportion and a general favorite of the ladies. I considered myself in great luck in getting him for a bunk mate, for he was scrupulously clean, healthy and good natured. These three, with Oscar Lamson the saddler, Pat Kalga and myself, comprised "Our Mess," while camped near Jackson, Tennessee.

Charles F. Herbert was transferred to the Battery from an Illinois Infantry Regiment about the time I joined it at Shiloh. He was of good proportion and form, had a fair education, much natural talent, and was chuck full of the devil throughout his whole six feet of length. Before he came to the Battery he was on special duty at Regimental Headquarters as a sort of aide-de-camp to the Colonel, whose favorite staff officer was a woman who passed as his wife. She was something less than thirty, a good looker, had fetching ways and was especially flirtatious. The natural result was a popular place to call, for an Army officer who is debarred from female society for a month or more will walk two miles to look at a pretty woman.

The colonel could not always remain near his quarters for he had duties to perform. Charles Herbert's special duty was to look after the madame during his absence.

And it happened that the Colonel's civil wife left in Illinois wrote him that if he could not obtain leave to come home and see her she would join him at Pittsburg Landing. So he hastily got permission and started down the Tennessee River, leaving his military wife in charge of his trusted aide Charles Herbert.

After an absence of two weeks the Colonel returned to camp. He found that Charles had faithfully carried out his orders to give the madame every proper attention and supply her with every reasonable want, but learned from some source that he had exceeded his instructions and furnished her with luxuries that the colonel did not wish the lady to enjoy during his absence. So a coldness sprang up between them which resulted in Charlie landing in McAllister's Battery on both feet, right side up with care. Herbert called himself "Charles de Moore, the Robber of the Hatchie," but he would shine as a Robber Chief only in comic opera, for he was really a tender hearted fellow and full of fun. He seldom cracked a smile, never at his own drollery.

It was here at Jackson he held his mock dress parades that drew crowds to witness them. He would get as many of the Battery boys as he could persuade to fall into line, a few out of other commands, then all the Darkeys, cooks and teamsters of the Brigade and have them arm themselves with sabers, muskets, brooms and trail handspikes.

We would generally select a very decent looking chap to act as the colonel, but upon one occasion he put up our gigantic cook, Jack Jackson, in soldier's clothes. The bottom of the trousers came down about half way between his knees and ankles and the lower edge of his jacket didn't reach the waistband of his breeches by a foot. The sleeves of the jacket stopped somewhere between his elbows and wrists, and on the shoulders were a couple of old sardine boxes to represent epaulets. Rigged out with sash and saber, Charles would perform the duties of Adjutant in a masterly manner. When he sang out "Troop, Beat Off," a couple or more coons would come pacing down the line blowing willow whistles, followed by a half dozen others pounding on old mess-pans and camp kettles. The exercises in the manual of arms were too ridiculous for description.

At "Attention to Order," Herbert would produce a bunch of manuscript and entertain the crowd with general, special and court martial orders, correct in form but devilishly humorous in content and composition.

We had begun to anticipate these harmless entertainments much as a country boy does the coming of a circus, and the grotesque exhibition was drawing larger crowds at each succeeding dress parade. Then some of the higher officers had to butt in and knock it out. They were always interfering with our wholesome amusements.

When I joined the Battery it was officered by First Lieut. George J. Wood and Second Lieut. Edgar H. Cooper. I never saw Captain McAllister [first Battery commander] for he resigned in May. I do not know if he was at Shiloh or not. It must have been held-and I think with reason-that neither of our lieutenants was competent to command the Battery. Captain Henry H. Rogers, was given command and proved himself a brave, earnest and competent officer.

About the 28th of July, [1862] we left our pleasant camp, and followed the Hatchie River road down to Bolivar-about a day's march. General John P. Post was in command. He located us in a large open field, about as near the river as we were at Jackson, with no scattered trees or timber nearby. Here we constructed a sort of fort for our guns with cotton bales for protection.

Near our camp was a hundred-acre field of white sweet corn just coming into roasting ears. It supplied our wants until it became too hard for table use. The balance was fed to our horses and mules, fodder and all.

Memphis, about sixty miles west of us, had been ours (Union) since June, but there had been much raiding on all sides of us and many a morning we stood at our guns at the approach of daylight in anticipation of an attack. Our cavalry was kept busy, and it was not far from Bolivar where Lieut. Col. Harvey Hogg of Bloomington went down, as reported to me by one of his men.--

"We met a detachment of Rebel Cavalry, each side drew in line with an open field between us. One of our sergeants sang out, `Now that we are ready, let's run as we always do.' This fired Colonel Hogg, who immediately ordered a charge and took the lead."

Payday came in October when I raked in a sergeant's pay as usual. That evening I entered Captain Roger's tent and protested against being carried on the detached roll now that I had been transferred to the Battery. This was agreeable news to the Captain for more men was the Battery's greatest need. Lieut. Wood, who knew of the failure of my application made while at Jackson, had resigned and gone home, and Lieut. Cooper had heard a mention of the incident and that was about all. He was called in and said he had heard of it at the time and believed I was correct in the matter. Search was made through the company files for a copy of the order and of course none was found, or there was never any such order made. But I had in my knapsack a comment that said that I was not transferred, but of this I made no mention.

The conclusion arrived at by Captain Rogers was that the order had been carried away by Lieut. Wood with other company papers that he had no personal right to. He never for one moment suspected that I was lying my way into his Battery.

At my suggestion he wrote the captain of my old Company K that if he had not already done so, to drop my name from his company rolls, as I had been duly transferred to his Battery. And it was done accordingly.

This was not the only lie I told while in the army, but I think it the best one, for it benefitted the service as well as myself. A soldier should not be required to serve under an officer for whom he has no respect, and certainly an officer should consent to the transfer of somebody whose good will he cannot retain.

CHAPTER XXVIII

Late in 1862 General Grant felt it about time to get on and do something with his Army, so brought the numerous detachments together at Grand Junction and LaGrange, Tennessee, and prepared for an advance on Vicksburg, via the Mississippi Central Railroad. This started about November 1, 1862. Over the various routes traversed about everything that would burn was torched off, including the fences.

It was said that a squadron of Kansas Cavalry that led our division was responsible for the stifling smoke on our route, but be that as it may, we were innocent of any incendiarism, for everything combustible had been ignited before we got to it.

This led to the issuance by Gen. Grant of General Orders No. 40, which said that "The Commanding General is astounded at the vandalism displayed by his forces on their recent march. etc.etc.etc.," and then went on talking about it until the writer ran out of paper. It was directed that this long, dull and stupid composition should be read to each command at nineteen (more or less) successive roll-calls. No exception was made for such command as our own who had patiently suffered from the smoke, without being in any way responsible for it.

We listened to the first reading with smiling equanimity, but scowled on the last paragraph and swore we wouldn't stand for it. Orderly George Cunningham threw us a wink and said "Never mind boys, I'll fix it all right."

At the following roll-call this absurd order, which required nine minutes to read, was over in a few seconds and a new record was made at each succeeding roll-call. George had converted this bore of an order into genuine entertainment. At the 19th, or last infliction, he shoved his hands in his trouser pockets and reeled it off from memory in seventeen and one-half seconds by a stop watch.

A mania for gambling had hit the boys, and we kept the pasteboards warm. We had come to the conclusion that square games, honestly played, were impracticable; that the party who depended upon his nerve and luck was generally the loser. A couple of card-sharps were barred from our games and played outside the Battery, often with the officers. A few of our boys were frequently caught cheating, conspicuously among them Bully Rhodes. So it became a rule with us that a hand got unfairly was a good hand, if the jugglery was not detected on the spot and proven.

Some obtained marked-back cards, while others marked the backs of the common kind of cards. Some would be stolen from the deck-one or two at a time-until there would not be enough in the pack to deal around. Then the game would be held up until they all disgorged, when they would start in with a full deck again, and resume their stealing. Many of them carried cold decks in their pocket or boot top ready for an opportunity to use them. This sort of play eliminated the too frequent accusation of cheating, for there was no satisfaction in accusing a fellow of skulduggery who would promptly acknowledge it and give you the laugh. So it resulted in hilarious good humor and much fun.

Many of the boys were too sharp for me and I soon found that I could not play even. Still it was not practical to keep out of the games entirely. Bully Rhodes was constantly laying for me and was five dollars to the good, when I got a clip at him one evening with a cold deck and got four of it back. He swore he saw me deal the hand from the bottom of the deck, when I drew from my boot-top the cards we had been playing with, and he had to subside.

I went over to the "Old Eighth" and took a walk with Sergeant Marion of Co. K. He was quite an expert and explained to me many of the simplest gambling tricks that he thought I might use in the Battery. Only one of them appealed to me and I went to work at it as soon as I returned to the Battery.

Lamson the saddler had taught me a little of harness repairing so that he could leave his business with me when he wished to take a scoot, and so I had the run of the Battery wagon.

While in the Army I did many mechanical jobs for others as well as myself. Out of a tin can I made two patterns. One had parallel sides, about one sixteenth of an inch narrower than a playing card: the other was a shade wider at the center and as much narrower at each end, giving it an unnoticeable oval form. I then put a true and smooth surface on a piece of hard wood and fastened an abutting strip on one edge. When any of the boys came around I would be engaged on a checker board, and so this job occupied nearly one day of my valuable time.

The next day being pleasant, I fished out of an obscure corner of the large implement box the stripping-block and put it in the breast of my jacket and dropped a shoe knife and whetstone in a pocket. Passing the sutler's tent I left four bits for two packs of cards, and then strolled out into a little grove nearby. I continued through this grove and out into a large field where I found a position that was not visible from the camp, and where no one could approach me without being seen.

Then I sat down on the ground, put a razor edge on the point of the shoe knife and got to work. I extracted three Jacks from a pack of cards and cut the remainder to the width of the straight edged pattern, one at a time. The three Jacks I made correspond to the oval edged tin. Then I shuffled them and drew out the three Jacks the first pop. I was delighted and I sat there and played for two hours against an imaginary gambler and beat him most shamefully. According to my reckoning I was at least five hundred dollars ahead when it occurred to me I was getting hungry and must soon return to camp.

So I put a new edge on the knife, cut the other pack on the same plan, placed them back in their wrapper as I had found them, and got back to camp just in time for noon roll-call.

There was a middle-aged man serving in the Battery whose name I cannot recall, who said he was raised in a country tavern in New York. He was a constant, successful card player. When his roll of the ready green became cumbersome, he would send a few hundred home by express. His favorite game was Old Sledge. He was a very companionable fellow and induced me to sit in with him once for small stake, and of course I came out the loser.

On account of his amiable disposition and his former winnings of about two dollars, and the further fact that he claimed intimate knowledge of card-sharp tricks, I concluded he would make a first-class experimental subject for my strippers, for if I could beat him without having my game detected, I need have little fear of others. So I said to him--

"Seven Up has never been my game: There you are too strong for me. I was brought up to play Euchre, and the rules of that little game I understand. Whenever you get lonesome and want to try my game let me know."

He smiled blandly and said he remembered something about Euchre; believed they played it with bowers or something of that sort; could soon catch on to it he thought, and he was about as lonesome now as he would ever be.

Then I suggested we stroll off in one of the fields and have a good time all by ourselves, to which he readily assented.

I steered him past the sutler's tent where I got a pack of cards, which I dropped into my right-hand coat pocket. When we came to a pleasant place we sat down on the ground and I drew forth a pack from my left-hand coat pocket. The Jack of Clubs was turned on the back, and as they had been handled only in the process of stripping-and this with clean hands-there could not be the slightest suspicion that these cards had ever been out of the wrapper.

We discarded everything lower than seven and agreed on a five-point game at a dollar. When I dealt he often made a point, and possibly two, but when he dealt I would get the three Jacks on top during the cut and they would come to me. If he played the trump turned, I would Euchre him. If he turned it down I could make the trump and a point or two on it. Needless to say, he could not get a game.

After ten or more games had been played I began to regret that the stake we were playing for was so small. Had I at the outset suggested a larger one, he would have readily assented to it, but now when I mentioned it he glumly shook his head. Such is human nature; the stakes are too small when you win and too large when you lose.

I had heard him say that he never jumped a game while he had a dollar, and mentally sizing his roll at two hundred, concluded it would take me about two days to bust him.

So we went on at the old gait until I had won twenty-five straight games, and then he commenced a critical examination of the cards. He failed to find a thing wrong with them, and if he had I was safe for I was playing within the rules of the Battery. If he could have produced a new pack of cards there would have been an immediate change, and he no doubt would have recovered his twenty-five. But he could not see through it and he got up and commenced stretching himself.

After waiting a reasonable length of time I remarked,

"Well, sit down and let us go on with the game; I have no intention of jumping it because I have a streak of luck. You told me you were a stayer, and I intend to stay with you like a man to the finish."

But he would not sit down again. He said that this was the most peculiar game he had ever been engaged in; that it was too onesided to be at all interesting; that when a fellow couldn't come within three points of getting a game out of twenty-five, the thing got monotonous. He could see clearly enough how I might enjoy it, and would be glad to stay in 'til he got finished, but was quite sure he had enough of it already.

I suggested that it probably came from his trying to play a game that he did not understand, and he replied--

"Hell, boy! I played Euchre before you was born."

I never got another crack at his roll. From that time on I kept ahead of the game, but not very far. I only cared to play this game on the winners, and for some reason I could never play it twice on the same party. I got a clip at Bully Rhodes with the strippers at straight "draw" to the tune of seven-fifty, and he would never sit in a game with me after. I did not want him to for I was now five ahead, and he was big and disagreeable anyhow. Lige Craig ranked as a professional, and could not get a sitting with us common boys. One day an opportunity offered and I caught him for a ten spot. Then he examined those cards for ten minutes without making a discovery, while I could detect the oval edges of these strippers across the tent.

Not a member of the Battery ever caught on to my little game, though it was believed I had one up my sleeve. I brought those tin can patterns home with me, and many years ago gave them to Bill McGaw of Monterey, Michigan, but I think he never used them.

CHAPTER XXIX

In December 1862 our Army started from Grand Junction and LaGrange, Tennessee, via the Mississippi Central R. R. for Vicksburg.

Our supplies came down this railroad from Columbus, Kentucky, which gave us a long line of communication to keep open.

Our depot of supplies should have been at Memphis, a hundred miles by rail nearer Vicksburg and the railroad from Columbus to Holly Springs, Mississippi of 140 miles should have been abandoned. The large force guarding it then should have joined the main Army.

If General Sherman with the considerable force under his command had been placed in charge of our line of communication instead of being sent down the Mississippi on a tom-fool expedition, we could have gone through to Vicksburg without a hitch. And from the day we reached there we could have received our supplies from transports on the Mississippi. But a large depot of stores was established at Holly Springs, Mississippi, and a small specimen of a colonel placed in command with an inadequate force and no fortifications.

Near the Tallahatchee River we halted one drizzly afternoon with our Battery beside a fine mansion that had been abandoned by its owner. It was stripped of most of its furniture. A few of the heavier articles remained such as the large canopied bedsteads, a book case still containing many volumes, a few common chairs, and a fine piano.

I could play a few airs I had taught myself on an old melodeon when a small boy, among which were "Hail Columbia," "Yankee Doodle," and the "Camptown Races." This last I sang with my own accompaniment and the boys said it was great. Soon the mules standing about got enthused and began to join in the chorus. Then I selected a book from the library and kept quiet.

Soon an order came to go into camp for the night and there was a general hustle for material to keep us out of both mud and rain. The doors and sash were the first parts of the house taken, and then the siding commenced coming off. The bedsteads were utilized and the inside trimwood was promptly ripped off and carried away. The vitals of the large square piano were destroyed with an axe and the case shoved out of a window. The mansion was at last razed to the foundation blocks and the blocks were rolled away to furnish fuel for the camp fires.

George Potter and I quickly secured a bunch of rails from the roadside fence, and on which we sat and watched the boys hustle. Rails were "toted" in from a distance of a half mile or more. As night drew near, George and I started a fire, made a couple of quarts of coffee, fished out hardtack and fried bacon from our haversacks and supped sumptuously. When it was time to turn in we laid several of these fence rails side by side, the ends farthest from the fire on a cross-rail to keep them off the wet ground and give the head a little elevation. We then spread our blankets upon them, placed an extra rail or two on the fire, used our boots for pillows and crawled in between the blankets. I drew my heavy rubber [rain protection--like a poncho] over the whole business, including our heads, and were soon into the land of pleasant dreams. We didn't care how much it rained--none of it could reach us.

Our division, under General McPherson, was about ten miles south of Oxford, Mississippi, with our cavalry still farther south at Coffeeville. Our advance was 60 miles below Holly Springs, when C.S.A. General Earl C. Van Dorn dropped in on them one morning and burned up all our supplies.

General Grant says [in his *Memoirs*] he did not know then as much about subsisting off the country as he did later on, or he would have gone ahead [after losing the supplies]. But his head was exceedingly thick; he was learning fearfully slowly, and at a terrible expense to the Government. Just that bunch of supplies burned at Holly Springs was worth a million and a half, but it was a small part of the loss that this incident cost us. Colonel Robert C. Murphy of the Eighth Wisconsin had misbehaved at the battle of Iuka, Mississippi and Gen. William S. Rosecrans wanted him skinned. Grant didn't like Rosecrans and let Murphy off. Then he placed him in command of the most valuable and important point of his line of communication. What could have been expected? Why, just what happened at Holly Springs.

Grant says that he notified Murphy to look out for General Van Dorn, but this may reasonably be doubted. Up to that time Grant had never looked out for himself, and it is unreasonable to suppose, and impossible to imagine, that he was astute enough to foresee any of the dangers that menaced his subordinates. Murphy should have looked out for himself. He should have thrown rifle-pits around his camp and supplies, and kept his cavalry scouting the countryside for miles about. As a matter of fact, he was as unconcerned about his situation as Grant was about his before the battle of Pittsburg Landing. Murphy was merely dismissed from the service after Holly Springs when he should have been shot. But he did not merit rebuke or criticism from the commander of the Army of the Tennessee at Shiloh.

So we commenced falling back and the evening our Battery reached Oxford, Mississippi we were out of rations and hungry. Four of our mess started out to find something and the other two stayed behind to pitch the tent and start a fire. Jack Jackson had been conscripted to drive our Battery wagon, and we were again doing our own cooking.

Our new location adjoined the residential district of Oxford, atop the bluff in plain view of the railway, though just at this time we could see nothing for it was as dark as our prospect was for a supper. By aid of a lantern we took a southerly course along the bluff, and when near the outskirts of the village left flanked into a street.

We came to a gate and entered. Built up to the sidewalk line was a low, brick house and here we knocked. We got a reply from inside from an evidently old Negro couple who seemed too frightened to open the door. We talked to them through the panels and when they learned that we were simply after something for our supper, they gave us exactly the information we needed.

The Master's house, also of brick, stood fifty yards back. In front of this was a handsome shade tree up which I went, followed by messmate Lamson with the lantern. There were a bunch of chickens roosting there, just as the old Darkey prophesied-and I adroitly sent them one after the other to the lawn, minus their heads. One of them sat far out on a limb with its head where I could not reach its neck with my hand and so I drew it in by the tail. It at once gave forth a despairing squawk which brought an old gentleman to the front door.

"What are you fellows doing here on my premises at this time of night? Go 'way at once or I will get my gun and hurt some of you," said the old southerner.

"Don't get excited, my friend," replied Clark Grim. "These are fine chickens you are raising; the Dominique take the premiums up in old Illinois where I hail from; say, have you got any yams lying around loose anywhere?"

"No, I haven't; are you going to leave here, or will I have to bring out my gun and drive you away?"

"I wouldn't try that, old man, if I were you," said Clark, "for Yankees won't drive like cattle. Say, how was the cotton crop about here last season?"

After I had sent down the last pullet from the tree, Clark whipped out his .44 and examined it by the lantern. At this, the old gentleman hastily stepped inside the door and slammed it.

We all started back to the rear of the house and found the cotton basket where the old Negro said he had left it, then passed through a gate in the garden fence just as the old Darkey told us to do, and soon came to a large pile of sweet potatoes under a shed at the spot the venerable old man had indicated. Packing as many as two men could carry we retraced our steps, picked up the fourteen nice, fat chickens, and returned to camp. We halted a moment at the front gate and told the old Negro couple that if they would open the door we would pass them in a chicken.

"Fur de lub ob heben dont lebe any chicken 'bout he'ah mistah, an dont say nufin, cos yer see yah gets me an my ole woman inter truble," pleaded the old man.

Another bucket of water was wanted and I took up the pail and lantern and started after it, following a path that led down a small ravine to a spring at the foot of the bluff. I saw a Darkey crouching behind a clump of bushes a few feet from the path. It was merest accident that the light and my eye turned on this object at the same instant, and when I held the lantern to his face he tried to turn white but was not altogether successful.

He asked me not to kill him and I promised I wouldn't 'til I had a chance to look him over by daylight and see if he was worth saving. Our cavalry that had gone the farthest south had not reached his plantation by ten miles, and when he heard that we were on the retreat he lit out to overtake us. He had heard tough stories about the Yankees and was a little dubious about us.

He was not at all sure that we were of the same form and features and talked the same language as the southern Whites, but when I spoke to him in a mild and gentle tone of voice in a familiar tongue, and he saw by the reflection of the lantern that I had the usual physical construction with benevolence and nobility plainly stamped on my serene countenance, he took to me at once, picked up the pail and followed me to the spring.

When we got back to the camp he pitched into those chickens and yams, and had a quantity of them cooking in short order. He had a personal interest in that supper for he had had nothing to eat for twenty-four hours and had walked forty miles of railroad ties.

And how we did wade into that midnight supper. It was more than 45 years ago and yet the recollection of it is so vivid that it makes me chicken hungry to recall it. If the market man will be kind to me and mark it down, I will have a fried pullet for my supper tonight to satisfy this craving and commemorate that Oxford, Mississippi supper - so help me God! From that time on "Bragg" was the cook for our mess.

Although we were ready to move out at nine o'clock the next morning, we did not get started until nearly noon. Our Battery was strung out on one of the residential streets, and opposite our gun resided a dashing young woman who did not hesitate to chaff us about making a retreat, and then enter the house and sing the "Bonnie Blue Flag" with piano accompaniment. We gave her a round of applause after each song, and another when she appeared at the door again. We lined up along the sidewalk and by general consent to let Dave Ocher hold up our side of the conversation.

She would fire off another volley of wit and sarcasm to which Dave would, with more or less skill, reply, and then she would return to the piano and sing "Dixie," then back again she would come and give us another chaffing. She was a good looker and sang well and we were just enjoying the entertainment when General Logan came walking down the sidewalk to see what was going on.

We made room for him at the gate and while the young lady was pounding out the "Marseilles," I explained to him the nature of the entertainment.

If this had been Grant or McClernand, they would have moved on as soon as the last notes of the piano had died away but Logan was not that kind of a general. He wanted to see the young lady and was willing to chance an attack of her raillery and sarcasm, surrounded by his boys, as he was wont to receive the attack of the enemy on a battle field. So the next time she appeared in the doorway she was confronted by a swarthy and gallant brigadier general.

"Why, good morning General," said the surprised but unabashed young lady, "I am delighted to see your Yankee Army on the retreat. What keeps you waiting so long; why don't you move on? Are you not afraid our soldiers will catch you before you get out of the city?"

"My dear young lady," answered John A. with a very grave face, "I am sorry to say to you that your soldiers will never again see this beautiful little city of Oxford."

"Why, general, I hear they are only ten miles away and are making all haste to catch you."

"If that is the case we would not move until they came up but, my dear, your information is not reliable. We have just let up after a fifty mile chase of your men, and during all that distance they would not stop and fight at all. But you seem very unconcerned; has not this part of the town been notified yet?"

"Notified of what," said Miss Secesh, exhibiting a slight shade of surprise.

"The torch will be applied to every building in this city at exactly twelve o'clock," gravely answered the general as he drew out his watch, "and, my dear, you have only a half-hour to gather your wardrobe and get to a place of safety."

For an instant the young lady was petrified. She tried but could not speak. Then she turned on her heel, entered the door, and gave it a violent slam. That was the last we saw or heard of her.

General Logan turned to us and grimly remarked,

"Boys, you had better get back to your guns now for the show is over."

CHAPTER XXX

A few days later we arrived at a small burg a short distance west of LaGrange, and many of us took possession of the lower story of an old building that was without floor, but from which the stringers [floor joists] had not been removed. They were small trees hewn on one side, and we cut them in short lengths to use on a fire in the center of the building for the weather was freezing cold and the ground covered with snow.

That afternoon when we halted beside the mansion near the Tallahatchee River I took from the library a full set of Sir Walter Scott in calf binding, and therefore adapted to military purposes. These I conveniently stored in the battery-wagon, and that it not increase the load on the team, I threw out the larger jackscrew that we had been lugging around, which we could have no possible use for. This was more than equivalent in weight if not in value for the books, and I left it on the site of the old mansion. It might have stood there yet if its master had remained at home and invited General McPherson to abide with him while we remained in the vicinity. The destruction of that grand old piano grated on my nerves, for it was not one of those pianola pianos of the present days.

So I put in much time during this bad weather reading Scott. While here an old Negro of the neighborhood called my attention to a stone under one corner of the building we were occupying. This stone was about a foot square. He said our building was built by the Masons when he was a boy. The upper story was their lodge room. The old man said there was money in that corner stone for he had seen it put in with a lot of papers. I also learned from this old Negro that our troops had never molested the room above, which was reached by outside stairs.

Remembering the fate of the non-coms who were connected with that Odd Fellows fracas near Jackson, I did not interest myself with the upper story of this old building, but determined to investigate that corner stone and hoped to get it slick enough to avoid detection.

I selected four boys to assist and about midnight, when every one appeared to be asleep, we carried out one of the stringers for a lever and readily got the stone. The cavity, which was about six inches each way, was filled with ice, so we were compelled to carry it into the building in order to move it near the fire. The papers had rotted, but we got between four and five dollars in American and Spanish silver. We placed the stone back again bottom side up, carried the sleeper back into the building, and then rolled up in our blankets for a nap.

The next day we met in an old stable nearby and divided the plunder, and we believed that closed the incident.

It was here we found a vacant room in a nearby house, and one evening held a stag party. I could play a few cotillions and call them off, too, and all the boys needed for a good time was a few girls.

After we had returned to our quarters one of the men remarked "That last hornpipe you gave us was a good one; where did you learn that?" and I told him,

"I picked it out of a book, but I will tell you how it became a favorite of mine. I was working at the carpenter trade in Chicago in the summer of '58 or '59, and boarding on the north-west side. At the corner of Kinsey and Wells was a wooden hotel building with dining room on the first floor, nearly on a level with the Kinsey street sidewalk. I was passing there one day and saw three gentlemen step into this room and one of them held by the hand a very pretty little girl. One of the party lifted a violin out of a case, perched on top of a cupboard, and played this piece the sweetest I ever heard, while the little miss danced the Highland Fling. The lower sash was raised and I saw and heard it as if standing there in the room. I remember it as the greatest performance I ever witnessed."

"I can tell you who that party was," said one of our boys who was sitting near and listening to the conversation. "I was working at the hotel at that time and remember the incident. The gentleman with the little girl was Mr. McVicker, and the child his daughter, Mary. The violinist was the leader of his orchestra, and the heavy gentleman with the plug hat was a New York manager. All but the latter were boarding with us."

This was the little girl who bloomed into a lovely actress and became the second wife of that prince of actors, Edwin Booth.

First Lieutenant James A. Boreland had returned to the Battery while we were camping at LaGrange. At Donelson he had been a sergeant-a brave one, too, was seriously wounded, and at once promoted for gallantry. He was a quiet, even-tempered officer who had the respect of his superior officers, and the good will of all the boys.

He had occasion one day to chide Bully Rhodes for imposing on one of the small boys, and I knew that Boreland would have an enemy in the Battery from that time on. Had I told him the nature of the fellow, and suggested that he have him relieved from duty in the Battery and sent back to his company in the Eighth (Illinois), which he could readily have done-he would have looked at me with astonishment-possibly with contempt-for he was afraid of no living man. But this is what should have been done.

Soon after, Boreland's boots were taken from his tent during the night, as he lay asleep on his cot. Boreland borrowed a pair from one of Logan's staff officers-who happened to own an extra pair-and we soon after moved up to the outskirts of Memphis, which gave Jim a chance to fit himself into some new boots.

This outrage caused great indignation in the Battery, and the unknown perpetrator was repeatedly denounced in the most violent and insulting terms that the Battery vocabulary afforded. I watched Rhodes closely during these remarks and noted that they made him very nervous. He knew very well that I suspected him, but he knew also that there was no proof against him, and so in a degree he enjoyed the situation.

I ventured to say to him, "Bully, I have heard every boy in the Battery denounce that dirty piece of thievery but you; what do you think of it, anyway?" And he answered,

THE UNION BLUE BOX: MAJOR CORNWELL'S OFFICER'S FIELD DESK

This desk was issued to Cornwell by the district quartermaster at Vicksburg, Mississippi, in 1864. To this day it holds a remarkable collection of original Civil War related documents—promotion papers, orders and Union Army items originating in Washington. There are also copies of books dealing with Cornwell's official responsibility and lighter works of period fiction.

The contents of this desk comprise a remarkable wealth of background material at Cornwell's grasp as he wrote his memoirs.

"I think it is none of your damn business what I think of it."

I had some respect for Rhodes because he was a gritty scamp and would hold his own in a battle with the best of them, and coming as we did from the same company I did not think it quite the proper thing to go square back on him. So I kept my suspicions-which in my mind amounted to a certainty-to myself.

Boreland soon after resigned, much to the regret of every man in the Battery but Bully.

We had no sooner settled in our new camp near Memphis than the five of us who had engaged in that corner-stone job at LaGrange were ordered before Major Charles J. Stolbrand, our Chief of Artillery. This was another one of Bully's jobs-I was quite sure. On the way over we agreed to tell the major nothing, and let him do his worst.

The Major was occupying a small house and was alone in his office. He called us in one at a time and I sent the others in ahead of me. As the boys came out they indicated by word or sign that they had denied all knowledge of it, and I passed in and by invitation took a chair. He asked my name, when and how I had joined, questioned me about my career before joining the Battery and pumped quite a bit of personal history out of me. I watched him closely and as soon as he had exhausted the subject I broke in,

"Major, I have taken pleasure in answering your questions so far because they relate to myself only, but I trust you will ask no more about that cornerstone incident. I cannot tell of that without giving evidence against myself and implicating others. Self respect will scarcely permit me to do either. Nor would you if you were in my place. Near the Tallahatchee River we tore a fine mansion down to its very foundation to get material to keep us out of the mud and rain for one night, and no officer chided us for it.

"We did not tear this old shack of a building down, but might have if we had wished. Then, would anything have been said about that little excuse for a corner stone? You have liberal pay and comfortable quarters; we rough it on thirteen dollars a month. We are willing to take hard knocks from the enemy, but don't deserve them from our own officers. We are their friends, and they should be ours."

The Major arose, strode to the door and called out,

"Boys, you are dismissed and can return to the Battery."

Then he turned to me and gave me his hand saying, "You are all right. If you think I can do you a good turn at any time, come and see me." I thanked him and joined the boys. It was not long before the Major had an opportunity to make good.

Amos Neal was a young light-weight lad who was the Battery bugler. When he was unwell or absent I blew his calls for him. His eyes were weak and the surgeon advised him to give up the bugle. Orders now were given to replace the horses of the Battery-wagon with a six mule team, and these mules had to be taken wild from the post quartermaster corral. Neal was not equal to the job of breaking in such a team but thought if he could get them broken to drive with cross-lines from the tool box [limber chest] instead of from the saddle of the near mule with a jerk-line, that he would like the job of driving the new mule team. So it was arranged that I would get the job, break in the mules, and trade jobs with him.

I went to Captain Rogers and told him I wanted that mule team to drive. He looked at me with much surprise and asked what I knew about handling mules. I told him I was competent to fill any position in the Battery except that of farrier.

"You wouldn't even except my position?" said the captain. And I answered,

"No sir, I would not; I could command this Battery or a regiment of infantry with credit if I had a chance."

"Well, it is not likely you will ever get a chance to try either, but as you seem anxious to boss something, you may take the mules. Look out and don't get your head kicked off. My, but you have a queer taste, man."

"Taste, nothing; I am tired of sitting 'round playing cards. It will be just fun breaking in those wild mules, for they say they are wilder than deer. Much obliged, Captain."

I got the sergeant to give "By" Beard my place on the gun crew and engaged "By" to boss the job of securing the mules and breaking them. Lamson readily consented to my making the cross-lines, but after we got to work breaking in the team he made them himself.

A gang of us went over to the corral in a commissary wagon with plenty of rope and halters, and found two hundred or more mules surrounded by a strong high plank fence. "By" picked the team and we managed to lasso them after a fashion. We could not walk up and halter any of them, but could lead them when haltered. We got them to camp, and then I engaged as many men to break them as we had mules. The result was that we drilled those mules from morning until night until they became tired and gave up. Soon a team was ordered to the city for supplies, and at my suggestion "By" put a team on the army wagon and drove them, he having broken the near leader to the jerk-line. "By" was the most accomplished and fearless mule puncher in the division, but had turned his team over to big Jack Jackson and refused to drive any longer. He said it [driving] had kept him out of two fights and that he was surely going to take a hand in the next one.

The new team were beauties and "By" straightened them out on the road in fine shape. Everything went well until we were headed for a railroad crossing, and then the train went by lickety-split. We were nearly forty yards away but those infernal mules took a notion to run and away they went. "By" stuck to the saddle, but the four of us in the wagon jumped out. When the mules crossed the tracks the off-wheeler went down, and as he could not get clear of the harness he soon brought the team to a standstill. We yanked off the harness, got him on his feet, and saw that one of his legs was broken. We gave him to a Negro who happened by and went over to a battalion of cavalry camped nearby to borrow a mule. They gave us a tall, rawboned cross between a camel and a jackass and told us to send them a quartermaster's receipt for it. We said we would but really intended to get another mule from the corral that afternoon, and send the old caricature back to them.

But here we slipped up, for while we were away, marching orders had reached the Battery, and we had to send the receipt for the old giraffe and keep it.

I had been down to the city [Memphis] once on a genuine pass from the Captain, countersigned by Major Stolbrand and Gen. Logan, but after that I wrote dozens of them just as good for myself and the other boys. I did not succeed in getting into city society, however, and so passed away most of the time sitting in the park, watching the antics of the squirrels and feasting eyes on the pretty women who tripped by.

CHAPTER XXXI

It was about the middle of February 1863 when we boarded a transport and started down the Mississippi. Tom Henry and Dave Ocher-the sergeants who were reduced to the ranks for that harmless raid on the Odd Fellows' Lodge near Jackson, Tenn., that talented scamp, Charles Herbert, [Charles DeMoore, the "Robber of the Hatchie,"] and a very common-place young fellow by the name of Dickert, remained behind near Memphis.

I recall nothing of interest connected with our trip down the river, for there was no pleasant scenery and it was only a monotonous old thoroughfare at best. The water was bank high, grey and dirty, racing from bend to point at a six-mile rate. There is scarcely a straight stretch in it a mile long. The pilots knew it by its bends, points and islands-all of which have a name and number. As its entire length is a constant succession of bends and points, the channel constantly changes through the violent action of the current on the soil. It is wonderful that a pilot can learn it in a lifetime. And yet Mark Twain says he did, but it is difficult to imagine him standing alone at the wheel guiding one of those large river boats down the Mississippi on a dark, rainy night. However, he says he became a full-fledged pilot, and his veracity being unquestionable we are bound by honor and inclination to believe everything he says, even if we know some of his statements must be untrue.

In due course we reached Lake Providence, Louisiana, and pitched our camp on its southwest shore. The large scattering of trees along its bank made this an ideal campground. This lake was about a mile wide, and four or five long as I remember it, and the water was clear. It was a good depth from the very shore and we could run and dive from the bank. I cannot remember that we caught any fish there.

At Memphis I had gotten "By" to drive my team to the boat with the jerk-line, but when we disembarked here at Lake Providence I had the cross-lines on them and drove to our campground from the limber chest in great style. Amos Neal went at once to Captain Rogers, obtained his consent to the trade, and turned over to me his horse and equipments, tent, cot, and bugle, and I cheerfully gave up the mules.

I had had the fun of breaking one of the mouse colored leaders that was wilder than a deer and I had driven the team just a mile. But I got much amusement out of this mile for we passed the old Eighth [Ill. Vols.] sitting by the roadside, and the boys guyed [kidded] me unmercifully.

My tent was pitched next to the Captain's, and after sounding the retreat that evening Captain Rogers called me in and said,

"Dan, why didn't you tell me what you were figuring when you asked me for that mule team?" I answered,

"You did not ask me. Did you think I wanted it for a steady job?"

"Zounds! What could I think except that I had sized you up wrong. Now you have a slick, clean and easy berth and I want you to content yourself until something better turns up."

While we were leaving camp at Memphis, Neal picked up a tongue-chain that had been discarded on the ground, and put it in the battery-wagon, saying that it was a better one than we had and that he would have it put on our rig the first opportunity. We had been here but a day or two when Neal came up while we were at dinner, crying mad. He reported that he had left that chain with Whistler, the blacksmith, to be put on his rig, but Collins the big burly mule puncher who had thrown it away, claimed it as his own and had ordered Whistler to put it back on his wagon again.

"The hell he has" I said, and started for the forge.

"Look out, Dan," called Grim, "Don't let him get hold of you. He's the strongest man in the Battery." This opinion was derived from his having outlifted the heavy weights on a gun carriage.

I found Whistler at the forge and Collins standing near with the chain lying at his feet.

"Collins, what is the trouble between Neal and you about that tongue chain?" I asked.

"No trouble at all Mr. Caverno [Cornwell]; it is my chain and is going on my wagon," he replied. And I told him,

"You threw that chain away at Memphis, and Neal put it in his wagon after you left the camp for good. Now, who does the chain belong to?" And I stepped up within arm's length of him.

"To me, unless you are a better man than I am," and he stooped over to pick up the chain.

He was without a hat and that shock of red curly hair within reach was irresistible. Into it to the wrist went my left hand, and I sent the right to his ear with such force that he dropped to his knees and would have gone flat on his face if I had lessened my hold. As he did not struggle to get to his feet, I asked,

"Whose chain will you say that was?"

"Neal's."

"You are a liar; you said it was your own."

"I have changed my mind."

"Then you must have met a better man than yourself?"

"I guess I have."

"Whistler, will you put that chain on the Battery wagon?"

"You bet I will."

I strode back to the mess table the proudest boy in the division. My comrades had watched the fracas with much concern and were now bubbling over with satisfaction-all but Bully Rhodes. The expression on his face showed all too plainly his disappointment and chagrin at the result. I looked him square in the face until he dropped his eyes, and he soon left the table.

"Rhodes didn't seem to enjoy the fun," said Grim drily.

"I saw he didn't. The first pretext I get I will put him in the Collin's class."

That afternoon the boys deluged me with cigars, but Captain Rogers felt it his duty to issue a company order against fighting. There is no doubt the Captain would have given Neal the chain if I had carried the case to him, but Collins would have remained the same overbearing bully. The only way to squelch such fellows is to thrash them or get some one to do it for you.

I cared nothing for the Captain's order. Order statutes will never deter a man from resenting an insult or opposing a bully. A lack of confidence, strength or skill, may produce hesitation. But if you think you are equal to the occasion you should promptly sail in, and no matter how it terminates, if you did your level best you will be a winner.

I liked the position of bugler for it gave me a fine saddlehorse, a tent of my own in the officers' row and freedom from details of any sort. At drill, parade, review, or battle I rode near the Captain to hear and repeat his orders whenever a bugle call would express them. I did not have to change mess, or lose Potter for a bunk mate. And being more by myself I played cards less and read more. Neal cheerfully sounded the calls when I was absent. And the battery wagon was still at my service for stowing away books and other plunder. Each morning the boys of our mess would in turn give our Colored cook "Bragg" a dollar, and he would keep us supplied with milk, butter, eggs and other luxuries. The weather was delightful. I hark back to this period of the service with unusual satisfaction regretting only that it was not of longer duration.

We were still in General Logan's Division, and learning that a foraging train was going out one morning, I concluded to go with it. When I saw Neal about pumping out the bugle calls for me, he suggested that I get "By" Beard to take his team to one of our company wagons. They needed the exercise, and he added that there might be just a chance of his trading off "Pokahantas" for a decent mule.

"By" agreed to the arrangement and while he and Neal were coupling up the mules I rode over to the cavalry battalion that was to furnish the escort to the train and borrowed a carbine.

This train was made up of wagons from various commands in the division, with a detail of a couple of soldiers to each rig to lead the plunder, and they were all in charge of one Lockwood, the division wagonmaster.

I did not join the cavalry escort but remained near our team, and when we were about six miles out we halted opposite a plantation house around which loitered a few Negroes.

While waiting here for orders, a middle-aged Darkey came along, and as he caught sight of our saddle-mule he broke out into a mournful wail. He walked directly up to this mule and, putting his arm about its neck, he called it his "Deah ole Pomp" and burst into tears. And "Pomp," being a well-bred, amiable Missouri mule, with no prejudice against coons, did not resent this friendly familiarity, but to the contrary lowered its head and rubbed its nose up and down the Darkey's shirt front and exhibited much evidence of sympathizing with him in his distress. By looking sharp I thought I discovered a tear in each of the mule's eyes.

"Did you ever see that mule before?" asked Beard who was standing with his right foot on the hub of the near front wheel of his wagon.

"-if I eber seed this mool afore," said the fellow, "I recon Ise seen im afore an a hine too ebry day for abot six weeks. Pomps de bes mool wats eber on dis plantation, an now you sojes dun gone an got im, wen I 'lowed I hed im were nobody cud fine im cept my ownself."

I sat there on my horse watching this scene and was greatly puzzled over it. I knew the old man was talking nonsense for I had slung the lariat over that mule myself and led him out of the corral at Memphis. I was about to butt in when I glanced toward "By" and observed a slight shake of the head and unmistakable vibrations of the winkers of his left eye. I interpreted this to mean "keep quiet" and so I kept quiet.

"See here, old man," said "By," "we are friends of the Colored folks and don't intend to rob them, so if you will prove this is your mule by taking us to the place where we found him you can come to camp with us and bring him back with you."

"Will yer do dat now sojer? Den come right 'long an 'I shows yuh zackly whar yuh got im."

Beard slipped a bridle from one of the swing mules, and then I caught on and rode after them. The coon led us across a large field in the direction of a piece of timber about a half mile away. Then we followed him into this timber for another half mile and came to a high bayou bank. I dismounted here and, tying the horse, followed the others over on a down cottonwood. About eighty rods farther we came to a piece of dense undergrowth and here we struck a mule track. "By" sprang to the front and was soon out of sight. The Darkey appeared puzzled and slowed down. Then he stopped. I kept about the distance of a rod between him and the carbine, and neither said a word. We stood there about five minutes and then heard a mule whinney. Then, that coon stood on one foot and changed the shape of his countenance every few seconds until "By" came out with Pomp under him. We reached the bayou without a word being spoken, though I expected an outburst of pleading, whining and lamentation. But, here I was fooled, for the Darkey proved game, and failed to utter even a mild protest. But as we were about to cross the bayou he did say,

"Geman I doesn't want to go back wid you'ns, cos I bleve dem nigahs back dar didn't see me come out heah wid yer, an I don't want um to know I fool ole Pomp away cos yer see I'se boss ob dis yere plantation an I don't wan um to get to unrespecting my 'thority an interfluence." Then he skipped at a lively gait along the bayou so as to reach the plantation from a different direction from the one we would take, while "By" with a lead-line swam Pomp across.

When we reached the forage train our wagon was being loaded with sweet potatoes. Beard immediately cut Pokahontas out of the team, turned him loose, and threw the leader on Pomp. Now Neal had a pair of wheelers that were perfectly matched for when a coon mistakes one mule for another they have got to be exactly alike. He knows a mule as we know a person by countenance and voice, and it is not at all probable that such a droll incident of this nature ever happened before or since.

Before we left there I observed "de boss ob dis yere plantation" slyly slip a halter on old Pokahontas and lead him away to a stable. For a fact they were a sorry looking pair.

On this place was a shed two hundred feet long, and thirty wide and under it a windrow of yams, or sweet potatoes, its full length. We had not enough teams in our whole train to haul them all.

But we took a few hundred bushels of them with several barrels of white beans and much other truck. Part of the train went on to other plantations, and many of the wagons were loaded up with corn fodder, which the horses and mules ate with relish. When the grain commenced to harden, the farmers here would cut the top of the stalk off just above the ear, and strip the lower leaves. They would tie this in convenient bundles and keep them under cover as a substitute for hay. When they wanted any they got it by boat from St. Louis, for they made none themselves.

On these plantations we often found quantities of twisted leaf tobacco, "Good to smoke or chew," which was valuable plunder for us. No one occupied one of the mansions here and it was nearly destitute of furniture. I got a handsome curtain cord for the bugle and a can of pulverized sugar for the mess. We ate up the sugar, but I have the bugle and its cord yet [Now in the possession of the editor].

Going out we had noticed a bunch of cattle grazing by the roadside. My old chum and bunkmate of Co. K., Bill Miller, was in the party, and I got him and another fellow who was handy with a skinning knife to slip ahead with me. I downed a three-year old steer with the carbine and those handy boys dressed it in a jiffy and threw half in our wagon when it came along and the other in their own. It was a strange oversight by the officer in charge that these cattle were not all driven into camp, though they may have been sent for later.

When we got in I turned the half beef over to our quartermaster sergeant, reserving a nice chunk of sirloin and a soup bone for our mess. It was worth a dollar to see the smile across Bragg's face when he got that choice piece of beef and can of pulverized sugar. Those Darkeys had appetites as well as ourselves and liked to see the good things come in. An Army baker had his machine running here at that time and we were getting bread and living high. Hardtack, if not too hard or wormy, is all right on the march because it is a condensed ration and a small bulk goes a good way. But in camp where one can get a little fresh beef we needed bread to absorb the gravy. I have had hardtack that was no more porous than a piece of Bessemer steel, the same shade of blue, and quite as hard to break. I gave one to a mule one day and it was funny to see him shut his eyes and try and nip it in two. Failing in this he put the edge on the ground and endeavored to break it, but instead broke two of his teeth. That made him mad and I stepped back for fear he would strike me and was just in time for he missed me but knocked the hardtack back under his heels.

Quicker than lightning he kicked that hardtack through the blacksmith's tent into the lake, and it went to the bottom like a stone. We sometimes succeeded in breaking such on the anvil fine enough to feed into a coffee mill and after grinding it into meal and letting it soak over night, we would make griddle cakes of it for our breakfast. But they were not near so good as the buckwheat article.

CHAPTER XXXII

Directly after roll-call one morning near the lake one of the boys remarked,

"Bully Rhodes was shooting off his mouth in a bragging way last evening, and among other things he said was that at Donelson you were out together on a skirmish, and that you and the other three dropped behind a down tree and did not dare to go farther, while he jumped over, ran to a standing tree and plunked a reb.

"Did he say that?"

"Yes, and George Cunningham told him he believed it a damn lie and ought to be ashamed running down a boy of his old company who had always said that he was a good fighter."

This was a welcome piece of tale bearing for I felt unusually fine that morning. Since the Collins affair I had been trying to devise a pretext for a quarrel with Rhodes but could never bring it about so that he would appear to be the aggressor. Now he had tumbled into it in a manner that left him no chance of escape, and so I thanked the boy for the information and added that if he wanted to see a little fun to be around when Bragg called us to breakfast and he would see Bully put though his paces on an empty stomach.

A half hour later the six of us were standing around the mess table, and Bully and I were opposites. I at once introduced the subject.

"Jim, do you remember that little skirmish party the last day at Fort Donelson?"

"What of it; it didn't amount to much anyway."

"Then why were you talking about it last evening?"

"Because I'd a mi'nt to. It is none of your dang business what I talk about."

"But as you connected my name with it I am going to make it some of my business."

"Well wasn't you there?"

"Yes, but not behind the down tree where you was."

"I don't care where you was nor what you done, so shut up and mind your own business. Here Bragg, bring along my coffee."

"Never mind his coffee, Bragg, I'll give him mine," and I gave it to him in the face.

Bully was now trembling from head to foot, for all hope of avoiding a scrap had vanished. I walked back to a level piece of ground near the cook shanty and handed my jacket to one of the fifty boys who had gathered about. Jim came shambling up to the scratch, very nervous and covered with coffee grounds.

He would not come within reach, so I stepped up quickly and planted a right hander on the mouth, and ducking an awkward swinging blow, I got in a left to the jaw. This was repeated three times and the claret was running down Jim's front and mixing with the coffee grounds in a fine blend.

He took wind for a minute and then commenced edging up again, and I could read in his eye that he intended to try his big boots on me. I thought I could catch his foot and dump him, in which case I would be justified in fixing him so he would have to be taken to a hospital, but one of the boys in the crowd read his intentions as clearly as I did and instantly cried out,

"Rhodes, if you kick that boy I will smash in your head with a club."

Cries of "shame" and "Stand up and fight it out like a man, you big hulk," and much unintelligible buzzing in the crowd removed all danger from that source. Jim was cowed and the battle was practically won. Urged by the crowd to "Wade in and finish him," I sailed in with a jump and smasher to the chin, and Bully fell over a chunk of wood on his back. He got up so far as to get himself seated on the wood, and there he sat 'til we all went to our breakfast. Bully never came back to our mess again.

A couple of hours later the Captain ordered Lieut. Cooper to find the culprits and punish them for violating his order. He went to Rhodes, saw his condition, heard him acknowledge that he had been fighting, and had him tied to a fifth wheel. Then he came to my tent and found me smoking a cigar, and noticed a lot more scattered over the cot. I handed him one and while lighting it he remarked,

"You had a nice little scrap this morning and did Rhodes up in fine shape."

"Who told you so?"

"I saw it all myself, but then that don't count, you know. Jim said you and he had been fighting and so I had him tied up. Rogers had questioned several of the boys but none of them knew who Bully had his fight with, so his word is all the evidence we have against you."

"Well, I challenge his statement for he is the biggest liar in the Battery. It was on account of his lying that he got the drubbing he did. And he is a thief also, for he is the fellow that stole Boreland's boots."

"Then his statement won't go with me, and as you are as clean as a whistle and no proof against you, you go clear and that settles it."

Jim must have been hungry when he was turned loose, for they kept him there with nothing to eat 'til sundown. And he would have enjoyed every minute of the time if I had been tied up also. But the very idea is too absurd to think of. Such a service as I had performed for the company in knocking the stuffing out of two overgrown bullies merited a corporalcy, at least. I soon discovered that Captain Rogers was well pleased with Lieutenant Cooper's ingenious settlement of the matter and vindication of his order against fighting, for he had a smile for me and was unusually affable for several days thereafter.

General Sherman's corps now was fifty miles below us, above and in sight of Vicksburg. Nearly a year before, [Union] General Thomas Williams had come up here from New Orleans with 3,000 men and invested some time and much hard labor in a vain attempt to divert the channel of the river across the neck of Young's Point. If successful, Vicksburg would suddenly have become an inland city and her batteries useless. Sherman's men took up the job where Williams left it with no better success. The irresistible current of the river tore its way through a few years later and left Young's Point an island. That old river has been in the habit of going where it pleases, and objects to being driven, coaxed or led.

When this scheme was abandoned it was determined to investigate a route through Lake Providence and a string of bayous beyond. One end of the lake was not much more than 80 rods from the river and was about on a level with it at low water stage. The river was bank high now with barrels of water to spare and so the Army dug out a channel, cut the levee and gradually changed the complexion of this pretty lake to the color of Missouri mud.

The violent action of the water soon tore out a respectable channel and then down came a tugboat from the river with a lot of officers and a cornet band aboard and circled around the lake. This lake was normally about six feet below its bank, and as it was now steadily rising it was evident that our pleasant camp ground would soon be submerged. So we soon were hustled aboard a transport lying below the cut in the levee and taken a few miles above and set off at a place known as Berry's Landing, where it was believed the overflow would not reach us.

I afterward wondered why they did not let us go up there by land as the distance was only six or seven miles and the roads were fine. It would have been a nice little jog for our animals, which needed exercise, and could have been made in half the time it took us to stow our outfit on that steamer. They were always making queer moves in the Army, and it was as difficult for a private to comprehend the strategy of our generals as it was for Admiral Schley's subordinates to see any sense in the wide, circular swath he cut at Santiago [Cuba] in '98.

Before we left Tennessee we had loaded ourselves up with Confederate currency that engravers and printers in St. Louis were turning out in unlimited quantities, all complete except for the number and signature of the register and treasurer. Why they hesitated to commit this trifling forgery I cannot explain but we were quite equal to the labor of correcting the omission. With never a scruple to deter me I signed "P. Hill, Jr.," for register and "R. M. Payne" for treasurer so many times it became a habit and on more than one occasion I caught myself unconsciously signing one or the other of those illustrious names on passes that required countersigning by Major Stolbrand and General Logan. For numbering I used red ink and slug in any of the old numerals just as they came to mind at the instant of jotting them down. I think it was generally admitted that the St. Louis engravers could not do quite such coarse work, nor the printers obtain as poor a quality of paper as the Richmond mechanics. But they were so near alike and of so little value that no one gave them a close scrutiny.

We were supplied with fake bills from one to one hundred dollars each, assorted to order, at about two and one-half genuine dollars per one hundred bills, without regard to denomination. We had a way of rubbing this illegal tender on our heads until it had the appearance of having been passed over the bar many times.

One of the many schemes used to get this stuff into circulation was to approach a Southerner in a confidential manner and say that we had taken a little of it from Confederate prisoners for articles that they sadly needed for their comfort. This was done at great risk of arrest and punishment as our orders were to destroy it at sight. We therefore had to get rid of it at the first opportunity. And then if he would make us a decent offer he would find himself possessing the roll.

Sometimes these conversations would lead to an apparent serious discussion of the principles involved in the war. In the interest of commerce the idea would be conveyed that we were drafted men serving under compulsion contrary to our will and principles, and that our sympathies were wholly with their cause. If the negotiation was successful we would adjourn to our quarters, select another bunch of these promises to pay "six months after the ratification of a treaty of peace between the Confederate States and the United States of America," and proceed to give our skulls another polishing.

One of our fool generals had some of our soldiers arrested and court martialed for using this stuff, and he succeeded in convening a court composed of officers who were asses enough to convict these men of a crime. When a record of the proceedings reached Army Judge Advocate General Joseph Holt, this is what that level-headed old Kentuckian said of the matter:

"The circulation of Confederate notes assists in sustaining the financial credit of the rebels, and to that extent gives aid and comfort to the rebellion. The circulation of counterfeit Confederate notes could not properly be treated as a criminal offense. To punish for the circulation of these notes because they are counterfeit would be to give direct aid to the rebellion and would be a recognition of the authority of the rebel government to issue such a currency, which of course cannot be permitted."

The amount got rid of by the soldiers was a very small figure. I know of none who made enough out of it to buy their discharge or a commission, but many a card sharp succeeded in stacking up a poker debt against his commanding officer that was in the end liquidated by official favors of this sort. It served a useful purpose in furnishing a medium for a little harmless devilment and a cheap currency to gamble with, all of which kept some of the boys healthy and free from homesickness and the blues.

Northern cotton speculators and Southern bankers were the parties that put this stuff into circulation in large quantities. It was estimated that they shoved about $300,000,000 of it. A patriotic New York City genius demonstrated to his own satisfaction that he could get possession of all of the cotton in the Confederacy, ruin their currency, and end the rebellion and, incidentally, save a moderate competence for his old age. He called on President Lincoln and elaborated his scheme, but that astute lawyer and statesman had no time to consider such a proposition and referred him to Secretary of War Edwin M. Stanton. Stanton said that it was a matter that had no logical connection with the War Department and suggested that he counsel with U. S. Marshal Sharp of his own city. Then the speculator returned to New York and called on the marshal and found him too sharp to commit himself on so delicate a subject.

The New Yorker had not a word of discouragement from either of those officials and he could only infer that they were not averse to his plans though they would not openly sanction them. So he went ahead, and with the assistance of Southern bankers and speculators inflated the Rebel currency until three months' pay of one of their cavalry captains was not sufficient to buy him a pair of boots. That it assisted in breaking the rebellion can scarcely be doubted, and that this genius New Yorker made a good thing out of it leaves room for even less doubt.

Soon after pitching camp at Berry's Landing, [Louisiana], a bright looking middle aged Darkey came along and said he had a horse to sell. I had no earthly use for another horse, but said I had and went with him to a nearby plantation. The planter and his family had disappeared and left this man in charge. From a stable he led out a very fair looking nag and I made a critical examination of him. I tried his eyes and found them good. Then I opened his mouth, which was proof that he didn't have lockjaw. I ran my hands down his limbs in search of splints, spavins and ringbones, though I did not know one from the other. I gave him a poke in the ribs with my thumb because I had seen jockeys do so, though I had not the remotest idea what they did it for, and finished my diagnosis by giving his tail a vigorous and steady pull. After finding some fault with his color, weight and general proportions, I said,

"Do you warrant this animal to be kind and sound and to work both in single and double harness?" I had once heard a man say this when buying a horse, and was not glad that I remembered it.

"Wy, ese as kind as my ole woman dar an e aint got a spint no splasm on im, but he don't knoe nuffin 'bout haness cos ye see boss ees a saddle oss. He can fox trot, single foot, an go any gait dere is."

"All right! I'll take him" I said, and handed him a "Confed" fifty and was about to lead the animal away when he exclaimed,

"Hold on dar boss, yer can't hab dat oss fer cotton basket full eb such money, as dis yere. No sah! I takes nuthin but de genwine Lincum greenbacks. Dis yere kine ah money aint no good, no how; taint good fer nuffin: yer cant get nuffin fer rebel money 'round ere no moah. I tell yer it aint good fer nuffin."

Protesting that I had no other kind of money but would give him enough more to make it an object, he replied,

"Yer cant meck no object ob me wid any sich money as hat dere fer I wudnt gib yer de rope on dis oss fur all yer go fur it aint good fer nuffin anymoah roun heah."

Then I said I supposed he was transacting business for his master, and as the old judge was away in the Confederacy where this kind of currency was legal tender, I was sure that it would be quite acceptable to him.

"But yer see boss ders nobody my master no moah an dat money I gets must be cepterbol to my ownself."

I then arrived at two wise conclusions...

First: I did not want another horse anyway.

Second: That Darkey did not need a master to take care of him.

CHAPTER XXXIII

One morning early in 1863 Clark Grim, "By" Beard, a boy from an adjoining battery and I rode out of camp with no object in view except to exercise ourselves and nags. We went up the river through the camps until we came to an open thoroughfare leading in a westerly direction and followed this a few miles past some very fine plantations. We struck out across country in a southerly direction, not wishing to return to camp by the same road we had come on, and found a road leading back that would apparently bring us to the river again south of our starting point. So we trailed along this road and when a couple of miles from the river we found it covered with water from the overflow of Lake Providence.

As we proceeded the water gradually became deeper until it reached our horses' knees, and then we began to see among the floodwood near a rail fence the backs of some large fish. I tried to persuade one of the boys to get one of them, claiming I was afraid of cramps, rheumatism, couldn't swim, and all that sort of thing, but they didn't care for fish and stuck to their saddles. I said that it was humiliating for a musician like myself to have to hustle for grub when there were privates about, but they reminded me that a musician got one dollar less a month than a private and so they all ranked me. That came very near being a fact and so I humbly slipped off into the water and started for the rail fence.

Using a piece of fence rail I quietly moved along the drift wood until I got a whack at the back of one fish, which stunned him so that I easily captured him. I strung him up to the saddle by a blanket strap and we moved through the water until we reached a planter's mansion with the usual outhouses and a double row of Negro cabins flanking a wide avenue. Here the ground was somewhat higher than the general level and the water did not overflow the premises. I recognized this place, having ridden out to it while we were camped on the bank of the lake, and remembered seeing a fish spear in one of the outhouses. There were a few Darkeys here yet and one of them got it for me.

Then we started for camp a couple of miles away. There was water for a mile and then we had dry land. On the way I planned a fine outing for the day following and enjoined the boys to keep very mum about the fish we had seen and make up any kind of an old lie about the one we had. This one was of the buffalo variety, and its gross weight was about thirty pounds. We had a good supper from it and when the scales were dry they were picked up by the boys and used for poker chips. They were about the size of a silver half dollar.

That evening "By" and I secured a flat-bottomed scow and quietly loaded it into one of the company wagons and engaged a little fellow that drove horses for caissons to take us down to the water and come after us in the evening. We didn't expect to be all day filling the boat with fish, but we intended to put in a full day spearing, and when the boat got full we could run to land and heave them out. With good luck we might catch enough to fill the wagon box. Our mess cook, Bragg, had breakfast ready at the break of day, but Grim didn't care to go for some reason and as the other Battery boy did not show up, Beard and I had the expedition all to ourselves, much to our satisfaction. Never did two fellows start out with finer prospects of sport.

The water had risen perceptibly during the night and we soon reached the overflow and nervously yanked the boat out of the wagon. "By" seized the pole and I grabbed the spear and we pushed for deeper water. It was about a half hour before I struck one, which I think was about a hundred pounder, but I did not have the satisfaction of estimating him out of the water for he rushed under the boat and tore himself loose. Then I had a faint impression that I needed a harpoon. Still, the whole day was before us with plenty of fish in sight and we would get a boat full anyway. Or so we thought.

The water was deeper now and the fish did not lay around in the driftwood over the ditches as they had the day before. They now scurried about the flooded fields and seemed to keep an eye on us and kept well out of our way. Some of them were veritable whales and when they struck out under a full head of steam, they created a swell that would rock our boat like a passing transport. I believe that we saw fish that day that would have measured seven or eight feet long and weighed up to five hundred pounds.

And we were after them with a common fish spear; a carving fork would have done as well. Had we brought along a couple of muskets or carbines we might have broken the back bone of a few of the smaller ones, but one of our 24-pound howitzers would have been about right for the big ones. Through the livelong day, without a mouthful to eat, we poled over those flooded fields, and got nothing but a gar about three feet long. One third of this was head and bill and the other two thirds worthless.

A few years later I caught a catfish in the Mississippi that for a time I could not handle. I had a half-inch rope stretched from the bank to a snag one hundred yards from shore in a strong current. Two heavy sinkers held a section of this line on the bottom, and between these were tied strong hooks about six feet apart baited with meat. I caught nothing with this layout but catfish, and they ran from eight to thirty pounds, with one exception. In about every case they were caught at one side, or the corner of the mouth. Many of the hooks would be gone and I was told by old river men that that was the only sure hold on a catfish of any size.

Overhauling my line one morning I brought up an unusually large one. He came to the surface without a flounder, but the instant his nose reached the atmosphere, he turned and went steadily and surely to the bottom of the river again. So strong a pull did he make that I did not dare to try and hold him back. I paddled to the bank and again overhauled the line. When he came to the top this time I fired a shot from my .30 caliber pocket revolver into this head. But he went to the bottom again just as before. I repeated this performance four times with the same result, and my pistol was now empty. Then I went to shore again and up the bank. I had a long iron poker with an eye in one end into which I drove a handle. The other end I inserted between the logs of a block house and bent it until I had a substantial gaff hook. Then I picked up a hand axe and a Darkey, went back to the boat, and proceeded to overhaul the line once more.

The old fellow came up as steady and quiet as usual, and when his head came into sight I sunk the hand axe into it up to the eye. He did not drop back again and so the coon gaffed him, but did not attempt to pull him into the boat. And I again paddled to shore. It took two Darkeys to "tote" him up the steep bank and hang him to a cotton tree limb the proper height for skinning. I circled the hide just back of the head, cut it in strips from neck to tail, and skinned it with a pair of pliers. This hide was much tougher than any incident I have related in this book. In fact, none of those pistol shots made a hole through it. When dressed, the net weight was an even hundred, which would have made it about 150 gross. But this was only a minnow compared with the largest we saw in the inundated cotton fields near the Mississippi River banks.

As the sun was setting, down came the team after us and we pushed the boat over to the pike and met it. The driver took a look in our direction and roared out,

"Where in hell is your fish?"

I held up the gar and said it was all we had, and that he might have it for his trouble. And, then without waiting for any further explanation, and when he plainly saw that we were tired, hungry and humble, he swore and abused us most shamefully. I believe he intended to drive back without us. But when he backed up the wagon at a cramp to turn on the narrow pike, the back wheels sunk into the water up to the hubs. We then shoved the boat into the wagon before he could get away. As I tossed the gar out of the boat, the driver turned in his saddle and commenced abusing us again.

"You thought I was such a damn fool that I would take that gar. I guess I know as much as a pair of smarties like you two. You were going to surprise the boys with a wagon load of fish, weren't you? They will be surprised all right when they see you sneak into camp without a fish. You are a sweet scented pair you are."

"Say, Ted, let up will you? Each of us will give you a dollar when you get to camp and that will pay you well for your trouble," said I.

"Hell! I wouldn't do it for ten," said the aggravating rascal, "It's worth more than that to get a whack at a pair of conceited asses like you two." Fortunately, the water by this time was so high that we did not have far to go, but he had us roasted to a turn by the time we reached camp.

We dropped the boat between the levee and the river bank, and found our supper ready for us with plenty of fried fish on the table. We learned from Bragg that the boy from the other battery, who was out with us the day before, went out with a gang from his own company. They went where the water was not so deep as where we were, and they got a lot of the smaller fish in the ditches by wading side by side, driving them into shallow water, and then throwing them out on the pike by hand. In this way they soon filled a wagon and supplied our Battery as well as their own.

--- ------ ---

Going back to the night I found Bragg hiding in the ravine at Oxford, Mississippi. The next morning there came into our camp a nondescript little Darkey whom Bragg said was his brother, John. He was then taken in by a mess of four boys who had no cook. And he remained with us.

During the winter ('62-'63) John was the dullest coon in camp. He would sit on a stick of wood near a fire by the hour, apparently asleep. If he was touched on the lips with a finger or stick while thus hibernating, he would snap at it like a turtle. Bragg would then remark,

"I tell yu-uns John aint well. Wen ese well ese de liblist niggah you ebber see."

John had now got thawed out and he was making good. Here [at Berry's Landing] Darkey John enlisted into his service all the little coons of either sex that could be found in the vicinity and made them report to him every afternoon for drill. They were required to furnish their own arms, which were represented by brooms, mopsticks, hoes, old umbrellas, and articles they could pick up about their cabins. He would march them about on the unoccupied strip between the levee and the river bank, just back of the Battery. He would swear at them like a steamboat mate, make them stand guard duty, and for imaginary infractions of discipline, would buck and gag them or tie them up by the thumbs. Then one of us would attract his attention, while another would cut the culprits down.

I had put the fish spear under my cot, but one day John sneaked it out and tied an old shirt to it to represent the colors on one of his dress parades. The levee was lined with spectators and we enjoyed his parade exceedingly, but the little black devil was having so much fun that he didn't know when to stop. Our fishing boat lay nearby and he had to yank the shirt from the spear while jumping into it and then told the crowd that he would show them how "By" Beard and Dan Caverno "got dat wagon load ob fish de odder day."

"Cut that out, you son of an ape," I growled, but the crowd told him to go on with it and so he paid no attention to me. Of all the silly, absurd performances I ever witnessed, that took the cake. He got one of his little coons in the rear end of the scow with a mop stick to do the pushing act, while he stood at the bow giving orders and keeping a lookout for the fish. Presently he made a stab at one, lost his spear, fell overboard, and swam back to the boat on the sod. I could see no fun in such silly gymnastics, but the fool crowd thought they did and yelled him encouragement to go on with it. One of the little pickaninnies happened to be sitting near and he hooked the barb of his spear in her frock and hauled her into the boat. Then he held her up before the crowd by the heels and declared that she was a female catfish, chuck full of eggs.

This utterly disgusted Beard and me and we adjourned to my tent and turned the atmosphere purple. We swore we would kill that detestable little Darkey if it was the last thing we ever did, and planned to take him with us in the boat some evening and lose him in the river. But he would never go with us.

CHAPTER XXXIV

The overflow through Lake Providence as a means of getting steamers and supplies below Vicksburg proved futile and our 17th Corps, commanded by General James McPherson, dropped down the Mississippi River to Milliken's Bend, Louisiana. Grant was with Sherman's Corps at Young's Point, ten miles below us and in sight of Vicksburg.

At the beginning of the war, the position of Adjutant General of the Army was held by Lorenzo Thomas with the rank of Colonel, or a notch below. He had attained the position by long service and fawning around old General Scott. While he may have made a fair adjutant of our little Army in peaceful times, he should have been retired with Scott as soon as the fun began, for they were both back numbers and quite out of date.

But at the suggestion of retirement Thomas would fly into such a rage that to get rid of him, or how to get rid of him, puzzled President Lincoln and Secretary of War Simon Cameron for a long time. The Adjutant General issued orders for the War Department such as "By Order of the President" or "By command of the Secretary of War," but these two were new to this business, and Thomas was allowed to promulgate orders unilaterally without waiting for suggestions from his official superiors.

As an example of his officious "astuteness" he incorporated in a War Department General Order of July 19th, 1861, the following:

"In future, no volunteer will be mustered into the service who is unable to speak the English language."

However idiotic this may have been in point of policy, it was certainly plain English and no one could possibly have misunderstood it. Yet, twenty days later this followed:

"Par.3, Gen.Orders No.45, from this office, which prohibits volunteers who do not speak the English language from being mustered into the service, is not intended to apply to regiments or companies of foreign nationality-in which men and officers speak the same tongue-but to prevent the enlistment into regiments or companies whose officers speak the English language only, of men not understanding it, and to induce such persons to enlist under officers whose language they do understand."

What stuff. There were very few, if any, commissioned officers in our service who could not speak or understand our language, and of necessity it had to be the language of command and record. But a moment's reflection will make it clear that it would have been far better if the foreign elements had mixed with the native, as the former would have learned our language as rapidly as they could have acquired the drill. Three years of field service with our boys would have rubbed off their foreign clannishness, and made Americans of them, while if segregated their social intercourse would have been entirely in their native tongues. And they would have become familiar only with the phrases used in military parlance.

Five days later Thomas must have received an emphatic command from his superior for in another order he says:-

"Par.3, of Gen. Orders No. 45, from this office, having been misunderstood"-(as if anyone could possibly have misunderstood it) is hereby repealed."

The Army then put E. D. Townsend into the Adjutant General's office to keep things straight, but did not succeed in prying Lorenzo out until sometime in October 1862, and then only by giving him the rank of brigadier general and sending him out on special duty.

It will be remembered that when President Andrew Johnson had a row with Secretary of War Stanton, he replaced him with Gen. Grant, but the latter was made to realize that it would be in his interest to "run with" the radicals. Grant got into a disagreement with Johnson wherein a question of veracity was involved, and he was turned out. Then Lorenzo Thomas was made Secretary of War-pro tem. After that he was dubbed "Pro. Tem. Thomas."

We were just comfortably settled in our camp at the Bend when General Thomas came down the river on a special mission from the President and explained the matter to General Grant.

Grant sent him to General McPherson and by request Mack assembled his corps (without arms) about a large platform built on top of a few army wagons. After the troops had all taken position, the platform was occupied by McPherson and Thomas, followed by the division and brigade commanders, and many staff officers.

They sat and talked among themselves for a few minutes while a tardy regiment was dressing up in its place, and then Mack stepped gaily to the front and called his corps to "Attention."

He then proceeded to say that Gen. Thomas was here on a special mission from the president to recruit and organize colored men into a military force for garrison duty, so that more of the white troops might be available for field service. In anticipation of a possible objection to this policy from a few of the officers, he had been instructed to muster them out of the service. And he called any and every officer present who felt disposed to condemn this policy of President Lincoln to step forward at once and let it be known.

If this scheme disgruntled any of our officers, they kept it strictly to themselves. So Thomas did not have to exercise his authority as a muster-out officer in our Corps.

General McPherson was in fine humor and seemed to enjoy this talk, of which I have given only an outline, for he talked all around it, on all sides of it, over it and under it and elaborated on it until it seemed that nothing more could be said on the subject. And then he introduced Lorenzo as follows:

"With these few remarks-officers and soldiers-I will now present to you Brigadier General Lorenzo Thomas, Adjutant General of the United States Army and Special Commissioner of

President Lincoln. He will now eloquently explain to you the details of the great mission with which he has been entrusted." Then he waved his gloved hand gracefully for Lorenzo to come forward.

Imagine his predicament when every word of the speech he had prepared had already been delivered, over and over again. Because he was shy, his ability to articulate his position was truly pitiful. He came shuffling up and mumbled in a low voice something to the effect that Gen. McPherson had unkindly taken advantage of him and told them all about his mission, and had left him with nothing new to tell them. But as his orders were to deliver the message to the troops himself, he would be obliged to repeat it to us although we had already heard it three or four times.

I was standing quite near the stage and sincerely sympathized with "Gen. Pro. Tem." in his embarrassment. I wondered how the handsome and gallant James could find it in his heart to play such a scurvy trick on this insignificant old veteran, and wondered again how he could sit there in plain sight of us all, seeming to enjoy the old fellow's discomfiture.

Thomas repeated about as much of the business as I have detailed and took his seat. Mack came up again, smiling as sweetly as a high school graduate, and called on Gen. Logan for a few remarks. John stepped out promptly and delivered a rattling ten minute speech, and being without arms must have reminded him of his political campaigns in Illinois.

After our dismissal, Thomas, Logan and McPherson adjourned to the latter's tent. It was a hot day and John A. quickly slung off his hat, saber, sash, coat and vest and straddled a chair. The others divested themselves of some of their surplus toggery at a more leisurely pace.

"Mack, why in the name of the devil did you play that dirty trick on me today?"

"Why in the name of St. Patrick didn't you give me that thirty-day leave I asked for last fall?" said Mack.

"You might have forgotten that when I sent you your Major General's commission," returned Thomas, "but you Scotch never forget anything except to send for a bottle and some glasses when your guests are famishing."

A Darkey soon brought in the liquid refreshments and after they had been lubricated, Lorenzo again referred to his grievance by saying,

"That was a scurvy trick, Mack, to introduce me to your Corps as an eloquent speaker after you had stolen my speech and fired it off yourself. You knew I couldn't say anything new after you had told it over two or three times. I asked you to assemble your Corps and let me talk to them, but you did all the talking yourself." And General "Mack" answered,

"Hardly. I made only a few preliminary remarks and then introduced you, but as you had but little to say I called on John, and he did the talking."

"I think it was very unkind of you to put me in such a hole, and I believe it will be my duty to report the matter to the President."

"Do," said Logan. "It will furnish him with a good story for a cabinet meeting; let's take a bumper to Honest Old Abe."

Without a word they filled their glasses and drained them standing.

"I say, John," broke in McPherson, "if we succeed in getting this Army in the rear of Vicksburg, we will send the old man some news that will cheer him up."

"Sure thing, Mack," replied Logan, "and if General Thomas will rush his scheme we will give him the post of honor, won't we?"

"What is that?" asked Lorenzo.

"Command of the African Brigade at the head of the advance column," said Logan.

"I've not the right complexion," retorted Thomas, "but you could take that position without violating the harmony of colors."

This was a score for Lorenzo at which they all laughed, and upon which they took another drink. And as Thomas wrapped his sash about his waist and buckled on this saber belt before departing he said,

"Mack, that is a mighty fine old whiskey of yours, and if you will send me over a half dozen to keep me alive until my supplies arrive from St. Louis, I'll forgive you and call everything square."

And "Gentleman James" replied,

"It's a go, Lorenzo. You shall have the whiskey."

--- ------ ---

Of the four of our boys who remained behind when we left Memphis only one ever returned to the Battery to my knowledge, and that was Dave Ocher. He was the duty sergeant that was reduced on account of that escapade near Jackson, Tennessee, when the boys came in loaded down with Odd Fellows paraphernalia.

He came back to us at Milliken's Bend, very grave and sober. He had been one of the most cheerful and sporty of the old boys, one whom the blues or ill nature could never make an impression upon. He was very fond of the female sex and never failed to make love to any pretty woman with whom good fortune brought him in contact. His speech was smooth and his manner insinuating. He would not hesitate to assure Southern ladies that his sympathies were with them and their cause, declaring that he entered the Union service involuntarily and only awaited a favorable opportunity to go over to their side and take with him a squad of men who shared his feelings and were quite ready to share his fortunes also. He made love to scores of them, a few of whom gave him letters of introduction to Confederate officers. He took many risks visiting outside our lines, but luckily escaped capture. Of his adventures in Memphis, he told the following story...

Dickert, one of the boys reduced in rank after the Odd Fellows caper, was found in an old well with this throat cut. Tom Henry and Ocher were tried by a court martial for the murder, found guilty and sentenced to be hung. They were both on the scaffold when Henry acknowledged his guilt, clearing Dave from any part in the crime. Ocher was set free, took the first boat down river, and joined us after an absence of about a month.

During this time Ocher was posted on the company roll as a deserter, and through neglect this was never corrected. As he returned of his own accord, it was a simple case of absence without leave for which he was never brought to account, and ought not to have been either. He had creditably passed through the battles of Donelson and Shiloh and had suffered sufficiently while under sentence of death at Memphis. Then he served gallantly through the battles of Port Gibson, Champion Hill, Jackson, Big Black, and then rammed up against the fortifications of Vicksburg and was killed there while tossing hand grenades over the parapet.

And still he is reported in the state (Illinois) records and no doubt in Washington, as a deserter. He might as well have been hung with Tom Henry and be done with it. The boys all agreed that he was as brave in battle as he was in a lady's parlor, and ought not to have been reduced for that harmless escapade at Jackson. A Rebel Odd Fellow was no better than a Rebel even fellow, and should have been shown no special favors. Clannish fraternal humbuggery had no proper place in our Army, and it was unmanly to give or take advantage of such relations. I would have been proud to command a Battery composed of boys such as Dave Ocher. Had he never returned to us and been a deserter in fact, he would have been a better man than thousands who got honorable discharges but never got near enough to the front to draw the fire of the enemy.

Since the above was written, I have received a letter from one of my old comrades, John T. Weisman of Lincoln, Nebraska. John was a corporal in Company D, 8th Ill. Infantry, and like myself got a detail into McAllister's Battery in which he served during the campaign and siege of Vicksburg. He says that when he learned that Dave Ocher was in military records as a deserter, he took the matter up with the State and National authorities and got these records corrected. He was with Dave in the trenches and had personal knowledge of his having been killed there. For this service Comrade Weisman is entitled to the warm thanks of every living member of that fine old Battery.

--- ------ ---

Since coming down the river we had received a number of recruits, and a few of them were quite toney young chaps who sang the new war songs most charmingly. They made up a quartette and warbled for us every evening, and a few of the old boys who had but little taste for music were inclined to ridicule this entertainment. Others would on occasion stuff them with the most absurd yarns about matters of the military service.

That all-around handy fellow Byron "By" Beard got up a mean scheme on one of the daintiest of them, held a mock election one evening, and had him promoted to a "third corporal." Although he was but a stripling of a boy who had not been with the Battery more than two weeks and knew nothing about drill or duties whatever, he thought it was the real thing. Presuming, no doubt, that he had won the boys' hearts with that squeaky little tenor voice of his, he took his promotion very gracefully and like a politician promised to fulfill the duties of his office to the best of his ability.

They represented to him that he would need to appear at roll-call the next morning with the chevrons on the sleeves of his jacket, and as luck would have it, "By" happened to have some tape on hand and was also flip [handy] with the needle. He kindly offered to sew them on for him. So the nice boy sat up with Beard while he was engaged on the job and put in time until after midnight writing letters to his family and friends at home. Of course, he informed them of his sudden, unexpected advancement, and no doubt modestly gave them a sly hint that in the future they might direct his letters to Corporal so and so. "By" easily induced the new "corporal" to give him these letters to mail and he awoke Orderly George Cunningham who took them and slipped them into an inside pocket of his jacket.

At the morning roll call, Captain Rogers noted these new chevrons, and told the boy to report at his tent when the men were dismissed. As soon as the captain had dismissed him, he cut for the orderly's tent to recover his letters, but George told him a whopper about having mailed them on an early boat, when the scamp had them snug in his jacket pocket all the time.

After breakfast I saddled my horse and rode over to division headquarters with George as I was in the habit of doing, and on the way he took these letters from his pocket and slipped them into a haversack with the other mail, remarking that there were six of them. I said,

"It's too bad to put up such a scurvy trick on the little cuss; why didn't you give him back his letters?"

"Give back nothing; all the mail that falls into my hands goes through."

"But when he gets mail addressed to a Corporal you will not call it out before the whole Battery?"

"Won't I? Just wait and see. I don't pass a title-even that of third corporal. You need not fear I will spoil your fun."

"But it is none of my fun. I rather like the little fellow."

"Of course you do. "By" said you gave him the stamps to mail those letters. By the way, there is not room in this Battery for the exercise of all your accomplishments. Why don't you apply for a commission in one of these colored regiments. Ayers says you know all about infantry, and it would be just fun to drill the Darkey's."

"Gad! I hadn't thought of it," said I, " and I suppose it is because I have no strong desire to leave the Battery. But a commission is worth going after, and if you think I stand any chance I will try it."

"You will have as good a show as anyone and if you will hand in your application I'll bet you a dollar that you will win."

"What makes you think so?"

"Because Major Stolbrand was asking me about you yesterday."

"What has he got to do with it?"

"He will pick the men that go from the artillery."

"The devil he will; then there is no show for me. The only time I ever had a talk with him was when he had me up on that corner stone deal, and I declined to give him any information whatever."

"No matter, that hasn't hurt you any. Say, I will tell you something on the quiet and you must not give me away. He wants your application but doesn't want you to know it. I think he would like to get you a commission, but he wants you to ask for it."

"Well then, he won't have to wait long, for I would drill a company of alligators for a hundred and twenty a month. A fellow can't save anything out of thirteen. He will get one this morning if I can get a good place to write it out."

When we reached Headquarters a quartermaster furnished me the conveniences and I wrote as follows:

Milliken's Bend, La., Feb.--1863

Major C. J. Stolbrand,
      Chief of Artillery.
Major,
      I have the honor to apply for a commission as captain in one of the colored regiments about to be organized.
      I understand the Infantry service from A to Z and have a fair knowledge of Light Artillery. I was once refused the loan of a copy of the Army Regulations by my captain with the remark that I already knew too much of them for a sergeant, but that objection will not hold good if I secure a captaincy.
      For reference I respectfully refer to Captain Rogers of Battery D. and Captains Dennison and Wheaton of the 8th Ill. Infantry.
      I have asked for a captaincy because that will give me an opportunity I have long craved of commanding the best company in a regiment. But should such a position not be open to me I will cheerfully accept a lieutenancy, and patiently await for promotion to the rank I wish to obtain.
      Yours,

I am Major very truly, Dan Caverno, [Dave Cornwell]
Private, Battery D, 2nd Ill. Lt. Art.

George [D Company orderly] came in, read it, laughed heartily, and remarked,

"That's the stuff Dan. You are as sure of a commission as if you had it in your pocket, but it will probably be a second lieutenancy for there are more than a thousand applications in ahead of yours."

"Well then, I guess I am left."

"Not a bit of it," replied Cunningham, "don't seal it; take it as it is and hand it to the Major."

I met Stolbrand at the flap of his tent and handed it to him. He quickly ran his eye over it and said,

"This is all right, Dan. I'll attend to it."

--- ------ ---

Major General John A. Logan was democratic and hospitable to a degree, and the officers of his division felt free to drop in on him at any old time with no more important business in mind than to sample his whiskey or burn one of his stogas.

Logan was a fluent talker and in the use of strenuous words has no rival in the Army of the Tennessee except Colonel John A. Rawlins, Grant's Asst. Adjutant General.

We had just had a review of the division in honor of Governors Richard Yates of Illinois and Oliver Perry Morton of Indiana, and General Logan had repaired to his tent, accompanied by these worthy civilians to refresh themselves with lemonade. John was a little hot about something that had been said of him, and broke out,

"Dick [probably Col. Oglesby of the 8th Ill.] some of them ---- sons of ---- reported that I would not recommend a man for promotion if he was not a democrat, when as a matter of fact the first name I sent in to you was that of a --- ---- Black Republican."

In Logan's quarters that evening, the proposed colored regiments were the subject of conversation. Lockwood, the division wagon-master, whose complexion was about as dark as John A.'s, with dark hair that curled slightly, remarked that he would like a commission in one of those regiments himself. Logan said that would be impossible as the President would commission only white men.

Pay day came around and with it an appointment for me of First Lieutenant in the new colored 9th Regiment of Louisiana Infantry. The battery boys flocked about with congratulations, and gave me a goodly roll of greenbacks in payment of money loaned and poker debts. They exhibited more evidence of good will than I really deserved. I was loathe to leave the Battery for I had become strongly attached to it. But there was no hope of advancement here, and this seemed to be my only show for getting a start upward. Could I have qualified for the Orderly's position offered me at Jackson, Tennessee, I might now have expected a commission in the Battery upon the first vacancy in the officer ranks.

So this was my opportunity for a hundred and ten per month instead of thirteen. I wrote and thanked the Department for the appointment and added that it was cheerfully accepted. Then I called on Major Stolbrand and thanked him also and in the course of our conversation he said that the Captains I had referred him to had assured him that I was capable, but Dennison had added that I was as willful as hell and would do as I pleased no matter where I was. Capt. Wheaton had said that he knew but little of my disposition, but that I had habitually drilled Co. K [8th Illinois] while a member of it, and put them through their paces correctly. He had also noticed me on the field at Shiloh, and had wondered why I was not an officer in my old company and regiment, instead of a private in the light artillery. He thought there was something wrong somewhere and believed the appointment would be a good one. He [Stolbrand] therefore sent in my name and trusted I would never give him cause to regret it.

CHAPTER XXXV

Sergeant Corydon Heath of Major Stolbrand's Battery G [2nd Illinois Light Artillery] received an appointment of captain, and Edward P. Smith from an Ohio or Indiana battery got a second lieutenancy. These two, with myself, filled the quota from the light artillery, and it was arranged between Stolbrand and Major Herman Lieb of the 8th Illinois that we three should serve in the same company of the new 9th Louisiana Infantry Regiment (African Descent) so I might help with the infantry drill, which they knew nothing about.

The three of us got together and called on Major Lieb of the "8th" who had the appointment of colonel of the 9th Louisiana and it was decided that we would establish a camp in tents on the Richmond road about two miles from the river. So there we moved our traps and settled down to business. We got blue flannel blouses and shoulder straps from the sutler and made a hustle for horses that would be required for recruiting purposes. Captain Heath secured a good saddle horse from his battery but I was not so lucky and took a mule. Smith did not succeed in getting anything. He was rather heavy and slow anyway but handy about quarters, and as we had no servant we let him remain in camp to keep things in order.

There was no surplus of Darkeys hanging around our camps for most of them had been run off by their masters, and we soon found that we were up against a stiff proposition. While we were recognized as commissioned officers we could not get mustered in and draw officer pay until we had the prescribed number of men enlisted. Forty would admit the muster of a first lieutenant and when the minimum number for a company were enrolled, which I think was about sixty-four, the captain and the second lieutenant could muster. Up to this time we were still members of our old organizations, and entitled to our old pay only. We three happened to be flush of funds and were buying our rations though still entitled to them free from the commissary.

Big Darkey Jack Jackson jumped his job driving mules and joined us with a couple of others he had managed to pick up somewhere, and I got the captain to appoint him first duty sergeant. We hoped to get white boys to fill the positions of orderly as they needed to have a common school education. I expected to have Bragg (our Battery mess cook) for a servant and he was anxious to go, but the Battery D boys could not spare him. I told him to stay with them until he could get their consent to skip, and then hunt me up.

As soon as our camp was established, Captain Heath and I started out for recruits. At the first plantation house we came to there were six or eight eligibles loafing around and we dismounted and proceeded to business. We found them much interested in the subject but could get no decisions from them. They would not say they would not go. Neither would they say they would. But they were willing to listen and talk, for they had nothing else to do and seemed to enjoy the importuning of commissioned officers, as it created a new sensation that was flattering. When the captain threw them a pretty slick bait at which they seemed inclined to bite, their wenches, who stood about, would shake their woolly heads at them and they would back off. Then they would commence to talk the subject all over again.

They tired the captain out at last and he told them to think it over and he would see them again the next day. Then we moved on, visiting three more plantations that day, and everything passed off so near like the first that I do not recall a variation worthy of note. Heath was a candid, honest fellow of unlimited patience, and a persuasive talker. Among white men he would have been a successful recruiting officer. I therefore said but little, but on one or two occasions I got a coon off to one side and stuffed him with argument until he would agree to go if his wench would consent. But of course she never would and I had no more success than the captain.

When we returned to camp that evening Heath seemed quite confident that we would get some of them the next day, but I was not. We were hungry and tired, and after demolishing the good supper that Smith had prepared for us, and smoking a cigar or two, we rolled up in our blankets under a beautiful shade tree in front of our tent, and a mockingbird lit in its branches and sang us to sleep.

We arose early next day and after breakfast started out as we had the previous day. We worked the same territory, talked to the same men, used the same old arguments and many new ones, answered the same questions over and over. We got plenty of talk but not a recruit. When the captain told them he would not be back again, they were evidently disappointed. They enjoyed these visits and would cheerfully have talked until the war closed.

This time Captain Heath returned to camp quite dispirited - so much so that he did not refer to the subject that evening.

When the other two turned in for the night I lay down also but with a fresh cigar lit for I was not ready to go to sleep. I had studied the situation carefully and arrived at the conclusion that these Darkeys were now having the time of their lives. Their masters had left them plenty of provisions so they had nothing to do but sit around, talk, and have a good time. Our Army was advancing, would surely win, and their freedom was assured. What need had they to "go sogering?" Wouldn't some other nigger get their wench if they did? That not one of them had the slightest intention of enlisting, I felt quite certain. It was equally certain that they liked to talk about it, but I swore that none of them would ever get very much entertainment of that nature at my expense. At this rate we would never enlist a company, and if it was going to be a failure the sooner I got back to the Battery the better.

As soon as I felt sure that Heath and Smith were asleep, I slipped away and hunted up Big Jack. I had a scheme and explained it to him and he said it was the only thing and wanted to help carry it out for he had only a half dozen Darkeys to boss. He was crazy to get more of them. As soon as our plans were arranged I returned to my blankets, and this time slumbered off with the other boys.

At breakfast next morning I asked Captain Heath about the program for the day. He said he had not decided anything and asked for a suggestion. I told him,

"You had better stay in camp today. Let your mouth rest and loan me your horse."

"Good boy. Nothing could suit me better; try one of my smokers."

"Don't you want me to go with you?" broke in Lieut. Smith.

"Not today," I replied. "I'll take an orderly with me."

The Captain brought up his horse and as soon as Jack saw me mount he rode up on my mule with his musket and cartridge box. His large bare feet just cleared the ground and the sleeves of his jacket, which bore a sergeant's chevrons, stopped about half way between the elbow and wrist, while his trousers were practically knee pants. His general appearance was extremely grotesque, but Jack himself was quite insensible to it.

There was a dubious look on the Captain's face when we started off, and I imagined that Smith felt hurt that I should prefer the company of Jack to himself. But between Jack and me there was a perfect understanding, and we agreed to a plot on the proper method of obtaining recruits for a "Company of African Descent."

We struck out for the farthest plantation. When we reached it the gang swarmed out of their cabins and gathered around us with unusual celerity, for Jack was a drawing card. They did not pay much attention to me but riveted their eyes on Jack, whom they must have thought a brigadier at least. Jack soon dismounted and proceeded to set these fellows up in line with about as much ceremony as he would use setting up so many tenpins. He reached for one on the left and hustled him up near the right with the remark,

"Yu wants tah gets yrsef in line cordin' to yer rank."

Jack meant all right, but he thought rank and height synonymous terms. He soon had them marking time and then marching about the grounds. I cut out an old fellow who was about seventy-five, and then Jack started down the road with the whole bunch, while I followed behind leading the mule. When the wenches discovered that the men were being marched away they set up a terrible howl, but this did not bother Jack. He kept them going and they were soon out of sight and hearing.

We stopped at three other plantations, gathered more Darkeys in, and reached camp in time for dinner with twenty-one very green, black recruits. Jack lined them up in front of the Captain's tent, and the sight of their familiar faces nearly paralyzed him. I dismounted, took their names, and asked the captain to swear them in, which he immediately did. Then, I quietly told Jack to keep his eye on them and see that none of them got away.

And the singular part of the transaction was that none of them seemed to want to get away; none of them ever complained about the manner of their enlistment. None of them ever deserted. In every respect they were just as contented and just as faithful as if their enlistment had been voluntary. Later I found that I had the good will of these men to an unusual degree, and it is not an unreasonable conjecture that they were grateful that I had taken the responsibility of settling the question of enlistment for them.

Being uncertain how the Captain would view such proceedings, I gave Jack all the credit for getting these men. In return for our success Heath gave me an even-up trade of his horse for my mule, and then gave the mule to Jack. Then he went off and got himself another horse. From that time on Jack and I attended to the recruiting, and we had only to find the Darkey to get the recruit for the new 9th Regiment of "Volunteers."

The Confederate Vicksburg batteries had been successfully run early in 1863 by many of the Union gunboats and numerous transports loaded with supplies. The Army had marched around by land, crossed the river into Mississippi, and taken Port Hudson at the mouth of the Big Black River. We had picked up all the recruits we could find within range of our camp in Louisiana and had less than 200 for the entire regiment.

Colonel Lieb selected a few officers to accompany him and started around after the army on a recruiting expedition. When about five miles from camp he for the first time noticed Big Jack, in all his glory, bringing up the rear. He asked me who was responsible for bringing along such a menagerie, and I pled guilty. He expressed his astonishment to find me so destitute of every sense of propriety, and ordered me to send him back to camp.

"If you wanted a servant or an orderly with you, why did you not select one that could get shoes, a uniform to fit, and ride the mule without crooking his legs? Why damn the fellow - just look at him! He is riding at the head of the other orderlies and thinks he is in command of them. What in hell did he want to bring that musket with him for? See the way he carries it; instead of having the muzzle down like a cavalryman's carbine, he has got it at a right-shoulder-shift with bayonet fixed. That fellow will bring ridicule on the whole Colored Service, and we will be a laughing stock all along the route. Send him back, Lieutenant, and my boy will take care of your horse while we are together. We are not out with a show, but are after recruits."

I said I understood that to be our object and that was why I had brought Jack along; that it would be soon enough to send him back when we got to Richmond, Louisiana, and in the meantime I would tell him something about the fellow. So I proceeded to give him much of Jack's history, which he listened to with great gravity. He did not even smile at the Irishman's discomfiture when Jack brought in the bee-hive that evening at Jackson, Tennessee. This gave me an insight into Herman Lieb's taste, disposition, make-up, or whatever you may call it, and I never wasted any more funny stories on him. Yet, with his nervous German-English speech, he was himself quite droll at times, but seemed to be utterly unaware of it himself.

I concluded the story with Jack's success in landing those twenty-one recruits before dinner when the captain had labored two whole days without securing a man. But I did not go into details about our methods; that was a scheme we were not bragging about. We rode along in silence for a half mile or so, and came in sight of the village of Richmond. Then Colonel Lieb remarked,

"At the first opportunity you get that colored sergeant a uniform that will fit him and a pair of shoes to cover his feet, and say, I wish you would drop back and tell him to unfix his bayonet and carry it in the scabbard, and to strap his musket to his saddle, muzzle downward, so that he will not attract quite so much attention." No more was said about sending him back.

We stopped the first night out in an extra room or two in a house occupied by General Thomas E. G. Ransom, who had lost an arm in battle and was now constantly accompanied by his young and beautiful wife. The General from Illinois was young and handsome and there was no unusual disparity in their ages. He was a high-bred officer and had the reputation of being both brainy and fearless, the two indispensable requisites of a general. His quartermaster supplied us with fodder for our animals, and his commissary with hardtack, coffee and sugar without charge. And we bought sardines and cigars from a sutler.

The second night out we accepted the hospitality of an artillery battery. Col. Lieb got into a game of draw poker here with the first lieutenant where the ante was five dollars. This lieutenant drank heavily of straight "Commissary" whiskey, and as they were sitting and dealing on the ground floor of the tent, there were no backs to their seats and his Darkey servant had to sit behind him and hold him up. Lieb had been losing right along, but as he kept sober and the lieutenant was getting drunker every minute it seemed only a matter of time when he would get his money back. And he no doubt would have but for the fact that the drunker this lieutenant got the more reckless he played, and the more certain he was to win. I was fool enough to stand there and watch the game and so when Lieb went strapped [broke] I had to lend him fifty, which went into the lieutenant's pile in about that many seconds. Then the coon let his boss tumble over, stuffed the winnings into his own pocket for safe keeping, covered his lieutenant with a blanket, and the game was over. Ten months later Lieb repaid the fifty. He played a square game and depended upon his nerve and was therefore no match for a professional gambler.

About noon the next day we crossed the Mississippi River at Port Hudson, Mississippi, and had dinner with a cavalry regiment, after which we received our orders and separated. I accompanied Lieb about ten miles and then found my old Battery B and remained with the boys overnight. When I saw Lieb in the morning he informed me that he intended to make the present campaign with the Army, and told me to gather up all the recruits possible and take them up to the Bend, back across the river.

I immediately struck out for Rocky Springs, Mississippi, near the advance positions of our Army, and then pushed on a few miles farther until I caught up with some advance cavalry. Turning back we enlisted every available Darkey we could find and drew the line sharply on chin music [very little discussion]. Jack did most of the talking and about all he said was,

"Git in dem ranks dar; faud ma'ch."

If a fellow hesitated, Jack picked him up and set him down in the line according to his "rank," and the column moved on. We reached Port Gibson, Mississippi, late in the evening, tired and hungry with about sixty recruits. I had called Lieb out as we passed Gen. Stephenson's quarters to see the gang, and he told me to turn them all over to the chief quartermaster at the landing to handle the supplies. I found the Q.M., who took charge of the men and me also.

In the morning I started back over the same route, intending to cut a wider swath this time, but was cautioned by some cavalry officers to keep near the main road used by our troops for fear of capture.

General Grant was quartering nearby and had his oldest son with him. He was a fair, average kid to all appearances. Somebody had picked up a shetland pony for him to ride, and it was turned loose here to graze on the lawn. It was a stallion, well along in years, and when I attempted to pay him my respects by stroking his mane the little beast wheeled and gave me a vicious kick. I was so incensed that I told him to go to -- back to the Shetland Isles. Then I went on to the stable and robbed Lieb's saddlebags of a half dozen cans of sardines.

About a half mile farther on I saw Billy Sherman [General W.T.] sitting in front of his tent with nothing on but his shirt and trousers. "Tecumseh" was not pretty at his best and looked very unlovely in this rig. Hours later while on my way back, he and his staff were lounging on a lawn in front of a mansion. I dismounted and sauntered up the walk intent on getting a glass of water, when off the front porch stepped an elegantly gowned lady who walked directly up to the party and inquired for the commanding officer.

Uncle Billy slowly arose and asked how he could be of service to her.

"By calling off your men who are running down my chickens," replied the lady.

"There it is, chickens again," replied Sherman. "My dear Madam, this is a grand campaign that we are engaged in and I have something of more importance to attend to than the protection of your henroosts. One would think from the complaints you people make, that chickens were the principal product of your plantations. You will certainly have to bear these little annoyances until this terrible war is over."

And she tossed right back,

"Well, I am going to tell you General that if your Yankee soldiers had charged on Richmond [Virginia] as valiantly as they do on my chickens this terrible war would have been over long ago."

Sherman could not appreciate or enjoy this sally, and his staff officers had to turn their backs to him or forego a smile, as he would stand no merriment at his expense. One of the pictorial artists sketched him one morning while he was standing around in his shirt tail, and by an unlucky chance Uncle Billy saw it and fired the gentleman out of camp.

This night I stopped again with the Battery boys. The next day I reached the river [Mississippi] with a dozen recruits. The other officers of our party had reconnoitered the country in other directions with fair success, and so we did not go out again.

Aboard one of the steamers lying at the landing I saw Colonel John P. Post, now commander of the "Eighth." He was the major at Donelson who strolled off when the regiment was hotly engaged and got captured. He remained a prisoner so long that his conduct was overlooked and upon the resignation of Col. Frank Rhodes in Oct. 1862, he became colonel of the 8th Illinois Volunteer Infantry. The command was now well out to the front in the charge of the plucky Lieut. Col. Josiah A. Sheetz, with the talented Major Loyd Wheaton next in command. And here was the colonel of this fine regiment walking the cabin floor of this steamer in full regimentals, making trips to the bar as often as once every ten minutes.

I took a seat and watched this man for more than an hour, and wondered what sort of material he was made of. I could imagine how a private soldier with no hope of notice or preferment --no matter how bravely he might conduct himself --might take an opportunity to escape the dangers of a vigorous campaign such as this was sure to be. But for a full-fledged colonel with a dubious reputation to clear up, to slink out in this contemptible manner was something quite incomprehensible to me.

What would I not have given for his privilege of conducting such a fine organization through the campaign now before them. Could he not see that a man had better die a thousand deaths than live without the respect of a living person, including himself? Why didn't he tear himself loose from his absurd fears, mount his horse and make a run for his command while the road was open to him? He had worn the uniform of a field officer for two years, and acted badly in the only engagement that fell to his lot. For all of that time he drew a field officer's pay and allowances of several thousand dollars without returning to the government a dime's worth of service. Had he no self respect, no sense of honor, no shame?

CHAPTER XXXVI

A couple of days later, the line of communication with the Army was broken, and the Quartermaster turned over to us about two hundred recruits, which we at once put enroute for Milliken's Bend, and they reached there without incident.

This bunch was distributed with a view to making the companies about even in numbers, and it gave us about forty men to the company. We at once commenced drilling them and found that in the marchings and company maneuvers they [Black soldiers] taught about as easily as white men. The discipline of the camp became very slack during our absence. Wenches had flocked in until they were nearly as numerous as the men.

Heath and Smith now became the recruiting officers for B Company, while I handled the management and drilling of the men. One of our Darkeys told Capt. Heath he knew of a magnificent stallion hidden in a swamp some twenty-five or thirty miles back from the river and offered to pilot him to the place. Heath was very fond of a fine horse and it was a temptation that he could not resist, notwithstanding there was much danger in venturing so far from our lines. So they hiked out and at the end of the second day the Captain returned with the frame of what might once have been a fine stallion. But the colored man did not return as he had drowned in crossing a bayou. Heath was much affected by this incident and turned what was left of the horse loose to roam in the Bermuda grass, remarking that he did not care what became of him. For reasons that will soon appear, I can give no further history of this stallion.

The Army of the Tennessee had thrashed Confederate generals, Johnston and Pemberton, wherever they had met them in the field, and had driven the latter inside the fortifications at Vicksburg. Had Grant been content to stop there, fortify his lines and give his tired troops a rest, he would for the first time in his military career have done something creditable. The contending forces here were so near even in numbers that any attempt to carry the Rebel works by assault was simply idiotic. We would have needed five men to their one to give us any hope of success, and then with a certainty that the loss of men would be nearly all on our side.

There was no exigency in the affairs of our Army or of the nation that required the immediate capture of this stronghold "at all hazards." Our connection with the river on our right furnished our supplies in convenient abundance. Our gunboats held the river below and above, and our troops lined the western shore. The enemy was absolutely cut off from all hope of obtaining additional supplies to feed their Army and the many inhabitants of the city of Vicksburg.

If the commanders of our Armies--like our Naval officers--were compelled to share the dangers of their men, no charges on these fortifications would have been made. It was a heinous crime to issue such an order, for the enemy suffered only a trifling loss while our boys were destroyed by the thousands. Bear in mind that these men had fought their way from Grand Gulf to Vicksburg via Jackson, and were tired and entitled to a rest and a small show for their lives.

But it was little of either for many of these old regiments. Civilians may have thought Grant a very brave man in their ignorance of the fact that he never would expose his person to any danger, and that it does not require personal courage to make other men fight. Often, the more timid a man is, the more desperate he wishes to appear; and if he is an army commander the more eager he is to have his men do something heroic for which he can get credit without sharing the personal risk.

So those fine boys were repeatedly ordered to charge the formidable Vicksburg forts and rifle pits to gratify the ambition of a heartless, brainless commander. Our men were mowed down by the hundreds, while the Confederate loss was insignificant. When Pemberton's last mule had been eaten, and all prospects of relief had vanished, he surrendered, and not because of those deplorable frontal assaults. At the end of each of them Pemberton had been the gainer, and Grant the loser.

Colonel Lieb took part in the first assault and then came back to us at the Bend. He was terribly put out with Grant and denounced such assaults as wholesale murder. He liked a fair fight but would not buck an impossible proposition. If cornered, Lieb would fight any odds; otherwise he wanted at least an even show. He was also disgusted with the condition in which he found his regiment [9th Louisiana, African Descent], and immediately hustled us to the river, leaving the women behind. Here he established an orderly, well-laid-out camp, and began running things with some system.

I soon called on him to convince him that our men should at once be taught to shoot for they knew nothing whatever about firing a musket. Before I had gotten half through what I had intended to say he sent an orderly after the Quartermaster and asked me how many cartridges we needed. I said 20,000. He told Orderly Clark to go with the requisition, and bring them back. Then Lieb turned to the Adjutant and directed him to make a special order appointing me instructor of target practice, and suggested I have targets made at once and get the boys all busy.

As I bid the Colonel good morning I mentally repeated an expression from Victor Hugo, "Vendee has at last a Commander."

I at once made a target and the other accessories and got the Regimental officers out for a drill of instruction. One lesson was sufficient for them and I went to work on my Co. B.

The target was a light frame - like that of a screen door - 22 inches wide and six feet high, about the size of a man. This was covered with canvas or sheeting with a large black bull's eye in the center, and set up in the field 200 yards from the levee. Immediately in front of it a pit was dug deep enough for a man to sit in out of sight and danger. He was provided with a flag on a rod sharpened at the butt to stick in the ground and when this flag was in sight no firing must take place. On the end of another rod was a disk of six-inch diameter, white on one side and black on the reverse. After each hit this would be held for an instant over the spot, so the firing party could at once see the result. By this method several shots can be made with short intervals, and when the ball holes in the target become too numerous to remember, the pitman would raise his flag [to stop the firing] and paste bits of paper over them.

We commenced by teaching aiming, and for this purpose made a tripod of sticks six feet long tied together a foot or more from the end. Spreading out the feet sufficiently to stand firm, we placed on the upper part of this simple contrivance a sack of earth into which a musket could be pressed so that it would point to the center of the target. Then we would call up the men in succession and tell them to place their muskets on this dirt sack so the sights would line up with the bull's eye. But few could do it.

Then we would point their piece for them and have them squint through the sights and see that they were in line with the bull's eye. They would brighten up then and declare they could do the trick correctly every time now. Then we would derange the musket and ask them to prove it. They would again commence squinting, squirming, wriggling, patting their gun into the yielding dirtsack, and after an exasperating wait, exclaim,

"Dar, Lutent, I'se got it right dis time; dat make hole fru middle dat bull's eye, suah."

But it wouldn't. It would only make a hole through the atmosphere fifty feet above and twenty to the right of the target. He had left the rear sight of his piece quite out of the calculation. Then I would make him get his eye in line with both sights of his musket and own up that it was not pointed at the target at all. But he felt "suah" he could do it the next time "cos yer see dis hind sight's got ter be tended to an' I ferget all 'bout it afore." But the next time he forgot all about the front sight and his piece was pointing to the ground not more than fifty yards away.

Then I would call him a woolly headed nincompoop, aim his gun correctly for him again, and tell him if he did not do it right the next time I would kill him. This time he was likely to be successful, but if he was not I didn't kill him, of course. I had no recruits to spare and knew he would learn after a while.

During this instruction there was a bunch of coons at my rear squinting, listening and catching on, and soon they commenced stepping up and pointing their pieces correctly at the first and second trying. So the next day I had some of them shooting at the target, and when one of them would accidentally hit it, he would be as proud as if he had killed his overseer, and would strut back and tell all the other Darkeys just exactly how he did it.

In a week these fellows would have been doing some very good shooting if something had not happened just at this time.

CHAPTER XXXVII

In the Spring of 1863 E. Kirby Smith, Lieutenant General, C.S.A. was in command of the Confederacy's Trans-Mississippi Department, which included all territory west of the big river between Cairo, Illinois and the Gulf of Mexico. His headquarters at this time was at Shreveport, Louisiana, 150 miles west of us, on the Red River, near the Texas state line.

In his command was one Major General Richard Taylor, a son of Old Zachary Taylor and brother-in-law of C.S.A. President Jefferson Davis. He sent this officer with a division, 5,000 or more strong, to clean out the colored troops along the west bank of the river, and if possible communicate with the besieged Confederate garrison of Vicksburg under General Pemberton.

Taylor reached Richmond, Louisiana with his division on April 5, 1863. A Rebel battalion of cavalry was a couple of days ahead of him, and we had got wind of them.

Our territory was called "The District of North Eastern Louisiana" and was in the charge of Union Brigadier General Elias S. Dennis, with headquarters eleven miles below us at Young's Point. For forty miles above us, to Lake Providence, were our Darkey recruits, stationed at a few selected points to protect the Northern planters the Treasury Department had encouraged to work abandoned plantations.

Our camp at Milliken's Bend was between the levee and the river, a distance of about 100 yards. The force here consisted of black soldiers the 9th Louisiana, Colonel Lieb, 400 strong; 1st Mississippi Battalion, 175 strong; 13th Louisiana Battalion, 125 strong and the 11th Louisiana, Colonel Chamberlain, 800 strong. These units composed the Milliken's Bend African Brigade.

The evening of June 5th General Dennis sent up to the Bend a Battalion of the 10th Illinois Cavalry under Captain Christ A. Anderson, about 200 strong, and ordered Lieb to cooperate with them in a reconnaissance westward toward Richmond. With the 9th Col. Lieb started at the break of day on June 6th, Capt. Daniels of Co. A leading with his men mounted on mules. I came next with Co. B, and a few hundred yards in rear came the other eight companies of the 9th.

We proceeded in this order until we were about two miles from Richmond, where the mule cavalry was fired into by some Rebel pickets from behind a bayou levee. Lieb came back and asked if I thought my company could charge that levee and drive the Rebels out. I said I thought they could if there were not too many of them, and so hastened forward out of the timber, deployed the men as skirmishers under fire, and rushed them over the levee.

We saw the Rebels mount their horses and escape without loss, and we came out equally well. It was fun to see those Negro recruits run for that levee. Each tried his best to get there first.

The rest of the Regiment came up and we were about to move forward again when a Darkey slipped out from behind a hedge and told us that the enemy was near by in great force. Lieb whipped out his field glasses and discovered a body of cavalry skirting around a piece of timber with the presumable intention of getting in our rear. He immediately faced us about and we started on the back track.

I now took up the duties of rear guard and after we had made about a mile and were in a heavy piece of timber I met the battalion of the 10th Illinois Cavalry, and steered my boys to the side of the road to let them pass. I politely saluted the officer who was riding at the head of the column, but he disdained to notice me. The troopers were more sociable, however, for I overheard the following remarks,

"A man ud be a damn fool to try to make soldiers out ah niggers."

"Anyone ought to know a nigger won't fight; they're running now before they seen a Reb."

"We will show them how it is done if we find any of them."

I shook my head at my boys and they made no reply. As we moved on I could hear a buzz of undertone talk among my men, and when I turned in the saddle they dropped their eyes and I read in their faces and manner evident dissatisfaction. They thought their white officers were making a cowardly sneak while they were itching for a fight. As a consequence, their gait was slow and their manner sulky. I knew better, and dropping back where they could all plainly hear, I broke out,

"Step up lively, bullies, and let's get over that bridge. Then if they hit us we will have a fair show. That cavalry talk don't touch me, I've seen cavalry before today. I could clean out that whole bunch with this company and would like the fun of doing it, only we are not here to fight one another. When our time comes, they will have to sing a different song." This outburst had the desired effect. They at once brightened up and struck into a brisk walk.

We passed on through the timber, over the bridge, and came into open fields in sight of the Regiment, which was about 400 yards in the lead. Then 1,000 yards from the bayou a roar came from the rear resembling distant thunder. Turning in the saddle I saw cavalry coming over the bridge at their greatest speed, and facing the boys about I started them back on the run for a block house that stood close up to the roadside. I quickly divided them into two bunches and placed them at the corners with strict orders not to fire until I gave them the word.

When the head of the cavalry column reached us they called out,

"Save us boys, for God's sake save us!"

The day was hot. Their jackets had been discarded, and most of them had lost their hats. They were lying on their animals' necks, wildly driving their spurs into their flanks, hanging to the pommels of their saddles for their dear lives and imploringly, piteously bawling, "Save us, save us, save us."

There was no interval between our cavalry and the Texans, and from their appearance as they flew by they could not be distinguished, but it so happened that the leading Texan took a revolver shot at the man directly before him when fifty yards away and I kept my eyes fastened on that fellow while I repeated the caution to my men, "Don't fire 'til I give the word."

As the last Illinois troopers passed by I yelled "Fire," and off went the muskets. These Texans were so excited with their chase that they had not noticed us at all. As my guns exploded they made a right turn into the field, received a harmless volley from our 9th Regiment at long range, and leisurely returned to the bridge where they found their regiment in line of battle with their backs resting on the bayou.

Not more than a dozen of these plucky Texans came as far as the block house. And they all went back again for my boys fired their guns before they were brought down to a level sighting condition. All balls traveled far overhead of the Texans.

That regiment of Texas cavalry was nearly our equal in numbers and had there been a Sheridan or Kilpatrick at the head of them, we might have had a serious time in getting back to the Bend. We could have withstood cavalry charges, but if they had surrounded us and poured in a steady fire we would have been nearly helpless because our men could not hit anything smaller than all out-of-doors.

But it is not at all likely that the Rebs had any officers of that caliber in the Trans-Mississippi Department. And so we plodded along toward camp in company with many of the 10th Cavalry boys who walked along leading their winded plugs and trying to make amends for the mean opinions they previously had of us by being sociable and praising us to our faces. And these are fair specimens of many remarks I heard on the way to camp:

"I say Lige, no one can tell me now that the colored men won't fight."

"Nor me nuther, for they saved our lives."

These cavalrymen had endured a terrible fright and for the moment were boiling over with gratitude.

We wended our way to the Bend, which we reached without further incident and commenced making preparations for an attack that seemed imminent. A report of the reconnaissance was at once dispatched by courier to General Dennis with an urgent request for reinforcements.

To our extreme disgust and mortification we found that during our absence from camp thirty yards of the hedge in front of the levee on the left of our line had been cut down, and I have never been able to find out who was responsible for this deplorable blunder. An ex-officer of the 11th Louisiana who was in camp that day recently wrote me that it was done on the order of one Col. or Gen. Shepard, who claimed to have some authority over the troops along the river and that it was owing to his protest (from the 11th Regt.) that this nefarious work was abandoned. But this same officer when writing of matters with which I was familiar, proved himself such an abominable liar that I find myself unable to credit his mildest statement.

That evening Major General Richard Taylor, occupying comfortable quarters in the village of Richmond, sent his army to wipe out the Negro troops at Milliken's Bend and Young's Point. He did not go himself, but entrusted the job to another major general by the name of J. G. Walker. This Walker had the true instinct of a major general all right, for when he got five miles away from Richmond, where a road branched off toward Young's Point, he pitched his tent, set out a box of cigars and a bottle of whiskey, and engaged in a battle royal at checkers with his Asst. Adjutant General. He had two brigadiers to do the work and it could not be expected that he would bother himself with the details.

He therefore told Brigadier J. M. Hawes to take a few cavalry troopers and his three regiments of infantry -- the 8th, 18th, and 22nd Texas, make the march of twenty miles to Young's Point during the night, and clean out the little garrison at the break of day. Then they all took another drink and Hawes with his little army struck the pike for the Point.

To his other Brigadier, Henry E. McCulloch, he gave the 16th, 17th, and 19th Texas Infantry, and a detachment of cavalry, and left the fate of Milliken's Bend in his hands. McCulloch was only five miles from his victims and so he brought his brigade down the road until his advance butted against our picket line. Then he sat down to await daylight.

General Dennis did not fully appreciate our situation, for he sent us only a light battalion of the 23rd Iowa Infantry...105 men, and a gunboat. He could have obtained more men from the right of Grant's line during the night, and should have done so if he had been a general in fact as in name.

CHAPTER XXXVIII

The levee in front of our camp was an embankment of earth about six feet high, sufficiently wide at the top for a wagon road, with sloping sides of about 25 degrees. At the foot of the exterior slope ran a thoroughfare for teams and wagons, while from choice horsebackers usually took the levee top. Next came a fine osage orange hedge with many gaps cut out for passages to the musket targets being erected by the company commanders. Beyond this, for about 1,000 yards to the next hedge parallel with our camp, was open field. Opposite our flanks were perpendicular hedges, the south one along the Richmond road. And right here the levee made a left angle and ran to the river bank. To equally protect our right flank we had thrown up a rifle pit, and another across the center of the camp.

Rebel encounters with our pickets during the night assured us we would be attacked at daylight, and so the first break of dawn found us in our places quite ready for them. Many officers and men were absent recruiting and on other duties, while a few were sick in hospital or camp, so of course we could not put the number in line that we had on our rolls.

The 9th La. under Col. Lieb took the left of the line with 285 officers and men. Next on the right was a battalion called the 1st Mississippi with only 153 men. Then the 13th La., 108 strong, and next a gap was left for the 23rd Iowa, which was still aboard the transport that had brought them up the river during the night. They got ashore just in time to keep the enemy from pouring through the interval that had been left for them, and put into the fight 105 officers and men.

The 11th La. of Col. Chamberlain held the right of the line. This regiment was filled to the minimum or better, for eight of their companies had been mustered in, and they furnished 680 men -- more than half of the whole Union force at Milliken's Bend.

As soon as it was light enough to see the farther hedge, we got glimpses of the enemy forming his line of battle. His front covered the field from hedge to hedge, double rank, elbow to elbow. They soon commenced advancing over this smooth open field, without an obstacle to break their step, until they reached our trifling target pits, and they had the appearance of a brigade on drill. What would I not have given to see them break into column by division, or assume any other formation that would put a check to their farther advance, for although I had been in battle before, we had no line of retreat here except to swim the Mississippi, and were evidently up against something this time that was extra hazardous.

Captain Heath, our "B" Company commander, had taken a musket and stepped into the ranks at the angle of the levee on the left, and Lieut. Smith had taken his place at the head of our company for I had been given a division (two companies) in reserve to watch the line where the hedge had been cut down, with orders to smash any force that gained a foothold on our side of the levee. Lieut. Charles M. Clark, our Regimental Quartermaster, had been the second duty sergeant in Co. K of the old 8th, and was appointed Q.M. Sergt. of our [9th La.] Regiment. His duties had kept him away from the battlefield so far in the war. But he was of Irish extraction--had a liberal supply of pride and pluck--and had sworn that he would have a hand in the next fight that came his way...and this was it.

He had recently made a trip to Memphis after supplies and had brought back many things for our officers, among them a few revolvers. One of the largest and best of these was for himself, and there he stood at our right, a few paces away in the front and only rank of our line, with his hands on his hips, and a revolver in each of them.

Colonel Lieb was astride his large, fine old war horse, "Jim," and was every inch the commander. No other field officer on our side of the levee mounted his horse during the fight. And I don't blame them much for it was rather conspicuous. But that did not faze Lieb. He was born conspicuous - would never take a back seat among men, and on a field of battle he was always in sight. No one ever had to ask where he was keeping himself. If they were anywhere near the firing line they had only to look about them to see him. Pythagoras said he would not ask another to do what he was unwilling to do himself. Lieb would never send a man where he was unwilling to go himself. If officers had to fully share the dangers of their men they would shy the hot corners and use their brains - if they had any - in maneuvering so as to get the enemy into the hot corners. We were now in a mighty hot position, but it was not of our seeking. The Army should have sent us a thousand or more good white soldiers, for these Darkeys knew practically nothing about using their muskets. We were sent only a hundred and were up against it good and stiff, for the enemy had nearly reached the levee.

After passing our musket targets 200 yards away the Rebels took the double quick and came forward in great shape. Not a shot was fired by us until they reached the near hedge row, and then most of the shots went into the air. Where the hedge was down the Rebs sailed up the exterior slope of the levee to meet our thin line on the top with empty guns and lowered bayonets. Those who hit the hedge near this opening came around through it but did not deploy to their left to obtain their original position in line. Instead, they rushed the levee at this point. Their guns being loaded, they shot the men facing their front and slowly moved down the interior slope, loading their pieces as they came.

It was time for my men to take a hand now. I had seen the weakness of the men at the levee and ordered my men to save their loads and not shoot a man if he could bayonet him, and not to fire a gun until the muzzle was against a Rebel. They were intensely excited and could not stand still. I guess I was a little excited myself, for instead of saying "Battalion, Charge Bayonets, Forward, Double Quick, March," as I ought to have, I simply said, "Now bounce them Bullies."

Big Black Jack Jackson passed me like a rocket. With the fury of a tiger he sprang into that gang and smashed everything before him. My whole reserve was onto them before they were aware of it and spread terror through that portion of the Rebel line. There was nothing left of Jack's gun but the barrel, and he was smashing in every head he could reach. He had repeatedly been bayoneted, but seemed unmindful of such injuries. The levee was soon cleared of the Rebel gang and I withdrew my men to our own side. But for Jack I could do nothing. On the other side they were yelling, "Shoot that big nigger, shoot that big nigger," while Jack was daring the whole gang to come up there and fight him. Then a fatal bullet reached his head and he went down full length on the levee.

The Johnnies, officers and all, threw themselves flat on the ground, out of sight, and there was no more bayonet fighting in that part of the line. We could hear their officers importuning them to jump up and rush us again, and to their implorations we added a warm invitation to the same effect, but nothing could induce those Texans to engage in any more bayonet exercise that day. But the plucky ones would raise up and shoot. I think a large majority of them did not rise up at all. I instructed my men to keep down and shoot only when one of them came in sight.

At my right I saw Clark with one hand on the top of the levee cracking his revolver almost in their faces. His hand did not tremble either, and he proved his nerve that day if any man did. As far as I could see, the officers in our regiment did not lie down, but I could see none of the enemy standing on their feet. I saw a Johnnie come in sight and told the Darkey near me to plug him. He was too slow and the fellow plugged me. The ball shattered the bone of my right arm at the shoulder. Hard luck you will think, but it was not as bad as it might have been. An inch to the right or left would have been my finish, for I was standing with my right side toward the Texan.

Colonel Lieb was spending much of his time on our right for conditions were not satisfactory to him on that flank. Colonel Chamberlain, commanding the 11th Louisiana, had gotten possession of a skiff or dugout and paddled himself out to the gunboat. When the gunboat captain saw him coming he should have told one of his gunners to drop a solid shot through the bottom of the skiff and drown the pusillanimous cuss. But he didn't. He politely received him on board and allowed this deserter to remain there until the battle was fought out. That captain had possibly served under old Commodore Foote and been taught to kick a humble Jackey [sailor] whenever he felt like it, but to treat a pair of epaulets with respect.

There were left with the 11th Regiment two field officers: Lieut. Col. Cyrus Sears and Major Cotton. The latter was a brave, manly fellow. He stood by his men at the levee and was killed early in the action. As the fight progressed here [on the right flank] Lieb could see but few officers with their men. This worried him for he thought the line here might give way at any moment. He could not be sure but that the officers had been killed. He had no time to investigate the matter. His left wing was standing solid, so he kept his eye on the right.

This spasmodic firing over the levee was kept up for a couple of hours or more. Lieb got a ball in the hip early in the fight but was still in the saddle. Our men were getting the worst of it because the Texans were good marksmen, while our colored troops could not hit the broad side of a cotton gin. Lieb rode up and said we must go to the river bank, that we could not stand this any longer: That the movement would commence on the right and must be executed rapidly. I agreed with him and then he noticed my condition and exclaimed,

"Good God! You can hardly stand up. Go to the river. I'll tell Smith," to which I replied,

"Get away from here or you will be shot. I'll tell Smith and then go."

He took my word for it, and while I was posting Smith I saw the line break at the center. Not being able to run I at once started and reached the river bank a moment ahead of the men.

A concerted effort to follow us was not made. The Johnnies had hugged the ground so tightly that we very nearly escaped without their knowing it. Two or three spasmodic rushes were made, but no Rebs ever reached the river bank. The enemy opposite us got about half way when our boys sprang up the bank and with a tigerish roar made a rush for them with their bayonets down. The Texans immediately wheeled and were soon tumbling over the levee out of sight. Those Negro bayonets had got on their nerves.

Failing to promptly follow us to the bank and shove us into the river, the enemy had virtually lost the battle. Our men could now stand and load their muskets below the danger line and fire with but little exposure. The Johnnies were a respectable distance away and our men cooled off and shot with greater care. We had now but to keep up a steady fire and tire the enemy out.

Up to this time the gunboat *Choctaw* on the Mississippi had not fired a shot. They were so low in the water that they could not see the levee, and could not help us, however much they might have wished to. Now they began sending shells over our heads and the levee into the field beyond. They could not hit any of the enemy, but sometimes a bombardment of the atmosphere has a salutary effect, and I have no doubt it was so in this case, inasmuch as it gave them a plausible pretext to give up the fight. The Rebels could never acknowledge defeat in a square stand-up fight with a lesser number of green Negro troops, but the gunboats were a different thing. So while we enjoyed hearing those large shells split the air above our heads, Gen. McCulloch must have gained much comfort from them also.

It might have been two or three hours after we took shelter under the river bank when the enemy withdrew. Another gunboat or two had arrived from below and they kept up a lively bombardment. I never could learn whether their shells killed anyone, but it was no fault of theirs if they didn't. If the river had been high so they could have got a fair rake at that levee behind which the enemy lay, and the field beyond, the fight would have been over in less time, and no doubt with much less loss to us and more to the enemy.

While we were at the levee there was no shirking of either officers or men in my vicinity, except in one instance. A middle aged Darkey of my company named Daniel Smith was making a sneak, and I called him back. He was frightened nearly to death and said he could not stand it any longer. I said,

"Shame on you, Daniel, to be a coward. This is only a skirmish; we will soon have them whipped and then you will be sorry you ran." I was lying to him for at that time I had not the remotest notion we would ever whip them. But I knew Smith to be a pious black and believed he ought to be willing to make the journey to Paradise with the rest of us. He at once resumed his place in the line and came through with the wounded. Later Daniel took much pride in telling of this incident, and two years afterward I overheard him relating it to some of the men. And he finished the story by saying,

"I tell yer boys its er fack; if it hadn't bin fur Lutent Caverno I'd bin a coward."

One of our most heroic white men at the Bend was John W. Ayers, a tall, clean cut, fine looking youth of 18 or 19 when he joined Company K (8th Illinois Infantry) at Cairo, in August of '61. He too had been detailed to serve in McAllister's Battery soon after Shiloh, and was returned to his company before we went down the river. He went through the battles of Fort Donelson and

Shiloh without a flinch and was one of the memorable "thirteen" who returned with me to camp after that two day [Shiloh] fight. With the "Old Eighth" he had participated in several engagements preceding the siege of Vicksburg and was also in the first silly attempt to carry that stronghold by storm.

Lieb was there, knew Ayers to be a first-class boy, and got him detailed for service in his new regiment (9th Louisiana Infantry). Then he sent him up to the Bend with a few recruits that had been picked up, and a temporary appointment of Orderly Sergeant. Such appointments were expected to be - and were in fact - only temporary, for Orderlies acted in the capacity of commissioned officers and very soon all of them who remained with the regiment were commissioned lieutenants, and their places filled with the most intelligent of the colored men.

On our left, at the angle in the levee, Captain Heath had planted himself, and with several men near him was cut off and taken prisoner. Ayers was near there in command of a company, but would not permit them [the enemy] to gather him in. He stubbornly fought them back to their own side of the levee. When we all fell back to the river bank he had had a bullet through each hand and was helpless. He returned to the regiment about October 1st minus a hand, a finger or two on the other and in poor health. Our Surgeon told him he must go back home and remain until he got well. On account of his condition he would not ask Lieb for a commission, and quite likely for the same reason, Lieb did not offer him one. He accepted a discharge and returned to his home in Bloomington, Ill. He should have been given a commission and a leave of absence, and then permitted to resign when he thought it his duty to do so.

He was of good stuff throughout, for in spite of the disadvantages that beset him he became a successful businessman and for the past twenty years [just prior to c. 1905] has been in the service of the Texas Pacific R.R. Co. At the present time he has charge of their most important station in Texas at Dallas.

John McElroy, in his incomparable history of the opening of the Mississippi, says when writing of this fight,

"All our troops at Milliken's Bend were under the command of Brigadier General E. S. Dennis, formerly Colonel of the 30th Illinois Infantry Regt." This is true inasmuch as he was in command of the geographical district, but it might be inferred by the young reader, or one unfamiliar with army organization, that he was on the ground and in command during the battle. As a matter of fact he was never at Milliken's Bend from the time we established the camp of colored troops there until after the fight. I did not hear of his going up there afterward. Gen. Dennis, while a Colonel, made a gallant fight against odds in Tennessee and won a star, but I do not remember that he did anything after that worthy of mention.

When Dennis received Colonel Lieb's report of the battle he made up a report of his own, using details given him by Colonel Lieb, very nearly in identical language. Dennis sent this report forward to Grant. So the report of this general who was a dozen miles away during the battle got into the Army records. Lieb's own report never turned up. If Dennis had been a gentleman he would have forwarded Lieb's report to Grant with a letter of transmittal. It would then have gotten into the

Army records as a report written by an officer who fought in the battle and knew of what he was writing. I do not hesitate to denounce Gen. Dennis' report of that fight as a contemptible fraud. I am glad of this opportunity to give Lieb's report as he wrote it while lying wounded on a cot in his tent, in the camp he had defended with such fearless gallantry and skill. He had an enemy bullet still in his hip as he wrote:

"Head Quarters, African Brigade, Milliken's Bend, La., June 8th 1863

General,
    I have the honor to report that pursuant to orders and instructions from Brig. Gen. E. S. Dennis, commanding Dist. of N.E. La., I made a reconnaissance in the direction of Richmond. Leaving camp at 2 o'clock a.m. of June 6th, I came up with a small force of our cavalry, encamping in the timber, three miles from the Bend, under command of Captain [Christ A.] Anderson.

    It was agreed that he should take the left side of Walnut Bayou and pursue it as far as Mrs. Ames' Plantation, while I with my command -250 strong- proceeded along the Richmond road.

    I then started marching leisurely forward to the railroad depot, within three miles of Richmond, where I encountered the enemy's pickets and advance which we drove in with scarcely any opposition, but anticipating that the enemy was in strong force, I retired slowly in the direction of the Bend.

    When about halfway back, a squad of our 10th Illinois Cavalry came dashing madly up in our rear, hotly pressed by the enemy's cavalry, reported to be in strong force.

    I immediately drew up my regiment in line across an open field and fired one volley, which was sufficient to send them [Rebels] back in disorder. But anticipating a flank movement in order to contest our passage over Walnut Bayou bridge, I again took up my line of march to the camp, where I arrived without further incident at 12:40 p.m.

    I immediately dispatched a courier with intelligence of the facts to General Dennis, who immediately started to my assistance the Navy gunboat *Choctaw*, and a detachment of the 23rd Iowa Infantry.

    Shortly after my arrival in camp I proceeded to double my pickets, and sent a squad of mounted infantry from my regiment to act as videttes. I immediately issued orders to the different Regiments of African Descent in my command to be in line of battle within the entrenchments at 2:00 a.m., leaving the 23rd Iowa - who were without tents or other shelter until 2:53 a.m., when I ordered them to move in double quick time to the breastworks.

All my orders were promptly obeyed. After a few minutes the pickets came in reporting the enemy rapidly advancing in strong force on the main Richmond road. At the same time heavy firing was heard in that direction, verifying the report. I immediately disposed my regiments in the rifle pits as follows:

The 9th La. Infty., 285 strong, on the extreme left; the 1st Miss. [BN.], 153 strong; the 13th La., 108 strong; the 23rd Iowa, 105 strong, in the center; and the 11th La., 395 strong, on the right.

The enemy advanced on the left of our front in line of battle, throwing out skirmishers in front, with a strong force of cavalry on his right flank, marching in close column by division, until within 3/4 of a mile of our works in an open field, where they deployed to the right and left, marching boldly on our works. [According to C.S.A. General H. E. McCulloch's battle report the action opened about 3:00 a.m.]

Our men were ordered to hold their fire until the enemy was within musket shot. The first volley was delivered when they were about in this range, which made them waver and recoil, a number running in confusion to the rear, the balance pushing on with intrepidity soon reached the levee, where a charge was ordered by the leaders and they came madly on with cries of "No quarters for white officers, kill the damned abolitionists, but spare the niggers, etc."

Our men being unaccustomed to the use of muskets - some having drilled only two days - the most proficient not more than three weeks in the manual of arms, they [Rebels] succeeded in getting up to our works and a number of them on top of the levee before any of our men could succeed in reloading their pieces. Many of our guns were Austrian Rifles and failed to fire, owing to deficiency in manufacture.

Here ensued a desperate hand-to-hand fight of several minutes duration with bayonets and clubbed muskets, the blacks exhibiting unprecedented bravery, and standing the charge nobly until the enemy in vastly overwhelming numbers succeeded in gaining a position on the levee on our extreme left from which they poured a murderous enfilading fire along our line, directing their fire chiefly to our officers who fell in numbers. Then, and not until they were overpowered and forced from their positions, were the blacks driven back, when numbers of them sought shelter behind wagons, piles of boxes and other objects. The others sought shelter behind the river bank and all poured volley after volley into the advancing enemy, and doggedly contested every inch of the ground.

At this juncture a broadside from the gunboat [*Choctaw*] checked the enemy who soon disappeared behind the levee, keeping up a constant fire on our men, and appeared to be extending their lines to our extreme right, although keeping up the heaviest fire on the left. They, however, attempted to cross the levee on our extreme right, but were held in check by two companies of the 11th La. Infty., which I had posted behind cotton bales and part of the old levee. In this position the fight continued until near noon, when the enemy suddenly withdrew. Our men, seeing this movement on the left, rushed after them and poured into their retreating ranks volley after volley while they remained within gunshot.

The old gunboat *Lexington* also gave the retreating rebels her farewell compliments, their scattering masses showing where the shell and shot struck with telling effect. All thanks to the staunch and noble boats, *Choctaw* and *Lexington*: They will long be remembered by the officers and recruits of the African Brigade.

My entire force, officers and men, are deserving of high compliment and special notice. Such a hand-to-hand conflict, such feats of daring, especially when we take into consideration that they were raw recruits and opposed to vastly superior numbers of veteran Texan troops, has never in the annals of this war been equalled. The endurance of the men after being wounded, their persistence in doggedly fighting, after having been driven from the breastworks, and their eagerness to resume the conflict, can never be surpast (sp).

I would gladly mention the names of some of the officers who made themselves conspicuous by acts of daring, but for fear of doing injustice to others, I will omit mentioning them here. The majority acted nobly.

The enemy had in action one brigade of infantry, and about 200 cavalry, commanded by Brig. Gen. McCulloch, nearly treble our number with two brigades in reserve. His loss is over 100 killed, and a large number wounded. They succeeded in getting a large number of the wounded off the field. Among their killed is Colonel Allen of the 10th Texas.

The losses in my command are as follows:

9th La. Infantry

Lieutenants J. Bawner, H. Wetmore and Thomas L. Walters and 1st Sergeants John J. Wine, B. F. Perrine and C. F. Cady, Killed. Captains Hissong, Hammond and Dewitts, and Lieutenants C. M. Clark, Dave Cornwell, R. T. Pains, M. M. Miller, W. A. Skillon, and 1st Sergeant John W. Ayers wounded. Captain Heath is a prisoner now in the Negro prison at Richmond. 60 privates killed, 98 wounded and 21 missing.

1st Miss. Infty.

2 killed, 21 wounded, 3 missing.

13th La. Infty.

5 wounded

11th La. Infty

2 officers killed, 7 wounded and 1 missing. 31 privates killed, 112 wounded and 242 missing.

I can only account for the very large number reported missing from the 11th La. Infty. by presuming that they were permitted to stray off after the action, as I am confident that none of them were taken prisoner.

Soon after the engagement, Col. Thomas K. Smith of the 54th Ohio Infty. arrived at the Bend, and kindly proffered the use of his boat, the *American*, for the wounded and sick, extending great courtesy and attention to officers and men.

This report is in main a resume of regimental reports, I myself having in the early part of the action received a not severe but a very painful gunshot wound in the thigh, which soon incapacitated me for action. The command then devolved on Colonel Chamberlain of the 11th La. Infty., who was nowhere to be seen on the field. Lieut. Col. Page of the 9th La. Infty. then assumed command. The 23rd Iowa Infty. left the field soon after the enemy got possession of the levee, headed by their Colonel, and was seen no more.

The detachment of [10th] Ill. cavalry, commanded by Major E. P. [Elvis] Shaw, although posted quite near, took no part in the action.

H. Lieb, Col. 9th Infty., Commanding
African Brigade

This is not a model report, but it is an exceedingly modest one, inasmuch as Lieb says he was wounded in the early part of the battle, which soon incapacitated him for action, when as a matter of fact he did not go out of action until we all fell back to the river bank, when if he had remained in his saddle he would have been the only one on our side, wholly exposed to the enemy's fire, and he would have been riddled with bullets in ten minutes. And at the time he turned the command over to Lieut. Col. Page, the fight was virtually won.

There are immaterial errors in this report, but it is not at all surprising. Lieb had to take the regimental reports for granted, and base his upon them, and his knowledge of what transpired after he turned the command over had to be obtained from officers who remained in action to the finish. The errors he was led into about the volleys that were poured into the seats of the Johnnies' pants as they retreated from the levee, and of the havoc created by the gunboat shells, was no doubt the work of an enthusiastic and officious lieutenant by the name of Matthew M. Miller, who came from the 46th Ill. Infantry, known as the Washburn Lead Mine Regiment, whose home town was Galena. This officer had his hand tied up and got himself listed among the wounded for a mere scratch that his Orderly at that time, and later his lieutenant, said he gave himself while attempting to load a musket with the bayonet fixed. He wrote a letter to his aunt directly after this battle, describing his role in it, and the innocent old lady, fired with pride in her gallant nephew, persuaded the *Galena Advertiser* to publish the letter in full. I happened to get [a copy of] that issue and cut it out. When Miller learned there was a copy of it in the Regiment, the knowledge of it made him very unhappy. He said he wrote it to fool his aunt and did not think she would have it published. Later I will tell you how Lieb got rid of this pretentious fellow.

I knew General Dennis well by sight, and would never have picked him out for a brigadier general. He wore his hair long and in curls like a school girl, and had an insipid look. Like many another colonel who accidentally got a star, he probably became indolent and lazy and instead of spending time on horseback visiting his camps and pickets and occasionally accompanying his cavalry scouts so that he might be familiar with his command and their surroundings, no doubt preferred to sit in his tent and play poker or pinochle. If he had been on the job he would have borrowed three or four regiments from Grant's right, come up to the Bend with them himself and killed or captured every man in McCulloch's Brigade.

Lieb had had an idea about what was coming and asked Dennis for reinforcements. He sent us only 100 men and a gunboat. The men were all right as far as they went, but he should have known that the gunboat could only help us with noise unless they sent their Jackeys ashore with carbines and revolvers. They were mighty shy of taking any such chances, and yet Lieb thanked them for shooting off a few guns without the slightest risk to themselves, and Dennis copied his thanks and forwarded them to Grant as his own.

The battle report handed in to Lieb by the 11th Louisiana says the number they lost in the fight was 2 officers and 31 privates killed, and 7 officers and 112 men wounded, and 242 missing, leaving only one survivor.

That one must have been Colonel Chamberlain, who had safely stowed himself away on the gunboat. He must have felt lonesome when he got ashore. Lieut. Col. Sears was neither killed nor wounded, so he must be counted among the missing. There is no doubt that some of his officers knew where he was. But their knowledge came from their being with him, so they won't tell. A white soldier wrote me a few years ago that some of the colored boys told him that it made them feel bad to have their officers desert them the way they did. I did not believe him then but I do now.

Captain Frank Orm of company B (11th Louisiana) in a letter to me from Burlington, Iowa, dated April 6th 1902, said the regiment put into the fight 680 men, and that his own company furnished 85. So they did have a few left after all. Lieb could have scarcely believed himself when he said that he could only account for the excessive number of men missing from this regiment by thinking they were allowed to wander off after the battle. He must have known that they slipped away during the fight, but he did not like to say it. For years Lieb shielded this regiment. Nevertheless, Lieut. Col. Sears has within the last few years been getting affidavits from the officers who were with him under the river bank stating that he himself commanded the African Brigade during nearly the entire battle, and that it was owing to his courage, skill, and pluck that the fight was won. I have copies of some of these lying affidavits, and Sears wrote me that he had plenty more of them. I have several letters from him and these documents as a bunch are a funny lot of contradictions. Sears undertook to ventilate some of this stuff during the past year in the *National Tribune* and I took the trouble of calling him down. I did not regret it for the article brought me letters from many of the old boys that I had not heard from since the war closed.

Here is what was in the *National Tribune* of October 10th, 1907:

"Col. Cyrus Sears, 49th U.S.C.T., Harpster, Ohio, owing to the bad conduct of his colonel became the ranking officer in the bloody fight at Milliken's Bend, where most of the officers present of his regiment were killed or afterward hanged by the rebels. In spite of the enemy's overwhelming numbers and their vicious charges, Col. Sears managed so well that he got his men together behind the last levee and made a determined stand, repulsing the enemy with great loss. The [11th La.] regiment lost 62 killed, which comrade Sears believes is the largest proportion of killed in any regiment in a single engagement."

As soon as this appeared [in print] I wrote Col. Sears and asked him if he was responsible for its publication. He denied all knowledge of it when I sent him a copy and then he wrote back that he was not the author, but that every word of it was true. Editor McElroy said that it was probably made up in the *Tribune* office. No doubt it was condensed from a long self-glorifying letter from Sears that they would not furnish space for.

At once I sent in a reply, but McElroy as a brave soldier, and a kind-hearted old veteran has an aversion to skinning people alive. He sent it back and asked me to modify it. I did so - though not so very much - and it went into the *National Tribune* of February 13th, 1908.

I never heard of Col. Chamberlain claiming any special credit for the gallantry (?) he exhibited in that fight at Milliken's Bend, but I will tell you of something he did do. When Lieb joined the Society of the Officers of the Army of the Tennessee many years ago when they met in Chicago, a very distinguished appearing stranger stepped to his [Lieb's] side, and without introducing himself requested the honor of presenting him to the Society. He then took his arm, led him to the platform, and gave an oration that was astonishingly fine in language, accompanied with graceful gestures and delivered with much feeling. He said he had seen General Lieb ride his charger through a storm of bullets that would blanch the cheek of the bravest man, but in him there had been no fear. And that at the close of the war he returned to his family and friends the hero of a dozen battles, and had well earned the title of the "Marshall Ney" of the Western Army. He covered him all over with what Lord Macauley would call "hyperbolical adulation" and judging from his manner he [Chamberlain] believed and felt every word he spoke.

It took Lieb's breath away to the extent that he could scarcely speak when he arose to acknowledge the warm greeting with which he was received, but later when he learned that the finished gentleman and accomplished orator who so eloquently and feelingly presented him to the Society, was no other than "Gunboat" Chamberlain, he nearly fainted away.

The percentages of loss in killed and wounded in the various regiments engaged in the fight were about as follows:

9th La. 70%; 1st Miss. 15%; 13th La. 5%; 23rd Iowa, 80%; and 11th La., 20%.

No blame can be attached to the colored men of the 11th for skipping out as many of them did. If their Colonel was aboard a gunboat on the river and their Lt. Col. [Sears] with many of his company officers were behind the river bank out of sight, they would of course have felt themselves deserted, and the wonder is that they did not all hike out. And they probably would have if Lieb had not looked after them pretty close.

In his work on the *Opening of the Mississippi*, John McElroy says this about one of our Captains at the Bend fight:

"Many of the wounded were terribly maltreated, receiving a number of wounds. Conspicuous among these was Captain William A. Skillen of the 9th La., and formerly a sergeant in the 20th Ohio. Five Rebels dashed at him to kill him, but he killed or wounded three of them before he was himself struck down. He was bayoneted in several places, his skull fractured with a musket butt, and several shots were fired into his body. But in spite of all this he lived, being one of the worst wounded men who survived during the war. There were many other instances of a similar nature."

Captain Heath who commanded Co. B of the 9th, was captured and hung. And Clark, the plucky 9th La. quartermaster, died of his wounds.

CHAPTER XXXIX

It was a desperate emergency that brought a little band of veterans, what was left of the 23rd Iowa, to this terrible fight. It makes one's heart ache to know that such brave men were shoved into battle after battle, and given no chance for their lives at all, while many regiments slipped through the war with scarcely a serious engagement to their credit.

When the battle opened up a battalion of the 10th Ill. Cavalry, commanded by Captain Christ A. Anderson, was drawn up in line about 400 yards from our left flank near their camp by the river bank. The first question likely to arise in the mind of the reader is why were they not behind the levee and dismounted in order to render the most effective service?

I can answer that only by surmising that they were sent up from Young's Point by Gen. Dennis with instructions to reconnoiter in the direction of Richmond, without being told to report to Lieb for orders, in which case Lieb could assume no authority over them. But it might have been just as well, for they were then at liberty to pitch in at any point [during the battle] they might choose as free lances, and there was nothing to prevent them from seriously embarrassing the enemy except the risk of getting hurt. They did not have the nerve to take this risk. They were strangers to pride and self respect and chose the part of ingrates and cowards and abandoned us to our fate. These troopers saw the terrible hand-to-hand bayonet struggle on the flank of the levee nearest to them, heard the Rebel yell and the cries of, "no quarter to the damned niggers and their officers," saw the bayonet lunges and the clubbed guns circle the air, and yet sat there on their horses within rifle range of the right flank of the enemy, armed with sabers, revolvers and carbines, without firing a shot or being moved by a single manly, honorable impulse. The 10th Illinois cavalrymen remained fixed in their saddles, viewing the scene, a half hour or more, and then slowly and shamefully started off down the river and disappeared from our sight. Later in the day they heard the result of the engagement and then wended their way back to the river-side camp they had so ingloriously deserted in the morning.

One of these men wrote a letter to his wife the next day, and started out in this fashion,

"Talk about wars and rumors of wars, but I have been in a tight place without a doubt. The story I'll relate."

He said that when the battle commenced at the break of day, they were mounted and in line within one fourth of a mile of our camp in fighting (or running) trim. That three hours after it was over they returned to their camp and found nothing disturbed, and that had we been defeated they would have lost all their clothes and things, without an opportunity to fight for them. And, he said he did not write this for publication, but "if Pa wished he might show the letter to the editor of the *Journal*."

If we had but known that "the clothes and things" of this salubrious battalion that we had rescued the previous day were in jeopardy, what an incentive it would have been for bringing into play all of our reserve vitality to beat back those ferocious Texans, that they might not ransack this cavalry camp after they had got us all killed off.

Frank Leslie's Illustrated Newspaper, January 16, 1864, showing respectful sketches of Negroes

Captain Anderson of the 10th Cavalry is now a simple and pious old duck living on a generous pension. He is chaplain of a Grand Army Post, believes himself a poet, and whines because the printers refuse his doggerel for publication. I tried to convince him that at the very least, the commander of his battalion ought to have been shot for making that dastardly sneak, but my efforts were an utter failure.

And he finished a recent seven or eight-page letter to me by expressing his gratitude to God for His care in the dangers he had passed through during the days near the Bend.

I jarred him a little by telling him that he might think his peace was made with his Maker, but it wasn't...that the boys who died in the ranks fighting like devils for their country, while such humbug soldiers as himself and companions deserted them, would stand much the better chance on "The Great Judgment Day," for God hated a coward and would never go back on a brave soldier, no matter what his orthodoxy, and that it was quite likely He would desert them as they had deserted us in our time of great distress at Milliken's Bend.

This is the sort of report troopers of the 10th circulated about this engagement: That our [white] officers all ran away, and the Negroes fought until all were killed or wounded but one or two; and then that the gunboats had opened up on the Johnnies and slaughtered them like sheep. And that what was left of them skipped out.

Colonel Lieb went north for a few weeks and neglected to prefer charges against Captain Anderson, so he escaped the dismissal for cowardice that would have been his fate had his case been attended to.

The 10th Illinois Cavalry was organized at Springfield in November, 1861 under Col. James A. Barrett. It served four years, and its record is hardly a brilliant one. Barrett served through all the campaigns and battles of Camp Butler and resigned in May, 1862. Lt. Col. Dudley Wickersham then clapped on the spread eagles and wore them two years. When he resigned, the command fell to James Stewart, who appears to have been the best of the lot.

Their historian says they were fortunate in having a very efficient chaplain who preached to them at every opportunity. Whether this was a piece of good fortune or a calamity will ever be a matter of opinion, but his unbounded influence over them can scarcely be doubted as they appear to have served their Lord and Master with far greater fidelity than they ever did Uncle Sam.

At Cane Hill, Arkansas in July, 1862, they killed a man and "took many prisoners." A few days later they had another skirmish and here they winged two and got more prisoners. No losses were sustained in either of these actions. In October Stewart had them out and attacked a Rebel camp and killed four; an increase in regular geometrical progression. Then (they say) they captured a captain and twenty-six men, and had the first man killed and the first wounded. They did really, at long last, get in the way of a few bullets. My suspicion that Stewart was their pluckiest officer proved correct.

On November 7th, 1862 seventy of them were attacked and surrendered. They do not claim that any of these men resisted capture or got hurt. The commanding officer was kicked out of the service, which must have been a surprise to him, even if he did not feel any pain from the operation.

For the next five months the 10th succeeded in steering clear of the enemy. Then that little fracas occurred near Richmond June 6, 1863 where, their historian says, they had two killed and 21 captured. They made no pretense of having injured any of the enemy here. In fact they did not stop long enough to cock a gun on the route back from Richmond.

In August, at Bayou Metee, they ran onto a few Butternuts who shot two of them just for fun. The 10th boys were rapidly withdrawing from the front and had no wish to bring on an engagement.

In July 1864, somewhere in Arkansas, the Johnnies got after them and they escaped with all of themselves except 22. They say (in their history) two of this number were killed and the others taken prisoners.

I will not question the truthfulness of this regimental history but it does not accord with reason. It does not seem possible that such a large and expensive organization could have served in such a war and done less. Many a company has killed more men in four hours than this regiment of twelve large companies killed in four years. Many a company has had more men killed in one battle than this regiment lost during their entire service. Many a soldier has killed more of the enemy than this regiment ever did. It is a moderate estimate that the maintenance of this regiment cost our government over $2,000,000.

Under able officers the 10th Cavalry might have been a good regiment. The enlisted men can be held at fault only as they upheld and defended their pusillanimous commanders.

These statistics tell much about the 10th and its wartime record:

Dismissed and drummed out -10th Ill. Cav., 11; 11th Ill. Cav., 2; 8th Ill. Infty, 1.
Killed and died of wounds - 10th Ill. Cav., 10; 11th Ill. Cav., 41; 8th Ill. Infty., 165.
Deserted - 10th Ill. Cav., 244; 11th Ill. Cav., 141; 8th Ill. Infty., 118.

The following is an extract from a letter I recently mailed one of the 10th Cavalry boys who was at Milliken's Bend:

"While you boys were not responsible for it, your commanding officer was a shameless coward and ought to have been shot. If I were you I would not try to excuse him as you do. He and his memory are unworthy of the friendship of any living man. There could be nothing but wind in his talk about protecting that hospital [near Young's Point]. If those convalescents were depending upon such an officer for protection, they might as well have thrown up their hands at the approach of the first Rebel.

"I cannot modify my remarks regarding the officer who commanded your battalion on the morning of June 7, 1863. No previous orders could possibly bind him for one moment after we were attacked in plain sight of his command. That of itself nullified all former orders and there was nothing left for him but to pitch in and stay to the finish. There is no defense of such conduct as he was guilty of. It is more merciful to flay him dead than alive, but I presume he was living in 1885 and saw my letter in the *Springfield* [Ill.] *Monitor*, wherein I assumed the man Morgan was the battalion commander, and therefore dressed *him* down to a finish in that letter.

"I say again, you ought not apologize for such cowards. They did you boys infinite harm in teaching you to run whenever the enemy hove in sight. I say 'damn such shameless officers,' and you would be justified in repeating it every night as you go to bed, and again in the morning after taking a little tobacco to get the natural taste in your mouth. Officers who brought Illinois boys through such a war as we had, without giving them a chance to try their carbines on the enemy, deserved to have had them tried on themselves."

But the members of Company A of the Bloodless Tenth capped the climax when they met in reunion at Springfield, Illinois near the close of 1884, and permitted the following item to be published in the *Monitor* as a part of their military history. In it they claimed to have had a hand in the Milliken's Bend fight, and one J. H. Morgan, as their historian, made this statement:

"During the battle I was an eye-witness to a daring deed that I have never seen in print. General Lieb was in command of our forces and soon after the battle opened I saw him rush down the bank, spring into the river, and swim to a gunboat, leaving the men to take care of themselves. This same Lieb is now a prominent politician in Chicago. 'He who fights and runs away, etc.'"

Lieb sent me a copy of the *Monitor* containing this "history" and an accompanying note which said...

"Don't that cork you, Major? Please give that dirty slink a shot, and oblige."

I at once worked up a sketch of what transpired about the Bend on the 6th and 7th, and closed the article and Morgan as follows. (The article had called Morgan a captain and I assumed him to have been the commander of the 10th Ill. Cavalry battalion that had deserted us at the Bend. I have learned since, however, that he was a corporal and never held a commission.) I wrote,

"But where was this gallant dragoon, Captain J. H. Morgan, on the 7th with the cavalry we had saved from annihilation the day before? Just hold your nose and I will tell you. They were sneaking off down the river toward Young's Point and saw none of the battle but its commencement, and that from a distance. They had left the Negroes to take care of themselves.

"A brave officer will fight and run away with his command when it is judicious to do so, and fight again the next day if he has a fair show, or will fight any day or any minute if he is cornered. But this Captain J. H. Morgan of Petersburg, Ill. would always run and never fight.

"This is another piece of history that I hope he will have the pleasure of seeing in print, and I trust that it will be read by all his neighbors and that this unworthy whelp will be properly rated by them from this time forth.

"The wretch who could basely act the part that he did [on June 7th] in the vicinity of Milliken's Bend, and then pen the extract at the head of this article, certainly merits the execration and contempt of every man, woman and child in America."

The *Monitor* gave me a square deal in publishing the letter in full with attractive headlines:

MILLIKEN'S BEND
An Interesting Account of the
Fight, by a Company
Commander [David Cornwell]

How Company A, Tenth Illinois
Cavalry Came Over the
Bridge.

The Statement that General Lieb
Swam his Horse to
a Gunboat
Denied.

Something for the Boys
of Company A
To Chew.

When the *Monitor* carrying this article reached General Lieb in Chicago he handed it to his wife to read aloud, and at the finish they laughed until they cried. Their three bright boys, who had been eagerly listening, jumped up and with yells, kicked their chairs over, and then hugged the old hero until they had him nigh strangled. He wrote me that it was a happy evening for them, and that this was another proof that I could always be relied upon.

A few weeks later I had a letter from Morgan saying that he did not wish for any newspaper controversy, but mentioned in extenuation of their action that one of their men had once been badly treated by Negro troops. I knew nothing of it and sent the letter to Lieb. He also had never heard of the incident and advised me to let him [Morgan] sizzle. So I never replied to it.

Quite recently one of the 10th boys wrote me that an Irishman from their battalion while enjoying a little inspiration strolled into a Negro camp and frankly gave them his opinion of them as a race and as soldiers, and that he got pretty roughly handled. What could be expected if there were no officers about to protect him?

The defeat of McCulloch's Texas Brigade at Milliken's Bend was a stunner on their commander, and the making of his official report of the battle must have been a gloomy and difficult task. To have told the plain truth would have been disgraceful, incredible. There was nothing for it but to romance it from beginning to end.

It has been said that the most expert liar cannot succeed in condensing more than three lies in one sentence, but he would not have made that break had he known the facts about this fight, and had a copy of McCulloch's report before him.

In the representations of this doughty Rebel warrior, the field over which his force advanced to the attack was so full of obstacles and pitfalls that it was only with great difficulty that he reached us at all. Really, he had nothing of this nature to contend with except the hedge immediately in front of the levee behind which our troops were posted. Numerous hedges are shown on his map that had no other existence, and the position of his brigade advancing to the attack with two parallel hedge rows on his immediate front is simply ridiculous. In the Mississippi he has placed four gunboats and three transports. He massed a thousand more Federal troops on our right where there was nothing in fact but timber and bushes.

When he said, "The true Yankee White portion ran like whipped curs almost as soon as the charge was ordered," he doubtless referred to the battalion of the 10th Cavalry that was plainly in his sight, and which sneaked off without firing a shot.

If we had been re-enforced with three transports loaded with troops, as he says we were, but very few of the liveliest sprinters would ever have got back to tell what happened to the rest of the Rebels. McCulloch acknowledged a force of 1,500, so it can be estimated that he had 2,000; or 700 more men than we had. Judging from what actually took place, it is probable that had we been able to meet him on the levee man for man it would have been a bayonet fight to the finish, and all over before the sun rose.

The Confederate Generals involved were much like some of our own. One remained in Shreveport, another in Richmond, the third at the forks of the road several miles away, while the one in immediate command kept himself at a safe distance. Hawes' Brigade that started for Young's Point did not reach it until near noon, when they were bluffed off and retired without a fight.

CHAPTER XL

While destroying my usual number of buckwheat cakes this morning, Mrs. Caverno [Annie Cornwell] in a kindly tone remarked,

"You worked pretty hard yesterday, Dan [Dave], and I think you have earned a day off and might go fishing."

To be accused of doing a day's hard work seemed something of a joke on me, but she looked sincerely grave and so I said I had forgotten what I had busied myself about yesterday, but whatever it was, I was not feeling sore over it just then.

"Why, don't you remember, you took out all the screens, dusted them off nicely and stored them snugly away in the attic?"

"Oh yes! Come to think about it, so I did," I answered; "it very nearly done me up. I believe I will rest up today and finish Charles Bradlaugh's *Impeachment of the House of Brunswick*, that I began last evening."

"Shoot Bradlaugh's *Impeachment*; the Brunswickers have now a hold on England that a thousand Bradlaugh's can never disturb, and all through the reign of a sensible woman [Victoria?]. I think you had best go fishing."

This struck me as something stronger than a mere suggestion, so I made no answer but kept at work on the buckwheat cakes and did a little thinking.

Since attaining middle age I have been inclined to flatter myself into believing that I had reached a point in civilization that freed me absolutely from the influence of every superstition and all the conventionalities of society that were not based on common sense or sound reason. Mrs. Caverno thinks she has too, but she hasn't. She still believes that Friday is the proper day of the week to eat fish and be hung.

Now reason and common sense teach one to eat a nice fresh fish whenever one can get such, and none but an inborn idiot would enjoy hanging on Friday more than any other day. And that lingering superstition accounts for her planning a fishing trip for me when really I didn't want to go at all.

I said it was cold and I was afraid I could not keep my feet warm, but she reminded me that I had a pair of lumberman's socks and rubbers for rabbit hunting, and wondered if they would not do for fishing. She also gave me permission to wear an old overcoat that hung in the basement. And I told her;

"Gee! I wouldn't wear that old coat through the business part of the city [Allegan, Michigan] for a five dollar bill."

That remark rather pleased the Madam, for at times she had suspected that much of my concern for personal appearance had gone the way of my superstition. She at once suggested that I take the skiff, which was housed above town, and slip down the river to the dam, thus bypassing the business section of town.

This kind of encouragement rather appealed to me, and so when I was told that the pancake batter had given out and that I would have to finish my breakfast on something else, I immediately arose and, rigging out in the toggery prescribed for me, shoved a small can of angle worms, a box of hooks and sinkers and the reel in my pockets, and catching up the rod, started for the boat house. I had left a few nice minnows in a pail of water that I had not seen for ten days, and I was anxious to give them fresh water. When I reached the skiff and emptied the bucket I let the minnows go with the water, for they were all dead.

Then I hastily jerked the boat into the stream, and soon was scudding down the river, in rear of the business blocks toward the dam.

When I reached there I tied the skiff and crossed the dam. There was not a fisherman to be seen. I at once took possession of the deepest and best fishing hole, where there were bushes on either side so that another could not crowd in, placed the boat cushion on a boulder for a warm soft seat, emptied my pockets of the accessories, and proceeded to assemble my rod, reel and line. After baiting the hook I lit a fresh stoga [cigar] and went after a fish.

A glance at my Ingersoll [pocket watch] told me it was nine o'clock. The Allegan County Court House bell struck five minutes late this morning. That city clock is an erratic concern. When the dials [faces] are out of sight I can never tell within five minutes when it will go off. A clock of that size that cannot keep up with a dollar watch is unworthy of the high position it occupies.

At nine twenty-seven I got a distinct nibble and pulled up a little flat fish of some species about two inches long. With a warning that if I caught him again I would leave him on the bank to suffer a lingering death, I returned him to his native element and baited my hook for a new start.

While the court house clock was striking ten I got a savage jerk, which bent my slender pole beautifully, and I skillfully landed a rock bass of goodly proportions. This made me feel fine and I hastily rebaited my hook and sent it after another one.

The next thing I caught was a snag. Not being able to get free from it I sat there half an hour. Then a minnow came along and released the hook. By doing so he got caught himself, but I instantly thanked him and dropped him in the water again, though if I remember right I did chide him gently for being so slow about freeing my hook.

Then along came a middle-aged, pleasant looking German with a covered basket on his arm. He had a cane pole about as large at one end as at the other, and with fully as much elasticity as a house mover's crow bar. His line was proportioned to his stick. I took him for a carpenter out of a job utilizing his chalkline, for his sinkers were a couple of twenty-penny steel wire nails looped on the line at one end, while the other ends were left to dangle in such a threatening manner that the boldest fish would never venture within forty feet of his hook.

I felt sorry for this simple man out of a job, because I felt that he needed a fish and that it was impossible for him to get one with that outlandish rig - the sight of which would frighten a turtle out of its shell. If I was only having a little better luck now I might catch enough for both of us. But I surely would get none at all if he dropped in anywhere near me, and so I advised him to take the farther boulder toward the dam where I had never seen any fish caught.

Being honest himself, he imagined I was, and confidently located himself on the rock that I had indicated to him; and after stringing a few worms on his hook he slung it into the water, spike nails and all.

It is a comfortable sensation to feel that you are "It," and strictly onto your job. As a faint streak of sunshine pushed its way through the bushes in my rear and hit me on the back of my neck I felt as comfortable and happy as if I had four good drinks inside me, and the remainder of the flask in my pocket. I had the deepest hole in the old pond, a neat elastic rod with reel, and black silk line - an outfit worth about ten dollars - while the rig of the old man next to me was worth about ten cents.

My pleasant reverie was soon disturbed by the German pulling out a bass as large as my own - a pure accident, of course. For some reason I was not getting any bites, and as I tried to raise my hook to see if my bait had been disturbed, I discovered that I had something. After a long, strong, steady pull I brought to the surface about four feet of number ten telephone wire.

Disgusted with my luck I hastily rebaited my hook, spit on it, and refused to sit down again. It now seemed necessary that I fish in dead earnest, for it was nearly noon and I was getting hungry. I had to have two more catches for less than three fish of the class we were catching would not go around. I was not happy any more but was feeling as serious as a penitent sinner.

While the noon whistles were screeching, I got another bite and landed a small bass. It was under the legal limit but what did I care. Just then I would have hung onto a four-inch shiner -- anything that had scales on it. So I said, "Good! Now for one more." As I dropped my hook into the water again I noticed the old German tugging at something that had got fast to his old chalk line, and Gee Whilikers! He slung out on the bank a pickerel about twenty inches long.

I laid my rod down, went over and made a critical examination of that pickerel, and measured him. I wanted to kick him for ignoring my tasty outfit and permitting himself to be caught with such a clumsy, common rig, but I did not dare do it because the German kept one eye on me all the time. Suddenly an inspiration hit me and I imparted it to the German. It was that he take a nickel for his bass and let me go home and get something to eat. And he replied,

"I vud gif you bof of dem for one nickel," and he raised the lid of his basket and there were two bass there. He had caught one that I did not know about.

So I reeled in my line, disjointed the rod, shoved it into its case, then with my ten-dollar outfit and the four bass started for home by the river, as I had come. The only person I encountered on the way who recognized me was Judge Williams, and he roasted me most heartlessly. But I have already forgiven him, for I had pulled my old hat down on my face to hide my identity and must have presented a grotesque appearance.

At dinner that evening Mrs. Caverno remarked to the third party at the table that I was becoming a very successful fisherman, for recently I had got a mess nearly every time I went out. The innocent little woman had not a suspicion that when I can't catch them myself I will buy or steal them to save her disappointment.

David's "Annie," Sarah Ann Stanclift Cornwell, his third and last wife. They were married in December 1888 in the Herman Lieb home in Chicago. This and the following photo of David doubtless were taken on the occasion of their wedding (left).

David at age 50 when in Chicago to be wedded to Sarah Ann. They lived together as man and wife for 23 years...longer than either of his previous marriages (right).

The Cornwell store at Monterey Center, Michigan c.1883-1903 (top).

David and Sarah sitting on porch of the store about 1895. Much has been done to the store building and surroundings since the Cornwells began housekeeping here (bottom).

CHAPTER XLI

Back to the Mississippi River: Immediately after the Bend battle, I was taken aboard a steamer where I lay on the cabin deck until transferred to a hospital boat at the mouth of the Yazoo River. I had kept the wound constantly wet with cold water and was not eager for an examination by the surgeons. But they came at last - two of them and a young medical student who was quite sure in his own mind that he really knew more than both of the old timers.

This youthful would-be surgeon decided at once that amputation was the only hope for me. The older doctors expressed no opinions on that point but said they wished to find the bullet if possible and extract it. They said the operation would be quite painful and tried to apply a sponge of chloroform to my nostrils, which I brushed aside with the remark that the smell was very offensive to me and they were at liberty to go after the bullet -- that I would notify them when the pain became unbearable.

So one of them probed about a little, apparently with no hope of accomplishing anything, and without causing any pain worthy of notice. When he desisted, the student again butted in with the assertion that amputation was the only thing that would save me, to which I replied.

"You made that remark before and you need not repeat it, for there won't be any amputation in my case." Then addressing one of the elders, I asked him to keep me supplied with a sponge and a basin of ice water to keep down the inflammation, and I would take my chances on the result. It goes without saying that had I taken the anesthetic I would have been on the dissecting table in short order. A few days later they removed me to another boat loaded with sick and wounded, bound for the north.

This boat stopped at Milliken's Bend for a couple of hours, and a few of the officers and many of the men came aboard. Lieut. Smith packed my belongings in a knapsack and placed them under my cot.

In time we reached Memphis where I was taken to the officers' hospital. I kept up the application of ice water without troubling the attendants - except to have them keep me supplied with the material and give me a dry mattress every few days. But soon the constant lying on my back became very painful and I asked if there could be no relief from this position. They brought me a hospital chair to try, and it turned out to be exactly what I wanted. I could then sit and recline at any angle I desired, and it seemed that I could never again be induced to lie on a horizontal bed. But I was though, for a boy in the same ward who had a painful wound in the head wished to try it, and I agreed that he might have it half the time, there being no other of the kind in the hospital. So I took to the bed again and sent the chair over to him, not doubting that it would bring him the same relief it had me. But it did not, and he sent it back within an hour.

This brave fellow was an Orderly Sergeant of the 23rd Iowa, who got his wound at Milliken's Bend. His officers were all killed and he had assumed the captaincy of his company - and he deserved to be, and I hope he became a captain in fact in time. He called himself one then and the doctors seemed to have no inclination to go back on a wounded man's word and brought him to this officers' hospital. I am ashamed to remember that I was glad when he sent back the chair. It was so hard to be unselfish and generous while in a painful situation.

This hospital was a model of cleanliness and comfort, and the care was all that could be desired. The "Old Eighth" had fought beside the 18th Ill. Infantry at Donelson and Shiloh, and a warm friendship had grown up between the men of these regiments. When on patrol duty they might arrest men of their own regiment, but never one of the other. One of the attendants here happened to be a little Irishman named Tim from the 18th, and when he discovered that I had been with the 8th until after Shiloh he paid me every attention possible, and looked after my every want. He would quarrel with the cook until he had the best of everything in the kitchen, and plenty of it, and would hang about and steal what he could not get otherwise. A wounded man is not like a sick one; when he begins to heal his appetite comes back strong.

The Medical Director came in one day and looked me over. He found the bones of my arm knitting together and said I would come out all right. He also said that it was unnecessary to use ice water any longer and had an assistant bandage my arm and give me a dry wrap. Zounds! but I felt comfortable then.

It was not long before I began taking walks up and down the ward, supporting my right arm with the left. I could not yet carry it in a sling without pain. A lady visited the ward and offered to read to me. I was delighted and told her so and had Tim bring her a chair. She opened the volume she carried in her hand and started on some Presbyterian stuff - one of Doctor Dick's sermons I guess - and so I paid no attention to what she was reading but feasted my eyes on her pretty hands and graceful form. Her face was a pleasant one though not handsome. But for all that it was a female face and looked quite lovely to me at that time.

When she finished the sermon she closed the book saying she would come again the next day if I wished. I did, and thanked her for her kindness suggesting, however, that she change books, as there was so much profound theology in the sermon she had read to me, that it would take me a week to digest it thoroughly. I added that if she could find a copy of "Pendennis" I would like to hear it read very much as it was one that I had never read but wished to. I thought if I could get her started on that I would have her engaged for a couple of weeks.

She came again the next day but did not have anything Thackerish in her little hand. It was a lugubrious volume entitled "What's on the Mind" or "Mind on the What's," I forget which. The last I caught of it the author was explaining the difference between reputation and character, and not being overburdened with either, it did not interest me. So I went to sleep.

That infernal Milliken's Bend fight got into my dreams and I suddenly awoke with an exclamation and a start that brought a sharp twinge of pain to my wounded arm. And it also brought a laugh from several of the boys in the ward. The lady was gone, and I felt I would see her no more. The more I cursed my stupidity the more the boys enjoyed my plight.

But that charming young woman fooled us for she came the next day at the usual hour as if nothing had happened, and this time the joke was on me for she had with her a copy of Orpheus C.

Kerr's stuff, which made me laugh until I had to beg her to desist because of the pain it produced in my arm.

She smiled sadly and said it seemed as if her efforts to entertain me had proved futile. But I assured her they had not, and that I had enjoyed her visits exceedingly, that I hoped she would continue them and give me as much of her pleasant company as she could spare and talk to me instead of reading from books.

So we drifted into conversation and had several pleasant chats. If she had been a few years younger I would have fallen head over heels in love with her. As it was, on one or two occasions I caught myself unconsciously reaching out to get possession of one of her pretty white hands. I can half understand why so many matches are made in hospitals between convalescents and pretty nurses, for a man is then in a very susceptible condition; but I do not comprehend the other side of it so clearly. Possibly sympathy cuts a large figure there.

I was soon able to carry my arm in a sling, and I ventured on the street for a short walk. My, but the world looked bright to me again. From the moment I caught sight of that solid line of Confederates moving down on us at the Bend up to the day the Medical Director examined me and cut out the ice water applications, I had but faint hope for the future. I had not persisted in following the method of treatment I adopted, with full confidence that I could save myself by so doing, but because I preferred death to amputation. Had I known that I would be pensioned and practically taken care of by the government, I might have taken a different view of the matter. As it turned out I saved my arm and a snug sum of cash to the nation. Being a commissioned officer I did not dream of a pension and was indisposed to lead the life of a one-armed man. I had found it none too easy to support myself in comfort when I had both arms, and I did not propose to undertake the task minus the right one.

I now spent much time in the city park, enjoying being alive as I never had before. The people were very friendly, Northern and Southern alike, and I received many a good cigar from gentlemen and kind and sympathetic words from ladies. To the inquiry as to where I was wounded, I would say at Vicksburg. Generally speaking, this was correct. It was not necessary to hurt the feelings of these kind Southerners who were supplying me with cigars and flowers, by telling them that I had helped a lot of green plantation Darkeys whip a superior force of their best Texan troops. That would have been a cruelty of which, in my condition then and frame of mind, I was quite incapable of inflicting.

Previously, Colonel Lieb, who had nearly recovered from his wound and was on his way back to our regiment, stopped off two or three days at Memphis and made me several visits. I was about "busted" financially, and Lieb was in the same fix. He remained there an extra day trying to raise me the fifty he had thrown into the poker game months earlier, but was obliged to leave me without liquidating. I think he felt as grieved over the circumstance as I did.

I wanted to go north for a few weeks but could draw no pay because our regiment [9th Louisiana Infantry, African Brigade] had not been mustered in. The State of Illinois had a committee in Memphis looking after the welfare of its soldiers, and I asked them for a loan of fifty. They said the very best they could do for me was to give me ten outright, and I reluctantly accepted it. An

Illinois captain offered to take charge of me and see that I got to Bloomington. The steamer fare to Cairo was ten dollars, but he managed some way to "deadhead" me through, so I was able to buy my railroad ticket to Bloomington. That captain was a shrewd whole-souled fellow, and I much regret that I cannot recall his name.

I remained in Bloomington a while with my old landlord and friend, Mathews, and his lovely wife, hit him for a loan of a hundred, and left for Chicago. From there I drifted out into the country and whiled away a few weeks pleasantly, during which time I was initiated into the Union League, whose meetings were held in a little out-of-the-way country school house. About all they seemed to be interested in at the time was the re-election of President Lincoln.

The first night here I made the discovery that I could lie on my left side without bringing pain to my wounded right arm, and I can never forget the solid comfort I took that night. I wouldn't permit myself to go to sleep here as it would rob me of the consciousness of the enjoyment I was having out of the situation.

I kept in touch with Colonel Lieb and he urged me to return at the earliest possible date. I was anxious to go back for one reason: I was tired of going to the city every twenty days and procuring an extension of time on my leave, when it was evident that I would not have the use of my arm again for months. And the authorities could scarcely expect me to go on duty again until I could use my arm to draw a sword, and might have extended my time for months instead of days.

However, I started out about the middle of September, but on account of the river being extremely low, and the boats exceedingly slow, I did not reach Vicksburg until near the end of the month.

When Colonel Lieb went down the river after recovering from his wound he found his command still at Milliken's Bend, and in a most deplorable condition. His lieutenant colonel was trying to have a good, easy time and to this end had confiscated an old carryall and harness, and in this was having one of the remaining Darkeys drive him about the country behind Lieb's splendid horse, Jim. As he had not been mustered in yet, this officer was sent back to his old organization and out of the 9th in short order. Lieb went on to Vicksburg on the same boat in which he had come down, and immediately called on General Grant. The latter highly appreciated a good officer and told Lieb he could have anything he wanted.

"Select any piece of unoccupied ground you can find about the city for your camp, and bring down the remnants of your regiment and take possession of it. I will furnish you all the facilities for recruiting that you require. You may organize as Infantry, Cavalry or Heavy Artillery as you like, but I would rather you choose the latter and help on the new fortifications here."

"But I don't know anything about the artillery service," replied Lieb.

"That doesn't matter. You can learn," said Grant.

Of course, that settled it with Lieb. He had been given an option on any of the three branches of the service and was then told which one to take. This was fair enough, only a trifle funny.

In two hours Lieb had picked out a beautiful location on the river bank south of the city, and was back at the Bend with a transport. In two more he had all that was left of the regiment piled aboard that steamer, and an hour later the boat was moored to the river bank at this new camp. As soon as the camp had been established and everything put in good shape, he dispatched the officers in various directions after recruits. He took a special steamer for Natchez and intermediate landings. He had to have a lot of men now for it took 1800 to fill a Heavy Artillery Regiment.

And it was there I found the colonel when I reached Vicksburg late in September.

Two *Leslie's* sketches showing early 1863 deployments and occupations of Negroes in the Mississippi River Valley. Their heavy engagement as infantry at the Battle of Milliken's Bend June 7 had to be considered the centerpiece of the Black man's contribution to Union victory west of the Appalachians.
(Top) "In The Trenches"
(Bottom) "Govrnt. Blacksmiths' Shop"

CHAPTER XLII

I went directly to Regimental Headquarters, was warmly received by Colonel Lieb, and addressed as "Captain." I had scarcely thought of my prospects for promotion during my absence. So I was surprised as well as pleased with this. During most of my service I had acted in a capacity above the rank that I held, and at last I was to have a command of my own, a company to control. I would not have to depend on a subordinate to drill and discipline the men for me for I knew that as soon as I could get the free use of my arm again I would be quite equal to all the duties of a captain in either infantry or artillery.

Lieb kept me with him until his cook called us to supper, and during the repast he told me what was known of the fate of Captain Corydon Heath and a few other officers captured at the Bend. The only one who ever returned was the Captain of Co. I [9th La. Infantry], whose name I cannot recall. I remember him as of medium height, square and solidly built, with a strong fine face. He had been a sergeant in the 6th Missouri Infantry [Union] and still wore his old uniform with the chevrons on the jacket. Fortunately for him there was nothing about his person to indicate his rank or his connection with a colored regiment, and he was able to convince the Rebels that he just happened to be there when the attack was made, and felt bound to take a hand in it. So they let him off. He returned to the Bend, picked up his traps, and went back to his old regiment. He did not propose to take such chances again [with colored troops]; and who could blame him?

The remainder of the captured officers were hung. When these facts were reported to Grant, he wrote a letter to General Dick Taylor, and the latter denied all knowledge of any such executions, and I think he admitted in the same letter that they could not have occurred without his knowledge. Although Grant knew these men were hung he accepted Taylor's word and dropped the matter. It was just as easy for major generals in either service to lie as it was for a private. Taylor did not have the manhood and courage of old Putnam, or he would have said,

"They were captured as nigger officers, tried as nigger officers, convicted as nigger officers, and hung as nigger officers." But he sneaked behind a cowardly, dirty lie.

Grant should have selected the same number of Confederate officers of equal rank and given Taylor ten days to produce those he had captured at the Bend. When the ten days had expired he should have hung them. And every reader will exclaim, "Why didn't he do it?"

It was because he was indifferent and did not want to bother himself with it. What were a few low-rank officers anyway - he could make plenty more of them. It was not because he was sympathetic and tender-hearted that he neglected to take a stern and just course in this case for it is a well-known, indisputable fact that later on, when Commander-In-Chief of the Army, he let our boys rot in Andersonville and other Rebel prisons while we held double the number of prisoners that the Confederate Government would have cheerfully exchanged man for man. The reason given was that our men would come back to us so emaciated that they could render but little service in our Army again, while the Butternuts, who had been well fed and cared for, could at once take up arms again and face us once more.

It seems incomprehensible that such heartless reasoning would have been considered for a moment by our government at Washington, but the fact was that Grant had by the most stupendous run of luck that ever fell to a mortal man become virtually a dictator, and no one dared to override him.

The boys in the ranks would to a man have voted for an immediate prisoner exchange even if they had known it would have prolonged the war five years. But it is not probable that it would have extended it for five weeks. There was no necessity for leaving our men in Southern prisons until they were starved into skeletons. A prompt and regular exchange of prisoners would have ended such cruelty.

At no time did the North ever reach the limit in supplying soldiers for our army, but the Confederacy had conscripted everything that could carry a musket. The cruelties practiced on Union prisoners can never be forgotten. That the enemy were permitted to hold them for the length of time they did through the cruel and heartless reasoning of General Grant should never be forgotten.

I was told to take charge of my old company which had been given the letter B, and placed on the left. The two additional companies, L and M, which the artillery organization would require, had no existence at this time. I strolled through the camp, chatting with the old officers I found on the way, and as they all called me "Captain," I saw it was understood in the regiment that when I returned I was to have command of my old company.

When I reached the quarters of company B, there was the big, awkward, homely but darling Lieutenant Smith, who was so surprised and delighted at my return that he hugged me and cried with joy. A stranger by the name of Patton had been placed over him as a first lieutenant, and they did not get along together. Smith soon told me of this, and also that he had tendered his resignation, which he now very much regretted.

Later Patton came in and his deportment was so obsequious, strangely mingled with a manner so airy and flippant, that I at once took a dislike to him. When Smith stepped out he turned the conversation on him and told me in confidence that he was of no account, had handed in his resignation and that we would soon be rid of him.

Smith dressed and bandaged my arm that night with the care and skill of a hospital nurse, tucked the blanket about me when I had taken to the cot for the night, and then took a seat beside me and we talked of the fight at the Bend and the sad fate of our Captain Heath and the other officers that had been captured and hung. Patton was sleeping somewhere out of quarters, and so we were not troubled with his presence.

But he was there at the morning mess and I told him that as October 1st was only two days off, I would take over the company property and assume command on that date. Then I asked Smith to take a walk with me and we strolled up to the Adjutant's tent. There I got the Adjutant to write the Adjutant General of the Army for Smith, saying that he had tendered his resignation while laboring under a misapprehension, and that he now wished to recall it.

I took this to Lieb and he hesitated about approving it. I told him frankly that I liked Smith and he liked me, and I wanted to keep him and that he would make a good recruiting officer and we could keep him busy for a long time. After much talk on the subject he reluctantly promised to approve and forward it.

That day the regiment was paid off and I got myself mustered in to date back to the seventh day of August as a first lieutenant. I was not on the payroll and did not go near the pay table. When we sat down to supper that evening Lieutenant Patton related that one of the company was absent when his name was called by the paymaster, and the money was handed to him. Then the man afterwards came up and drew his money also. Then Patton slapped his hand on his pocket to indicate that he had it right there [had the man's money]. "Well, what are you going to do with it?" I asked.

"Turn it into the mess fund so we will all get the benefit of it," he replied.

"Not by a damsite," said I. "You are going to return it to Major Dickey (paymaster) and then hand your resignation to Colonel Lieb. You attend to it first thing in the morning, else I will prefer charges against you and have you placed in arrest."

The next day I took over the company and told Patton I had no further use for him. Smith was the happiest officer in camp and wore a broad grin for a week after. Lieb sent for me, and as soon as I convinced him that the fellow [Patton] was a contemptible slink and a disgrace to the service, he approved of his resignation and sent it forward. Army Adjutant General Thomas happened to be in Vicksburg at the time and promptly accepted it. So Patton was out of the service before he could turn around.

But the funny part of it was that he got the sympathy of the paymaster he had robbed, for that officer came to me and said I must be mistaken in the matter; such a transaction could not have occurred. I replied that Patton said it did happen and had offered to turn the money into our mess fund, and as he was either a thief or a fool liar I had no further use for him. I did not learn if Major Dickey accepted the returned stolen money from him or not.

There were several of the Milliken's Bend Darkeys in my new company, and they were pleased to have me back with them. They had all disliked Patton and when I ousted him so promptly I won the last one of them to perfect obedience through respect and good will. There was no question now but that I could get the very best of these boys that was in them and I determined to do it.

That the reader may note the names of these plantation Darkeys, I will include the roster of our company as it stood just before the Bend fight, as of June 6, 1863.

Jack Jackson	#Tobias Ora	#Lewis Yennel
Geo. Washington	#Henry Liles	Thomas Brooks
Albert Houston	#Warren Jones	Washington Brooks
#Daniel Smith	#William Thompson	Calib Stamps
#David Walker	Jordon Hutchinson	#Willis Woods
#George Boy	Toney Patrick	#Andrew Griffin

Thomas Warnic	#Nelson Trueman	Holland Vaughn
Andrew Jackson	William Holly	Frank Vaughn
William Chilles	Willis Jones	Jacob Wells
#Thomas Smith	Henry Newsom	Wilson Shelby
Randal Russell	Jack Jenkins	Geo. Alexander
James Henry	Sylvester Noble	Cyrus Cotton
#Henry Hunt	Daniel Giles	Lewis Oliver
Samuel Franklin	Austin Cuffee	John Hennison
Moses West	Isaac Armstrong	#Richard Alexander
Jackson Broadrick		

The fourteen men whose names are preceded by # were still with the company, the remainder having been killed, too severely wounded to return to duty, or having died of disease. A number of these fourteen had been wounded and recovered. It will be observed that there is little in this list of names to distinguish the roster from that of a white company. Washington appears but twice, Cuffee once as a family name and we look in vain for Sambo.

I found this roll among the company papers and took it to Colonel Lieb as proof that I was entitled to muster as first lieutenant June 1st, having issued clothing to these men on that date. He told me to make out the papers and he would sign them, which I did at once and then got re-mustered. This gave me two months lieutenant's pay, less that of a private, which was an additional two hundred dollars and more. I had previously drawn my back pay on a personal payroll and got one hundred in bounty, which did not appear my due after my re-muster back to June 1st, for at that date I had not yet served two full years under my last enlistment; but I got it just the same, and the Army never tried to get it back.

On October 1st I took over the property of the company, and on the 15th issued clothing to fifty men, all of them but Tedrow, the white Orderly, signing their name with an "X."

General McPherson was in command and was popular with both soldier and citizen. He would stroll about the city unattended by staff officer or orderly, and was always approachable alike by brigadier or beggar.

In addition to being a thoroughbred gentleman, McPherson was one of the ablest officers in our Army. He was cool and fearless on the field of battle, and could divine the movements and action of the enemy with wonderful precision. Had he been in command of the Union forces at Pittsburg Landing, General Buell would have found little to do when he reached there with his splendid army, for the Army of the Tennessee would have been securely entrenched. And if the Confederates had persisted in their Shiloh attack, they would have been destroyed wholesale. Before nightfall we would have had the larger force, for with the security and advantage of a fortified line our men would have remained with us instead of taking to the woods as they did. The enemy had only about 1/4 more men than we did, and with double our number they could have made no impression on a strong line of fortification in one day. The history of Vicksburg, Port Hudson, and all other sieges of the war will confirm this statement.

McPherson had laid out and was now constructing a line of formidable fortifications around Vicksburg from river above to river below of about three miles in length, containing twelve strong forts about 1/4 of a mile apart, connected by an excellent line of breastworks for infantry.

Payday came around again, which brought me another nice bunch of money, and I felt financially very comfortable. I immediately expressed a hundred with interest to Bloomington to pay off the loan I had negotiated while there, and when the old gentleman received it he wrote, "Thank God; you have proved true." Then I learned he was not expecting to get it back.

He was a religious old duck that I had worked for and boarded with, and he would have thought well of me if I could have forgotten the vocabulary of the Erie Canal and attended the Presbyterian Church where he and his attractive wife were members. His wife was much younger than himself, rather nice looking, of a literary turn, and had some ideas quite her own about the elect. She never chided me if I happened to drop a strong word in her presence; she knew it was a harmless accident and would only laugh if I looked embarrassed or attempted a stupid apology. And when the old gentleman was not about she would use a mild adjective herself in telling a funny story or quoting someone. For example, when the Dominie and Deacon did not agree on a matter of church management, the latter would urge the former to take certain action and the Dominie would reply,

"I'll be damned if I do," and the Deacon rejoined, "You'll be damned if you don't." Neither were profane, only silly. She enjoyed a funny story and would tell them most charmingly, was thoroughly honest, and free from the slightest taint of vulgarity.

While stopping in Bloomington when wounded, I was occupying the parlor bedroom and lying there one afternoon when their minister called. The madam was neatly gowned and looked very handsome, and the old saint caught her around the waist and attempted to kiss her. She gave him a slap, the report of which would have awakened me had I been asleep. But I was not, and as the door stood ajar I witnessed the skirmish, and chucking the corner of a pillow in my mouth, kept one eye on this Soldier of the Cross. From the combined effects of the slap and his mortified feelings, his face was as red as a chunk of Libbie's embalmed corned beef. He offered a stupid and ungraceful apology and was backing himself out of the room when the madam motioned to a chair and told him to be seated. Then she quietly remarked,

"You may compose yourself, Elder, for you have simply made a mistake which will not be worth while for either of us ever to mention. Have you met Mrs. Brown since she returned from Chicago?"

This estimable and childless couple finally moved to Ypsilanti, Michigan. During their first trip there to buy into a manufacturing concern and lease a dwelling, some scamps broke into one of their rooms at Bloomington where they had stored my plunder for safe keeping while I was in the army, and carried away a trunk of clothing, another of my books, and the greater part of my carpenter kit. As he was not a warehouseman, encumbering himself with my trunk for pay, I did not think of holding him responsible for the loss which amounted to about double the sum I had borrowed of him. Apparently he thought I would deem him liable and keep the hundred on account. Therefore, when he received back his cash with 10% interest, he possibly went on his knees and thanked the Heavenly Father for decreeing that he should not suffer this loss.

Upon his urgent invitation I promised to visit them when free from the military service, and in due time found them settled in Ypsilanti. He wished to own a modest home of his own, and could only accomplish this by selling some of the stock of the concern of which he was principal shareholder and manager. He proposed that I purchase stock from him to the extent of my pile, which was a very small one, and become the foreman of the plant at a fair salary.

I spent a forenoon inspecting machinery, tools and stock, and the afternoon examining the books. In the evening the old gentleman invited me to attend their Thursday prayer meeting, but I excused myself and his wife was not disposed to go out in the storm. I mentioned to her the business of my visit, and the desire of her husband in the matter, which seemed to be news to her. I told her I could scarcely decide what to do as the lease of the building would expire within a year, without any hope of renewing it, and the concern had no money on hand with which to put up a new building.

In reply she quietly remarked that her husband, Mr. Mathews, had made a very poor investment, and if I put any money into it I would likely lose it. Not a word followed on the subject, and this was in line with her deportment at Bloomington when her clergyman made that break. She knew it was probable I had witnessed that affair, but never once alluded to it.

The next morning I informed Mr. Mathews that I had another business proposition near Kalamazoo [Michigan] to investigate and would mail him my decision from there. I had hard work to get away from him, but succeeded in boarding the first train going west.

CHAPTER XLIII

One morning in early fall of 1863, Colonel Lieb sent for me and when I reached his quarters his horses were both saddled and held by one of his servants. The Colonel said we were to select three camps near the new line of works and told me to mount one of his animals. I asked him where he got that chestnut mare, but I do not remember his answer. Then I enquired if she was a good saddle nag and he replied, "Fine." I had seen him riding her once at a square trot and did not believe she had any other gait, and so I said Jim would do me and swung myself on his old horse. I knew "Old Jim." He was a large, powerful gelding; sure footed and thoroughly gaited.

We followed the line through, selected the camps, and returned on the outside of the works near our picket line to examine the ground over which an enemy would have to make an attack. On the way in, Lieb remarked,

"You must have a nice bunch of money now; can't you afford to buy you a horse?"

I said I could get a saddle horse if he wished, but the matter of forage would be quite a tax for the little use I could make of one. And his reply was, "Then get the horse and I will attend to the forage."

We at once moved to the selected camping spots and established Regimental Headquarters [5th U.S. Heavy Artillery (Colored)] on a vacant lot near the Court House, just east of the military prison, facing Grove Street. Company B and three others took the central camp north of the Jackson road, and this detachment was placed in charge of the senior Maj. J. G. Davis. Captain Hissong had just received a major's commission, and he took charge of the camp on the right. For a couple of weeks Smith and I ran the company and had a good time, except that he was just a trifle out of sorts physically.

Smith got a notion in his head that he wanted a goat that he could milk. Our mess cook was an independent sort of a Darkey. Smith's servant and my man Ben were kept busy at odd jobs. We did not need more than one, but had to keep two or forfeit a servant's allowance on the payroll, and there being a margin in the transaction, we each kept our man. This regulation was got around by many of our officers by their signing a fictitious servant name to the payroll.

I recall that in Co. K [8th Ill.] from the beginning of the three-year term, our company officers had but one servant, and each signed "Henry ------" to the payroll. Six or eight months later, this allowance was charged back to them and deducted out of their pay. It made them squirm, but they had to stand it.

Our cook said he could not stand the smell of a goat, and would not milk one. Smith proposed to milk it himself, but the Darkey would not have the milk about the cook tent. I "butted" in and told him he would have nothing to say about it, and calling in Ben, directed him to take charge of the kitchen.

"Why Captain, yer isn't gwine ter deschauge me is yer?" whimpered the coon.

"No. Just fire you out of the camp, that's all; now get a hustle on you."

My horse had been delivered and Lieb had sent me down a sack of oats and a bale of hay. A few days previous a friendly quartermaster had loaned me a handsome white mule with saddle and bridle, which he said I might keep as long as I wished as he was not responsible to the government for him, so I was now rigged out for a captain of cavalry in the field.

The next day was a very pleasant Sunday. Immediately after breakfast Smith disappeared on the mule. About ten o'clock Ben brought up my horse and I started downtown. When I turned into Cherry street the walk was lined with officers, civilians, and finely appareled ladies taking an airing, or on their way to church. And right here was Lieutenant Smith in full uniform astride the bare back of the white mule, dragging along after him at the end of twenty-five feet of stout cord, a large stubborn female goat.

Surely he was "the observed of all observers" for every person on the street wore a smile - except Smith and myself. When I met him, without looking in his direction, I said in a low stern voice, "Smith, drop that goat and get to camp damn'd quick." The lieutenant was so astonished that he nearly fell off the mule, but soon caught his breath and had the animal on the jump. Lieut. Col. Simpson stepped to the curb facing me, and I reluctantly pulled up. Then the following dialogue ensued:

L.C. - Good morning Captain.
Self - Good morning Colonel.
L.C. - Been getting you a horse?
S. - That's what I've been doing.
L.C. - Are heavy artillery captains mounted?
S. - I am.
L.C. - Yes, I see. What's the expense?
S. - Two hundred even. (Gave but half the amount)
L.C. - Pretty stiff, but you have a fine nag.
S. - A thoroughbred.
L.C. - Is he gaited?
S. - To trot and run, but I'll break up his trotting and make a single footer of him.
L.C. - How do you do that?
S. - With spurs and bit.
L.C. - Thank you. I know all about it now.
S. - Then you catch on easy.
L.C. - Say Captain, who was that officer on the mule leading the goat?
S. - I don't know.
L.C. - He was an artilleryman; didn't he belong to your regiment?
S. - There are light batteries in the garrison.
L.C. - I remarked that when you met him he suddenly dropped the goat and struck out for tall timber. How do you account for that?

S. - I don't account for it at all. It didn't concern me. You did not see me look at him nor hear me speak to him, so why should you think of questioning me about him?

L.C. - That's true. I see it is useless; drop in occasionally and see a fellow. Good morning Captain.

When I returned to camp I called up Ben and told him he would find Smith's goat browsing around the Court House, which he did and brought her in. I tried to convince Smith of the impropriety of making such a ludicrous exhibition of himself, but he could not for the life of him see anything absurd or funny in the affair. I intimated that on a campaign in the field, anything would go, while in garrison in a city like Vicksburg, an officer must pay some regard to the proprieties, and never subject himself to ridicule. But this kind of talk was wasted on Smith. He could not comprehend it at all.

I had recovered the use of my arm again and laid the sling aside. A first lieutenant named George W. Mossman was sent to the company with orders to take over the property and assume command. When this was accomplished I reported to Col. Lieb, and he handed me an order of detail as permanent officer of the day and drill master of the regiment, and told me to stake my tent at headquarter and join the field officers' mess if I wished.

On this order the regimental quartermaster supplied me with all the forage required. I at once set about arranging the guards on the dozen forts and batteries, and each morning would have an officer's drill in artillery. The sergeant's drill was given to Captain Lynch, a bumptious Irishman, but he made such a mess of it that Lieb asked me to take that over too.

So I had my hands full that winter ['63-'64]. I was supposed to make the rounds of the guards each day and night, and make a daily report to headquarters. The report would go in with great regularity, but I would not always make the night round, and would excuse myself by saying that I was the officer of the day, and not of the night. And so when the weather was very disagreeable I would often sleep the night through. There were a few dubious climbs on the route, and so the night trips were made on the mule. I did not care to risk my $200 thoroughbred climbing out of or sliding into those ravines.

I was about to remark that a mule never lost his footing, and this one never did with me, but he sent Ben over his head once in the city street and wrecked my fiddle. It was some time later that there was attached to Co. B a lieutenant who was something of a warbler. I had started down to spend the evening with this company, and it was pitch dark. Ben was following with the violin case under his arm. He could not tell what happened to the mule but he said he knew what became of himself. He explained it in this way,

"Yer see Catpin"

"Shut up; I'm no sea captain."

"Well, I didn't mean nuthin like dat but yer see Ize riden rite long arter yer on a little gallop like, cos I didn't know whare you's gwine an had to keep up yer know, an wen we git heah, Snow Ball fall down on 'is knees hard like; same as colored preacher at prar metin, an I went ober 'is ed. Ise goin to save th fidle but hit de ground too quick. When I rides dat mule wid fiddle box gin Ise goin affot." Ben was not hurt - except his feelings - and so we went on, and the lieutenant gave us "The Mocking Bird," "Sweet Annie of the Vale" and a few other choice selections, but the violin obligato was missing.

The guards were stationed at the various batteries by the company officers who had special charge of them, and the condition in which I would often find them upon making the nightly rounds was a corker. For some time my principal duty was to wake up the whole gang and ascertain which one of them was supposed to be standing guard. If the fellow could be designated, I would place him on his beat again and suggest that he try and keep awake until he was regularly relieved. And this would be about the answer I would get,

"Well Captain, I done keep wake mores as two hours, but de odder niggers all go't sleep an nebber pay no tenshun to me, so I has to just releb my own sef."

I often had to disturb the sleeping sentinels by applying the flat of my saber to the seat of their trousers, or giving them a few lusty kicks with the toe of my boot. In making the day-round I would call on the company commanders and ask for their assistance, as it seemed impossible to make good guards out of their men without their help. Some took these appeals in good part, and some did not. Captain Lynch entered a complaint against me for cruelty, and was summoned before the colonel with his witnesses. His own men did not bear out his charges and he left an apology and took back to his quarters a stiff reprimand. When I explained to Capt. Miller the condition in which I found his guards the night before he enquired in a sarcastic tone if I was having my principal trouble with his men. I replied that my main difficulty was with their captain, who did not seem to have a disposition to teach them the duties of a soldier, and if there was not a marked improvement in his command from that time on, I would try and find him another job and give his lieutenant a chance to show his mettle.

He replied that I was assuming too much authority and he would see if I could carry out such threats. Shortly after he called upon the colonel and reported me. And this reminds me of a homely, old fashioned story I heard when a boy.

A farmer was seen one morning hoofing it toward the county seat. His boots struck the graveled thoroughfare with distinct firmness, and his chin was well up in the air. A neighbor hailed him and asked him where he was going and his reply was, "To Law."

Toward night he was seen returning, but his general appearance had undergone a remarkable change. His boots were now scuffing the gravel with an uncertain step, and his chin rested on his hickory shirt. Another neighbor enquired of him where he had been and he drawled out, "Been to Law."

I had no further trouble with Capt. Miller. Later Lieb informed me that he also had found him a very disagreeable officer and for that reason got rid of him at the first opportunity.

Having now gotten my authority pretty well established in the minds of the officers, I called them together in one of the central forts with muskets, and put them through a course of guard drill. And here I introduced an innovation. I established the beat of the sentinel on the parapet and had the terminals plainly marked. When the sentinel arrived at the end of his walk he was to halt and bring his piece to a shoulder. Then face about, bring the gun to a right-shoulder-shift, or support, and step off, left foot first.

It was a nice drill and many of the officers thought it would work out all right, but one first lieutenant informed me that the Army Regulations prescribed the rules for guard duty and that I had no right to teach it in any other manner. I justified myself by saying that these regulations were made many years ago, and could not at the present time be literally followed, and I referred to several requirements that were from necessity violated every day. I added that when they were promulgated the Army did not dream of enlisting Negro troops, that we now had that proposition on our hands and must make the best of it. He said he did not think so and would still object, to which I replied that I would take his objection under consideration, and in the meantime he must follow the instructions literally and teach them to his men.

This fellow preferred charges against me for swearing at him and named two other officers as witnesses. The specification stated that when directing my conversation to him I said "God damn you." Now this was not strictly true, for he had substituted the pronoun you for it. The term was profane but could not be held insulting or offensive in an Army officer. Still, he and two other officers were willing to commit perjury to get me into trouble.

Lieb was a man who liked to have his swearing done by proxy and so he slung the charges in the waste paper basket and called for the lieutenant's resignation. After a few months of civil life he came back to Vicksburg and secured a clerical position at district headquarters and our meetings were always pleasant. If he had not been over-sensitive and a trifle foolish he could have become a captain.

I will mention here that the regulation about sleeping sentries called for a court martial under the 46th Article of War, and a conviction called for a severe sentence. Had I taken this course when called for my time would have been occupied mainly in preferring charges against the guilty and getting them into a military prison, thereby depleting the ranks of the regiment equal to the number of convictions secured. It was more men we wanted; we had none to spare. These green Darkeys knew nothing about that terrible Article of War hanging over their heads, and had no conception about the gravity of the offense as viewed by a stickler to form. They did not deserve punishment other than a good kicking, or bucking and gagging for a few hours.

After I had the company officers well drilled in guard duty as I wished it performed I told them that hereafter I should hold the company commanders responsible for the performance of their men, and if they did not want trouble they had better look after them mighty close. That nailed the business, for I never found a sleeping guard from that day on. It appeared that each commander put his men through a thorough guard drill, and the sentinels took much pride in strutting back and forth at a conspicuous elevation, and showing their skill in the manual of arms at each turn of their beat.

Late in 1863 we were several hundred men short of being filled to the regimental maximum, and General McPherson's Adjt., Gen. Clark, told Lieb there was a capable lieutenant in the Marine Brigade who would undertake to furnish what recruits were needed for the third majority. Lieb called the captains together and they all kicked at the proposition, except myself. I was too far down the line to be personally interested, and really thought it a good deal for the regiment. A full company could have two first and two second lieutenants, and this would send many of the latter up a notch, and make room for the white sergeants. As for myself, I wanted to get back to Co. B and stay there.

Lieb would have dropped this scheme but Clark was persistent, and so he consented. Then the Marine Brigade commenced raking in the contrabands [Negroes] at a lively rate, and Lieb requested the medical examiner to pass none but good sound men. The result was that fully half of them were rejected.

There was a grand review planned in February and Lieb asked me to take out Co. B. So one evening I rode down to the Co. B barrack they were then occupying, and told Mossman to have the boys polish up for the occasion. When I took my leave the boys were all in their bunks and the lights were out. I quietly walked down the center of the barrack and overheard one of them say,

"Did yer know Captin Caverno [Cornwell] wus down yere dis ebening?" And the answer he got was, "No, is dat so; wish he ud stay down heah all time cos nobody can't do nuffin wid dis cumpny 'cept him." That made me tired of the officer of the day business and I determined to get back again where I belonged ... to Company B.

When I reached my quarters I saw a light in the Colonel's tent and walked in. He dropped his paper, handed me a cigar, and asked if he could do anything for me. That gave me an opening and I said,

"Yes, you have called the turn exactly; you can do something for me if you will. It has been my ambition to command a company. I have now the rank of captain, but my company has been taken from me. Those boys all like me and I like them and they will do anything I ask of them. I can make top-notchers of them in thirty days if you will let me go back."

The Colonel looked me over through his glasses with a peculiar expression on his countenance, and replied,

"Wait a little while Captain, wait a little while; I can't spare you just now."

I did not then guess what was on his mind, but did not have long to wait before I found out. Ten days later he handed me an appointment to a majority and charged me to get mustered immediately. In two hours I was mustered and my commission dated from the last day of November, 1863. It was now February 2, 1864, and I was mustered from this date.

This 1864 photograph of Herman Lieb's staff was taken at Battery Castle near Vicksburg. All White officers of the 5th U.S.C. Artillery (Heavy) Regiment. The 3rd battalion commander, Major D. Cornwell, is the third figure in line with Lieb and to his left (to reader's right)..

CHAPTER XLIV

I was continued in my usual duties, which had become less arduous since the guards were giving me no further trouble. The drill of the officers now was with the heavy ordnance, which was mounted on various carriages, each of which required a special drill. To the question "How did you acquire the knowledge needed to conduct this drill?" I can only say I was obtaining it day by day by reading published works on heavy artillery tactics. Many very intelligent officers were minus the gift, ability or disposition to train themselves in that way. With me it came easy and I soon had the nomenclature of these armaments at the tip of my tongue and could explain the drill and put a gun squad through it with an appearance of having had years of practice at it. My natural bent was mechanical, and it favored me. I would have made a poor quartermaster, commissary, or adjutant.

Since the successful result of my guard scheme, which had attracted the attention and got the unstinted praise of both soldiers and citizens of the garrison, and my promotion to major, the officers took their instruction cheerfully and with little criticism. They understood however, that before or after drill, or at any recess, they were at liberty to express their opinions as freely as they wished. So I was getting along easily and pleasantly now and made the night round of the guards as often as I felt so disposed.

Then came an order to fire a morning and evening gun from the fort on the Jackson road. Here was mounted a 10-inch Columbiad with an ordinary powder charge of 28 pounds. To make it speak out strong we would cut a few pieces of sod to fit the bore and ram them down solidly against the powder. This gun was ten feet long, weighed eight tons, and was mounted on a center-pintle carriage, which permitted it to be fired in any direction.

Directly in its rear, at a distance of forty paces, stood a frame dwelling that we wished to get rid of as it occupied the spot selected by the engineers for our magazine. The occupants as I understood it had been told to get out, but had so far disregarded the order. Now that we were using this gun, the necessity for a magazine in which to store our powder, tools and implements was quite apparent, and Lieb asked me to attend to the matter. He said the agent of the treasury department would provide a building so the residents would not have to be turned into the street. And he added that the quartermaster would send teams to move them, if they desired.

When I got this order I did not see Lieb's face for his back was turned to me and he was nervously fumbling over some papers on his desk. So I said, "I'll attend to it," with about as much concern as if he had ordered a field piece moved to a new location. Singular as it may appear, I had scarcely noticed the house and had not the faintest idea who its occupants were.

The time to attend to a piece of business is when you have it on your mind, have nothing else to do, and feel just like pitching into it. This was precisely my fix at this time and so I vaulted into the saddle and rode out the Jackson road.

Arriving at the house, I tied my nag to the hitching post and boldly knocked on the door. Presently a face appeared at a peekhole that had escaped my notice, and then the door was unbolted, swung open, and I was invited to walk in by a female who was about forty, coarse and fat. She conducted me into a sitting room and invited me to be seated. I planted myself into the nearest chair and the madam plunked herself down on a mammoth hair-cloth sofa.

"Madam, you are the head of this family?" I modestly enquired.

"You've hit it, Major. Would you like to see one of the girls?"

"No thanks, don't call any of them in for I have not come a courting. Just a little business proposition I want to lay before you. We don't need any of the children about to interrupt our conversation. Let the darlings sleep and I will tell you what brought me here. We want the ground this house stands on for a..."

"Ah, give us a rest. That sort of talk makes me tired. I think I have heard it before." And then she commenced counting on her pudgy fingers, "There's the engineer who laid out this fort, and then there was a Captain Ferslow who had the gun put up - he was a dandy he was - and no gentleman either. He did not know a lady when he saw one. He told me right to my face that he was married and never entered such houses. I'll bet he never repeated what I told him. The next was the treasury agent who talked like a Sunday School boss, but he was a nice fellow. He came in, took a seat, and treated us with respect. He offered us another house, but I told him this place suited me and that I would stay here.

"Next they sent up the Provost Marshal, that black haired, heavy-mustached fellow. He was game the Marshal was; sent his orderly back with his horse and remained here 'til after dark. He visits us quite often now, but never says anything about our moving out. That's four. And then only the other day up rode that fierce looking artillery colonel that talks German. He wouldn't get off his horse but pounded the door with his sword. When I opened up he raised his cap and said, (This was Lieb)

"'Good morning Madam. I called to tell you that you must move out. We want this site for a magazine.'

"I told him that he had been wanting it for a long time, had not got it yet, and that it would be another long time before he did get it, that I should not move out 'til I got good and ready. He said, 'By Got I make you.' I told him that it was a better looking man than he that would make me and then he said, 'Jesus! if you was a man I would run my sabre through you'; and then he rode off swearing.

"That afternoon I sent a boy for a hack and called upon General Smith. (Morgan L.) He's a gentleman and knows a lady when he meets one. He said that he guessed there was no great rush for that magazine, and that I might see the Provost Marshal about it. I am solid with the Provost Marshal and there you have it. And now, my dear, I will remark that you are rather a young man for a major, for sticking a boy up too fast is liable to give him the bighead, but I don't see as you are swelled up much and I think we will be friends and get along nicely."

"We will," I replied, "If you will give us this site for our magazine."

"Oh, damn your magazine," replied the lady, "We won't have any here and we want you to fire some other cannon if you have got to shoot one, for this disturbs us just when we want to sleep. I must step out for a few moments but will send in one of the girls to entertain you 'til I return," and before I could fire a protest at her she slid out of the room and closed the door behind her.

A couple of minutes later the door opened and in glided a good looking, neatly dressed young woman of about twenty. She bowed as she carefully closed the door behind her, then brought up a chair and seated herself very close in front of me and began talking in a low tone.

"Major, my name is Maud. I've been sent here to coddle you about this house but I aren't a going to do it. The old woman takes half and then swindles us out of the balance and I am tired of it. Now I like the looks of you and believe you are all right, and if you will get me a couple of rooms down town and protect me, you can walk in at any hour and hang up your hat. I will make more money than any of them and will give you all you want. Then you may blow this old house up with gun powder for all I care."

I scarcely knew what reply to make, for in truth I felt sorry for the girl. She was of trim build, had rather a sweet face, dainty feet, and a pair of pretty little hands that were white and clean, all of which excite my sympathy. Had I met her amidst different surroundings, she could have commanded me. As it was I muttered something about taking the matter under consideration. Then the old boss re-entered the room, and I arose to go. I said, addressing her,

"I scarcely think it worth our while to discuss this matter further. I have notified you to move out as I was directed to do and must report your refusal to headquarters. Then I hope I will be through with the matter. Now, if you will be kind enough to show me out I will bid you a good afternoon and return to the city."

I followed her to the door with Maud hanging onto my arm, and she disengaged herself with an appealing look that nigh went to my heart. The madam expressed herself as pleased at our meeting, and intimated that I was certainly a gentleman who knew a lady when I met one.

I threw myself into the saddle and with head down walked the horse back to my quarters. I had made a complete failure of my mission, and the only consolation I had was that there had been others before me. But now I wanted to succeed where the others had failed, and how to do it was the rub. I did not want to report a failure to Lieb, and so I kept away from him, except at the mess table, and I was not afraid of his broaching the subject there.

My first inspiration was to have our men run a large open trench under the house and store a quantity of powder there. The danger of being blown up I thought would cause the girls to leave. And it no doubt would have if we had ever succeeded in finishing the ditch and getting the powder stored under the building. But what kind of a fight would these women put up while we were engaged in the operation? With clubs and a few buckets of hot water they could make us suspend work at almost any time. When I thought of the possibility of such stored powder going off at half cock and blowing all of those lovely females into disgusting fragments, I dropped that scheme quicker than a mule can kick.

I awoke the next morning with a new idea in my head, and it seemed practical. Whether I had caught it in my dreams or not I could not tell. I tried to drop it from my mind until I had breakfast and taken a little exercise, for sometimes what seems real and sensible in a dream for a short time after awakening, turns out upon later examination to be pure nonsense. Before the day was over I decided that if that was a dream, it was a practical one, and I would lose no time in putting it into operation.

So, the next morning I loaded the old Columbiad heavily and pointed it so that the sod chunks would pass near the rear of the Madam's house. When she went off, the only effect I could see on the building was that the shutters were all lying on the ground. I left the men to clean up the gun and rode away without seeing any of the inmates of the house. The colored sergeant I left in charge told me that two of the ladies stepped out in their night dresses, but retired a moment after without making any remarks.

The succeeding morning I gave the gun the same direction, with a charge of 40 pounds of powder and a double wad of sod rammed down to beat the band. For fear of the gun bursting I sent the gun squad and my horse down into the ravine directly in front of the battery. It never occurred to me that if the gun burst a piece of it might possibly go through that house and kill some of the ladies. I stepped over the parapet with a long lanyard in one hand and a watch in the other. When the moment arrived I made the jerk and, Heavens, what a report! I thought for a moment the gun had burst.

Every window went out, sash and all. And all the plaster from the ceilings and much from the side walls came down, bringing the pictures and mirrors with them. Two inside doors lay flat on the floor covered with plaster, and another struck a stove and upset it. The stovepipe all came down of its own accord.

Out from the building rushed all the ladies in angel attire. None of us were in sight, but that did not prevent them from giving me the worst lambasting I ever received in my life. And the cutting part of it was that I deserved it all. Hardened sinner as I was, the profanity of those ladies made my blood run cold. And to cap the climax of my humiliation the charming Maud applied to me every foul epithet that her pretty lips could formulate. I saw three officers and two soldiers slide out of the rear door and disappear into a ravine, and then I sneaked down the one behind me and also disappeared. During the day the ladies secured another dwelling. And they, too, disappeared.

My dastardly treatment of the lovely Maud lay heavily on my conscience until I learned that she had married an ex-lieutenant and gone with him to live on a plantation.

--- ------ ---

A few mornings later, being hurried for time, I neglected to run the gun forward in battery before firing, which resulted in this eight-ton monster turning a backward somersault and landing on the ground with its carriage on top of it. I at once reported the mishap to the depot ordnance officer, and he sent up a crew that mounted it again in time to fire the sunset gun. A few days afterward Col. Lieb heard of it and called me down for not reporting the incident to him. I excused myself by saying that I disliked to trouble him with unimportant details. But he knew very well that I simply had not wished him to hear of it.

These Columbiads were a conception of one Colonel Bumford years before the war, and a large number of them were cast for our coast defense. The Confederacy had possession of the larger share of them and distributed them about their defenses where they would do the most good. We were gradually getting back our own again, for we found a large number here at Vicksburg, and had mounted one in each battery on the line. When we took possession of the Vicksburg forts I found one of the Columbiads spiked. The vent of our cannon of all sizes was 2/10 of an inch [diameter], and they were spiked to render them temporarily unserviceable by driving a steel pin made for the purpose into this vent. If the spike (pin) proves too hard for a drill another vent is drilled near the old one.

I reported the condition of this gun to Colonel Lieb and he told me to blow it out. He had read somewhere about that sort of thing, and his recollection was that a couple of pounds of powder with a good wad would do the business. So I tried it his way and the powder scarcely blew the wads out of the gun. Then we loaded her up differently by putting in forty pounds of powder and filling her half full of sod tightly rammed down. I sent the horses down into a ravine out of danger, fired the fuse at the muzzle of the piece, and then adjourned to the ditch in rear of the fort. We waited a long time and were fearful the fuse had gone out. I said we would take no chances but remain in the ditch for an hour. A dozen of my officers were there and a lieutenant asked permission to take a peep and see if the fuse was throwing out any smoke yet. I told him to go ahead and he was boosted out of the ditch, reached the top of the parapet in a few seconds, and came back again in one. If the boys had not caught him, I believe he would have had a broken neck, for he was making for the bottom of the ditch head first. He was the only one who enjoyed the privilege of seeing the gun go off. It did not burst, but it shook up everything in Vicksburg, and it was generally thought that one of the larger magazines had blown up.

Lieb came riding out there as fast as Old Jim could carry him, and called me down handsomely. I felt so humiliated over it that I turned my back to him to conceal my emotions. Then he excused me to the department and district commanders by stating that I was carrying out his orders, but that he had scarcely expected me to produce an earthquake. The next day a couple of mechanics from the ordnance depot drilled out the spike in a few minutes.

The summer of 1864 was a busy one for Colonel Lieb. He now had 12 companies of 150 men, each with five commissioned officers and a white orderly. A company was assigned to each battery, near which was constructed commodious barracks and cisterns sunk in the solid clay that were 16 feet in diameter and 20 feet deep. I was given the third battalion with headquarters on the Chicasaw Bayou road. The detail of workmen from the regiment that had been organized to construct these buildings properly started in on those of the first battalion, but I judged if we waited for them to get around to us we would again winter in tents. They had taken my best carpenters, but in spite of this I got out a gang of my own, laid out the work myself, and got my battalion into quarters first. This ought to have pleased Lieb, but for some reason it did not. One of my captains was rather slow and negligent and it just so happened that I got my own quarters built before this captain had got his last chimney topped out. Lieb noticed this and sent me a letter, intimating that

I had more regard for my personal comfort than for my men. When he read my reply if he was not ashamed it was no fault of mine.

Lieb took possession of the first bottom land above the city and established a regimental farm as a home for the wives and children of our soldiers. He organized a drum corps, found a capable white man to teach them, and had him appointed chaplain for the regiment. The young darkies were easily taught and crucified us with their incessant pounding. It was impossible to keep them quiet. I had to send my detachment a mile from camp to practice. They were young, comical little whelps, and when they were not pounding the sheepskins they were playing marbles. Upon reaching the drill ground one morning with the battalion I said to the leader of the detachment,

"Josephus, you will cut out juvenile billiards today and keep two of your imps near each flank of the battalion. When I call for a marker, the one nearest to me is to come like a shot. When I call for two markers, I want to see a lively foot-race; do you understand?"

"Yessah, I knows wat yer mean; I'll hab 'em dar."

One of the most insignificant in the bunch shrugs his shoulders and remarked to the others in an undertone .

"We mout jes well be common solges."

Lieb was bound to have the biggest show in Vicksburg, and so he started out for a cornet band also. I don't remember how he got the money to buy the instruments, but the teacher was paid by a contribution from the commissioned officers equal to one day's pay per month. He was a German and rank Rebel and got to airing his opinions and prejudices among the boys he was teaching to such an extent that we cut off his salary. This made Lieb mad at us and he gave me "particular hell" on account of it. He said if I had ignored the matter the other officers would have passed it by. I said I did not want them to pass it by, I wanted the teacher kicked out. He had no right to laud Jeff Davis and belittle Lincoln before our men, and I wouldn't stand it. He kept on teaching the band just the same, but he also kept his mouth shut, and so we renewed our contributions.

Our dress parades were held in the street in front of regimental headquarters each Sunday afternoon, and the show was largely attended by officers and citizens. At the command "Troop Beat Off" the horns would take the lead with the drummers following. They would pound the sheepskins to the foot of the long line. Then they would wheel about and the horns would have their inning. It was great - so Lieb and many others thought - but I had an opinion of my own about such swell shows.

For drill, each company was divided into two sections. A full company was too large to handle as infantry, and this gave each major eight companies, which made a fine battalion to maneuver on the drill ground. When the three battalions met, they were handled as a brigade.

No doubt Lieb expected to mix us up when he sprung the brigade drill on us. He no doubt had had it in view for some time, and had studied it. We were of course taken somewhat by surprise. He closed his first drill by sending us from line into column by the following command:

"Close column by division - on the first division - first battalion - right in front."

We got there without making any bad breaks, and when the formation was completed, Lieb ordered us to close in mass on the leading division. I was in the center and I told my captains that our columns were already closed in mass, and to keep their distance.

The first battalion moved up a little and I brought mine up bodily within division distance. Lieb asked,

"Major, why did you not close your columns in mass when you moved your battalion forward?"

"Because they were already closed in mass," I replied.

"But they should have been at half-distance."

"You did not say half-distance in your order."

"It was not necessary; that is understood."

"I never understood it so and I don't think I will ever have to."

"What! I'll bet you a case of Catawby [wine] that your divisions should have been at half distance."

"I'll take the bet."

I left my companies with their commanders and accompanied Lieb to his headquarters. On the way he offered to bet the second case that he would win the first. I promptly took that bet also, for I knew it to be good stuff to keep around an officer's quarters. When we got there Lieb confidently picked up volume 3 of the *Drill Tactics Manual* as if expecting to produce his authority inside of a minute, but he didn't. He studied away for a long time while I puffed one of his cigars and enjoyed his eagerness to find something in the book that Casey had never put there. I think he spent a half hour at it and then said that he could not make out what the distance between the divisions should be.

"It wouldn't do any harm to take a glance at the little diagram that illustrates that maneuver," said I.

"Of course," he replied, "it won't do any harm as you say." And then he commenced to stare, and then to pull his mustache out by the roots. Suddenly, jumping from his seat he threw the book from him and exclaimed, "By got, Major, you haf won that Catawby; when in hell did you study brigade tactics?"

I said that I had not the pleasure of studying them well, but had looked them over occasionally while loafing about quarters.

"Vell, I was a dam fool to bet so much with you on tactics; I'll look a little out next time."

I told him to send up but one case as I couldn't use more, and then I lit another of his cigars and bid him good bye. He tried to smile as I withdrew, but did not succeed very well.

It occurred to me about this time that the general appearance of our men might be greatly improved...

1st, by having their wool closely clipped,

2nd, by wearing their caps with the forepieces turned up instead of down,

3rd, that the cartridge-box-belts that went over the shoulder might be dispensed with, as they never carried more than twenty rounds, and

4th, that light wood frames might be made for their knapsacks, which would give them a neat, boxy appearance with the blanket neatly rolled and strapped on the top outside. I had had one of that style in the 8th, had seen many others, knew they looked well and carried nicely.

In a letter to Lieb I suggested these changes and he immediately issued an order to carry them out. He had provided a fund from the ration surplus that furnished the men with white cotton gloves and shoe blacking, and when these innovations were put through we had the gamiest looking regiment of Darkeys in Uncle Sam's service. Next we worked in the direction of cleanliness and soon got them in such a way that they felt better when they were clean and well dressed than they had when they wore their wool long and were ragged and dirty. We actually got them to thinking it disgraceful to have a dirty dud in their knapsack, or a blanket that contained dust. And the time came when it was difficult to soil a white handkerchief on any of the belongings of one of them when he stepped out for inspection.

Soon you could never meet any of them off duty on the streets of Vicksburg except those in clean uniform wearing white gloves, polished shoes and waist belt with bayonet in its scabbard. Of course, Lieb was proud of his regiment as he had a right to be, but he had his weak points like other men. He enjoyed parade and show and would have the men taken by companies to church Sunday morning. They may have liked this, and they may have not, I never asked them and never went with them. The Captains usually sent them in charge of a second lieutenant, which gave him a chance to command a company on a march downtown and back, which they may have taken some pride in.

Our two bands contained 50 men, all drawing pay, yet none of them would have been on the firing line with a gun had we been attacked. As we were not, it was probably just as well. Lieb was a hustling officer and did not hesitate an instant in adopting a suggestion that he thought was good, and he was a fearless fighter from the first to the last crack of a gun. His weaknesses seemed trifling when his strong points were considered.

He organized a school in each battalion and soon we had colored men for orderlies, and the white boys all got commissions. The rapidity with which these Darkeys learned to read and write was astonishing. Some of them qualified for headquarters clerks in a year's time. I had one in my office keeping books who only a year before was taught the alphabet in my battalion school. One old wench who must have been past sixty hung around my battalion schoolhouse until she was able to read her Bible. Then she was satisfied and troubled the teacher no more. I never found out whether she was able to understand the Good Book after she read it.

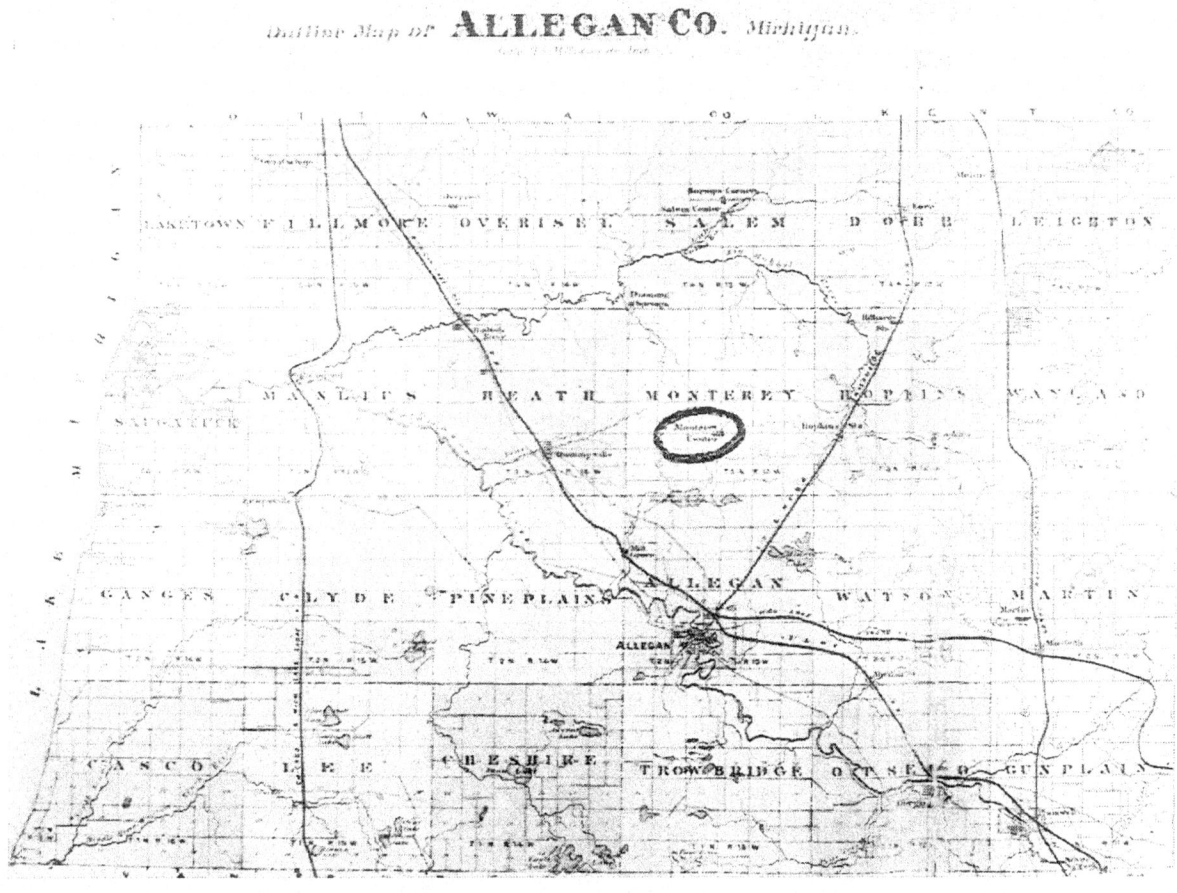

1873 outline map of Allegan County, Michigan.

CHAPTER XLV

When I took charge of the battalion I was given a white sergeant for a clerk (we called him a battalion adjutant) who bore the name of Victor M. Dewey. He had a long face, carried a grave countenance, was apparently free of the small vices, and the name on his mail bore the prefix of "Rev." In time I was called upon to recommend four sergeants for promotion to lieutenancies, and the Rev. V. M. Dewey came in on the draw.

Some time after he had donned an officer's dress I handed him a letter from his wife in Egypt, Illinois. As I passed from the tent he remarked in a sarcastic tone quite new to him,

"The Rev. V. M. Dewey -- that's a hell of a title for a commissioned officer; damn that woman, don't she know anything?"

Lieutenant Dewey was in due time attached to a company in the second battalion where I had occasion to call one evening. There sat Dewey at a table with three other officers, cap tilted on the back of his head, a lighted cigar in one corner of his mouth, and he was in the act of raking in a comfortable jackpot that he had won on three queens.

I had a colored wagonmaster named Wesley Sterrill who was proud of his piety. One Sunday morning he said that another Darkey who owed him thirty dollars had tendered him the greenbacks that morning. I replied, "That was lucky, did you get a little interest for the use of it?"

"Wy I didn't get nufin yet," said Wes. "Does yer spose dat I'd take money uf a Sunday?"

I told him that he was a poor financier and a stupid Christian also, for they habitually took up collections in the churches on the Sabbath. I asked him if he ever saw a preacher refuse money on any day or occasion. As he moved off with one hand in his wool I requested him to let me know when he got that money.

It was nearly a year later when the incident was recalled by my seeing him approach.

"Wes, how did you come out with that thirty-dollar loan?" I said. "You were to tell me when the man paid you, you know." And he said, "But yer see, dat nigger nebber paid me; twas just like you sed," replied he. "I didn't know nuffin 'bout de finansion bisness den cos yer see I nebber git any money afore. Dat nigger come all de way from de Barbour Plantation dat mawnin ter gib me dat munny, an dat ebening he tooks er boat fur Memphis an I nebber heared 'bout im since."

I do not remember exactly what time General James McPherson left us, but it was in October 1864 that Major General Napoleon J. T. Dana assumed command of the Department with headquarters at Memphis. He had been at Vicksburg in charge of the District since the middle of August, having succeeded Major General H. W. Slocum, who had been in command since the first of May, and was now called by General Sherman to take command of the 20th Army Corps. Now Dana took up his headquarters in Memphis, and sent down from there Cadwallader C. Washburn, Major General of Volunteers, who had had charge of that post for some time.

I heard the boys tell of a funny incident that occurred during Cadwallader's administration at Memphis. He was boarding at the principal hotel of the city called the Gayosa House, or something like that, and Confederate General N. B. Forrest thought it would be a good joke to capture him. So he came dashing into the city one night and missed his prey by a hair's breadth. Washburn had been aroused just in the nick of time and escaped to the fort in his shirt tail.

Lieb had served on General Slocum's staff as Chief of Artillery and Ordnance, and now Dana called him to Memphis as Inspector General of the Department. He characteristically pitched into his duties with a vim and had me detailed to serve in his department on General Washburn's staff.

Before going to Memphis, and while in command of the Regiment, Lieb rode out to my quarters one morning and invited me to take a ride with him. We went north past our line of fortifications, through our outer pickets, beyond the regimental farm and kept traveling until we reached Chicasaw Bayou where Sherman had made his disastrous attack and where that gallant and imperturbable Morgan L. Smith, now a Brigadier General in command of the Post and Defenses of Vicksburg, was seriously wounded in the hip.

Hitching our horses, we roamed about, guessing and speculating about this rash attack, and all the time keeping an eye out to get a glimpse of one of the alligators we had so often heard barking in that vicinity. Here Lieb presented a scheme for getting our regiment away from Vicksburg and into the field. He had already gotten weary of garrison duty and craved a new field to operate in.

I should have fallen in with his project at once. But I didn't. I said that we had by much hard labor got comfortable quarters and were under no obligation to vacate them as soon as completed for the use of other troops who had had no hand in their construction. And that we had the right number of companies and men to man the forts and that it would take new men a year to become as efficient in the duties as we were. I thought such a change would work injury to the service, but still if he wished to and could bring it about, I would make no opposition to it. And I was not to mention the matter to other officers. In answer to the intimation that there would be better chances of promotion in the field I said that I had been promoted rather rapidly as it was, and had already obtained a notch above what I had set my stakes for, and on that score was quite satisfied.

The next morning the regimental officers met at Battery Castle to be photographed. Here Major Hissong called me down into the magazine and introduced this subject. [Lieb's plan to get his regiment assigned elsewhere.] I assumed ignorance of the matter and indifference toward it when he expressed himself in strong opposition to such a move. Colonel Lieb had observed our movements, and having confided the project to none other than Lieutenant Colonel Owen (Erastus N.) and myself, he jumped to the conclusion that I had given him away to Hissong.

When we parted at his quarters he said that I was the last officer in his regiment from whom he would expect a betrayal of confidence, but now having gained in wisdom he would in future act with greater caution. The inference I drew at the moment was that he was offended at my expressed objections to his plans and I answered him by saying that my ideas were my own and I should not hesitate to express them when called upon to do so, that I knew of nothing that had yet transpired that should shake his confidence in me so utterly. And I added, "You are being sarcastic and mysterious, and I don't know what you are driving at. If you are now done with me I will bid you good day." Soon after, I saw clearly through his suspicion, but as he did not again refer to the matter it dropped there.

Not long after this Lieb told me that Lt. Col. Owen would like to get out, and suggested giving the vacancy to Major John G. Davis. I asked him if he could manage it so that Davis would never assume any authority over me, and he said that it couldn't be done. I said to him, "Then, get rid of Davis, too, for he is a low, ignorant, dirty whelp and a disgrace to your regiment. Hissong will fill the bill with credit." I guess this was Lieb's opinion, too, for it was exactly what he did. This left me the ranking major of the 5th U.S. Colored Heavy Artillery Regiment.

As an indication of the stupidity of this Davis, I will mention that one of his captains was in the habit of sleeping in a dwelling on the margin of his camp, and Davis placed him in arrest and preferred charges against him for sleeping out of camp without permission. While remaining in his quarters awaiting trial this officer asked permission to visit this same house to get his washing, and Davis replied over his own signature that he would require no permission as his house was within the limits of his camp. So the charge fell flat and the captain tumbled into his old habit again.

There were two inspectors general of the U. S. Army, with offices in Washington. One of them was General Marcy, father-in-law of General George B. McClellan, with whom he served as chief of staff while the latter commanded the Army of the Potomac. Then there were many assistants, regulars, who belonged to the staff corps but the bulk of them were details who still held their positions in their companies and regiments and were designated as Acting Assistant Inspectors General. This was a pretty long title and to represent it we used the initials, A.A.I.G.

To learn some of the details and requirements of this position I called at the office of the Inspector that my appointment had put out of a job, and found that without waiting for me to relieve him, he had skipped out for New Orleans to join his regiment and he had disposed of his office furniture and taken all the books and papers with him.

As I was leaving the building I met a young man who had been a member of Company K [8th Illinois Inf.] in the three months' service, but had since been clerking at various headquarters where he could pull a good salary. I told him of my appointment, and of my dilemma respecting office furniture and records. He said he could help me out on that and we walked back into the office, which was in a building partly occupied by the Treasury Department. One of their clerks was arranging the room for his own convenience, and had given me the misinformation I had obtained about my predecessor.

Said my clerical guide, "That office desk, that table, that revolving chair, those three common chairs, this box and this field desk were all in the service of Captain _____, as Inspector of this District."

"Is that true?" I asked the Treasury Clerk. And he replied,

"I guess it is. The captain told me he would send for them as soon as he got settled."

"Will you see that they remain here until I secure an office and send for them?"

And he replied, "Certainly I will."

After acknowledging my obligation to my friend of the Old Eighth, I called upon the elegant and high-bred Captain _____, who I knew had some experience in the inspectors department, for the purpose of extracting some information to assist me in starting out in my new line of duties, but I could not get a thing out of him except discouragement of ever taking them up at all. After he had given much talk of this sort I remarked that I thought it would have been better for the service if they had let me alone, for I was well acquainted with my duties in the line, and knew nothing about staff duty whatever. He said I had expressed a sensible view of the case and as a brother officer he would try and help me out of my predicament. Then he took pencil and paper and drew up the following letter:

Hd.Qrs., 3rd Bat. 5th U.S.Col'd.Art.H'y.

Vicksburg, Miss., Dec. 16th 1864
Lieut.Col.T.H.Harris
Asst.Adjt.General:

Colonel.

By special order No. _____, I am appointed A.A.I.Gen. of the District of Vicksburg. I would respectfully but most urgently request that I may be relieved from that duty.

I am at present in command of this Battalion of my Regiment, numbering between five and six hundred men. I am responsible for a very large amount of Ordnance and Ordnance Stores, which I will be obliged to turn over and give up my command. I have had no experience whatever in the duties of the Inspector General's office, and think it will be better for the interests of the service, and my immediate command, that I be relieved of that duty.

I therefore most earnestly hope my request may be granted.

I am Colonel
Your Obt.Servant

The Captain handed me this with a graceful flourish, after reading it with much unction and folding it, and intimated that if I would copy it in my poorest hand he would guarantee it would relieve me from an embarrassing position.

I slipped the draft into my pocket and asked the Captain what he was doing at present. He replied, "Not much of anything, mostly waiting orders."

Then I could read his hand as clearly as if I held the cards myself, and thanking him for his courtesy I immediately called upon the Regimental Quartermaster, and secured the assignment of two lower rooms of a large brick residence on Cherry Street, a couple of blocks south of District Headquarters. As soon as my servants had given them a thorough renovating, I sent a dray for the office furniture and then called upon General Washburn and presented my order of appointment. He was very nice and said he would take pleasure in announcing me in General Orders.

When I returned to the office the stuff was there. While Ben ripped the top from the box I picked the lock of the field desk, and we found them both full of books, blanks and all sorts of papers pertaining to the business of the office, as well as many private ones. The latter were never called for and were eventually burned.

It took me one day to turn over the battalion property and move down my truck, another to examine the books, orders and blanks, to get a feel for the business, and another to secure a competent clerk and a cavalry boy for an orderly. I don't remember that I felt any embarrassment over the prospects ahead of me: On the contrary, I was quite elated and tumbled into the business with peculiar enjoyment.

I soon found that the Inspector is held in high esteem on account of the independence of his position, and the fact that he reports regularly to a superior headquarters, not only on the efficiency and discipline of the troops in the command, but also includes in his criticism, every staff department, and the Commanding General himself who has announced him in general orders as a member of his staff. His assignment to duty is from a higher command level and he cannot be relieved from his position by the Commander on whose staff he is serving. The result of these conditions was that when I asked for anything, in or out of reason, I got it. And I got the big-head, too, to some extent without asking for it or having any use for it either for that matter.

A general inspection of all the troops was made monthly, and a detailed report forwarded to the Department. I had a reputation to make and went right after it. Several regiments I sent to their quarters to clean up, and made a new date with them. Some of the commanders were inclined to sulk at this, but I told them it would be better for all if I sent in a good report of them rather than a bad one, and they soon became reconciled to it. The Colonel of one white regiment thanked me most heartily for taking the conceit out of his captains, as he expressed it. He remarked,

"Now they will believe what I have so often told them, that they were not paying sufficient attention to the cleanliness of their men and their apparel."

CHAPTER XLVI

I held down this "I. G." position about a year, and during that time the following General Officers, in rotation, commanded the Vicksburg District:

Major General C. C. Washburn,
Brig. General Morgan L. Smith,
Major General Davidson,
Brig. General J. A. Maltby,
Brevt. Maj. General M. F. Force,
Maj. General P. J. Osterhaus.

I had much experience in many phases of garrison life, which is full of red tape, a record being kept of every transaction, as in civil affairs. Subordinate to me was one brigade and four post inspectors, whose reports were consolidated with mine and forwarded monthly. A written report covering specific points was made tri-monthly, and special ones when occasions required them.

Many matters that required investigation were referred to me and I was soon so busy that I kept two clerks and two mounted orderlies for most of the time on the jump. These were white boys. For servants I kept Ben to cook and another Darkey to care for the horses. I wonder now that I got along as well as I did, and held down the job so long, for I was young and willful, and no one seemed inclined to take exception to anything I did. If complaints were made against me they must have been turned down, for I never heard of them.

There was a regiment stationed 25 or 30 miles below [Vicksburg] that I wanted to inspect. It was at Davis' Bend, which was nearly an island, as the neck was but 200 yards wide while it was 30 miles around by river. By fortifying the neck and keeping a regiment of colored troops stationed there, and patrolling the river with a craft from the Mosquito Fleet, it made a comfortable and reasonably safe rendezvous for a few thousand Darkeys, old men, women and children. The Freedman's Bureau had control of them and cultivated the land, which was owned by Jefferson Davis and his brother Joe, unless our government had already confiscated it.

When a river steamer reached the neck of this bend it was the proper thing to run into the bank and let the passengers off to stroll about while the boat was going "round the horn." Across the whole front of Jeff's home mansion were letters formed of evergreen twigs, or leaves of some kind, which read, "The House that Jeff.Built." The "Mansions" were occupied by bureau officers, and large additions were made to the Negro quarters.

If I had depended on the regular boats I might have had to remain at the Bend a night or two, and believing that Vicksburg could not get along without me for that length of time, I asked the Quartermaster for a tug. He smiled a bland smile and said it would require an order from General Washburn to get one. "That's easy," I replied, "have her ready in the morning, will you?"

"When I receive the General's order I will send notice to the captain to have her ready for you."

The order was given without hesitation, and by invitation a few officers went along for a day's outing. While inspecting the regiment I was surprised to find an intelligent looking white man in a private's uniform standing in the ranks with the Darkeys. I noted that there had been chevrons on the sleeves of his jacket, and could scarcely refrain from smiling at the gall of a commander who would reduce a white orderly to a private in a colored regiment.

From investigation I found that this young man was from Boston, was well brought-up and educated, had all the conceit and assurance of a true native of the Hub, and was much too smart for confinement to any position that could be given him in our military department. He had tried clerking in several offices at Vicksburg, and was systematically kicked out for impertinence and inattention to his duties. After going broke and getting fired from several boarding houses he enlisted in this colored regiment and was made band master with the rank of sergeant.

The major in command here bore him a month or two and then reduced him to the ranks, since which he had been in the guardhouse about half of his time. Naturally a dude, he was now getting dirty and shabby, and probably lousy also. The major hoped he was and was trying as hard as he could to enjoy his discomfiture.

A large, stern looking captain attracted my attention, and I took him along for a walk. I soon discovered that he should have been in command of the regiment. He said the major was completely taken in by Young Boston, and gave him full liberty of the camp, including his own quarters. The rascal managed to dine with him nearly every day, and as compensation for his board would teach the major and his wife table manners and give them lessons in French to enable them to read menu cards and intelligently order a dinner at a first-class hotel or restaurant. Then he would suggest new dishes for the next dinner and hunt up material out of which to concoct them, all at the major's expense, of course.

Now this was not pleasing to the major for he was close-fisted and was trying to save a roll to take home with him after the war, but his wife enjoyed it and he permitted it to go on until he caught the scamp kissing her, and then he went into the air, and the band sergeant went into the ranks.

"I once told him," said the Captain, "that I would manage that fellow if he would give him to me. My Orderly had just been promoted and I had a place for him."

"Would you have made him your orderly?" I asked.

"I certainly would. I would not have a white man in my company below that rank."

"Well, Captain, please tell me in detail how you would curb him."

"I should first, simply as a matter of form, tell him that while he served with me he would be neither reduced to the ranks, nor sent to the guardhouse; that he should have a tent of his own, and should draw his rations and cook them himself; that his associates would be the white non-commissioned officers; that he must attend strictly to his duty, never get airy or shoot off his witticisms in any direction."

"But you would scarcely expect him to regard these instructions, would you?" said I.

"No. As I said, these would be simply a matter of form; something for him to remember later on :."

"Well, go on. I'm interested."

"I should expect the first day to have occasion to take him by the scruff of his jacket and slap him until he could not repeat his name. This I would repeat on every provocation. Legal punishments have no effect on him; I would give him a taste of the higher law that would paralyze him. He would have to behave or desert, and if he did not do one or the other inside of a month, I would be willing to throw up my commission."

I rather liked this strenuous captain and believed he had a level head on his broad shoulders. His was certainly the cleanest and most orderly company in the regiment, and I suggested to the major that he give him this man. He said if he did he would have to make a first sergeant of him, and that he would never do that. He had him in the ranks and there he should stay.

"Boston" filed a written complaint with me, and I gave him a private interview. He pled his own case very ingeniously and said the major's only grievance was jealousy, for which he was in no manner to blame. He said both the major and his wife insisted upon his dining with them each day, and as a compensation he had taught them table manners until they could get through the menu in very creditable style. The Boston man stated that when he joined the regiment neither the major nor his wife could eat a soft-boiled egg without besmearing themselves quite inelegantly. He was certain that everything would have been lovely to this day had the major not caught his wife trying to kiss him.

We got back to Vicksburg about sundown after a very pleasant trip. The following day I rode down to a hospital near the river and asked the surgeon in charge if he could use another man as nurse, or in any other capacity, and he said he could. So I got "Boston" detailed for this service, but he kicked up the devil in the hospital inside of two weeks, got the nurses all quarreling, and provoked the Assistant Surgeon and Hospital Steward into a fist fight. Then he sent a written statement to headquarters that the hospital was grossly mismanaged, and that all the officials were stealing.

Final result: "Boston" was discharged from the service and ordered out of the Vicksburg District.

I shall never forget the beautiful Mrs. Sloan whose neat cottage stood opposite my office in Vicksburg. She was apparently less than thirty, of medium height, oval face, elegant form, dainty feet, and a pair of the sweetest little white hands that man ever kissed. Can you wonder that her admirers were as numerous as the officers at the Post? It was said that her husband was a captain in the Confederate Service, but she seemed to have no prejudice against Union officers. She met them in society very pleasantly, but it appeared quite impossible to get on as good terms with her as one would wish.

At Vicksburg now was a captain in the Regular Army, who was mustering officer of the District. He was quite skillful in small talk and devoted much of his time to the handsome madam, but I don't think he succeeded in mustering her into his service. He was small and effeminate, seemingly amusing to her, but possibly she thought him insignificant also.

"Captain DeRussey, how do you like the colored service?" I overheard her say to him one evening.

"Zounds! my dear lady," he replied, "I am a captain in the wegular ahmy; wat put that wediculous notion in your head I'd like to know?"

"Why Captain! I read it only this morning in the *Herald*. It said, 'Captain DeRussey, 13th U.S.Colored Infantry, Mustering Officer,'" said the lady. "Now what is a mustering officer for, captain? What is mustering, anyway? Whatever it is you would be bound to make a mess of it. I never heard of your doing anything except to promenade the walks in your fine uniform and flirt with the ladies. You need not be ashamed of the Negro regiments, for General Washburn informs me that they are as good as any and I know some of the officers are very nice."

"Oh! hang the Negro regiments. I don't belong to them at all," replied the exasperated captain. "That duced editow put it in his paypa cos he didn't know any bettaw, don't you know. I've been in his dingy office a hundud times and tole him to take it out, but he nevah did it, you see, I'm going to get an awdah from the General and then if he don't change it I'll have him awested."

One day I met on the walk a married lady friend who said, "I shall have a little dancing party Wednesday evening, and wish you to come."

I asked her who would be there, and she mentioned the names of a few citizens and officers - mostly known to me - and among the ladies she mentioned the beautiful Mrs. Sloan. I at once said I would be delighted, and as I passed on I drifted into a monologue

"This will be my opportunity to make the acquaintance of this incomparable woman. There was not mentioned an officer that ranked me nor a citizen that could elbow me to the rear. I have a speaking acquaintance with her and will not have to secure an introduction. If possible I will engage her for the first dance and trust to luck to make a good impression. Why could not all women be made beautiful like her; it would be like heaven then for such superb women do not have to wear jewelry, because they are angels on Earth. It will be worth a year of one's life to hold those dainty hands for ten minutes, and who knows but I may get the opportunity. If I do I will improve it, and though the distance to her cottage is exasperatingly short, if she will permit me to cross the street with her when she gets tired of dancing there is a possible kiss for me, but pshaw that is too Heavenly to anticipate, though no one can tell what will happen."

I couldn't tell then, but I can now. This exquisite beauty floated into the room on the arm of that homely old General Washburn, who never left her side for an instant, barred all round dances, and saw her safely back into her little cottage again, at one o'clock a.m. But for the charming Mary Rates, with whom I was on excellent terms, I would not have had any fun at all.

I never laid this up against the General for he was a fine old fellow, and had a decided taste for the beautiful and elegant. General Washburn came into the service as Colonel of the Second Wisconsin Cavalry. He had a brother in the U.S. Senate, which will in a degree account for his rapid advancement to the rank of Major General. A Senator at that time was respected by the people, had influence with the President, and the same as now, senatorial courtesy did the rest. However, if he could handle a division of troops in the field with as much skill as he displayed in managing Mrs. Sloan that memorable evening, and had the courage to stay by them as closely as he did by her, he was justly entitled to the rank.

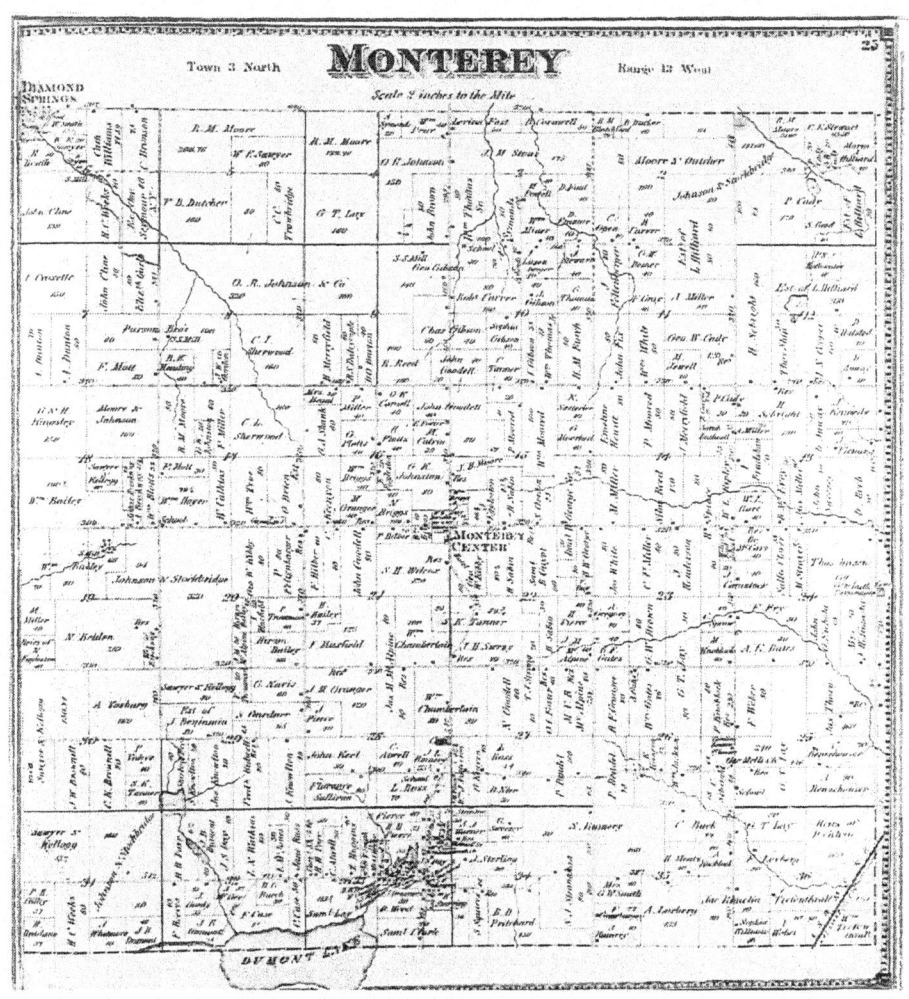

1873 map of Monterey Township, Allegan County, Michigan.

CHAPTER XLVII

It was about January, 1865 that I made my first inspection trip to Natchez, which post was included in my District. I took a regular boat with one of the cavalry orderlies, and landed at an early hour in the morning. I engaged a room and took breakfast at the principal hotel, which was run on the European plan, and about nine o'clock called at Post Headquarters.

I had never heard the name of the officer in command down there and was much pleased and surprised to meet the gallant Mason Brayman, hero of the battle of Pittsburg Landing, who was now a Brigadier General. By invitation I dined with him, and found the General and Mrs. Brayman a high-bred, elegant couple. They were occupying one of the best residences in a city of fine dwellings, and the General ordered Major L'Hommadieu [S.S. L'Hommedieu, Jr.] his A.A.I.Gen., to assign me a pleasant room in the building. This I felt compelled to decline with many thanks, saying that I had engaged rooms at the hotel and did not feel justified in giving them up. My duties as Inspector would scarcely permit me to be his constant guest while at the Post, as it might reasonably be held that it would have a tendency to influence my report.

I sent for the Post Inspector and we rode about the city while he gave me quite an insight into the affairs of the garrison, and we planned the order of inspection of the troops, to commence the following morning.

There were both white and black troops here and we commenced on a white light artillery battery. Of this I have only to say that the ammunition in the chests was actually wet, and the excuse given was they had repeatedly requisitioned tar paulins to cover the ammunition chests, but had never got them. A glance over the camp discovered a number of them in use as tent flies and awnings, and I was so astonished and disgusted that I told the Captain that his damned battery was not worth inspecting, but that I might possibly look him over again before I went back.

Then we tackled a regiment of Darkey infantry that was not in all respects disgraceful, but much inferior to anything at Vicksburg. The commander was a well-meaning man and supposed he had a superior organization, but I told him he had not and invited him to go back with me and look over the garrison of Vicksburg, then come back and go to work.

Then we ordered another regiment of Colored infantry to be in line at two p.m. and went to dinner. When we got back we struck a menagerie. There was not a clean man or musket in the whole circus. The men stood in all sorts of attitudes, and kept up a constant jabber. They were living in log quarters and some of them had to be shoved out of our way when we passed through. One of the captains explained the situation by saying that the old colonel was a pious "nigger lover," would welcome complaints of the men, and invariably decide in their favor against the company officers. It was therefore impossible to have any discipline in this regiment.

I called this old colonel down good and strong and told him that he was a disgrace to the uniform he wore and that I would recommend his immediate dismissal from the service. I expected to see a flare-up, but was fooled. He evidently thought a young man of inferior rank could not jar him, but there he was fooled. If he had temper I failed to draw it out, and doubt not I was remembered in his prayers when he turned in for the night.

I finished the day inspecting a light battery of white boys, and found everything in excellent shape. The post inspector said that the captain of this concern, although an educated man of much general intelligence, was a complete failure as a battery commander, and upon his recommendation was kept on detail so that the company might be left in charge of the first lieutenant.

That evening, with three members of the post staff, we called upon a few of the citizens and found them delightful entertainers. The chief medical officer of the post was our leader. He was talented and witty and could not be thrown into the shade by the brightest of them.

It was near midnight when I returned to the Post with the Adjutant and we sat down to smoke our last cigar. Suddenly, three officers in dark blue overcoats entered the office, and the leader asked for General Brayman. L'Hommadieu tilted back his chair and languidly informed him that the General had retired, and asked if he could be of any service to him.

"Yes you can. Just tell General Brayman that Major General Davidson has arrived from New Orleans to take charge of this District and wishes to see him at once."

It was funny to observe the lightning change in manner and movement as the Adjutant sprang from his seat and flopped out of the office. Then the General turned to me and asked what position I held at the post. After I enlightened him he said I need go no further with my inspection as Natchez was now a separate district, and that I could return to Vicksburg at my pleasure.

"Then it will be by the first boat," I answered.

"You may take the boat I came up on if you wish."

"Nothing could please me more," said I.

Turning to one of his staff he said, "Lieutenant, ride down to the landing and tell the captain of our steamer not to pull in his gang plank 'til Major Caverno [Cornwell] is aboard."

Then turning to me again he asked what I had done and how I had found things as far as I had gone. I said I had put in one day and then told him what I had found. I gave my opinion that General Brayman was not responsible for the condition of this garrison, but if he was in any measure it should be overlooked for on the battlefield he was simply sublime and deserved all the honors the Nation could shower on him for his gallantry on the field of Shiloh. He gave me his hand at parting and said he would repeat my testimony to General Brayman. A half hour later I rode aboard the steamer and a voice came down from the hurricane deck.

"Is that Major Caverno?" "Aye, Aye, Sir," I replied.

"Pull in that bridge. Cast off that line. Back on the laboard, forward on the starboard." And a moment later, "Forward on both," and we were soon scudding against the current at a twenty-mile gait.

I was in Natchez a few months later with General Dana and many other officers, and had a pleasant chat with General Davidson. He said he had made a captain of that lieutenant of artillery that I had spoken so well of and sent the old "granny" colonel home to the bosom of his family.

--- ------ ---

We had a battalion of regulars under Colonel Dudley at Vicksburg and I naturally felt a little uncertainty about inspecting West Pointers. But I had to report on them and could scarcely do it without looking them over. So I rode down to their camp one morning and told the colonel the object of my visit. He said if I would set the hour he would have the battalion in line ready for me. I said I would prefer to simply go through the quarters and note their every-day condition. As he was then conducting an officer's school I readily excused him and he turned me over to a first lieutenant doing duty as battalion officer-of-the-day. This officer made himself exceedingly agreeable and so I gained confidence and courage, and poked my nose into every nook and corner of the camp and asked a few hundred questions. I was much benefited by this tour but I could not see that they were.

Later they moved their camp from the vicinity of the ordnance depot to a vacant piece of ground on Cherry Street, and as I was riding past there one day I noted the colonel standing in front of his quarters looking my way and raised my cap to him. He then signaled me to ride up, and while thanking me for the gentlemanly report I made of his battalion his officers flocked about and gave me quite a reception. I recall this as one of the most pleasant incidents of my Army life.

Early in 1866 Colonel Lieb took a trip to Washington in view of having his regiment incorporated into the Regular Army. During this time his place was taken by Colonel Van E. Young of the 49th Colored Infty. I was back in the regiment at this time [No longer an Inspector General] and Lt. Col. Hissong not being well ordered me to attend a meeting of commanders at Post Headquarters in his stead.

There was to be a review the next day by General Gilmore, who was making a tour of inspection, and we were then to receive orders about our positions, and that sort of thing. Reviews are described in Army Regulations and the latest edition -1863- did not conform to the tactics we were using. And the question was repeatedly coming up:

"Shall we conform strictly to the words of command as laid down in the *Revised Army Regulations*, or shall we use the tactical commands that would have been in this book if proper attention had been paid to its revision?"

To use incorrect commands because they were left unchanged through neglect seemed absurd to many of us, but there were officers who held the book as sacred as many honest sincere Christians do the Bible, and who believe it inspired "from kiver to kiver," no matter how unreasonable, contradictory, absurd or impossible.

This point was discussed, and each of us gave his view as called upon by Col. Young, who had very properly left Dudley for the last, as he was of right the ranking officer, being a Brevet Brig. Gen. of the Regular Army. General Dudley said the best authority he knew of was the usage at West Point, and there they conformed to the tactics. That settled it - but not as the reader would naturally suppose, for Young at once gave orders to use the Regulation [1863 ed.] commands, totally rejecting General Dudley's sound opinions.

Some time earlier Young had been an Officer of the Day of the Post and had made an unfriendly report concerning the regular battalion, which had been shown to then Colonel Dudley. Dudley had served through much of the war as a Major General of Volunteers and unjust criticism from an officer of Young's caliber and reputation was a little trying to his disposition. Soon after he met him at department headquarters, and in the presence of the commanding general and many staff officers he cut him wide open, saying that he was a disgrace to the uniform he wore and to the Darkeys he commanded.

When we rose to go, General Dudley spoke up:

"Col. Young, you remind me of a Col. Wilson who commanded the 3rd U.S. Cavalry in the Mexican War. While in camp at San Miguel, Major Jones of the 4th Infantry, who had been detained on court martial duty and was now on his way to the front to join his regiment, came up with them and remained over night. Col. Wilson was known to the service as a parsimonious officer whose hospitality never made a perceptible inroad on his pay and allowances. When the Major mounted in the morning to continue his journey, he said,

"Colonel, if any of our boys should inquire about the color of your whiskey, what shall I say?" Then Dudley turned to Col. Young and said, "You are on the safe side; your whiskey is without color, strength or flavor."

Young made no reply and we left him scowling and biting his lips. A few of us felt the same contempt for Young. Our appreciation of this fine old Regular led us to escort him to his camp. When we bid him goodnight he said,

"Not so early, gentlemen, come right in and see the color of my whiskey."

We did, and found it a light amber with a heavenly flavor. The Perfectos were passed and when we had lighted up the general drifted into reminiscences of the Mexican War and entertained us for an hour.

When General Force was sent to Jackson I returned to duty in the regiment. But I had not been with the boys long when I got a special order from General Wood, the department commander, placing me on the staff of General Force again in the old position. For special reasons I did not wish to leave Vicksburg just at that time, told General Wood as much, and he let me off. [Early in 1864 Major Cornwell married Miss Frances Millen of Lake County, Illinois. She lived with him at Vicksburg for some time as an Army wife. Their first child, a son, Frank, was born January 29, 1865 at Vicksburg. Cornwell's memoirs do not mention this family life, but the "special reasons" mentioned here may reflect certain critical family "conditions"]. He said that Force had requested him to send him an inspector, and I was the first one that occurred to him. Later I saw Force's letter, which stated specifically that he wanted me. Had I known this I would have gone, for I had the highest regard for the General. He was an earnest, candid, considerate officer and gentleman who bore an unblemished reputation. His Asst. Adjt. Gen., Major J.E. Edmonds, was a high-bred young man of integrity, and never a suspicion of unfair dealing with officer, soldier or citizen was held against the Force administration of the District of Vicksburg.

The war had virtually closed. Property that had been used for military purposes was being returned to its owners; civil law was being re-established, and the commanders were daily meeting questions of administration that were really puzzling. A level-headed inspector who is not out for graft can be a great help to a commander in investigating cases and making a report of the facts and suggesting what would be the proper action to take. Force thought I was the right man for the job and wanted me. I have always regretted that I did not go to help him.

But I didn't, and Col. Van E. Young was dispatched in my stead. Later, with two other officers, I was elected to sit on a Court of Inquiry, and there came before us a Mr. Johnson, cotton speculator, and a businessman of Jackson, Mississippi whom we will call Mr. Holden, and Col. Van E. Young. And this is the story that was told under oath by the two former.

Johnson had purchased a large quantity of cotton fiber and when about to ship it to Mobile, Young put a guard over it under the pretense that he thought that part or all of it was Confederate cotton once sold to the Confederate Government and therefore subject to confiscation. Financial ruin stared Johnson in the face and he at once started for Washington to confer with the Secretary of the Treasury who had encouraged him to engage in the venture in the interest of the country as well as himself.

Holden happened to be on the same train and he confided his trouble to him. They did some figuring and then Holden said that he had sized Young up and found him on the make, and as the staple was on a steady decline, it would be in his interest to return and buy him off. Holden's figures supported this view and so they dropped off at the first station and took the next train back, Holden agreeing to negotiate the deal.

He at once called on Young in Jackson and a bargain was struck without difficulty. He met him again at midnight and gave him ten one thousand dollar treasury notes of consecutive numbers - of which he retained a memorandum.

Johnson was up bright and early to load and ship out his cotton, and finding the guards still on duty he sent Holden at once to Young to have him remove them so that he could commence moving the stuff. Holden found Van still in bed and in a queer state of mind. For the life of him he could not recall the deal that was consummated but four hours back. He was sure they had had no such meeting nor any such deal and refused to remove the guards. Then Johnson started for Washington again and reported the case to the Secretary of the Treasury. He took it to the Secretary of War, who at once ordered General Wood to investigate the case.

I never had the slightest doubt about the literal truthfulness of the evidence given by these two citizens. Young simply denied everything. After the case was closed, I knew well how the senior member of the court would act and also that the junior member would agree with him no matter how he went. My name or opinion would not appear on the records and so really it did not matter what I thought of it. However, my opinion was called for, and I said that Young was guilty of a piece of treachery that was evidently original with him, and stamped him a shameless and heartless knave who should at once be turned over to the mercy of a court martial. But he wasn't. The record and findings did not require my signature and the other two acquitted him.

About a year earlier than this I had served on a Board of Survey with Young. Now, not knowing that I strongly dissented from the recent findings in his case he brought to my office a carefully prepared statement of the findings of that Board, saying that the survey record had been lost and we now had to replace it from memory. I read it over very carefully, and then remarked,

"If we sign this we will be in a predicament should the original ever turn up, for that held the steamer to blame for the damage, and you here have saddled the loss of the oats on the depot quartermaster." Then Young replied,

"That's not as I remember it; I think we found the Q.M. at fault for not covering the sacks with 'paulins after they were stacked up on the bank. However, the original papers will never turn up; you may trust me for that." And I replied,

"I might trust you for it but I shan't. I think you have the original record in your pocket and are holding it over the boat company for a consideration. You will get no help from me, so good morning, Colonel."

I was told that after he left the service he returned to Wisconsin, invested his money in a woolen factory and lost it. It must have been about 1870 when there was a reform Mayor elected in Grand Rapids [Michigan] and he wanted a reform Chief of Police. And he got one in the person of Van E. Young, who possibly served a month or more before he was fired.

The year that Cleveland was re-nominated for President I saw Young hanging around a hotel in Grand Rapids. He was seedy, garrulous and full. The hotel clerk told me that he had not a dollar and was living with a married daughter.

CHAPTER XLVIII

The morning after our meeting at post head quarters, Hissong sent me a note saying he was unable to do duty and wished me to take charge of affairs until he got better. Brigadier General J.A. Maltby had been mustered out and had gone into business in Vicksburg, and having no use for his horse sent him up to my stable. I mounted him for the Gilmore review. He was large, coal black, and the finest show horse I had ever straddled.

Maltby was a plain, unpretentious man who would not endure his antics, so the horse had contracted the habit of carrying him about quite gravely, and I never guessed his possibilities until I mounted him one morning for an airing. When I reached the courthouse in town they were mounting the post guard, and I halted on the right flank to see the parade. When the cornet band started down the line the old fellow went into the air, and meeting with no discouragement, waltzed about on his hind feet, keeping very respectable time with the music. Unlike Maltby, who was middle-aged and heavy, I was only a hundred and fifty pounder with much more humor than dignity, and cared but little how much this horse cut up.

Between the two pieces of music, and while the band was reversing direction, the old fellow stood quiet with his neck on a slight twist and right ear thrown forward in a listening attitude. As the band stepped off on their return, and reeled off that hornpipe tune that was so great a favorite with them, the old rascal's hind heels went so high in the air I very nearly went over his head. Having found that he could play at either end, I was on the lookout, but barely managed to keep my seat.

I determined to give him the time of his life on this review, and my recollection is that he got it. No one recognized the animal as Maltby's, and thought I had picked him up somewhere and trained him to cut up. He would stand so erect on his hind legs, and stay in the air so long, that it seemed quite uncertain which way he would come down. But luckily each time he managed to hit the turf right side up.

Back of the reviewing party was an upward slope of ground covered with spectators. A lady questioned her escort,

"What General is it riding the beautiful black horse that cuts so many graceful antics?" And the escort answered in a tone of deprecation,

"That is no General, only Major Caverno [Cornwell] showing off."

It may be remembered that the company officers I most admired in the Old 8th for their intelligence and pluck were the lieutenants of Co. E.; Loyd Wheaton and Sam Caldwell. Sam was A.D.C. on General Oglesby's staff from Shiloh to Corinth where the General was seriously wounded and sent home.

The next I knew about Sam he was staff officer for that surly old humbug McClernand, who was sent into retirement by Grant during the siege of Vicksburg. Sam said that McClernand, in the presence of his staff after they crossed to the Mississippi side of the river near Bruinsburg, prophesied that the campaign they were engaged in would terminate in a disastrous defeat for the Union Army. But our boys fooled him; they sailed in and whipped everything they came to.

I heard from Sam next in 1864 in the Inspector's Department at Memphis, and in 1865, he came down to Vicksburg with General Dana, and was soon after announced Judge Advocate of the Department. We messed together several months, and I recall this association with much pleasure and satisfaction.

When Oglesby left the Army and became Governor of Illinois he asked Sam to come to Springfield and said he would find him a regiment. But for some unaccountable reason Sam would not go. My boyish blunder in refusing the 1st sergeantcy of Co. K in 1861 was not worthy of mention beside this. Caldwell was both brave and brainy and would have been a handsome and gallant commander, and even a general if he could have gotten into a lively campaign before the war closed.

Sam married a beautiful young woman of a well-to-do family, and they urged him to give up his commission and settle down to a civilian life; but he would not do that either. He returned to his regiment as Captain of Co. E of the 8th Illinois, some time before it was mustered out at Baton Rouge, in May 1866. Then he went home, was admitted to the bar, sent to the Illinois Legislature, and died at an early age.

Perhaps the ablest, all-around, most level-headed officer of the "Old Eighth," was Loyd Wheaton, who remained with the regiment throughout its five years of service, and reached the colonelcy in March 1866. That is the point Colonel Lieb would have touched in his stead, had he stayed with the old regiment. Wheaton got a commission in the Regular Army and rose to Major General. At one time he commanded about half the territory of the Philippine Islands. He retired a few years ago and makes his home in Chicago. When I last met him he was about seventy, but looked many years younger. It would take much travel to find another as sturdy, accomplished and handsome an old soldier as General Wheaton.

The "tall and short" men had reached Vicksburg by late 1865 and were nightly plying their trade. One of our captains was relieved of $400. The greenbacks were in his pants and the pants were under his head. The expert smashed a pane of glass and yanked out his trousers before he was fairly awake. The next day they were found in a nearby ravine with the pockets on the outside.

They made me a visit about a week later. This was a mistake for them for a national bank was then running in Vicksburg and I had an account there and less than twenty dollars in my clothes. I was occupying a barrack on Grove Street with the back side near the breastwork, and fronting toward the residence of an old Southerner named Randolph, who was then the city's mayor. This barrack had a covered porch and the front windows were of the French style running down to the floor. This night the window of my sleeping room was thrown open and covered by a couple of cloth half-curtains, and an old black hair-cloth sofa was backed up against it. The entrance door was from an adjoining room.

The head of my cot was against the back wall. Then came a chest, a chair and a desk. I had thrown my pants on the chair, laid a pocket six-shooter on the chest, set the kerosene lamp near the cot and read the latest daily 'til I became sleepy. Then I tossed the paper over the revolver, turned the lamp low, and went to sleep.

About two a.m. I happened to awake and open my eyes. I thought I saw a movement of those window curtains. Soon I was quite sure of it for they were moved wide apart and a man poked his head and shoulders into the room, then withdrew them and placed one eye to a gap left between the curtains. The situation then came to me clearly, and I did not dare move a muscle for he could see me lying there, but evidently could not see that my eyes were open.

If I reached for my revolver he would instantly disappear. I decided to wait 'til he was well into the room, just about to reach for my trousers, then make a spring for the revolver and wing him as he went back through the window. I soon saw that there were two of them, and they truly were the veritable long and short men sure enough. They dallied about the window a minute or more, tried the bottom of the old sofa to see if it was getting rusty, and finding that it gave out no sound the tall one held the curtains wide apart and the short one stepped over the back into it and moved across the floor without making a sound. And he came so rapidly that I nearly lost my uniform pants, for he was reaching for them when I sprang for him. "Halt, you son-of-a-gun," or something very nearly like it, I yelled, as he went through the window like a shot and was caught and set on his feet by the tall, slim chap. I was at the window as soon as I could pick up the revolver and get there, and saw them plainly by the light of the moon running for the nearest corner, side by side.

The pistol was not a self-cocker, and I got but two shots before they were out of sight. A few days later an officer and myself were standing on the parapet near the street walk, talking of this affair when I exclaimed, "There they are now!"

"Are you sure those are the men?"

"Positively certain," I said.

"Why, let's arrest them; what do you say?"

I shook my head. We eyed them sharply as they passed by, and I remarked in their hearing.

"Those are the boys all right."

But they did not look up. I explained to my brother officer that an attempt to arrest those men there would have got us into a pistol fight where we would have got worsted, no matter how it resulted. The civil law was then [late 1865 and 1866] paramount and we would be bound to get the worst of it. And I added that I held no grudge against them for I had as much excitement and fun out of it as they had.

While Colonel Herman Lieb was commanding the post he sent me a note saying that an officer would like to see me. I was there in a few minutes and found our old Swedish friend, Major

Stolbrand, who once had me up for stealing that corner stone, and later chose me for a first lieutenant. He said that he was pleased to find that he had made no mistake in sizing me up, for Lieb had informed him that I had made good wherever placed. He gave me some information about the movements and doings of old Battery B [2nd Illinois Light Artillery] after they left Vicksburg. We sampled Lieb's wine, which happened to be rather poor stuff, and at parting I again thanked him for giving me the upward start. I do not remember Stolbrand's rank at this time, but he closed his military career as a brigadier general.

As the end of our service drew nigh, discipline relaxed somewhat, and our officers would get themselves into comfortable citizen dress as soon as off duty. Then rank and title would be utterly ignored and we would accost each other with "Hello, Lieb; Good Morning, Lime [nickname for Lt. Col. Lyman J. Hissong]; which way, Shorty," etc., etc. This sort of freedom was very enjoyable after our five years of starchy military deportment, and seemed to breed a feeling of friendship among us, much warmer than had existed.

The prospects of our early freedom [beginning 1866] made us cheerful and chatty, and we discussed our futures and commenced laying plans for them. Lieb had been corresponding with Gov. Oglesby and decided to publish a German language newspaper at the state capitol; and as soon as this conclusion was reached he subscribed for a number of leading publications, and with the instinct of a born journalist procured a pair of shears with blades a foot in length.

Sam Caldwell and I made a couple of trips out to the "Magnolia Plantation," which was advertised for sale, and as soon as we made the discovery that our combined wealth was not enough to make the first payment and get possession, we lost all interest in agriculture.

Sam fell back to the reading of law, and occasionally sent a spicy article to the *Press and Tribune*. I formed a partnership with Lt. Col. Hissong to deal in general merchandise where we could command a large cash trade and make big profits. We had a mutual desire to get very rich mighty quick and decided to lay in a $10,000 stock as a starter, paying down what cash we had and running our handsome mugs for the balance. I have yet Lime's invoice of the stock we would purchase, but that is all the evidence that ever existed of that beautiful enterprise.

Lieb's suspicion that I had played him false at Battery Castle the Sunday morning we were photographed had never been cleared up, and as we were soon to separate, I wished to convince him that he had for a long time labored under a misapprehension. The three of us concerned were sitting in the Colonel's office, and as Hissong rose to go, I said,

"Lime, Lieb has been laboring under a delusion since the day we were photographed at Battery Castle and before we separate I would like to have his suspicion removed. I wish you would repeat the conversation we had at that time."

"I don't remember any except what passed between us down in the magazine," said Hissong.

"How did we come to go in the magazine together?"

"I called you down to tell you about a movement to take the regiment into the field."

"What was said?" I asked.

"I opposed it, but you didn't care, so you said."

"Did you know that I had heard of this before you mentioned it to me?"

"No - I supposed it was news to you, of course."

"Who told you of it?"

"Lt. Col. Owen."

"That settles the case; much obliged, Lime," I said and Hissong left.

Lieb jumped to his feet and paced the floor with much agitation, exclaiming,

"Why in the devil did I not know this sooner; why in hell did I make such a mistake?"

Colonel Lieb was impulsive, almost erratic at times. But he was an energetic, capable and serene fighter, so he had my respect and loyalty from start to finish. This ought to make up for my meanness and insubordination while a member of Company K, of the old 8th Illinois.

To the 20th day of May, 1866 I had served continuously five years and twenty-five days. [Cornwell commanded Negros troops almost continuously from May 1863 until May 1866...3 years.] On this date we were mustered out and made citizens again. Later I received a commission from the President of the United States of lieutenant colonel by brevet, U.S. Volunteers.

NOTE [By Cornwell]

General Herman Lieb was born in the Chateau Harl on the Swiss side of the river Rhine, a few miles from the old city of Constance, in 1826. His father was a manufacturer of cottons and established the first calico printing factory in the Russian Empire in 1808. In 1820 he drew out of business, returned to his family in Switzerland, where he died eight years later. Young Lieb was two years old then.

At age 19 Herman went to Paris, France, to assist an elder brother in his business, and was in the nick of time for the revolution of '48. He joined the Guard Mobile and served until Louis Napoleon was elected President of the French Republic. When the Guard was disbanded, Lieb came to America.

Here he dropped the patronymic Von Vasmer and used his middle name in its stead. He went from New York to Boston, and back to New York. Then he started for New Orleans via Cincinnati.

In the latter city he engaged with a French firm in the wine and liquor trade, and after a few years of service was sent to Decatur, Illinois to start a branch in that city. He was here when war broke out, and was among the first to enlist.

He served as a private in Co. B, 8th Illinois Infty. for three months, and upon re-organization for the three year service he secured the captaincy. To speculate a little, suppose he had not struck a job in Cincinnati and gone on to New Orleans as he had intended. There were many French there - the sort of people he was fond of - and whose language he spoke fluently. It is reasonable to think he would have engaged in some kind of business and have jumped into the Confederate Army with the same avidity that he joined the Union at Decatur, Illinois. There were people who say success in life depends only on brains and will power. Lieb was lucky to get into the right army, and luckier still to get out of it alive.

POST SCRIPT [by Editor]

The common Civil War experiences of Lieb and Cornwell forged a bond of deep respect and friendship that endured into the 20th century. On the surface they may have seemed an unlikely match as peers. However, the profound sensitivity of David Cornwell to the finer things of life made him a follower of aristocratic Herman Lieb's sophisticated and very literate life style. From a cabin boy on his father's Erie Canal boat in the 1840's and 50's to his adventures in Chicago (1854-61) construction, David Cornwell nurtured a talent and affinity for the refinement and sophistication of the outermost limits of what marked the character and taste of those who grasped and secured the best of what life had to offer on a raw and often brutal frontier life.

Herman Lieb and young David Cornwell represented extremes in American society during mid and late 19th-century years. In few other times and places could two such diverse personalities weld a long-term friendship based on respect and understanding that quite transcended the sociological and traditional society status measures of the times. Each took from the other and certainly each also gave to the other a respectful comprehension and sensitive understanding of life's qualities and values that sprung from the raw, vibrant, restless frontier of mid-19th century mid-west America and the comfortable entrepreneurial, conservative society of central western Europe. Perhaps only during the course of combat in the cauldron of the trans-Appalachian Civil War campaigns could a Lieb and a Cornwell complement and appreciate each other as did these two robust Union soldiers.

Their friendship continued and steadily increased following the war. They remained in contact for many years, and the pioneer farmer from southwestern Michigan often visited his old commander in his very comfortable Chicago home. And, in fact, Cornwell and Sarah Ann Stanclift were united in matrimony at the Lieb residence late in 1888. This was "Major Dave's" third marriage; the longest, and possibly most satisfying for the old soldier. "Annie," a school teacher in southwestern Michigan before the marriage, outlived her first and only husband and passed away in Medford, Oregon in 1940, outliving David 29 years, leaving no immediate survivors.

David Cornwell's evening years were full and productive. One incredible episode was his very active involvement at the turn of the century running lines for a rural telephone company owned by him and his son-in-law. In a diary he kept for 1901 the "old major" [as he was called by youngsters around his store about 1900] describes acquiring rights of way in Allegan County, Michigan for lines and poles. He helped set the poles by hand and then worked at running the wire. His diary shows the old vet had a fair understanding of the basic electronic-mechanical elements of telephonic communication. This business was a last hurrah for David. About 1903 he sold his little crossroads general store at Monterey Center and built a rather fine brick house about 1905 at 414 Cedar Street [still standing] in Allegan, near the county fair grounds. He lived in town until his death of natural causes May 1, 1911, leaving three children, of whom two were born to first wife Frances Millen (died 1879), and one to second wife Harriet Fox. Daughter Edith, born in 1872, died at about age 19 and was buried near her grandfather Joshua in Poplar Hill Cemetery near Monterey Center.

David rests now beside many Civil War comrades in the ancient, beautiful Allegan Town cemetery on "high school hill." Here he is outranked only by Brevet Brigadier General Benjamin D. Pritchard, the Civil War commander of the 4th Michigan Cavalry. His Union Army regiment gained a full measure of renown by capturing Jefferson Davis soon after Appomattox as he tried to flee his homeland and reach a place of refuge far from the authority of the Washington government.

From mid-1867 until early 1911 David was an enthusiastic citizen of Allegan County, Michigan. His inherited acres north of County Seat Allegan led to a comfortable business career by century's end. The discharged Union Army major threw his enthusiasm, energy, and integrity into a tough pastoral existence much as he had during his military service. The Cornwell farm is accurately sited in this 1873 Allegan County Atlas, which included this very Victorian title page.

This austere, prim-looking woman was David Cornwell's mother. The photo appears to date from the American Civil War period. It was taken at Picton, Prince Edward County, Ontario. Charity Conklin Lazier was born here about 1810. Her husband Joshua also probably was born here. At one time--1861-1862-- Charity Lazier Cornwell had two sons (David and Frank) and her husband Joshua in the Union Army of the West. Joshua served in the 3rd Michigan Cavalry, but was honorably discharged August 1862 because of service related injury. He died in Allegan County, Michigan in February 1867, leaving son David in possession of his very small farm.

Addendum A.

OBIT.

ANOTHER SOLDIER MUSTERED OUT
From *The Allegan Gazette,* May 6, 1911
Major David Cornwell, Stricken with Apoplexy, Died
in Few Hours--Had Long Services in Union Army--
Resident of Allegan County Since the War.

At about six o'clock last Sunday morning Mr. David Cornwell suffered a stroke of apoplexy from which he did not in any degree rally, but steadily declined until he peacefully died. He had been about his gardening the preceding day and was apparently in usual good health. Arising to shut a window he returned to bed; but as he laid in a peculiar position Mrs. Cornwell spoke to him. Receiving no answer, she discovered his condition and summoned aid. All was of no avail, however, and, not giving at any time the least sign of consciousness, Mr. Cornwell died at about seven o'clock Monday evening.

The funeral was held from the home at ten o'clock yesterday, Rev. A. V. Brashear officiating, and interment was made in Oakwood cemetery.

Mr. Cornwell was somewhat more than seventy-two years of age, having been born in Watertown, N.Y., Dec. 19, 1838. He passed his youth in Rome, N.Y. assisting his father who was a boatman on the Erie canal. When he was about eighteen years old he went to Illinois, and there became much interested in political questions of the days before the Civil war. He often heard Lincoln speak in public and was an ardent admirer of him even before his fame was wide.

Mr. Cornwell saw long service in the Union army. He was one of the very first to enter the volunteer host, enlisting in company K of the Eighth Illinois Infantry, and was mustered into service April 25, 1861, for three months. At end of that period he re-enlisted in the same company and regiment for three years. He served so as second sergeant until after the battle of Shiloh when he effected a transfer into battery D, First Illinois light artillery. He was with this battery until February, 1863, when he was given a commission as first lieutenant in the Fifth U.S. Colored heavy artillery, and became captain and major within the same year, and he remained in this command until mustered out May 20, 1866. They were brave men who became officers of colored troops, for they were specially hated and marked by the Confederates. During the last year of his army service he served as a staff officer in the inspector general's department, and received at the close a commission as brevet lieutenant-colonel.

For two years after close of his military service, Major Cornwell remained in Vicksburg, Miss. engaged in the fuel business, but then came to Michigan, to Salem township, Allegan county, and became a farmer. Following this occupation until 1884, he went to Monterey Center and kept a general store until nine years ago when he removed to Allegan, having taken an interest with M.D. Owen in a local telephone company which later sold to the present Citizens company. Since that time Mr. Cornwell had lived a retired life, building a home and enjoying its comforts. So well was he and so full of interest in life that he had determined to soon remove to Florida and take part in building a new town there.

Mr. Cornwell is survived by his wife and four children--Frank Cornwell and Mrs. Willard P. Blake of Hutchinson, Kansas; T.B. Dutcher (adopted) of Eagle River, Wis.; and Mrs. M. D. Owen of Allegan, all these by former marriages; also by a brother and two sisters. He was a man of force of character, one liked much by his many friends, for he was frank, companionable, and of unusual intelligence. He has written a book of his army experiences and quite lately placed it in the hands of the publishers. In its composition he showed how efficient a man may become in knowledge of letters who strives to overcome in later life the lack of early education.

Addendum to David Cornwell obituary

The widow, Mrs. Sarah A. Cornwell, was David Cornwell's third wife. Her maiden name was Sarah Ann Stanclift, formerly a school teacher, probably somewhere in Allegan County, Michigan. They were married December 1, 1888 in Chicago by the Reverend F.G. Nielsted at the home of David's old Civil War commanding officer, General Herman Lieb.

Cornwell's first wife was Frances Millen from the Chicago, Illinois area. They married about 1864. She died in Salem Township, Allegan County, Michigan at the Cornwell farm home in June 1879. She is buried near Deerfield, Illinois, probably not far from her childhood home. Their first child was Frank who was born in Mississippi (probably Vicksburg) January 29, 1865. The second child was Edith, born in 1872 in Salem Township. She worked as a clerk in the Cornwell store in Monterey, a crossroads community in Monterey Township, about 10 miles north of Allegan and died at about age 18 of dropsy (a heart deficiency) and was buried at Poplar Hill Cemetery in Monterey next to her paternal grandfather, Joshua Cornwell. The third child of the first marriage was Emma, born also in Salem Township at the farm August 11, 1876. Pension records for David hint that Edith was born July 1, 1872.

Cornwell's second wife was Harriet Fox, whom he married at Monterey November 9, 1881. Their only child was a girl (Grace) who moved to Hutchinson, Kansas in 1901, where she married Willard P. Blake... date unknown. She went to that place because her older half brother Frank had gone there also as a young adult.

There was no issue from David's third marriage. The widow Cornwell moved to Oregon a few years after David's death and died there March 3, 1940 in the town of Medford at 113 Cottage St.

David Cornwell's oldest child, Frank, came home to Michigan to attend his father's funeral. Frank returned to Michigan at least once more, visiting his sister, Emma Owen, and husband, Milton, at their home in Galesburg, Michigan about 1937. Nothing has been heard from him by family members since that time. According to Alice Owen Sanford, Mrs. Willard P. Blake visited Michigan relatives at least once and was an accomplished pianist.

It is known from local census records that Frank had children. In August 1991 John and Roberta Wearmouth stopped at the city library in Hutchinson, Kansas and researched all available local records looking for traces of the Frank Cornwell family. He was identified up to about 1920 by tax and census records...nothing after that time. During this visit John phoned all Cornwells listed in the Hutchinson phone directory. *None* of them were related to the Michigan Cornwells. Local library records show that Frank Cornwell at age 23 married in Reno County, Kansas, on November 9, 1888 to Miss Carrie Wray. They were married in South Hutchinson by the Rev. L. C. Buckles, minister of the local First Methodist Church. Census records for Reno County as of March 1, 1895 list Frank as a salt laborer and name his wife (at age 25) and three children: Calarance H. (perhaps a son Clarence...writing indistinct), five years old; Iva, three years old; Hazel, a year old. No effort was made in Hutchinson by the Wearmouths to locate descendants of Mrs. Blake.

Children and grandchildren of David Cornwell's daughter Emma Owen and husband, Milton D. Owen (all born in Michigan):

Grace Elizabeth, born in Allegan, Michigan June 27, 1899. She married John William Wearmouth in Windsor, Ontario, Canada September 21, 1921. Their children: John Milton born Allegan County, January 7, 1924; Elizabeth Jean born Detroit August 17, 1929; Robert Owen, born Detroit August 17, 1929; Alice Emily born Detroit November 13, 1931.

Ruby Helen, born August 29, 1902 in Allegan. Never married.

Alice Antoinette, born February 26, 1906 in Allegan. She married Charles A. Sanford May , 1936 at the M. D. Owen home in Galesburg, Michigan. Their children: Judith A., born Detroit March 26, 1937; David Owen, born Detroit July 24, 1940; Carole, born Jackson, Michigan October 11, 1943.

The above information was derived from the Cornwell obituary, Allegan County vital statistical and land records and U. S. Government records on file in Washington, D.C. at the Archives of the United States...Civil War and pension application records. As a matter of possible, somewhat related family history, Charity Conklyn Cornwell, mother of David, filed about 1890 a claim with the U. S. Pension Bureau for a pension based on her son Frank's death (1863) and husband's service-connected disability. Joshua, who had enlisted about August 1861 in Allegan somewhat fraudulently (lied about his advanced age), was injured when thrown from a mule while serving as an army cook with Union troops (3rd Michigan Cavalry) in Missouri. He served one year and was mustered out of service at Detroit in August 1862. Mrs. Joshua Cornwell was living near where she was born in Prince Edward County, Ontario when she filed for her widow's pension. She did get it...something like $8.00 a month. It is thought Joshua, too, was born in Ontario. He left his wife alone in New York State about 1860 and bought land in Salem Township, Allegan County, which property was left to his son, David, when he died early in 1867. Joshua's move to Allegan really was central to the later birthplaces of all those mentioned above who were born in Allegan County, Michigan from 1872 through 1924.

John Milton Wearmouth
March 25, 1998
Port Tobacco, Maryland

The Cornwells in their new brick home at 414 Cedar Street in Allegan about 1910...all very comfortable, steam heat, electricity, extensive library, and doubtless, a telephone (top).

Photo taken March 26, 1910 in front of the Mission at San Diego, California. Cornwells marked by arrows. All most fashionably "dolled up" (bottom).

Addendum B

Report of Brig. Gen. Henry E. McCulloch, C.S.Army, commanding Brigade, of attack (7th) on Milliken's Bend

HEADQUARTERS McCULLOCH'S BRIGADE,
Richmond, La., June 8, 1863

According to orders, on the night of the 6th my brigade took up the line of march for Milliken's Bend, to attack the Yankee force at that place.

We advanced to within about 1 ½ miles at 2:30 a.m. on the 7th instant, when the enemy's pickets fired upon my cavalry scouts and skirmishers. The cavalry scouts fell back precipitately upon the skirmishers, amid the fire of the enemy, which led the skirmishers to suppose them a portion of the enemy's cavalry; consequently they fired upon them, killing two of their horses and wounding a third. Fortunately no man was killed or wounded by this fire. My skirmishers immediately pressed forward, driving the pickets of the enemy before them. We advanced but a quarter of mile farther when the enemy's skirmishers in considerable force opened upon us under cover of a thick hedge. A portion of the command was immediately thrown in line, moved forward, and drove the enemy from his lurking place to the next hedge, about 600 yards farther; and thus the fight or skirmishing continued from hedge to hedge and ditch to ditch, until within 25 paces of the main levee on the bank of the Mississippi River, where the charge was ordered. Here we encountered a thick hedge, which could not be passed except through a few gaps or breaches that had been made for gates and pass-ways. These had to be passed by the troops the best they could, never fronting more than half a company, before a line could be formed to charge the levee, which was the breastwork of the enemy, 10 feet high, and in several places had a layer of cotton bales on top, making a very formidable and secure work of defense. The line was formed under a heavy fire from the enemy, and the troops charged the breastworks, carrying it instantly, killing and wounding many of the enemy by their deadly fire, as well as the bayonet. This charge was resisted by the Negro portion of the enemy's force with considerable obstinacy, while the white or true Yankee portion ran like whipped curs almost as soon as the charge was ordered. There were several instances in this charge where the enemy crossed bayonets with us or were shot down at the muzzle of the musket. No charge was ever more gallantly made than this, and the enemy were not only driven from the levee, but were followed into their camp, where many of them were killed.

In this charge Colonel [Richard] Waterhouse with his regiment distinguished themselves particularly, not only by a gallant and desperate charge over the levee, but they drove the enemy (leaving the camp covered with the dead) to the very bank of the river, and within short and direct range of the gunboats of the enemy. In fact, from the beginning to the end of the engagement, the colonel behaved in the most gallant manner, and his officers and men seemed to catch the enthusiasm of their commander, and did their duty nobly and gallantly upon every portion of the field.

Colonel [R.T.P] Allen's regiment was immediately on the left of Colonel Waterhouse, and Colonel [William] Fitzhugh's regiment (under the command of Lieutenant-Colonel [E.P] Gregg) was immediately on the left of Colonel Allen. Both of these regiments, officers and men, conducted themselves in the most praiseworthy and gallant manner, advancing coolly, and steadily, forming and charging in the most gallant style under a heavy and destructive fire of the enemy, during all of which the officers distinguished themselves for coolness and courage, and their men for a determination to conquer or die.

Colonel Allen was slightly wounded, but never left his post. Lieut. Col. Gregg and Major [W.W.] Diamond, of Colonel Fitzhugh's regiment, were both wounded too badly to admit of their remaining in command, which left the regiment without a field officer, but did not destroy their usefulness or dampen their ardor; upon the contrary, seemed to make them fight the more fiercely; and under the command of Captain [J.D.] Woods (senior captain) and their respective company commanders, they continued to fight steadily on until the close of the action.

Colonel [George] Flournoy's regiment was not in the principal charge upon the enemy's works, but performed good service afterward, assisted by small portions of the other three regiments, in driving the enemy from an angle in the levee, and log and brush barricade which commanded a considerable portion of our line, and from which they were pouring a heavy fire upon us. This position was of too much importance to the enemy to be given up without a desperate struggle, while we were suffering too much by its occupation by them to allow its continuance; hence they were driven from it by assault with considerable slaughter. During the balance of the day this important point was held by Colonel Flournoy's regiment, and although they were more exposed to the fire of the gunboats than other portion of my command, the regiment behaved itself well and sustained its character for courage and gallantry.

Major [R.D.] Allen, of Colonel Allen's regiment, was placed in command of the skirmishers during the advance, and as his command and that of Colonel Flournoy was not under my immediate observation during the whole engagement, I have called upon them for official reports, which I respectfully forward, and to which beg leave respectfully to call the attention of the major-general commanding.

There were too many instances of individual coolness, courage, and gallantry to mention in this report; but the services of Captain [G.T.] Marold, of Colonel Flournoy's regiment, and Private [A.] Schultz, of the band, of the same regiment, deserve notice. During the engagement some fears were entertained by a portion of the officers of the command that the enemy would or were attempting to turn our left flank. To quiet this apprehension and drive some Negroes from some houses from which they occasionally fired a shot at us, Captain Marold was sent out with his company and captured 19 Negroes, all of which were at or in the vicinity of the houses from which we had been several times fired at by Negroes. Some of them fired at officers of my staff while making reconnaissance of ditches, hedges, and fields in and about our battlefield. These Negroes had doubtless in the possession of the enemy, and would have been a clear loss to their owners but for Captain Marold; and should they be forfeited to the Confederate States or returned to their owners, I would regard it nothing but fair to give to Captain Marold one or two of the best of them.

Mr. [A.] Schultz being on duty with the surgeon's infirmary corps, he was sent with Dr. Cocke's horse to a house for some cistern water for the wounded. When he arrived at the house, he found himself surrounded by a company of armed Negroes in full United States uniform commanded by a Yankee captain, who took him prisoner. The captain asked him where the main body of our troops were. He pointed at once to the southwest, in an entirely different direction from where we were then engaged with the enemy. The captain then observed that, only a portion of our command being present, it might be possible for him to get through our lines to the transports. Schultz told him he could easily do so, and proffered to show him the way to avoid us. The Yankee suffered himself to be humbugged by our German youth, or young man, and he led him and his entire company of 49 Negroes through small gaps in thick hedges until they found themselves within 60 yards of Colonel Allen's regiment, who took them all prisoners without the fire of a gun. Thus by his shrewdness the young Dutchman released himself and threw into our hands 1 Yankee captain and 49 Negroes, fully armed and equipped as soldiers, and, if such things are admissible, I think he should have a choice boy from among these fellows to cook and wash for him and his mess during the war, and to work for him as long as the Negro lives. And as the horse of Dr. Cocke was lost in the praiseworthy effort to procure water for our wounded, another of these fellows might be well and properly turned over to him to compensate him for his loss.

My loss in this engagement was 44 killed, 130 wounded, and 10 missing. Several of the wounds are mortal, and many others so serious as to render recovery doubtful, while in proportion to the number more are severe and fewer slight than I have ever witnessed among the same number in my former military experience. This makes my casualties 184, embracing 2 officers killed, viz, Lieut. Thomas Beaver, of Colonel Allen's regiment, and Lieut. B. W. Hampton, of Colonel Fitzhugh's regiment, and 10 wounded, viz, Colonel Allen, Lieutenant-Colonel Gregg, Major Diamond, Captains [E.P.] Petty, [S.J.P.] McDowell, and [J.H.] Tolbert, Lieutenants [T.H.] Batsell, [D.M.] Waddill, [A.A.] Dickerman, and [James M.] Tucker, which is an exceedingly heavy loss, but nothing to compare with that of the enemy. It is true that no certain or satisfactory estimate could be made of the loss of the enemy, but I know, from the dead and wounded that I saw scattered over the field in the rear of the levee, and those upon and immediately behind it, it must have been over a thousand.

My full strength on the battle-field did not exceed 1,500 men, while that of the enemy must have been over twice, if not three times, that number, backed by three gunboats that were kept constantly playing shot and shell upon us during the whole engagement.

The attack was made under verbal orders from Major-General Taylor "to engage the enemy before day and carry his works at the point of the bayonet," which orders were doubtless based upon information received which led him to believe that there was only one battalion of Yankee cavalry and one of Negro infantry at the camp, without any batteries of field artillery or gunboats, while I have no doubt that the enemy were fully apprised of our approach, had made full preparations to receive us, and had received a reenforcement of three transport loads of troops during the night before. I was entirely misinformed by our guide with regard to the ground over which we had to advance. Instead of finding it smooth, open field without obstructions, I found the ground exceedingly rough, covered with small running briars and tie-vines, through which infantry could scarcely march, and so much cut up with ditches and obstructed with hedges that it was impracticable to make any well-regulated military movement upon it; and, under all the circumstances, I would not have been the least surprised if we had made an entire failure; and nothing but the best and bravest fighting, under the providence of God, could have crowned our efforts with even partial success.

During this engagement the officers and men of my command behaved most gallantly, deserving the gratitude of the country and highest commendation of their commanders; and I am perfectly satisfied that there is not a troop in the Confederate States of the same number that could have done better fighting under the same circumstances.

During the day's fighting Captain [Benjamin E.] Benton, assistant adjutant-general, and Major [J.H.] Earle, brigade commissary and acting aide-de-camp, and Maj. W.G. King, brigade quartermaster, of my regular staff, rendered me great service; and Capt. W. D. Mitchell, forage master, who acted as volunteer aide-de-camp, also, who bore frequent and important messages for me during the day to different portions of the field, frequently under heavy fire. Captain Benton and Major Earle were about my person except when absent under orders, and were exposed to the fire of the enemy from beginning to the close of the battle. Both of these officers acted with great gallantry throughout the day. Captain Benton participating in every forward movement and charge, moving amid the troops on horseback, constantly urging them on to the enemy.

Great credit is due the surgical corps of the brigade and Surgeon [E.J.] Beall, of the division, for efficient services to the wounded; especially to Dr. [William P.] Head, of Colonel Fitzhugh's regiment, and Dr. [William J.] Cocke, of Colonel Flournoy's regiment, who were not only the most active and energetic in their attentions to and operations on the wounded, but went upon the field at the beginning of the fight, and organized their respective corps and put them in operation. My thanks are tendered to the medical officers of Colonel Randal's brigade for the kind and efficient services rendered my suffering companions in arms on the day of the battle.

Accompanying this report will be found a complete list of the killed, wounded, and missing, made from the reports of regimental commanders. My loss is truly deplorable, and my very heart sickens at its contemplation. But the scathing ordeal through which my little brigade was compelled to pass has increased my confidence in and love for them, and makes me anxious to see them have at least one fair chance to meet the enemy where they can gain a complete victory to compensate them for the gallant fighting they have done and always will do when called upon to meet the foe.

Most respectfully, your obedient servant,

                        H. E. McCULLOCH,
             Brigadier-General, Commanding Brigade

Maj. R. B. MACLAY, Assistant Adjutant and Inspector General

Addendum C

HEADQUARTERS NORTHEAST DISTRICT OF LOUISIANA,
Young's Point, La., June 12, 1863.

COLONEL: I have the honor to report that, in accordance with instructions received from me, Colonel Lieb, commanding the Ninth Louisiana, African descent, made a reconnaissance in the direction of Richmond on June 6, starting from Milliken's Bend at 2 a.m.

He was preceded by two companies of the Tenth Illinois Cavalry, commanded by Captain Anderson, whom he overtook 3 miles from the Bend. It was agreed between them that the captain should take the left side of Walnut Bayou and pursue it as far as Mrs. Ames' plantation, while Colonel Lieb proceeded along the main Richmond road to the railroad depot, 3 miles from Richmond, where he encountered the enemy's pickets and advance, which he drove in with but little opposition, but, anticipating the enemy in strong force, retired slowly toward the Bend. When about half-way back, a squad of our cavalry came dashing up in his rear, hotly pursued by the enemy. Colonel Lieb immediately formed his regiment across an open field, and with one volley dispersed the approaching enemy.

Expecting the enemy would contest the passage of the bridge over Walnut Bayou, Colonel Lieb fell back over the bridge, and from thence to Milliken's Bend, from whence he sent a messenger informing me of the success of the expedition, and reported the enemy to be advancing. I immediately started the Twenty-third Iowa Volunteer Infantry to their assistance, and Admiral Porter ordered the gunboat Choctaw to that point.

At 3 o'clock the following morning the enemy made their appearance in strong force on the main Richmond road, driving the pickets before them. The enemy advanced upon the left of our line, throwing out no skirmishers, marching in close column by division, with a strong cavalry force on his right flank. Our forces, consisting of the Twenty-third Iowa Volunteer Infantry and the African Brigade (in all, 1061 men), opened upon the enemy when within musket-shot range, which made them waver and recoil, a number running in confusion to the rear; the balance, pushing on with intrepidity, soon reached the levee, when they were ordered to charge, with cries of "no quarter!"

The African regiments being inexperienced in the use of arms, some of them having been drilled but a few days, and the guns being very inferior, the enemy succeeded in getting upon our works before more than one or two volleys were fired at them. Here ensued a most terrible hand-to-hand conflict of several minutes' duration, our men using the bayonet freely and clubbing their guns with fierce obstinacy, contesting every inch of ground, until the enemy succeeded in flanking them, and poured a murderous enfilading fire along our lines, directing their fire chiefly to the officers, who fell in numbers. Not till they were overpowered and forced by superior numbers did our men fall back behind the bank of the river, at the same time pouring volley after volley into the ranks of the advancing enemy.

The gunboat now got into position and fired a broadside into the enemy, who immediately disappeared behind the levee, but all the time keeping up a fire upon our men.

The enemy at this time appeared to be extending his line to the extreme right, but was held in check by two companies of the Eleventh Louisiana Infantry, African descent, which had been posted behind cotton bales and part of the old levee. In this position the fight continued until near noon, when the enemy suddenly withdrew. Our men, seeing this movement, advanced upon the retreating column, firing volley after volley at them while they remained within gunshot. The gunboat Lexington then paid her compliments to the fleeing foe in several well-directed shots, scattering them in all directions.

I here desire to express my thanks to the officers and men of the gunboats Choctaw and Lexington for their efficient services in the time of need. Their names will be long remembered by the officers and men of the African Brigade for their valuable assistance on that dark and bloody field.

The officers and men deserve the highest praise for their gallant conduct, and especially Colonel Glasgow, of the Twenty-third Iowa, and his brave men, and also Colonel Lieb, of the Ninth Louisiana, African descent, who, by his gallantry and daring, inspired his men to deeds of valor until he fell, seriously though not dangerously wounded. I regret to state that Colonel Chamberlain, of the Eleventh Louisiana, African descent, conducted himself in a very unsoldierlike manner.

The enemy consisted of one brigade, numbering about 2,500, in command of General (H.E.) McCulloch, and 200 cavalry. The enemy's loss is estimated at about 150 killed and 300 wounded. It is impossible to get anything near the loss of the enemy, as they carried the killed and wounded off in ambulances. Among their killed is Colonel (R.T.P.) Allen, Sixteenth (Seventeenth) Texas.

Inclosed please find tabular statement of killed, wounded, and missing; in all, 652*. Nearly all the missing blacks will probably return, as they were badly scattered.

The enemy, under General (J.M.) Hawes, advanced upon Young's Point while the battle was going on at Milliken's Bend; but several well-directed shots from the gunboats compelled them to retire.

Submitting the foregoing, I remain, yours, respectfully,

ELIAS S. DENNIS
Brigadier-General, Comdg. District Northeast Louisiana

Lieut. Col. John A. Rawlins, Assistant Adjutant-General

* Or 11 officers and 90 men killed, 17 officers and 268 men wounded, and 2 officers and 264 captured or missing

TO AID IN THE PROMOTION OF AN INTERURBAN ELECTRIC RAILWAY

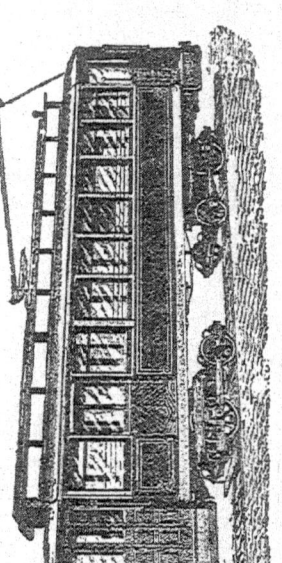

From Allegan, through Monterey Center and Burnip's Corners, to Jamestown or a point of junction with an Electric Railway from Grand Rapids to Holland, WE, THE UNDERSIGNED, hereby promise and agree, each for himself, to pay to David Cornwell and Milton D. Owen, the promotors of this enterprise, the sum of Ten Dollars, at the First National Bank of Allegan, on or before the first day of January, 1901.

It is also understood and agreed that each subscriber who fully pays his subscription according to the terms above set forth, shall be entitled to a pro rata return of any unexpended balance remaining in the Promotion Fund on the first day of July, 1902, if the construction of said railway has not been commenced at that date.

DAVID CORNWELL and MILTON D. OWEN.

Per..Solicitor.

Cornwell's last entrepreneurial hurrah dealt with ambitious plans to connect Allegan and Grand Rapids by rail. His 1901 diary shows clearly that acquiring railway rights of way for the new-fangled electric cars took a good bit of energy and enterprise. In the end all came to naught when capitalization fell short of needs.

Addendum D

Into the 20th Century. To mark the dawn of a new era Cornwell kept a diary for the year 1901. His introductory remarks on the first page amusingly reveal the character and spirit of the old veteran. He wrote in the introduction to the 1901 diary, "Will commence the new Century by opening a Journal, and resolving not to swear anymore, only upon fitting occasions, and to cease chewing plug tobaccos, smoking a pipe, and drinking gin cocktails. I like fine cut, and cigars best, and prefer my whiskey straight in the good old democratic fashion. I could not for a moment consider the question of dropping these latter luxuries, and thereby beating the Government on the intenal revenue sticker or doing anything so thoroughly unpatriotic. We must support McKinley and Mark Hanna at all hazzards for they have licked the Spanish and got the Filipinos and Chinamen on the run, and boomed business to beat the records. So, Hurrah for Uncle Sam and his Republican Empire. In a business way."

And for the 1901 record David announces his intention of going into the telephone business by seeking franchises to run poles and lines outward from Allegan and the central switchboard operated by son-in-law Milton D. Owen. The entire diary for the year is an account of a no longer young man running two businesses...the flourishing general store at Monterey and installation of poles and lines using the most rudimentary techniques and tools. Right-of-way permits took a lot of time and led to many humorous tales about how this was done. People in this part of Michigan were just beginning to appreciate the potential of telephone service, which was offered only to subscribers whose patronage came through a very hard sell pushed by a pretty tough man excited by challenge and technological innovation, still carrying around in his upper right arm a bit of lead to remind him of more hazardous times.

Amid all this enterprise the old major and son-in-law Milton were promoting construction of an electric railway from Allegan northward to Grand Rapids, the metropolis of southwestern Michigan. This "light rail" project was about a century ahead of times, however. Stock certificates were printed, but the anticipated rails never saw the light of approved rights of way.

Addendum E

The following letter by Cornwell, dated sometime late in 1907, discloses a few more interesting details about Milliken's Bend.
The Battle of Milliken's Bend.
Reputation Fakers

Editor, National Tribune.

I take the following extract from the Tribune of Oct. 10, 1907.

Col. Cyrus Sears, 49th U.S.C.T., Harpster, Ohio.

"He afterward became Lieutenant-Colonel of the 49th U.S.C.T. and owing to the bad conduct of his Colonel, became ranking officer in the bloody fight at Milliken's Bend, where most of the officers present of his regiment were killed or afterward hanged by the rebels. In spite of the overwhelming numbers and the vicious charges of the enemy, Col. Sears managed so well that he got his men together behind the last levee and made a determined stand, repulsing the enemy with great loss. The regiment lost 62 killed, which Comrade Sears believes is the largest proportion of killed in any regiment in a single engagement. Col. Sears well won a Medal of Honor, and has been for years a banker at Harpster."

Cornwell replied . . ."Now my knowledge of that engagement is not limited to what I saw of it myself, for during the past two years I have had much correspondence with officers and men who were there, and among them this Lt. Col. Sears himself. I have read the account of this fight as given by several historians, the best and truest of which is that of John McElroy in his "Opening of the Mississippi." I have Vol. 24 of the Rebellion Records and the official report of Col. Lieb, as made up from the [Brigade] regimental reports, and yet I think I can throw a little light on that affair that these reports and histories do not shed.

"First, bear in mind that the report of the Confederate General H.E. McCulloch is as false as the quotation at the head of this article. There were no obstacles or obstructions to his advance except the osage orange hedge, just outside the levee over which we fought. Not a shot was fired until the right of his line struck this hedge. On our left the levee made a right angle and ran to the river - say between one and two hundred yards.

"Unfortunately, while Col. Lieb with his regiment, the 9th La., was out on a recognizance [reconnaissance] the day before, someone cut down about 100 yards of this hedge on the left of our line. This was our weak point and Col. Lieb placed two small companies in reserve [commanded by Cornwell] to care for it. When the enemy's line reached us their right was slightly in the lead, and having clear sailing poured over the levee and was about crushing our thin line when these reserve companies came up on the jump and bounced them with the bayonet. Here a fierce fight was maintained for several minutes.

"The darkeys would not give way, and when the Texans got all they could stand of it, they fell back behind the levee and lay down. And after that, no amount of coaxing or threats could induce them to jump up and try us with the bayonet again.

"There was no other levee there than the one then separating us from the enemy. The fight continued across the top of this for about two hours, and we were getting much the worst of it for the Texans were good shots and our men could not hit the broad side of a cotton gin. There was nothing for it but to go to the river bank before our men were all picked off. It was a dangerous move but had to be made and it commenced somewhere in the center. A concerted Rebel effort was not made to follow us, but two or three spasmodic rushes were made and when our men jumped from behind the bank on the level, and started to meet them with the bayonet, they at once withdrew behind the levee again. Having failed to rush us to the river bank and shoot us into the river, which they might have done, the victory was practically ours. At this time Col. Lieb, who was wounded early in the fight, was assisted from his horse, and the command was assumed by his Lieut. Col. Page. We had no artillery, and the gunboat had not yet fired a shot, for the very good reason that their shells could not reach the enemy because the river was so low that the top of the bank hid the levee behind which they lay. However, they soon commenced dropping their shells in the field back of them and this furnished them with an excuse for going. They didn't want to be driven off by the "Niggers," but the gunboats were a different thing.

"At no time was the attack on our right, where Col. Sears' regiment [the 11th La.] was stationed, pushed with the vigor that it was on our left, and his loss was the lightest of any of the troops there, except in the number of his "missing." Here he came out shy 242 men and Col. Lieb says in his official report that he is quite sure that none of them were taken prisoner.

"The officers of the 9th [Louisiana] remained with their men from beginning to finish, and there was no straggling from their ranks. We were too hard pressed, and any shirking would have brought disaster. Our "missing" was 21 and many of these were cut out at the angle of the levee with Capt. Heath and were taken prisoner.

"F.W. Sedgwick of Parma, Michigan, than a member of the 10th Ill. Cavalry, wrote a long letter to his family the day after the fight, a copy of which I have. In this he stated that the white officers all ran and left the darkeys to fight out the battle by themselves. Knowing this to be untrue as to the 9th, who had 15 killed and wounded [white officers], I called him down strong and accused him of willful lying, and proved to him that with respect to the 9th it was a lie whether willful or not.

"He replied that the colored men themselves were his authority for the statement, for some of them had told him that it made them feel bad to have their officers all leave them the way they did. Now knowing that such a statement could not have been made by a darkey from the 9th La., and having a better knowledge than I had then of how things went on our right flank, I am convinced that Mr. Sedgwick wrote his family what he then believed to be the truth.

"Colonel Cyrus Sears now says that he lost 62 killed, though directly after the fight he reported 33. It is a simple question of mathematics [as to] how long it will take him to kill off the balance of his regiment, including himself. His colonel, Chamberlain, very properly passed in his commission [after the 33battle] and retired to civil life, and Lieut. Col. Sears very naturally, and properly, should have stepped into the vacancy. But not on your life. They [the Army] skirmished around and found one Van E. Young for the command and still Sears would not resign, but humbly wore the silver bars to the close of the war.

"Lieut. Col. Sears, being a banker, may outrank Gen. Lieb in the financial army, but in the Grand Old Army that put down the rebellion, he did not trot in the same class with that gallant Switzer.

"The old hero is still living in Chicago, is past 80 and has a reputation that does not have to be bolstered up with spurious statements and false affidavits.

"At no time during the fight at Milliken's Bend was Col. Sears the ranking officer, nor did he ever presume to command any officers or men other than those of his own regiment. It would have been much to his credit if he had attended to them better than he did. He may have a Medal of Honor and he may not: I am not prepared to take his word for it. But my word will hold good when I assert that he did not win one for any gallantry displayed at Milliken's Bend on the 7th day of June, 1863."

    David Cornwell
    Brevt. Lieut. Col. U.S. Vols.
    Allegan, Michigan

[At bottom of his copy of this letter Cornwell wrote: "Note, letter held to be too severe for publication. Sent a modified letter."]

"King Cotton" regions of the deep South were home to many of the Black troopers at the Bend confrontation. Life on cotton plantations was usually cruel and demanding. Cotton culture was very labor intensive and depended upon endless reserves of slave labor. Countless cotton-picking plantation legions were kept at needed strength primarily by Southern planters northward who often sold slaves to cotton plantation owners along the Gulf Coast, often at the highest possible slave price.

The tragic, often publicized July 18, 1863 Union attack on Fort Wagner has somehow dimmed the Trans-Mississippi Bend melee. Negroes debuted in battle as U.S. soldiers June 6 and 7, 1863, over a month before the Fort Wagner assault. Perhaps more significantly, the African Brigade included three Black regiments—about 1,100 men. By any rational measure performance of Black infantry at Milliken's Bend must overshadow any other Negro military action during the first year of recruiting and preparing Black men for Army service.

A comparison of Black soldiers training at the Bend with those serving along the east coast could have led Mississippi and Louisiana recruiters to doubt seriously that Black men actually abducted from surrounding plantations, totally illiterate, having no experience with firearms whatsoever, could ever be molded into effective combat troops. Perhaps even the Confederates felt there was nothing to fear from Union "Darkies" who surely would jump into the Mississippi River when hard pressed by veteran White Texas infantry. They allowed about four hours to gain a victory. Actually, ferocious combat lasted about eight hours with no Confederate victory.

Colonel Robert Gould Shaw's 54th Mass. was composed almost entirely of Black men who had never known slavery. Nearly all were literate. Some, like Frederick Douglass's two sons, were very well educated and had known sophisticated, comfortable New England life styles before their service. And 54th's 40% casualties at Wagner do not compare with the 70% casualty figure of the 9th Louisiana Infantry (A.D.) at the Bend. Lieutenant David Cornwell commanded a thin two-company Brigade reserve (about 160 men) close to the river. His reserves stopped a Confederate break-through on the Brigade left. The battle ended shortly after. Eye witness accounts of the Bend carnage seen afterwards can leave little doubt about the extremely vicious hand-to-hand bayonet and club action. Corpses were seen pinned to the ground by bayonets, and countless skulls smashed to a pulp by musket stocks.   —*Editor*

BATTLE OF MILLIKEN'S BEND

Addendum F

THE NEGRO IN THE WAR *

The negro will ever figure as a prominent feature in the present civil war. They have been caricatured in some cases and more fairly treated in others; but the gallantry of the men who fought at Milliken's Bend, who rushed to the assault of Fort Hudson and Fort Wagner, will stand as proudly in American history as the defence of the fort on the Delaware in the Revolution. Robert Small, in the capture of the <u>Planter</u>, did one of the cleverest feats of the war. We give our double page this week to a grouping of some scenes of the employment of negroes by the army, which will be of interest to many. It is not our part to discuss questions of political bearing, but simply to portray living history. The sketches here given are all, with the exception of the fight at Milliken's Bend, drawn from sketches made in the army of the Cumberland.

The women are employed in washing, and both sexes in cooking. The men not enrolled as soldiers drive cattle, make roads, load steamers, act as teamsters and do much of the blacksmith work. As soldiers we see them in the dangerous work of scouting, holding the riflepits, and, as at Milliken's Bend, charging on the enemy's works amid a storm of shot and shell.

* Appeared in <u>Frank Leslie's Illustrated Newspaper</u> for January 16, 1864. It explained why <u>Leslie's</u> chose to honor Black Americans for their Civil War services. Black soldiers and sailors had served on active duty in uniform only since April 1863.

Detail from Augustus Saint-Gaudens' splendid 1897 Boston bronze memorial to the 54th Massachusetts and its commander, Robert Gould Shaw.

Addendum G

EPILOGUE

Those who have read the Cornwell Chronicles might well ask the question...if the Black troops trained and led by Union commanders like Cornwell performed so well and heroically, as at Milliken's Bend, why have they received such sketchy, dismal recognition for their Civil War service? After all...and most pertinent...how could two centuries of slavery produce men who only days out of servitude could stand and completely stall an advance of experienced White Confederate infantry in their first combat experience? From the 9th Louisiana Infantry at Milliken's Bend, Louisiana, in 1863 to the 92nd Buffalo Division on the west coast of Italy, 1944-1945, American Black soldiers held their own around the world in combat with the best troops other nations could put in the field.

The true and shameful answer has recently been spelled out by Joseph T. Glatthaar in his Forged in Battle...The Civil War Alliance of Black Soldiers and White Officers. Spurious, much less than professional studies of Black soldiers by members of the American medical establishment followed the war. Several studies by recognized authorities indicated that the Black man simply was not an equal to the White man in several respects...including intellectual capacity. Publication of such views even warped the attitudes of White service veterans who had fought alongside Black troops and seen them perform very well under a variety of demanding combat conditions. Within a few years Whites dismissed many accounts (official and otherwise) of the excellent war record of American Blacks. Even the Grand Army of the Republic accepted ever increasing intoleration toward their wartime Black service comrades. Besides the tainted "medical authorities reports" the 19th Century Civil War historians often did not recognize, or often belittled, the war contributions of Black soldiers.

In his Regimental Losses in the American Civil War, 1861-1865, author William F. Fox indicated the incredibly high losses (70%) of the 9th Louisiana (African Descent) Infantry at Milliken's Bend. Oddly, to say the least, Fox entirely omitted mention of the 9th later in his section on Union Army regiments with the greatest number of casualties in the war in a single battle. How could any writer of history intentionally be responsible for such an abominable "oversight"? In fact, the Black soldiers of the 9th Louisiana at the Bend holocaust had suffered the most terrible battlefield losses by one regiment in any single engagement of the American Civil War.

In all accounts of the Milliken's Bend fight published after the war no author pointed out the magnificent role of Colonel Herman Lieb, commander of the African Brigade at the Bend. Lieb went into battle as commander of the 9th Louisiana. David Cornwell in these Chronicles puts Lieb in proper focus for the first time. Lieb and Cornwell were both wounded in the nasty Bend scrap. They remained close friends for nearly half a century. As commander of Lieb's reserve force on June 7, 1863 David Cornwell earned the right to be a recognized authority on the battle, as tacitly admitted many years later when Cyrus Sears (49th USCT) crossed swords and words with both Lieb and Cornwell over Sears's published alleged Union command problems during the Bend battle.

Editor

FULLNAME AND SUBJECT INDEX

----, Alick 62-64 Arabella 15-16 18 George 11 13 15 192 Henry 249 Maud 259-260 Rose 107 Sam 54-55 57-58 60 Sambo 246 Tim 238

1ST Illinois Cavalry 77 79 Illinois Infantry 35 Illinois Light Artillery 87 293 Mississippi Infantry 207 211 217-218 221

2ND Illinois Light Artillery 79 103 114 191 195 288 Michigan Cavalry 141 Regiment Illinois Light Artillery 88 Wisconsin Cavalry 277

3RD Michigan Cavalry 139-140 292 295 U S Cavalry 282

4TH Illinois Infantry 18 Infantry 282 Michigan Cavalry 291

5TH U S Heavy Artillery (Colored) 249 269-270 293 White Officers 255

6TH Missouri Infantry (Union) 243

8TH Illinois Infantry 19 67 69 73 79 90 94 102-103 109 115 122 132 140 145-146 164 189 191-193 195 200-201 214 226 249 264 269 290 293 Illinois Infantry (Old 8th) 118 154 169 211 215 238 270 285-286 289 Texas Infantry 210 Wisconsin 158

9TH Illinois Infantry 67 Infantry 35 38 48 Louisiana Infantry (African Brigade) 192 195 198 204 207 209 211 217-219 221-222 239 243 303-304 309-312 315

10TH Illinois Cavalry 207-209 216 219 223 225-226 228-229 303 311 Infantry 35 Texas Infantry 218

11TH Illinois Infantry 67 79 226 Iowa Infantry 117 Louisiana Infantry (African Brigade) 207 209 211 213 217-222 304 310

13TH Iowa Infantry 117 Louisiana Infantry 207 211 217-218 221 U S Colored Infantry 276

14TH Illinois Infantry 67

16TH (17th) Texas 305 Texas Infantry 210

17TH Corps 185 Texas Infantry 210

18TH Illinois Infantry 79 97 117 120 130 132 238 Regular Infantry Regiment 19 Texas Infantry 210

19TH Texas Infantry 210

20TH Illinois Infantry 83 Ohio Infantry 222

22ND Illinois 38 Texas Infantry 210

23RD Iowa Infantry 210-211 216-217 219 221 223 237 303-304

29TH Illinois Infantry 79 121

30TH Illinois Infantry 215

31ST Illinois Infantry 67 Illinois Infantry Regiment 99

46TH Illinois Infantry 219

49TH Colored Infantry 281 U S C T 221 309 315

54TH Massachusetts 312 Ohio Infantry 219

92ND Buffalo Division 315

94TH Illinois Infantry 33

ACHLEY, Adm 177

AFRICAN BRIGADE, 188 218-220 304

AFRICAN DESCENT, Regiments Of 216

ALBANY, 7

ALEN, R T P 298

ALEXANDER, Geo 246 Richard 246

ALLEGAN, Michigan 105 140 231 294-295 311

ALLEGAN COUNTY, Michigan 91 107 265 290 292-294 Settlers From Holland 146

ALLEGAN TOWN CEMETERY, Michigan 291

ALLEN, Col 218 299-300 R D 299 R T P 305

ALTOONA PASS, 34

AMERICAN, Boat 219

AMES, Mrs 216 303

ANDERSON, Capt 225 303 Christ A 207 216 223

ANDERSONVILLE, 243

APPOMATTOX, 291

ARKANSAS, 226

ARMSTRONG, Isaac 246

ARMY OF THE CUMBERLAND, 132 137

ARMY OF THE POTOMAC, 269

ARMY OF THE TENNESSEE, 135 145 192 203 221 246

ASHLEY HOUSE, 4

ASHMORE, Capt 44 115 James M 21

AYERS, 215 John W 131 214

AYRES, John W 218

BACON, John 91

BAKER'S DRAGOONS, 48

BARBOUR PLANTATION, 267

BARNARD, James S 44

BARRETT, James A 225

BATON ROUGE, 286

BATSELL, T H 300

BATTERTON, 118 Ira A 100 116 John 131

BATTERY CASTLE, 268 288

BATTLE CREEK, Michigan 105-106

BAWNER, J 218

BAXTER SPRINGS, Kansas 103

BAYOU METEE, 226

BEALL, E J 301

BEARD, By 167 171-173 181-182 184 190 Byron (By) 189

BEAUREGARD, 10 G P T 134

BEAVER, Thomas 300
BECK, 91
BELLEVILLE, Ontario 58
BELMONT, Missouri 83 84 88
BENTON, Benjamin E 301
BERRY'S LANDING, Louisiana 177 179
BIG BLACK, 189
BIG BLACK RIVER, 198
BIG MUDDY BRIDGE, 36-37
BIRD, Col 35
BIRD'S POINT, Missouri 35 37 38 73 76 79 81 85 88 103 142
BISHOP, A G 44 Squire 30-31 105-108
BLAIR, Gov 141
BLAKE, Mrs 295 Mrs Willard P 294 295 Willard P 294
BLOOMFIELD, Missouri 80-81 84 116
BLOOMINGTON, Illinois 3 4 22 39 43 45 48 61 83 139 150 215 240 247-248
BLOOMINGTON PANTAGRAPH, 26
BOLIVAR, 150
BOOTH, Edwin 164
BORELAND, 166 176 James A 164 Matthew W 88
BOSTON, 273 289
BOY, George 245
BRAGGINGTON, John 142
BRASHEAR, A V 293
BRAYMAN, Gen 280 Mason 119 121 279 Morris 135 Mrs 279
BROADRICK, Jackson 246
BROOKS, Thomas 245 Washington 245
BRUCE, Lt 44
BRUINSBURG, 286
BUCKLES, L C 295
BUCKNER, 135-136 Gen 102
BUELL, 130 Don Carlos 127 129 132 Gen 128 133-134 145 246
BUFORD, 85
BUMFORD, Col 261
BURLINGTON, Iowa 220
BURNIP'S CORNERS, 92-93
CADY, C F 218
CAIRO, Illinois 14 19 21 26 35-38 42-43 61 67 69 73 79-80 87-88 90 94 100 140 207 214
CALDWELL, Lt 74 Sam 102 145 285-286 288 Samuel 44 68
CALIFORNIA, 64
CALKINS, Rev 16
CAMERON, Simon 185
CAMP BUTLER, 225
CAMP DENNISON, Cincinnati 87

CAMP DOUGLASS, 24
CAMPION, Lt 83
CAMP YATES, 18
CANE HILL, Arkansas 225
CAPE GIRARDEAU, 79-81 83 85
CARLSON, R 13
CARR, George W 116
CARVILLE, Illinois 51
CASEY, Silas 61
CASSIDY, Hugh 139 Sgt 120
CAVERNO, (Annie Cornwell) Mrs 231 (Cornwell) Capt 254 (Cornwell) Maj 280 285 (Cornwell) Mr 32 170 (Cornwell) Mrs 105-106 108-109 234 Dan (David Cornwell) 31 184 191 231 Lt (Cornwell) 214
CENTRALIA, 61 65
CHAMBERLAIN, 304 Col 207 211 213 219-221 311
CHAMPION HILL, 189
CHARLESTON, Missouri 21 83 95
CHATEAU HARL, Switzerland 289
CHATTANOOGA, 141 145
CHICAGO, 6 10 21 27 30 45-46 51-52 62 164 221 227-228 234 240 286 290 294 311
CHICAGO BATTERY, 88
CHICAGO RIVER, 6
CHICASAW BAYOU, 268
CHILLES, William 246
CHOCTAW, Gunboat 214 216-218 303-304
CINCINNATI, 6 46 289-290
CLARK, 213 222 Adj Gen 254 C M 218 Charles M 211 Orderly 204
CLAY, Henry 36
CLEVELAND, President 284
COCKE, Dr 299-300 William J 302
COFFEEVILLE, 158
COLFAX, Schuyler 4
COLLINS, 170-171 175
COLUMBUS, 84 88 90 Kentucky 69 83 157 Mississippi 145
COLUMBUS-BELMONT BATTLE, 85
COMPANIES, Naming Numbering And Positioning In Regiment 22
CONSTANCE, Switzerland 289
COOK, John 19
COOPER, Edgar H 150 Lt 151 176
COOPERS, Lt 177
CORINTH, Mississippi 118 128 131 133-135 140-142 145 285
CORNWELL, 109 122 132 165 289 309-310 Annie 290 Calarance H (Clarence?) 295 Carrie 295

CORNWELL (cont.)
  Charity Conklyn 295 Charity Lazier 292 Dave 218
  David 131 138 228 234 290-296 306-307 311-312
  315 Edith 291 294 Emma 294 Frances 138 282
  291 Frank 9 67 87 89 91 138 282 292 294-295
  Grace 294 Harriet 291 294 Hazel 295 Iva 295
  Joshua 6 291-292 294 Maj D 255 Mr 294 Mrs
  293 Mrs Joshua 296 Sarah A 294 Sarah Ann
  Stanclift (Annie) 234
CORNWELL STORE, 235
CORWIN, Tom 5
COTTON, Cyrus 246 Maj 213
CRAIG, Lige 156
CRITTENDEN, 129
CRUMP'S LANDING, 133 137
CUFFEE, Austin 246
CUMBERLAND RIVER, 94-95
CUNNINGHAM, 192 George 146 153 175 190
DALLAS, Texas 215
DANA, 268 Gen 281 286 Napoleon J T 267
DANIELS, C W 103 Capt 207
DAVIDSON, Gen 281 Maj Gen 273 280
DAVIS, David 3 J G 249 Jeff 9 262 Jefferson 207
  273 291 Joe 273 John G 269
DAVIS' BEND, 273
DAWSON, John B 131 Johnny 68
DAY, Samuel 75
DECATUR, Illinois 6 18 21 38 111 290
DEERFIELD, Illinois 294
DENNIS, E S 215-216 Elias S 207 305 Gen 209-210
  220 223
DENNISON, 115 193 Capt 146 191 Charles E 19 21
  Lt 130-131 Noah W 44
DERUSSEY, Capt 276
DETROIT, Michigan 295-296
DEWEY, Victor M 267
DEWITTS, Capt 218
DIAMOND, Maj 300 W W 298
DICKERMAN, A A 300
DICKERT, 169 189
DICKEY, Maj 245
DOC, 47-48
DOLE, Charles 60
DONELSON, see Fort Donelson
DONELSON CAMPAIGN, 87
DOOLITLLE, Sen 4
DOUGHERTY, 85 Henry 38
DOUGLASS, Frederick 312 Sen 4-5 Stephen A 3
DRAKE, James W 131
DUDLEY, Col 281 Gen 282
DUTCHER, T B 294

EAGLE RIVER, Wisconsin 294
EARLE, J H 301
EDDY, Albert (Dell) S 23 Dell 25-26
EDMONDS, J E 283
EGYPT, Illinois 267
ELECTRIC RAILWAYS, 306-307
ELLSWORTH, Elmer E 9
ELLSWORTH CADETS, 24
ENGINEER CORPS, 95
ERIE CANAL, 7 69 247 293
EVANS, 116 118 Fighting Bob 88 Jim 139 Walter F
  100
EVANSTON, 60
FERSLOW, Capt 258
FINNEY, Mr 106 108
FISH, 51
FITZHUGH, Col 300 302 William 298
FLORENCE, Tennessee 135
FLORIDA, 294
FLOURNOY, Col 302 George 298-299
FLOYD, Gen 102
FOOTE, Andrew 34 Andrew H 89 Commodore 213
FORCE, Gen 282-283 M F 273
FORREST, N B 268
FORT DONELSON, 94-97 100 102-104 109 112
  114-116 118 132-133 135-136 139 141 144 164
  175 189 200 214 238
FORT HEIMAN, 94-95
FORT HENRY, Tennessee 94-96 100 111 116 135
FORT HOLT, Kentucky 26 87 88
FORT HUDSON, 313
FORT SUMTER, 10 Attack 9
FORT WAGNER, 312-313
FOWLER, C S 64
FOX, Harriet 291 294 William F 315
FRANKLIN, Samuel 246
FREDERICK THE GREAT, 24
FREEDMAN'S BUREAU, 273
FRENCH, Gen 34
GALENA, Illinois 219
GALESBURG, Michigan 295
GATES, Oswald 109
GAYOSA HOUSE, 268
GIBSON, Charles 92 Clinton 93 Fletcher 93 Isaac 93
  Jasper 93 Mr 93 Uncle Charlie 94
GILES, Daniel 246
GILMORE, 285 Gen 281
GLASGOW, Col 304
GLENCOE, 60
GRAND GULF, 203
GRAND JUNCTION, Tennessee 145 153 157

GRAND RAPIDS, Michigan 106 123 141 284 307
GRANGER, 141 Frank 105-106 Mrs 109
GRANT, Ulysses S 19 36 69 81 85 88-90 96 100-101 111 115 122 129-130 132 134-138 140-141 145 158 160 185 192 203-204 210 215 220 243-244 285 Gen 83-84 95 102 133 153 186 200 240
GRANT'S *MEMOIRS*, 84 88-89 95-96 129 133 135-136 158
GRASS, Daniel 22
GREGG, E P 298 Lt Col 300
GRIDLEY, Banker 3
GRIFFIN, Andrew 245
GRIGGSVILLE, 21
GRIM, 148 170-171 Clark 147 149 159 181
GRUNDY, Robert L 131
GUARD MOBILE, 289
GUMBART, Conrad 103
GURNIES, 60
HALLECK, 141 Charles 88 Gen 140 145 Henry 139
HAMBURG, 139
HAMMOND, Capt 218
HAMPTON, B W 300
HANDENBURG, 23
HANKS, Old Man 4
HANNA, Joseph M 21 44
HARDEE, 24
HARDING, Col 35
HARPER'S WEEKLY, 8
HARPSTER, Ohio 221 309
HARRIMAN, 51
HARRIS, T H 270
HART, Hannibal 92 Judge 92
HARVEY, 37 101 Capt 23 26 36 43 49 67 73 77 97-100 118 139 Mr 15 William 115 William H 22
HATCHIE RIVER, 145 150
HAVERY, Wm H 44
HAWES, J M 210 305
HAWES' BRIGADE, 229
HAYDEN, Charles 120 139
HAYES AND EVANS, 139
HAZELBAKER, Sid 104 Sidney 103 Sidney J 131
HEAD, William P 302
HEATH, 203 Capt 196 198 211 215 218 222 244 Corydon 195 243
HEMLINE, Lytle R 131
HENNISON, John 246
HENRY, James 246 Thomas 145 Tom 169 189
HERBERT, Charles 139 145 150 169 Charles F 149
HESSING, A C 60
HIGHLAND PARK, 5 59 62 64
HILL, P Jr 177

HISSONG, 269 285 289 Capt 218 249 Lt Col 281 Lyman J 288 Maj 268
HOGG, Harvey 150
HOLDEN, Mr 283
HOLDSWORTH, Jim 109
HOLLY, William 246
HOLLY SPRINGS, Mississippi 157-158
HOLT, Joseph 178
HOPKINS STATION, 105-106 109 Allegan County 142
HORSE, Prince 79
HOUSTON, Albert 245
HOWELL, Joe 49 68 71 77-78 83 97 101 Joseph G 44 Lt 70 95
HUBBARD, Elbert 119
HUDSON, 125-126 Mr 123
HUNT, Henry 246
HURLBUT, 129
HUTCHINSON, Jordon 245 Kansas 92 294
ILLINOIS, 43 293 Gov 286
ILLINOIS RIVER, 18
INDIANA, 88
IOWA, 88
IRISH BILLY, 60
ISLAND NO. 10, 139
IUKA, Mississippi 158
JACKSON, 150-151 189 197 203 282 Andrew 246 Andrew (Old Hickory) 147 Jack 147 150 158 167 195-196 198 245 Jack Death Of 212 Michigan 295 Mississippi 283 Tennessee 145 149 169 188 193 198
JARIS, Indiana 149
JENKINS, Jack 246
JESSEE, James W 131
JOHNSON, Andrew 186 Mr 283
JOHNSTON, 134 203 Albert Sidney 133 135
JOLIET, Illinois 88
JONES, 108 Bill 105 E 44 Joseph B 44 Lt 75 Maj 282 Warren 245 Willis 246
KALAMAZOO, Michigan 248
KALGA, Pat 147-149
KANSAS, 91 Hutchinson 295
KANSAS CAVALRY, 153
KEITH, Doc 23 Price 22
KENTUCKY, 73
KILPATRICK, 209
KING, W G 301
KINGSTON, Canada 57
KRUG, Amos 105-106 108 Liz 106
L'HOMMADIEU, 280 S S 279
LAFOLLETTE, Robert 3

LAGRANGE, Tennessee 153 157 163-164 166
LAKE MICHIGAN, 59-60
LAKE PROVIDENCE, Louisiana 169 177 181 185 207
LAMON, Ward H 9
LAMSON, 154 158 167 Oscar 145 147-149
LAUMAN, 85
LAWLER, M K 79
LAWRENCE, Jonas 28-29 39 42 Justice 46 Squire 40-42 Toll 39 42
LAWRENCEVILLE, 22
LAZIER, Charity Conklin 292
LESLIE'S ILLUSTRATED, Newspaper 122 224 241 313
LEXINGTON, Gunboat 218 304
LIEB, 200 215-216 220-221 223 241 250 253-254 257 262-264 268-269 288 Capt 117 Col 198-199 204 207 211-213 225 239-240 243 245-246 249 251 260-261 281 286 289 303-304 309-310 Gen 227-228 H 219 Herman 30 44 103 130 195 234 254 287 289-290 294 315
LILES, Henry 245
LINCOLN, 262 Abraham 3 Honest Old Abe 188 Mr 4 6 9 President 113 179 185-187 240
LINCOLN, Nebraska 189
LOGAN, 6 43 84-85 102 128 141 145 164 188 Capt 168 Col 101 Gen 146 160-161 171 177 187 John A 5 67 99 127 192
LOMBARD BOYS, 4
LONG BRANCH, New Jersey 70
LONSBURY, Family 45 Mr 45
LOUISVILLE, 137
LOVEJOY, 6 Owen 4-5
LYNCH, Capt 251-252 John 21
LYON, Nathaniel 65
MACK, Mrs 124
MACLAY, R B 302
MACON COUNTY, 75
MAGNOLIA PLANTATION, 288
MALLORY, Andrew 107 Mandy 107
MALTBY, J A 273 285
MARCY, Gen 269
MARINE BRIGADE, 37
MARION, 119 George 118 Sgt 154
MAROLD, G T 299
MARSH, Capt 18
MARTIN, Lt 44
MATHEWS, 240 Mr 248
MCALLISTER, 114 Capt 150 Edward 88
MCALLISTER'S BATTERY, 140 189 214
MCALPINE, James 32

MCCLELLAN, George B 36 269
MCCLERNAND, 85 100-101 122 129 134-136 140-141 160 285 Gen 120 John A 90 116 121
MCCLUNG, 115 Lt 131 Thomas J 77 118
MCCOOK, Gen 129
MCCRAMER, Andrew J 22
MCCULLOCH, Brig Gen 218 Gen 214 H E 217 302 305 309 Henry E 210 297
MCCULLOCH'S BRIGADE, 297
MCCULLOCH'S TEXAS BRIGADE, 220 229
MCDOWELL, S J P 300
MCELROY, 221 John 215 222 309
MCGAW, Bill 156
MCLEAN COUNTY, 6
MCLEAN REGIMENT, 33
MCNULTY, Col 34 Lt Col 33
MCPHERSON, 145 188 247 Gen 146 158 163 186-187 246 254 Gen James 267 James 185 James B 95 133
MCVICKER, Mary 164 Mr 164
MCWILLIAMS, 21
MEDFORD, Oregon 290
MEEKER, Mr 55 58-59
MEEKER HOUSE, 54 57 60
MEMPHIS, Tennessee 150 157 164 166 168-170 188-189 212 237 239 267 268 286
MERCER, Robert 131
MERSEY, Augustus 35 Lt Col 38
MEXICAN WAR, 18-19 22 29 36-37 282
MEXICO, Gulf Of 207
MEXICO/MEXICAN WAR, 35
MICHIGAN, 43 88 94
MILLEN, Frances 282 291 294
MILLER, Bill 76 114 119 128-129 173 Capt 252-253 M M 218 Matthew M 219 William 131
MILLIKEN'S BEND, Louisiana 87 108 185 186 188 191 203 207 209-211 225 227-229 237-238 240-241 243-245 297 303 305 309 311-313 315 Battle Of 212-224
MILLIKEN'S BEND AFRICAN BRIGADE, 207
MINNESOTA, 90
MISSISSIPPI, 91
MISSISSIPPI RIVER, 21 37 70-71 83 90 157 169 182-183 185 199-200 211 214-215 222 229 237 297
MISSISSIPPI RIVER VALLEY, 241
MISSOURI, 295
MITCHELL, W D 301
MOBILE, 283
MONTEREY, Michigan 156 294

MONTEREY CENTER, Allegan County Michigan 92 94 105 107 123 235 290-291 293
MORGAN, D J 67 J H 227-228
MORTON, Oliver Perry 192
MOSSMAN, 254 George W 251
MURPHY, Robert C 158
MYERS, Dr 59 Hank 59
NATCHEZ, Mississippi 14 241 279-281
NATIONAL TRIBUNE, 220-221 Newspaper 309
NEAL, Amos 166-167 169-171
NEGRO, Ben 249-252 271 273 Bragg 160 171 173 175 181 183 195 Henry 73 76 John 183-184 Josephus 262 Lockwood 192
NEGRO TROOPS, 210 214 224 227-229 241 253-254 276 279 289 297 299-301 310-313 315
NELSON, 129 134
NEW JERSEY, 52
NEW ORLEANS, 177 269 280 289-290
NEWSOM, Henry 246
NEW YORK CITY, 46 154 289
NEW YORK STATE, 88 296
NIELSTED, F G 294
NOBLE, Sylvester 246
NORFALK, Missouri 73
NORWALK, Missouri 73
OCHER, Dave 145 160 169 188-189
OGLESBY, Richard J (Col Dick) (Uncle Dick) 6 18 19 22 36 43 44 67 68 81 82-84 94 102 104 109 112-113 122 127 128 141 145 192 286 Col 23-24 36 61 79 97 99 101 103 111 Gen 285 Gov 288
OHIO, 88 94
OHIO RIVER, 21 26 56 70-71 89
OLD BREWERY BATTERY, 21
OLIVER, Lewis 246
OLNEY, 21
ONTARIO, Canada 88
ORA, Tobias 245
ORM, Frank 220
ORME, William W 3 33
OSTERHAUS, P J 273
OWEN, Alice Antoinette 295 Emma 295 Erastus N 268 Grace Elizabeth 295 Lt Col 269 289 M D 294-295 Milton 295 Milton D 307 Mrs M D 294 Ruby Helen 295
OXFORD, Mississippi 158 160 183
PADUCAH, Kentucky 69 83 135
PAGE, Lt Col 219 310
PAINE, E A 67
PAINS, R T 218
PALMER, J M 67
PARIS, France 289

PARMA, Michigan 311
PATRICK, Toney 245
PATTI, Adelina 13
PATTON, 244 Lt 245
PAYNE, 19 38 Eleasor A 35 Gen 36 R M 177
PEKIN, 18 21
PEMBERTON, 203-204 Gen 207
PENNSYLVANIA, 88
PEORIA, 19 21 38
PERRINE, B F 218
PETERSBURG, Illinois 228
PETTY, E P 300
PHILADELPHIA, 43
PHILIPPINE ISLANDS, 286
PICTON, Prince Edward County Ontario 292
PILLOW, Gen 102 Gideon J 69
PIPPS, John M (Quinine) 80
PITTSBURG LANDING, 112 132-133 135 139 145 149 158 246 279
PLAINFIELD, Illinois 88
PLANTER, 313
POLK, Leonidas 69
POPE, Gen 139 John 19
POPLAR HILL CEMETERY, Monterey Center Michigan 291 294
PORT CLINTON, 59
PORTER, Adm 303
PORT GIBSON, Mississippi 189 199
PORT HUDSON, Mississippi 198 199 246
POST, John P 18 150 200 Maj 102
POTTER, George 147-149 157
PRENTISS, 19 Benjamin F 35 Benjamin M 136 Gen 37 Tipp 38
PRESS AND TRIBUNE, 288
PRINCE EDWARD COUNTY, Ontario 296
PRITCHARD, Benjamin D 291
PUGH, Capt 44 Isaac C 18 21
PUTNAM, 243
QUINCY, Illinois 35
RAIDERS, Missouri 77
RAILROAD, Chicago And Milwaukee 59 Illinois Central 36 51 61 Mississippi Central 145 153 157 Texas Pacific 215
RANDAL, Col 302
RANDOLPH, Mayor 286
RANSOM, Thomas E G 199
RATES, Mary 277
RAWLINS, John A 192 305
REARDEN, James S 79
RED RIVER, 207

REGIMENTS, Naming Numbering And Positioning Of Companies 22 Numbering Of 19
RHOADS, 69 Col 68
RHODES, 147 Bully 154 156 164 166 171 175 Col 113 140 146 Frank 79 201 Frank L 18 James (Bully) 149 James M 131 Jim 148 Jim (Bully) 176 Lt Col 67 112
RICE, Dan 69-70
RICHMOND, 178 210 216 223 226 229 303 Louisiana 198 207 297 Negro Prison 218 Virginia 200
RIDDLE, 98
RILEY, 111-112
RITTER, 98
ROBERTS, Joseph W 44 Lawrence 61
ROB ROY, 79 Steamer 73
ROCHESTER, New York 57
ROCKY SPRINGS, Mississippi 199
RODERICK, Mr 106 108
ROGERS, 176 Capt 151 167 169 171 177 190-191 Henry H 150
ROLLA, Missouri 33
ROME, New York 12 69 293
ROOSEVELT, Theodore 137
ROSECRANS, William S 158
ROUGH RIDERS, 137
ROWETT, Richard 34
ROXEY, The Pig 7-8
RUSSELL, Randal 246
RUSSIAN EMPIRE, 289
SAINT CHARLES HOTEL, 21 25-26 43 47
SAINT JOHNS, 59-60
SAINT JOSEPH, Michigan 59
SAINT LOUIS, 11 45 88 173 177 188
SALEM TOWNSHIP, 123 Allegan County Michigan 138 293 294 296
SAN DIEGO, California 296
SANFORD, Alice Antoinette 295 Alice Owen 295 Carole 295 David Owen 295 Judith A 295
SAN JUAN HILL, 137
SAN MIGUEL, 282
SANTIAGO, Cuba 177
SAVANNAH, Tennessee 133
SAYER, Daniel 44
SCHLOSSER, Peter 44
SCHULTZ, 300 A 299
SCOTT, Gen 185 Winfield 24 Winfield (Fuss And Feathers) 36
SEARS, Col 310 Cyrus 213 221 309 311 315 Lt Col 220 222
SEDGWICK, F W 311

SEWARD, Gov 7-8 Mr 7 William H 6
SHARP, U S Marshal 179
SHAW, E P (Elvis) 219 John L 44 Robert Gould 312
SHEETS, Josiah 44
SHEETZ, Josiah A 201
SHELBY, Wilson 246
SHENNISY, Corp 77
SHEPARD, Col Or Gen 209
SHERIDAN, 209 Philip 140-141
SHERMAN, 129 134 137 185 268 Gen 157 177 267 W T 200 William Tecumseh 135
SHERMAN HOUSE, 6
SHILOH, 109 116 119 121-122 127 131-136 140-141 145 149-150 158 189 193 214-215 238 246 280 285 293
SHILOH CHURCH, 112
SHREVEPORT, 229 Louisiana 207
SIMPSON, Lt Col 250
SKILLEN, William A 222
SKILLON, W A 218
SLAVE HUNTERS, 38
SLOAN, Mrs 275-277
SLOCUM, Gen 268 H W 267
SLYBOOTS, 28-29
SMALL, Robert 313
SMITH, 136 196 203 213 249 C F 83 133 135 Caleb B 5 Calvin 139 Charles F 69 Daniel 214 245 E Kirby 207 Edward P 195 Lt 197 211 237 244 250 Morgan L 137 258 268 273 Thomas 246 Thomas K 219 Uzziel P 88
SNAKE CREEK BRIDGE, 137
SOPER, Thomas H 46
SPRINGFIELD, 4 18 33 42 225 286
SPRINGFIELD (ILLINOIS) MONITOR, Newspaper 227-228
STAMPS, Calib 245
STANCLIFT, Sarah Ann 234 290 294
STANTON, Edwin M 179 Sec'y Of War 186
STARS AND STRIPES, Newspaper 82 116
STARTSMAN, Luther 44
STEPHENSON, Gen 199
STERRILL, Wesley 267
STEWART, James 225
STODDARD COUNTY, Missouri 80
STOLBRAND, 192 Charles J 146 166 Maj 168 177 191 193 195 288
STRYKER, John 12
STURGESS, Capt 115 117 R H 44
SUTHERLAND, George 131
SUTTON, W P 44
SWARTZ, Adolph 79 103

SWETT, Leonard 3 33
TALLAHATCHEE RIVER, 157 163 166
TAYLOR, Dick 243 Maj Gen 300 Richard 207 210
    Zachary 207
TEDROW, 246
TENNESSEE, 8 88 177 215
TENNESSEE RIVER, 8 34 91 94 96 111 132-135
    149
TEXANS, 208-209 213-214 218 223 239 310
TEXAS, Illinois 149
TEXAS TERROR, 10
THOMAS, Adj Gen 245 Gen 188 George H 137
    Lorenzo 185-187
THOMPSON, Jeff 77 79-81 Polonica Cristine
    Abigail Cameron 63 William 245
TILGHMAN, 135 Gen 96
TOLBERT, J H 300
TRANS-MISSISSIPPI DEPARTMENT, 207 209
TROWBRIDGE, Silas T 80 Surgeon 114
TRUEMAN, Nelson 246
TRUMBULL, Sen 4
TUCKER, James M 300
TWAIN, Mark 169
VAN ARNUM, 69-70
VANDALIA, 22
VANDORN, Earl C 158
VAUGHN, Frank 246 Holland 246
VERMONT, 88
VICKSBURG, Mississippi 33 37 56 88 90 153 157
    165 177 185 189 198 203-204 207 215 239-241
    245-247 251 253-254 261-262 264 267-268 270
    273 275-276 279-283 285-286 288 293
VON VASMER, Herman Lieb 289
WADDILL, D M 300
WALKER, David 245 J G 210
WALLACE, 101-102 136 Lew 128-129 137 W H L
    79 135
WALNUT BAYOU, 216 303
WALTERS, Thomas L 218
WARNIC, Thomas 246
WASHBURN, 268 C C 273 Cadwallader C 267 Gen
    271 276-277
WASHBURN LEAD MINE REGIMENT, 219

WASHINGTON, Geo 245
WATERHOUSE, Richard 298
WATERTOWN, New York 293
WAUKEGAN, 64
WEARMOUTH, Alice Emily 295 Elizabeth Jean 295
    Grace Elizabeth 295 John 295 John Milton 295-
    296 John William 295 Robert Owen 295 Roberta
    295
WEISMAN, John T 189
WELLMAN, Capt 78 83 Robert D 77 79
WELLS, Jacob 246
WENTWORTH, (Long John) 6
WEST, Moses 246
WESTERFIELD, Henry P 21
WETMORE, H 218
WETZELL, 75 Capt 77 102 John 44 74
WHEATON, 68 Capt 191 193 Lloyd 44 Loyd 68 102
    117 201 285-286 Lt 74-75
WHELAN, Tom 51-55 57-60
WHELIN, Mr 52
WHISTLER, 170
WICKERSHAM, Dudley 225
WILCOX, Sam 105
WILEY, John S 131 Thomas J 131
WILLIAMS, Judge 234 Thomas 177
WILSON, Capt 100 Col 282 Robert 44
WILSON'S CREEK, Missouri 65
WINDSOR, Ontario Canada 295
WINE, John J 218
WISCONSIN, 67 284
WOOD, Gen 282-283 George J 146 150 Lt 140 151
WOODS, J D 298 Willis 245
WRAY, Carrie 295
WYOMING, 88
YATES, Dick 5 Gov 15 Richard 192
YAZOO, Mississippi 147
YAZOO RIVER, 237
YENNEL, Lewis 245
YOUNG, Col 282 Van E 281 283-284 311
YOUNG'S POINT, Louisiana 177 185 207 210 223
    226-227 229 303 305
YPSILANTI, Michigan 247-248
ZEIGLER, Wm 44

www.ingramcontent.com/pod-product-compliance
Lightning Source LLC
Chambersburg PA
CBHW080407300426
44113CB00015B/2433